ALLERGIC TO CRAZY

Other works of interest from St. Augustine's Press

Peter Augustine Lawler, *Homeless and at Home in America:*
Evidence for the Dignity of the Human Soul in Our Time and Place

Philippe Bénéton, *The Kingdom Suffereth Violence:*
The Machiavelli / Erasmus / More Correspondence

Albert Camus, *Christian Metaphysics and Neoplatonism*

Rémi Brague, *On the God of the Christians (and on one or two others)*

Rémi Brague, *Eccentric Culture: A Theory of Western Civilization*

Edward Feser, *The Last Superstition: A Refutation of the New Atheism*

H.S. Gerdil, *The Anti-Emile: Reflections on the Theory and Practice of*
Education against the Principles of Rousseau

Gerhard Niemeyer, *The Loss and Recovery of Truth*

James V. Schall, *The Regensburg Lecture*

James V. Schall, *The Modern Age*

Pierre Manent, *Seeing Things Politically*

Josef Kleutgen, s.j., *Pre-Modern Philosophy Defended*

Marc D. Guerra, *Liberating Logos:*
Pope Benedict XVI's September Speeches

Peter Kreeft, *Summa Philosophica*

Ellis Sandoz, *Give Me Liberty:*
Studies on Constitutionalism and Philosophy

Roger Kimball, *The Fortunes of Permanence:*
Culture and Anarchy in an Age of Amnesia

George William Rutler, *Principalities and Powers:*
Spiritual Combat 1942–1943

Stanley Rosen, *Essays in Philosophy* (2 vols., *Ancient* and *Modern*)

Roger Scruton, *The Meaning of Conservatism*

René Girard, *The Theater of Envy: William Shakespeare*

Joseph Cropsey, *On Humanities Intensive Introspection*

Allergic to Crazy

Quick Thoughts on Politics, Education,
and Culture, Rightly Understood

Peter Augustine Lawler

ST. AUGUSTINE'S PRESS
South Bend, Indiana

Manufactured in the United States of America

1 2 3 4 5 6   19 18 17 16 15 14

Library of Congress Cataloging in Publication Data
Lawler, Peter Augustine.
Allergic to crazy: quick thoughts on politics, education, and culture, rightly understood / Peter Augustine Lawler.
pages cm
ISBN 978-1-58731-021-8 (paperback: alkaline paper)
1. Popular culture – United States. 2. Politics and culture –
United States. 3. Education – Social aspects – United States.
4. Conservatism – United States. 5. United States – Social conditions
– 1980–. 6. United States – Politics and government – 1989– I. Title.
E169.12.L355 2014
306.0973 – dc 3   2014009622

ST. AUGUSTINE'S PRESS
www.staugustine.net

Table of Contents

Introduction

The title *Allergic to Crazy* might seem to be my demagogic effort to get identified with likes of Glenn Beck, Bill O'Reilly, Mark Levin, and Ann Coulter. But am I really saying all liberals or all progressives or whatever are crazy because they disagree with *me*? Well, no. Have I picked a title that will push the book to the top of the best-seller lists? I hope so. For me, though, the opposite of crazy is being realistic or sharing joyfully what we can know together about the real world, especially the world of real, particular persons open to the truth about who they are and what they're supposed to do.

The definitive refutation of existentialism, nihilism, and most varieties of postmodernism was noticed by the philosopher-novelist Walker Percy. Even the existentialist Sartre—who was all about absurdity and hell being other people and all—experienced the joy of shared discovery. He spent the best parts of his life communicating to others what he believed to be the fact that, deep down, we're locked up in ourselves. The most unjustly neglected American philosopher-poet (and the man who raised Walker Percy) William Alexander Percy similarly thought that the fundamental fact about his life and human existence was loneliness. Still, he wrote that he spent the best parts of his life imagining that there were lots of other people who shared his experience, and that his poetry was a successful way of allowing them to share their unrequited longings. Then the members of that community so formed even discover that common hungers for beauty, love, and understanding are not completely unsatisfied.

The being with complex language or speech, it turns out, is not an absurdly isolated individual but part of a world that's more than some arbitrary construction. That world isn't necessarily defined by time or place. Every poet or philosopher or novelist or theologian or true lover of greatness—every true "natural aristocrat"—is necessarily to some extent a displaced person. The members of his intimate community are rare souls scattered across history. Robert E. Lee, the southern aristocrat Will Percy imagined, would have been perfectly at home with General Washington and Marcus Aurelius and Pericles, but not so much with the men who happened to surround him in his time and place.

That introduction, of course, would have been the most laughable form of vanity if I thought it really had anything to do with me. This book won't be confused by any reader with great or even bad poetry. It's just that today's high technology has made the joy of shared discovery possible even for guys like me. This book is the result of the quick sharing of discovery made possible by the Internet. I watch a movie or a TV show, "get it," and write my thoughts down on a blog. Then, I imagine that I'm sharing my discovery the very same day with people all over the world. What I imagine becomes real when those who share my joy respond by clicking on the Facebook "Like" button. Often there's no need to say more, although many have added words in the "thread" or just by emailing me a quick "thumbs up" note. Blogging makes it a lot easier for me to get instant (and certainly less deserved) gratification than it was for Sartre or Will Percy. Or, at least, I have to rely a lot less on my imagination, which is a particularly lucky break. For displaced persons, having Facebook "friends" might be a necessary supplement to the real friends he has in his particular time and place.

The thoughts presented here are quick, but I hope they're informed by what I've learned over a lifetime (well, I hope not literally a lifetime). I've been teaching for over thirty years, written a bunch of books and hundreds of articles, and have expressed my opinions on all sorts of subjects. That doesn't mean I'm "interdisciplinary." It means that I have, in the good and bad senses, no discipline. I can brag that I'm not confined by the scholarly "scope and methods" of political science or philosophy. Or, I can shamelessly confess that I have the kind of attention deficit disorder that causes me often to be inattentive to detail and inept at revision. If I told you I was a "big picture" guy, you might confuse me, for no good reason, with either Newt Gingrich or Einstein. My pay grade is much lower than even Newt's. I'm certainly not obsessed with the "vision thing," and nothing I write is inspired.

Every one of these quick thoughts is about human psychology or the human soul—maybe the only genuinely strange, and certainly the most wonderful being in the cosmos. The title *Allergic to Crazy* is taken from the legendary Nashville songwriter Don Schlitz. Its choice is partly just coincidence: Last November, passing through Nashville, my wife and I visited the Bluebird Cafe. Don happened to be playing. It turns out that he's about my age and has written all kinds of funny and oddly tragic songs with very clear and intelligent lyrics. He's shy, he's anxious, and he's amazed and grateful when real love comes his way. He's about as nerdy and semi-unmanly as a country artist can be. He displays his flirtations with imagining he is crazy by talking about his sessions with his psychotherapist, which were clearly harder on the therapist than him.

Don's tune "Allergic to Crazy" is about leaving a crazy woman—not crazy in the clinical or the Patsy Cline sense, but crazy in the bizarrely unpredictable sense. Craziness can be cute and even erotic, but a reasonable man or especially a reasonable and anxious man can't live with it day in, day out. I might even be more allergic to crazy women than Don, but fortunately I don't have any in the refuge of home (except the random-biter dog). For me, "allergic to crazy" is all about a kind of gut-level reaction against the craziness just beneath the surface of what seems to be ordinary civilized sophistication these days. That means, of course, that plenty of sophisticated people are allergic to me. Not so long ago (in the 1992 presidential campaign), pundits observed that we had two Country Music candidates—Bush the elder and Perot—and one rock (or, more precisely, Fleetwood Mac) candidate—Bill Clinton. And both Bush and Perot proudly played Patsy's "Crazy" at their rallies.

Any kind of politico-musical analysis has to begin with the ironies: Ross Perot was actually crazy. Thank God he was unable to hide *that*, or he might have been elected president. Clinton was Governor of Arkansas (the home of the Razorbacks), but he was the candidate of liberal sophistication. And, Bush is the most old-money aristocratic president we've had lately, but he wanted us to believe that he was spiritually a Texan (Waylon and Willie, among others, weren't fooled).

But, finally, the choice for Patsy's "Crazy" (or even Willie Nelson's "Crazy") is against the flatness or banality of rock. It's country music that sustains better the depths of the human soul—the longings associated with love (including all manner of dangerous liaisons), God, country, family, and, more generally, living homeless and at home in America. So, country crazy is less crazy than sophisticated rock because it attempts to give voice to the longings that can easily be seen as the irreducible craziness of being a particular being, a searcher and seeker, wondering and wandering on the road to being at home. Country music, at its best (as Don reminded me), is about telling a story, as Walker Percy puts it, about being a particular being born to trouble and facing a predicament not wholly of his own making. Country music so understood points to the joy of shared understanding when we know who we are and what we're supposed to do. (That's even true of the effect Taylor Swift's high-school-diary songs have on barely teenage girls.)

Pointing away from that shared moral understanding is the sophisticated self-understanding of many Americans today. Just beneath the chatter of their happy-talk pragmatism, Solzhenitsyn claimed, is the howl of existentialism. A howl is the inarticulate noise that comes from the desperate experience of being deeply contingent and deeply alone. It's a noise that we share with the animals not hardwired for complex language or speech. But, the instinct-generated howls of the other animals have no existential dimension; they aren't caused by truthful and terrible experiences of who they are.

Walker Percy added that Americans today are crazier than ever, because they can't really account for themselves as more than inexplicable leftovers in a world more completely explained by modern science. They, for example, have become more self-confidently atheistic because they're more confident than ever that Darwin—or, more precisely, a combination of evolutionary psychology and neuroscience—explains it all. But, they're also autonomy freaks, refusing to be reduced to their biological inclinations. They really know—or hope—that the scientists can't explain what they experience about their freedom. Insofar as they're the social animals Darwin describes, they should be all about doing their duties to their families, tribes (or countries), and species. But, every free individual—beginning with every liberated woman—knows that she's more than that. And, she feels, our Supreme Court protects her liberty to choose not to be primarily species or country fodder, to have the freedom not to reproduce and to be replaced as nature intends.

Our sophisticated transhumanists even claim that we have the freedom to choose not to be determined by our bodies at all; we're on the way to becoming conscious machines that can exist an indefinitely long time. What about the good stuff about having a body, such as having sex and having kids? Well, don't forget we're already well on the way to separating sex from reproduction in the pursuit of perfect health and safety (see President Obama on the right of women to free contraception). And, if sex no longer has any purpose beyond momentary pleasure, then what kind of future can it possibly have? All kinds of writers—such as Plato and Shakespeare—talk about the twinship of erotic love and death. Who wouldn't surrender love—which is always distressingly out of our control (we can't, as Elvis sang, help falling into it)—to be free from death? Any Darwinian would have to concede that the natural point of having kids disappears if we stop reliably dying. Maybe that'll wreck nature's intention that species either improve or die out. But, what free individual doesn't want to be free from nature's indifference to anyone's particular existence? It might almost go without saying that the line of thought in this paragraph is certifiably *crazy*, but who can deny that it's carrying the day these days?

Our sophisticated autonomy freaks actually seem to be living less by their principles and more by their inclinations. Their marriage rate is high, their divorce rate is low, and they're even attracted to churches (if not to religious *dogma*) for the support they provide for family life. They're a bit weak from a species-preservation view when it comes to reproduction. They're typically having only one or two kids, mainly because they think raising kids has become hard. That's partly because, in the name of autonomy and luxury, both parents usually work. It's also because they think the future is going to be tough for kids these days, and so they must be equipped with education indispensable for membership in our productive meritocracy. It might be that, while their lives are objectively in many ways easier than ever, they rather crazily perceive the demands on them as unforgiving and unyielding. They're kind of crazy, because they understand their very beings to be both so contingent and somehow capable of being brought under their conscious control. They even think being itself depends upon their staying about; there's nothing, the thought is, after I'm gone.

Our sophisticates don't believe that autonomy trumps productivity. So, they don't think being bohemian—or all about the joyful art of life—trumps the personal responsibility to be bourgeois. They are particularly judgmental on themselves and their children when it comes to health and safety. They aren't easygoing when it comes to diet or exercise or safe, responsible sex. They're transhumanist enough to connect untimely death with unsafe choices—and so not with nature, bad luck, or God's will. They're particularly tough on themselves when it comes to avoiding smoking and obesity, and when it comes to securing one's own financial future. It's wrong to say that, in deed, they neglect moral virtue; it's just that their idea of virtue doesn't have room for courage, charity, or chastity. Those old-fashioned virtues are dangerous, impossible, and unnecessary these days.

Our sophisticates, to repeat, talk autonomy more than live it, and they certainly don't live the Sixties dream of doing your own thing. So, the good news is that our sophisticated meritocrats *are* better—in the sense of being dutiful social animals—than they *say*. They're all about relativism and non-judgmentalism in speech, but they're quite responsible and judgmental in deed. They seem, for the most part, more decent than crazy; although one definition of crazy surely is an extreme lack of correspondence between words and deeds. What does it means when people lack the words to explain to themselves who they are and what they're supposed to do? Are they being deprived of the joy that comes through shared responsibility, shared discovery, and shared love? Well, not completely, of course, but more than makes any sense at all.

Meanwhile, our sophisticates have distanced themselves more than ever from ordinary Americans—those who are getting less industrious and skilled at mental labor and so who are much less productive. The income gap between our classes widens, but so too do does the behavior gap. Ordinary Americans—non-college graduates with jobs that aren't about mental labor in the obvious sense—are getting less reliably productive, more often getting divorced, disconnecting parenthood from marriage, less grounded in churches, more disorganized and chaotic, and generally find living well as social animals more difficult and rare than ever. Their values are still relatively traditional or directed toward God, church, family, and country, but their behavior increasingly less so. We also notice, of course, that the social safety net of every sort—beginning with family and ending with unions, pensions, and government entitlements—on which they have come to rely are collapsing. Craziness, of course, is caused by being too lonely and disoriented or too much on one's own. Meanwhile, sophisticated meritocrats are nonjudgmental about or indifferent to the ordinary guys' moral and economic collapse, while being more contemptuous than ever of their allegedly unenlightened and allegedly desperate attachment to their God, their guns, their country, and so forth. They, crazily enough, are uncritical when they should criticize, and they criticize what remains of ordinary life and virtue that is genuinely admirable and valuable. One reason they think that ordinary Americans are crazy—or stupidly fat, poor, and superstitious—is that they've managed to convince themselves that they have so few shared experiences with them.

These kinds of questions—about the seeming paradoxes in how we live and who we think we are, and the kinds of everyday craziness we live with as modern and postmodern humans and Americans—are the subject of this book.

Most of this book is composed of my posts on the BIG THINK website, a collection of blogs and interviews. Centered in New York City, BIG THINK has been ranked by *Time* magazine one of the best websites for news and information. Almost all of the site's bloggers are progressive when it comes to, say, Obamacare, and equally uninterested in knowing or doing anything about the pathetic lives of the ordinary, unmeritocratic middle class. They think that religion and even moral virtue disconnected from productivity equals repression, and that there's no good reason—and so there's only anti-gay animosity—for being anything less than enthusiastic about the emerging constitutional right to same-sex marriage. They are also entrepreneurial, techno-enthusiastic, aggressively atheistic, urban and urbane, personally libertarian, and singularly transhumanist. I couldn't be more out of place. I'm a token, and it goes without saying that the guy who hired me doesn't work there anymore.

I've used this blog to record the joy of my discovery of something true and significant in all sorts of places—including, of course, movies and TV shows I just happen to see. Because the BIG THINKERS do nothing if not celebrate what the fashionable experts and their studies say, I try gently to defend unfashionable or more realistic views of education, happiness, technology, and so forth. I haven't, in truth, tried to convey in words the itchiness and scratchiness of my allergy to craziness. I've actually tried to be sympathetic and persuasive, with less than mixed results. Sure, I've pulled my punches and not spoken my whole mind. But I still find more freedom on BIG THINK than on some conservative blogs. Because the BIG THINKERS take it as a given that I'm pretty crazy, they aren't so judgmental about what I say. I certainly am under no pressure to adhere to a party line.

I've also included in this book some of my posts and short essays from other places on the Internet—including the excellent *First Things* blog POSTMODERN CONSERVATIVE. They have a different tone, because they're often directed against conservative craziness of various kinds. I'm allergic to conservative craziness too, whether of the libertarian or excessively traditionalist or agrarian variety.

I have to thank the appreciative readers of both blogs, who have contacted me just enough for me to be able to imagine that I really am sharing some good in common. I also have to thank lots of students at Berry College, for whom I came up with some of these pop cultural examples, to help me look cool, "with it," or whatever. The truth is, of course, that most intelligent and involved young people watch a lot less TV and many fewer movies than I do. So I mostly come up short of impressing them.

Several Berry students worked hard to get a mess ready for real publication. They include Kristian Canler and Beth Anne Dunagan. Jacob Stubbs made the most indispensable contributions and is the main reason this book will be published in my lifetime. Stephanie Tomys attended to the proofs with expert care and saved me from myself in many ways. Last and most, I have to thank Bruce and Benjamin Fingerhut for their confidence and patience, and Adam Keiper for his kind imposition of a crucial bit of last-minute competence.

Movies and TV

Limitless

I just saw *Limitless*, which isn't actually that good of a movie or even good science. But it did provoke me to some relatively obvious thoughts.

The premise of the movie is that one reason we fall short of our goals is that we only use 20 percent of our brains. That's not really true; roughly speaking, we use all of our brains, but not all at once. Don't you wish you could put more of your brain to work for you right now?

Let's say that you could take a pill that would allow you to immediately access and put to good use every memory you have of each of your experiences. And let's add that you can employ that information with perfect deductive logic.

Let's say, as the film does, that you're a smart—but not that smart—"blocked" writer wallowing in depression that's really contemptible self-pity. You have a book contract, but you haven't written a word. You're living in squalor, drunk a lot, and your almost endlessly patient, loving, beautiful girlfriend has finally just dumped you. Getting a job doesn't really occur to you as a viable option, and you seem very short on moral fiber or even ordinary decency. You certainly seem unfit to reproduce.

You take the pill: One result—you write that novel in four days. Does that make sense? Is novel-writing really about memory and deductive logic? Surely, those qualities by themselves couldn't produce a great novel. But this guy is writing a sci-fi thing about a future utopian society. That kind of book often really is a combination of ripping off stuff from various genuinely great books and deducing your way to futuristic mutations on perennial themes. And of course, perfect memory of even carelessly read

⁓9⁓

books is bound to radically upgrade your style, diction, and all that. So, I buy it. It's not a great book, but it's bound to be an impressive—if grandiose (as his agent says)—one.

After finishing the novel, he carelessly and somewhat ruthlessly tries to get really rich and powerful very quickly using his unearned advantage shamelessly to benefit himself. And he's no techno-entrepreneur aiming to invent stuff that will improve the lives of millions or billions, no Bill Gates; he's all about outwitting the other players on the stock market, on big mergers, etc., etc.

The only thing that "humanizes" him at all is that he wants to impress the girl who loved him, and he, in fact, now finally appreciates her love. But that's not enough. She dumps him again after seeing how addicted he is to the limit-busting drug. He, in fact, is no longer lovable. She's stuck with taking the drug once to get out of a jam he got her in. But, like any realistic woman, she knows enough not to take it again.

Is all that realistic? Maybe. He hasn't been chastened by experience. He forgets that he's still limited in many ways, and that the limits associated with our embodiment are the true sources of much of our happiness. He's not going to become more moral—or more relational or virtuous—just by getting real smart real fast. In the most important senses, he remains a contemptible slacker.

His constant calculation turns him into a control freak always on the move. He has no time to enjoy, no serenity now. He has no sense that his advantage is unearned, and so his victories are nothing more than immoral exploitation. He has no time for self-reflection, no spiritual depth, no leisure. So despite his unparalleled brainpower, he's far from living in the truth about what he can really know about himself.

From this view, the film is a criticism of our Adderall-addled, Achievatron techno-meritocracy. The film instructively highlights through exaggeration some of the implications of the techno-fantasies of our time. The society of the future to which it points is, in no proper sense, a utopia.

The King's Speech vs. *The Social Network*

There have been a lot of words trying to explain why the Academy chose the last noteworthy King of England over the founder of Facebook. Here's one explanation:

> "The King's Speech" is an anesthetic movie, "The Social Network" an invigorating one—and their scripts' departures from the historical record serve utterly divergent purposes. The tale of royal triumph through a commoner's efforts expurgates the story in order to render its characters more sympathetic, whereas the depiction of Mark Zuckerberg as a lonely and friendless genius (when, in fact, he has long been in a relationship with one woman) serves the opposite purpose: to render him more ambiguous, to challenge the audience to overcome antipathy for a character twice damned, by reasonable women, as an "asshole." [Hertzberg, "Royal Pains," *The New Yorker*, February 1, 2011]

Actually, the Facebook founder (Zuckerberg) is described at the film's end as a guy who wants to be an asshole; he lacks the guts even to achieve that low but often memorable goal.

The King's Speech is actually aristocratic history; the hero is made better or nobler than he really was through highlighting his singular greatness or admirable individuality. It's true he's no ordinary aristocratic hero insofar as he has to struggle so hard to be a king in almost the most minimalist conceivable sense. He doesn't rule his people, but only reads speeches written by others to bolster their morale. In doing so, however, he performed a perhaps indispensable if minor role in winning a war that saved not only his country but perhaps civilization itself. There's more than a trace of magnanimity in this rather unexceptional (certainly not brilliant) family guy with unheroic self-esteem issues.

Getting an audience to appreciate nobility requires highlighting it, especially in this case. In this case, members of the audience have to come to appreciate the heroic dimension of the King's struggle to do what almost every one of them could have done fairly effortlessly and probably better.

It's hard to see why the film's portrayal of the Facebook founder can be called ambiguous. It's not surprising that in real life he's better with "relationships" than he is in the movie. Who isn't? Probably almost everyone in the audience is. The point of the film is, surely, that those who pass for heroes these days—those at the top of our meritocracy defined largely by productivity—display none of the virtues of the heroes of the past, and even none of the virtues displayed by ordinary people, such as ordinary family guys in stable marriages. (The hapless but loving and faithful enough husbands and dads we see in *Hall Pass* are, in the decisive respects, paragons of virtue by comparison to most of the characters in *The Social Network*).

By the standard of heroic virtue, the old hereditary aristocracy looks much better than our democratic meritocracy. It's the characters in *The Social Network* who lack real vigor; their lives—despite all the techno-innovation and the creation of billions of online friendships—seem diverted from everything genuinely important or deeply animating in human life. Compared to the stuttering king, they're wimps. They don't exhibit any magnanimity or greatness of soul.

Here's one astute account of how the Facebook founder looked to many people in the audience:

> In *The Social Network*, a socially inept computer geek becomes an accidental billionaire making many enemies along the way. It was a brilliantly scripted story, but we don't really care much about the fate of Facebook founder Mark Zuckerberg (played by Jesse Eisenberg); indeed, we probably feel that all those billions in the bank have provided an enviably comfortable cushion against the vicissitudes he's faced. [Lee, "Why *The King's Speech* Beat *The Social Network*," *Telegraph*, February 28, 2011]

The Virtue of *True Grit*

Let me recommend to you this fine review of this season's best movie (Barra, "*True Grit*: The Coen Brother's Great Adaptation," *The Daily Beast*, December 25, 2011). Once again, I think the Coen brothers more than flirt with nihilism. The murderous violence of the film is, deep down, senseless, and the girl's quest for justice defined as vengeance most misguided.

Still, two bounty hunters operating as fairly lawless (and murderous) officers of the law are raised to the heights of courage and honor by their service to the spirited and uncannily eloquent young woman. They perform ably and nobly as warriors when it counts, and they save her even as she proves herself to be at least as manly (if physically weaker) as they are. The Coens allow us not to be that skeptical about the sheer beauty of their Homeric deeds.

Sure, we're constantly reminded of the disrespect for human life of these ex-Confederates (the Bridges/Cogburn character rode with the notorious Captain Quantrill of Missouri—the state where all the rules of war vanished into bloodlust). But we're also constantly reminded of the strange sort of cultivation that made these manly men (and woman) more able to articulate who they are than we are. The language of the film echoes that of the novel, where basically unlettered men speak with a formal and precise pagan grace. There's something civilized and even lawful in the violently state-of-nature Indian territory. These men and especially the very young woman are in some ways more civilized than we are, although, of course, not in many ways.

The film shows us what's to be said for and against the virtue that animated the Confederacy and the post-bellum southern frontier. It doesn't varnish the truth about honor, even as it displays the virtue it can become when ennobled by personal love.

The review is right to say that the beautiful language of the film is of the Americans who once were full of the language of the King James Version of the Bible and Shakespeare. But it would seem that the lives of the characters were hardly governed at all by the New Testament. It's true enough that the best of our southern warriors have always been only superficially Christian. Still, the novel or the Coens themselves allow us to leave the film wondering, at least, if there's room for grace in a cruel and violent world, just as we wonder whether there's room for real men and spirited women in our seemingly hyper-civilized world, where every effort is made to expel cruelty and suffering and all risky business from our lives.

More Gritty (Fishy?) Truth

So, my *True Grit* post got a lot of response on Facebook and by email and all that—mostly critical. One particularly astute critic, Ken Masugi, accused me of being in the "bad company" of that celebrated postmodernist-wrongly-understood Stanley Fish.

According to Masugi, Fish manages to make the film (and novel) both religious and nihilistic. It celebrates the religious devotion of Mattie while making clear that there's no reality that corresponds to it. Postmodernists like Fish say that people have narratives by which they make sense of the world, but there's no objective way of privileging one narrative over another. So Fish might be accused of ruining liberal education by saying the great teachers can't, in fact, tell the truth about who we are and what we're supposed to do.

If that's so, administrators respond, then real education comes from those who can back up what they teach with measurable, quantitative results, results that lead to the real production of power. The sciences are real; the humanities are, finally, edifying baloney that help us get through our, in truth, deeply meaningless lives. Fish often writes in favor of being religious, but at the expense of showing that "religious truth" is a self-deceptive oxymoron.

Let me save Fish from his nihilism by giving a different interpretation of some of the facts about the film and the novel he so perceptively notices: Mattie is a very clever and spirited young lady, all about "rational control." She wants to make the world make sense. She thinks she's smart enough and resolute enough to employ the law and contracts to gain fearful and mercenary control over dumber (but physically stronger and more capable) and emotionally weaker men to achieve justice.

She achieves enough success that she forgets the words she mouths at the film's beginning about grace being a limit to human merit or retributive justice and pride.

In truth, she gradually loses control of her situation or over men in the lawless state of nature of the wild Indian territory. She becomes more dependent on the natural strength and skill graciously given her by increasingly honorable (or non-mercenary) men. At the moment of her greatest triumph—the shooting of the man who killed her father—she falls into a pit of snakes.

That great moment, of course, was pretty fortuitous, not mostly her own doing. It was the two men in her life who won a most noble and quite improbable victory over the outlaws—a victory certainly inspired by her but not controlled by her. Mattie, in her vanity, almost deserves to fall into a pit of snakes, where she will surely perish on her own.

But she is rescued by Rooster, who graciously—or completely voluntarily or animated by some mixture of nobility and love and at great risk to himself—rides her to a doctor who can save her.

So Mattie was saved by grace: not the grace of God in any obvious sense, but by the gracious act of a free man, which was more than mere charity. Mattie had forgotten that she is a creature—a personally dependent being. It's impossible to make the world make sense all by oneself. But what (who) saved her was no random act in a merely chance-and-necessity universe.

The least we can see is that Christian humility is a realistic corrective to pagan—maybe Stoic—pride. But does humility—or recognition of personal, relational limits to our individual freedom—obliterate the greatness of human individuality? No, the greatness of Mattie and the noble warriors who won a seemingly reckless victory over evil outlaws still stands.

I could qualify this interpretation in many ways. Let me conclude that the film, maybe against the intention (for all I know) of the famously nihilistic filmmakers, does display some realistic (and so somewhat Christian) psychology. To some extent at least, the Bible does tell the truth about who we are.

Does any of this depend on the real existence of a personal God? Not in the eyes of the Coens, at least.

The Crazy, Stoic Heart

After saying something really controversial like Tea Partiers aren't Fascists, I thought it safer to return to a relatively trans-partisan commentary on a good movie. This is part of my emerging series of movies about Stoic Americans. It's also part of my series on movies about Stoic Americans played by Jeff Bridges (see my BIG THINK reviews of *True Grit*). It's also, finally, part of my series on movies that are supposed to remind you of one of the very best American movies ever: *Tender Mercies*. You might be offended that this review could be regarded as last year's news. But there are, of course, many ways you could still see this movie today.

Crazy Heart is supposed to remind you of *Tender Mercies*. There's another old-guy, almost has-been brilliant country singer/songwriter turned around by a beautiful single mom with a father-starved little boy. Robert Duvall, who plays the redeemed country singer in *Tender Mercies*, shows up in *Crazy Heart* as the only real friend of the Bridges character, and he sings just enough to remind us that he really can.

The first thing to be said is that Jeff Bridges and Robert Duvall are arguably the most effortlessly manly American actors, although they both are also exceedingly subtle masters of their craft. The second is that the musical performances by Bridges are utterly convincing as grizzled Texas greatness, as are the ones by Colin Farrell as today's country slickness. All the songs are good, and a couple you like more and more as you hear them sung repeatedly. Go to the movie just for the music.

The Bridges character, even at his most drunken, is a real gentleman, a dignified man in full (or as full as possible given his circumstances). He treats his fans and his old songs with the class they deserve, and he knows (except when really, really drunk) how to treat women. He can even figure out how to puke with dignity in the middle of a performance. He's also lonely beyond lonely, a fact that both is the cause of and caused by his being drunk for decades.

The Duvall character in *Tender Mercies* is redeemed by the woman and her boy, reconciles with his daughter (for a while at least), gets baptized, and his whole personal life is restored intact. It's quite a story about grace.

The girl dumps Jeff Bridges's character once she realizes that he's dangerous for her boy and can't get anything going with his son whom he hasn't seen for twenty-four years. He is returned to physical, mental, artistic, and financial health after turning himself over, not to God, but to rehab experts. The single mom, quite reasonably, still doesn't take him back, but he manages to stay on the wagon. The movie ends with his being reconciled with his uncompensated loneliness and even with the woman he loves getting what she needs and deserves (a good, presumably younger, reliable guy). It's quite a Stoic tale.

Overall (and although *Crazy Heart* is not as good as *Tender Mercies*), these two films display the twin peaks or fundamental alternatives to dominant American Lockeanism found in our South and its music–evangelical Christianity and Stoic philosophy (on the latter, see William Alexander Percy, *Lanterns on the Levee*).

The last thing to be said is that this is a very *erotic* movie—much more erotic than, say, the more graphic *Blue Valentine*. All of Bridges's longings (and hers) are animated in his relationship with the Maggie Gyllenhaal character (an aspiring writer with a love of a man of beautiful words, music, and deeds, but a mom above all else). This is the most credible and tragic film couple in a long time. Love doesn't conquer all, as both the old Stoic poet and the realistic young mom know. Maggie G. deserves the big awards as much as Bridges for getting so much across in so few words.

Men: Single and Serious

Both *A Single Man* and *A Serious Man* are about sad professors with seemingly really bad luck teaching in America in the Sixties. Both are single in the sense of lonely and not deeply in love with anyone still alive. The single man is the example of a good English teacher—erudite, charming, has "something to say." The serious man is the example of a bad physics teacher: too nerdy, self-absorbed, and motor-mouthed to get anything across in class. The (gay) single man is lonely because he oriented his whole life around a single young man who died in an accident. The (heterosexual) serious man is lonely because he's contemptibly weak in a world very short on love, and so everyone around him shamelessly exploits him. The single man, who spends most of the movie contemplating suicide, gets a pagan insight into the fact that everything is as it must be and gives up on suicide. He immediately dies of a heart attack.

The serious man—having been as tortured as the Bible's Job—finally catches the break of getting tenure, although he's done nothing to deserve it. He immediately gets an ominous call from his physician about something on his X-ray; he had provisionally been given a clean bill of health. That piece of bad luck, of course, can't be traced to any deficiency in character.

The single man—played expertly by Colin Firth—claims that his life was complete or lacking in nothing in love with another single man. He tells his woman friend, whom he loves but can't take seriously as a lover, that his life was complete without women and children. A single man was enough to make his life whole. Whatever might be true for most men and women, a general "natural law" theory of human longing can't comprehend the single life of this single man, who claims to be no more than a real and noble human exception to the bourgeois rule (well, he and the filmmaker do show far too much undeserved contempt for the way most people live). The movie is too serious and somewhat preachy, but there's no denying that it's pretty thoughtful on the mixture of the beautiful and the awful in the experience of this singular man. In some ways, this eloquent character is the opposite of the stuttering, family-guy king Firth plays in *The King's Speech*. Both characters, thanks to Firth, are full of class.

A Serious Man is one of the Coen brothers' explorations of the meaninglessness of life and the point that is there is no point. It's very funny, and I, for one, prefer a relatively subtle view of sordid suburban Minneapolis to the overbearing, deterministic bloodiness of *No Country for Old Men* or even the more morally charged murders of *True Grit*. Still, everything is ugly and tasteless—the homes, the landscape, the schools and synagogues, the people. (New Urbanists, agrarians, and so forth will love what they might regard as a candid exposé of what the 1967 suburbs were really like.)

The Jews are mostly self-absorbed and grasping. The gentiles are portrayed in terms of stereotypes—shamelessly corrupt Asians and gun-loving, violent, anti-Semitic working-class whites. (The movie might be regarded as anti-Semitic if it wasn't made by Jews.) The Rabbis are complacent and theologically clueless and don't work to make personal connections with the unfortunate. There's the occasional moment that might be interpreted as the Coens showing some affection for their childhood, but not many. (The Bar Mitzvah scene is genuinely touching and suggests that the mangled ritual somehow reflects something real—if only the shared identity of members of a tribe.)

The main character—who isn't evil at all—does manage to get your sympathy, until you realize that what happens to him isn't really bad luck at all but the result of his being really, really short on manliness. That seems to be an obvious, Nietzschean shot at taking too seriously the morality recommended by the Bible. The Coens might be praised for not following Woody Allen in combining existential meaningless with liberal platitudes and the promise of liberated sexual healing. They are also more seriously nihilistic than the makers of *A Single Man*, who aren't pagan or Nietzschean in their sentimental belief that personal love might be real and might be enough.

Mad Men

It's the season for highlighting the best that was written, said, and done in 2010. The consensus is emerging that the most thoughtful TV show (and so the one that most deserves critical analysis) is, once again, *Mad Men*.

From our view, people not so long ago lived somewhere between contemptible self-indulgence and inexplicable insanity. Advertising executives in Manhattan around 1960 really did give themselves the cool nickname "Mad Men." But the show's barely concealed message is that they really were mad. That madness is displayed for our complacent horror.

The Mad Men smoked like chimneys and almost routinely got drunk on multiple martinis. They ate huge pieces of red meat together with lots of refined carbs. They even had those martinis at lunch, right in the middle of the workday. So they got back to their offices sick, sleepy, and moody. Occasionally they didn't even return at all. They exercised rarely or only for fun and never scientifically. Blood pressure standards were much more lax in those days than they are in ours. Men weren't as focused on either health or productivity as people are today.

Rather than have sensible, emotionless, safe, and deeply consensual hook-ups, the Mad Men had complicated, emotionally sloppy, and altogether needlessly dangerous affairs. They found it almost impossible to think of women as autonomous individuals, and so they were guilty of all kinds of double standards and the cause of unplanned pregnancies. They weren't as enlightened as we are about either *safe* or *consensual* sex. Really smart wives were stuck frustrated at home with multiple kids, and so they ended up abusing substances and having dangerous liaisons too.

It's altogether too easy for us to see that the lives of those men and women were needlessly risky and obsessive. Sometimes we just want to scream at the screen that you guys just got to get control of yourselves and be more responsible. Lives today are more calculated, more controlled. They are, as David Brooks wrote, bourgeois bohemian. People have their tasteful fun, but not at the expense of ignoring risk factors or undermining their productivity.

We also see how hellish it was to live as a woman in more unliberated or less enlightened times. Ambitious women had to be much more skilled, industrious, and thick-skinned to have careers thought to be reserved for men. The civil rights movement was just beginning, and there's some sensitivity at the agency to the African-American advertising market. But there weren't any African-American Mad Men, and nobody was talking about remedying that situation. The intelligent and caring black woman in the show is underemployed as a domestic, and she is fired capriciously by a lazy and neurotic white housewife. And the gays, of course, remain desperately closeted, frightened of being anything but invisible. Our country, in general, is more just than it was in those comparatively cruel days.

We postmodern conservatives can see that there's been lots of progress in living as a free individual since the early 1960s. People really are less determined by race, class, gender, and sexual orientation, and particular individuals are enjoying longer, healthier, and freer lives. (Actually, the obesity "epidemic" is a reminder of the continuing relevance of class, but that's a story for another time.) The world is more a genuine meritocracy based on productivity than ever.

We can also see a narrative of decline in *Mad Men*. The early Sixties was the beginning of a kind of decadence that continues to progress today. The Mad Men were, compared to us, pretty classy and creative; they knew how to dress and were more certain about how to act. Although the new generation at the agency is markedly inferior in certain respects to the more "paternalistic" old men, they still knew how to handle themselves as ladies and gentlemen better than we do. They were comparatively attuned to their social (if not their environmental) responsibilities.

Those men were certainly less *bourgeois* or selfish in a petty way than we are. They weren't afraid to let themselves go and have those multiple kids, and they weren't obsessed—at the expense of enjoying life— with living forever. And the show often reminds us that there's a connection between romantic indifference to risk and the liberated creative imagination and the highest levels of real productivity. Women, from a cynical or Marxist view, were just beginning to be liberated to be wage slaves, just like men. And that liberation, we have to remember, gave women new choices but made the "traditional" ones harder. It's harder not to think of oneself as, most of all, a free individual these days. Even or especially Darwinians might have to agree that we've become too self-obsessed to reliably do our duty to the species as social animals.

Country Strong

Country Strong *hasn't been taken seriously by film critics. I'm not going to review what they've said or speculate on why they said it. I'm just going to explain why I enjoyed this very thoughtful film.*

The four major characters—two men and two women—are all extremely attractive. The women have all the longings of real women, and so they are sexy within the context of the whole of human eros. The men are virile and passionate and quite conscious of what's required to be real men. The longings of men and women, it goes without saying, overlap in many ways, but any Darwinian knows that they remain distinct and com-plementary. Most American art these days is erotically lame compared to this film.

The country—meaning the rural South and anyone who identifies with the rural South—is much more Christian and more patriotic than the rest of America. And so too, of course, is country music.

This movie doesn't include any obvious displays of patriotism. A huge American flag flows down at the beginning of spectacular display that Kelly's (played by Gwyneth Paltrow) concert is meant to be, but the char-acters aren't thinking or singing about their country. Still, the movie is a kind of defense of the American way of life as imagined in the more noble of the country songs.

None of the characters are obviously Christian. The fake former beau-ty queen singer with seven self-constructed smiles says that Jesus is her hero, but she does that for the fans who are her judges. And the Tim McGraw character says he's never been much of a church man. He also says that if he and his wife had stayed at home, she would be singing in the church choir. But they didn't.

Still, the two themes of the movie are quite Christian. The first is the importance of forgiveness for redeeming us from our sinful, self-destruc-tive brokenness. The Paltrow character can't forgive herself for killing her unborn baby in a drunken fall. She truthfully says not long before her sui-cide that she can't change her past, but she mistakenly believes that there's no way she can get past it but by ending herself, by disappearing. Her hus-band, James (McGraw), can't forgive her either. So he can no longer love her as a husband loves his wife, although he often remembers loving her more than anyone, just as she remembers loving the baby more than any-one. Perhaps she might have been redeemed by his love. He remained determined to do everything he could to protect her, but he didn't do enough.

The explicit and repeated theme of the film is the choice between personal love and fame. It's the choice, St. Augustine explained, that the noble Romans faced, the fundamental choice faced by anyone blessed with extraordinary abilities. James pulled Kelly out of rehab early in pursuit of fame, for a concert tour that would revive her career. It seemed, at first, a rather despicable act. But if both love and fame are roads to a kind of human flourishing, if there are two ways of avoiding self-destruction, he seemed to have no choice but to try to cure her through reattaching her to fame. Sure, it didn't work, but he still was working for her. One critic says McGraw is no Richard Burton, and he really isn't a great actor. But he brings a kind of tragic gravity to his role that's not all that distant from a kind of Christianized Shakespeare.

I still haven't talked about the two most attractive and deep characters in the film—both of whom choose love over the virtually certain prospect of fame and so are both personally and artistically redeemed.

Please Give

So, in the wake of the boring—yet annoying—*Golden Globes,* I've been asked what movies of last year I'd recommend that the foreign correspondents slighted. Let me say, to begin with, that my list of last year's bests probably wouldn't include the award-winning film *The Social Network.* How significant can a film be, finally, that centers on someone who's not even an "asshole," but only wants to be one? Sure, he's a really, really rich asshole wannabe, but still. I guess I could add that the film does well in highlighting the flat-souled narcissism of our techno-meritocracy—a narcissism that's more a fearful pose than a mirror of the Facebook inventor's soul. But *The Social Network* is far inferior to, say, Whit Stillman's *The Last Days of Disco*, where the characters have some genuine (if fading) class and a better sense of the price they're paying for having been morally abandoned. Maybe the irony of *The Social Network* is the word "network"; the film is about people for whom networking and hooking up have largely replaced real and lasting friendship. And there's no point making the hyper-obvious point that Facebook friends aren't real friends.

The Golden Globe people totally discredited themselves by ignoring *True Grit*, which seems stranger and more wonderful—if not exactly all that enjoyable—the more I think about it. But I actually really enjoyed the neglected *Please Give*. Let me share with you some thoughts about that film I wrote down last June, because you're in a great position to Netflix it (or whatever) now.

Please Give considers with great sensitivity many politically correct topics without supporting the politically correct conclusions. The central couple makes big money by buying the furniture of the newly dead (and formerly elderly) from their grieving children for very little and then selling it in their trendy shop as either antique or retro. The husband sees no problem with this, realizing they are being justly compensated for performing a valuable service from which everyone benefits. The wife is overly guilty about being a parasite and compensates by giving homeless people twenties and trying to volunteer to help out the unfortunate. She breaks down in self-indulgent sentimentality while observing a group of happy, athletic Down syndrome kids playing basketball. She so obviously doesn't have what it takes to work with those loving kids that she's asked by the professional caregiver to leave. The kids end up comforting her.

Meanwhile, she's pretty oblivious to the needs of her own daughter, who has her own issues.

Liberal guilt, we learn, is usually caused by being abstracted from those you actually know and love. The wife and mother's (very petty) redemptive moment is at the movie's end, where she loosens up enough to buy her self-esteem-challenged daughter some very expensive and flattering jeans as an act of love. The result, of course, is that the homeless who depend on her like domesticated cats will be short a twenty or two.

The husband, meanwhile, lonely with a wife who has become merely his abstracted partner in business, is generous and attentive to the daughter. He buys her nice stuff without worrying about how the injustice affects her soul. He has a fairly pathetic—even perfunctory—affair, but he never stops thinking about his wife and kid. And he's fairly okay with being somewhat fat, and that fact makes him very attractive to compulsively thin women.

The best thing about this movie is its unflinching portrayal of the lives of two very old (and very near death) women. One maintains her dignity by being brave and upbeat, the other by being smart and astutely critical of everything. They both are touchingly dependent on the unconditional love of a single grandchild, and that love is the most wonderful thing in the movie by far. In general, the movie shows us how hard it is for the old to be loved these days for all sorts of reasons. One, of course, is that people fear and work against aging and death more than ever.

There's other great stuff: We get a real feel for how tough and inconvenient it is for even pretty prosperous people to live in the city. And the fairly claustrophobic apartments make the case for the suburbs and their trees and square feet and huge laundry rooms indirectly but insistently.

Also, we're shown how dependent an only child is on his or her parents for altogether too much.

The self-obsessiveness of Manhattanites restless in the midst of prosperity reminds us a little of Woody Allen, but not much. This movie is way too pro-family and unsentimental; it's toughly critical of those who wallow in the misery of their mortality. It might be the type of movie Walker Percy would make if he were a woman and not particularly religious.

Holiday Movies

So it turns out there are actually three outstanding holiday movies—*True Grit, The King's Speech*, and *The Fighter*.

True Grit is, as I've said, very ambitious and philosophically pretentious. It makes broad claims about human nature, and it causes us to wonder whether everything we do is, finally, both insignificant and ridiculous. Its characters are sort of epic caricatures or not quite fully fleshed-out human beings; they're not quite realistic.

The King's Speech and *The Fighter* are based on true stories, and the characters are both more modest and more complete. One result is that those two films are both more realistic and more enjoyable than *True Grit*. They're about families, friends, and a man's dependence on the love of a beautiful and loyal woman. Neither includes even one murder, although *The Fighter* is, as you might expect, full of violence. (And the gathering storm of world war is the background of *The King's Speech*.) They are, we might say, less about death and more about love.

The King's Speech and *The Fighter* have strangely similar heroes. Each of those decent and gutsy family men frees himself from being dragged down by the pathologies of quite dysfunctional families to figure out for himself who he is and what he's supposed to do. Neither selfishly liberates himself from his familial responsibilities, though; each ennobles rather than runs away from the place imposed on him by birth.

Their backgrounds, of course, are radically different. The fighter grows up in a fairly squalid part of the Irish working-class rust belt; the king admits he knows nothing about such common people. The fighter's greatness depends upon his fearless and savvy use of his exceedingly powerful fists; the king needs all the courage he can muster to gain minimally functional use of his tongue. But both display the greatness that comes from displaying grace in public under pressure.

We actually are reminded that George VI was the last great English king. He proved classy and resolute enough to become a symbol of unified national resistance against Hitler. Kings had been reduced from rulers to actors, but the ruler—Churchill—still admired and was properly deferential to the actor who provided what the people needed.

There's a lot more to say about the fighter's complicated friendship with his crackhead half-brother, and the king's friendship with an actor/Shakespearean psychologist posing as a speech therapist. In both cases, though, the advice of the friend was indispensable, as was the different kind of endlessly supportive friendship of the woman who served the cause of his life's purpose.

Colin Firth has provided us a marvelously nuanced and sensitive portrayal of a real gentleman for the second year in the row. But the two gentlemen—the king and the cultivated gay professor in *A Single Man*—have quite different virtues and understandings of who they are. Both characters manage to be quite singular and quite credible.

Jeff Bridges also has two consecutive fine holiday performances. But the characters he portrays in *Crazy Heart* and *True Grit* are pretty much alike; both are quite memorable in that grizzled sort of way, but neither is quite credible.

Blue Valentine

Blue Valentine is a psychologically ambitious and impressively subversive effort by a new filmmaker. It is, in a subtle but clear way, a pro-life movie. It's quite jarring and claustrophobic; the psychological intensity and instability surely are meant to keep viewers from relaxing and just enjoying themselves. Still, in a subtle but clear way, the film is quite pro-enjoyment.

The basic message is that the instinct or, better, natural guidance we social, personal, relational beings are given to find life good lacks articulate and powerful defenders these days. That's why the two central characters, husband and wife, are much more broken—more screwed up—than people need or ought to be. Their little girl, meanwhile, seems very happy and very trusting—or not broken at all. But we're not given much reason to believe that she's going to stay that way. She's going to be stuck with a broken home, and with parents who even together—but surely not apart—won't give her anywhere near what she needs to find personal happiness. The film is also, of course, about how badly children are raised these days.

The wife, we learn, comes from a cold family with an at least verbally abusive father. A lot of her history is revealed during what seems to be pointlessly intrusive questioning at an abortion clinic: She started having sex at thirteen, had between twenty and twenty-five sexual partners, and the one who got her pregnant doesn't care about her. Her father says that she isn't the type to bring her boyfriends home. We're shown, surely with more detail than is necessary, that she enjoys twisted sex—sex more about bodily domination than personal love. She's especially attracted to a physically abusive and physically strong—a champion wrestler control freak, who, in any deep sense, isn't erotic or interesting at all. We see just enough to know that she remains more attracted to him than to her husband, and one plausible scenario we're left with is her return to that guy. Her husband says, on their last night together, that he won't hit her and won't rape her—no matter how much she enjoys it.

Her future husband futilely courts her for a while; he finds her very physically beautiful (which she is) and charmingly insane and full of herself (as beautiful women are). She finds him charmingly ineffectual and so a waste of time. She becomes interested in him only after she finds out she's pregnant by the other guy. She knows she needs a friend to get through the abortion, and we see no evidence that she has any other friends. She bails at the last minute from the abortion procedure, explaining that she has to talk to her friend. The doctor is vaguely disapproving, but, sticking with the protocol of consent, lets her go. Her future husband comforts, in many ways, this tearful girl he barely knows. On the bus ride home, he says let's be a family, and she cuddles up against him in something close to the fetal position. So it seems like he's saved her and her baby. And he's not vain or "manly" enough to care that the baby is not really "his."

What we learn about him is that he never graduated from high school and was abandoned by his mother. He's a lot like his father, who's a very multi-talented musician but works as a janitor. The husband tells his wife he didn't know he was looking to be a husband and father. But it turns out that being the family guy is all he wants. Despite his many talents, he is satisfied painting houses and devoting his real energies to loving his family. He's all about enjoying all the good things of life in quite unsophisticated ways. His wife asks him if he's really satisfied with a job that causes him to be drinking at 8 a.m. His very funny and memorable response is that it's a luxury to have a job that allows you to drink in the morning. Drinking fairly heavily is supposed to be a sign of despair. But not for him: He enjoys alcohol and tobacco and playing with his daughter and making love and all the enjoyments available to the ordinary guy; he's really content. His life is plenty good, and he doesn't need more.

But his wife has grown tired of him. She's pretty ambitious; she works as a nurse, and she's focused on her career. We see her, with some irony, performing ultrasounds on women who really want to have babies. But it turns out that the doctor who wants to promote her isn't mainly interested in her professional competence. Her husband isn't envious about her success, and someone might say he's a perfect husband for a career woman. She's dissatisfied with him, she says angrily, because she's more of a man than he is. That is, in a way, true enough.

More reasonably, she's frustrated because he won't really talk with her; one reason his contentment seems unmanly is that it's so inarticulate. It seems to her that she has two children, and she's tired of both their silliness. And so, her mothering is pretty perfunctory and joyless. She's neither a caring wife nor a caring mom, but only her husband feels the rejection (thanks to his protection of his daughter). We have to say she isn't wrong to be unhappy with a husband who's not in every way a grown-up, but she's living too distantly from the goodness of genuinely erotic and relational personal life to appreciate properly what's really good about him. Maybe we can say that he, most of all, can't give her the words she needs, words she wouldn't have heard in biology class either.

Someone might say it would have been better if she had had the abortion instead of being stuck with a husband and a kid she chose for the wrong reasons. What makes that conclusion implausible is the real presence of the little girl, who is the most compelling character in the film.

There's a lot to think about here regarding how hard it is to be happy these days, and this film doesn't turn our thoughts in a feminist or "autonomous" direction.

Groundhog Day

BIG THINK's great little interview with Danny Rubin got me thinking about the relationship between happiness and mortality. His very philosophic film is all about our "rightly understood" theme of the connections between virtue, happiness, and personal love.

Groundhog Day, of course, is all about the Bill Murray character. Bill very often plays (brilliantly) the same guy. His moods are irony that masks depression, or just depression. (The most full developed version of this interplay is the Bill of *Lost in Translation*.) We usually get the impression that Bill is, as a searcher or seeker, detached from ordinary human satisfactions. The main thing is that he just isn't happy, and we kind of buy into the thought that his misery must flow from superior insight. So it's understandable why he doesn't act like such a good guy.

Certainly *Groundhog* Bill begins the film by affecting that air of ironic superiority. He wants to appear to live without order and necessity to his life, like Socrates' democrat or the guy living under the unobsessive communism Marx describes. But Bill isn't easygoing, he's screwed up; he's just tone-deaf to love. All in all, his life isn't impressive to grown-ups. (But we moviegoers aren't quite grown-ups.)

We like to think people are screwed up because they're going to die. Free them from the misery of their mortality, and they'd be fine, unalienated. The Bill character probably would have bought into that "transhumanist" insight (see, for example, the more explicit whining of various Woody Allen characters).

But mysteriously freed from time and death or stuck in the eternal return of the same 24 hours, the Bill character soon becomes suicidal. Life is hell if other people become mere playthings at your disposal and if your life is deprived of any weight or point or purpose beyond enjoyment. Hell is being freed from the necessities of birth, love, work, and death. And the experience of hell is the remedy for self-indulgent, self-denying irony.

The Bill character doesn't have the option of suicide, and so he has to invent order and necessity for himself to make life endurable. He begins to practice the virtue of charity for people who can't have any enduring meaning (in the ordinary sense) for him. He devotes himself to cultivating his untapped talents. He masters the piano and even finds the joy of life in music. Of course he discovers personal love through his meticulous attention to the details of the longings of a particular woman. She becomes more strange and wonderful to him as she continues to elude his complete comprehension and control. And he becomes more strange and wonderful to her as he becomes more virtuous and talented and loving—as he becomes more than a typical *Bill Murray character*.

So being mortal isn't the deepest cause of our misery. And our happiness is found in understanding who we are—our personal longings in relation to our capacities. That means, of course, that happiness is found in discovering and performing the responsibilities we've been given.

The immortality or indefinite longevity promised by the transhumanists might make human happiness harder to find than ever. But it is not impossible, as the Murray character discovered.

His reward, the film concludes in a pretty corny way, is time and eventually death.

Diner and *The Last Days of Disco*

Now that summer's here and the time is right to turn to reruns of various kinds, I'm trying to spend the ample time I have as a tenured professor watching some of my favorite old movies (that were new when I first saw them). One advantage of being old is that there's plenty from which to choose.

So yesterday I revisited *Diner* (1982), written and directed by Barry Levinson. It turned out to be part of a trilogy, including *Tin Men* and *Avalon*, about the Baltimore of Levinson's youth or wonder years. Levinson made a fourth semi-autobiographical movie about Baltimore, *Liberty Heights,* but it doesn't fit into the whole. (It's still good.)

Diner is the best of the three, partly because it's the one that draws most immediately and "authentically" from Levinson's own coming-of-age.

One sign of its greatness is that it provided the first significant roles for the outstanding and wildly successful actors Kevin Bacon and Mickey Rourke. A case can be made that they've never been better than they were in *Diner*. The film also displayed the talents of the then pretty unknown Steve Guttenberg, Ellen Barkin, and Paul Reiser.

The movie focuses on young men in those ambiguous years right after college, when they can't be kids any more, but they haven't fully embraced the idea that they're stuck with being productive and probably being spouses and parents for the rest of their lives.

So the movie is dripping with many dimensions of selective nostalgia. First, there's the year: 1959. Things were better then (well, also worse, but we already knew that). Limits to our nostalgia being perfectly selective are all the smoking and the diner food (fries with gravy!), both of which seem scary and repulsive to us.

The movie overflows with dialogue, much of it at the diner, where the guys seem to meet every night and stay until 4 a.m.

The conversational film closest to *Diner* is Whit Stillman's *Last Days of Disco* (1998), where young people about the same age are in a very similar ambiguous situation spend all night talking at the *Disco* (where amazingly the music is not loud enough to stifle conversation). They're both among my favorite movies, although neither is action-packed.

One difference between the two films is that *Diner* is almost exclusively about male friendship; no women show up at the diner. The guys come by after dropping the girls off, and none of them seem to have a conversational friendship with a woman. (Actually, two of the guys have a rather intimate and candid conversation with a stripper they just met at a burger joint.) That's the difference between 1959 and 1982 (well after "the Sixties"). A careful viewer can notice both gains and losses in human understanding and emotional intimacy as a result.

Both films have really fabulous soundtracks, put together by someone who really knew and loved the music of the time and place. I can't help but prefer the Top 40 of the late fifties—or the time before the Beatles and Dylan—to Disco hits. But Stillman caused me to see more than a little good about *More, More, More*.

It's clear that *place* is indispensable for making a great conversational movie. Levinson's non-Baltimore movies aren't very memorable. In my opinion, Stillman's *Barcelona* (which, of course, takes place in Spain) isn't as good as either *Metropolitan* or *Last Days* (his conversational trilogy), and he hasn't shown us yet whether he can make a movie that's not rooted in people he knew and loved in Manhattan.

I can't help but prefer Baltimore to Manhattan. There's something more enduring and personal about all the row houses, diners, and (dare I say? "The Block?" In both films, churches show up in strange and oddly moving times, and we remember that cities are full of churches. (Levinson and his characters are Jewish, and he also reminds us, of course, that a large number of our immigrants were Jews.) In neither film is it clear that any of the characters are actually observant religious believers, although the deepest ones are haunted by what the religious believe.

Diner doesn't push it, but it's really about the descendants of recent immigrants who have no class (meaning deep culture) because they've become middle class. And so it highlights in a "nuanced" way (one of the characters in *Diner* rightly complains that you really don't know where you stand with the word "nuance") what's good and what's hard about being a middle-class American. *The Last Days* is not only about the decline and fall of disco, but the last, kind of abandoned, generation of American pseudo-aristocrats—those who haven't been shaped by any memory of being immigrants.

Parents—nice people who care about their kids (and bail them out more than once)—are around in *Diner*, but it's not clear they have that much influence over who their kids are. Certainly, their parents aren't talked about much at all at the diner, but maybe just enough. (Let me add here quickly that the students I teach at Berry College—southern, Christian kids, for the most part—talk about their parents a lot.)

In both films, the young adults begin with having little idea what they're supposed to do. Because there's so much serious talking in both films, it's impossible to say they haven't done much reflecting about who they are. The friends are closer in *Diner*, because they've known each other their whole lives. They are closer to being true friends, who care about each other and the good they share in common. When they take shots at each other, it's just to be affectionately funny and not to hurt or gain advantage. They're remarkably likely to tell each other the truth. Conversational friendship (as opposed to, say, *Facebook* friendship) turns out to be an indispensable feature of living a good life.

Conversational TV: *Men of a Certain Age, Friday Night Lights, The Big Bang Theory*

Now that the Emmy nominations are out, I can give my awards for the best "conversational" TV shows. My standard, of course, finds its peaks of excellence in conversational films such as *Diner* and *The Last Days of Disco*:

1. *Men of a Certain Age* is about three longtime friends around fifty years old. They don't act old and are charmingly and appropriately both ironic and serious about being stuck with not being so young. Each of them is working nobly to reinvent himself as what he was always meant to be (but failed to achieve earlier)—a golf pro (now on the senior tour), a film director, and a genuinely responsible leader of men (at an auto dealership). They meet now and again at something like a diner (and on hikes) to talk things through, and darn if the show doesn't capture perfectly the candid, casual manliness of talk among real friends. Their conversations with women are also quite memorable. They are guys who really like women as "whole persons," but they remain shy, confused, and vaguely guilt-ridden in their presence. It's one happily married guy, one divorced guy with kids, and one who has not grown up enough to have gotten married—that about covers the possibilities. (There's no gay guy, but one show can only do so much!)

2. *Friday Night Lights* is, of course, about the community of friends that is the rural Texas high school football team. The touching thing is that the guys usually half-way know that life will never again give them a challenge as noble and real as working to win "state," and that this life-transforming experience somehow has to last them their whole lives. Sadly, but predictably, the heroes usually don't do so well after high school. (There are some striking exceptions—such as the talent-challenged but big-hearted replacement quarterback who listens to Dylan and goes to art school) As befitting a show mainly (but not exclusively) about fierce men of action, their conversations are usually short on words and long on intensity of meaning. (The chatterbox male character, fan-in-chief Buddy Garrity, is not a player.) Almost the only job worthy of a man in this town is *coach*. The coach is a natural aristocrat of talent and virtue who's not from the town, and who could, everyone knows, distinguish himself anywhere. Maybe the most eloquent conversationalist in town is the coach's wife,

who is also a natural aristocrat that could flourish anywhere. She, a teacher in love with book learning, has her own ambitions for herself and the kids. An important lesson of the show is that the natural aristocrats who come to a small town to elevate the place remain aliens or insufficiently appreciated for who they are. The players sometimes properly appreciate the coach, but the evildoing oligarchs who run the town appreciate him not so much. Both the coach and his wife get one raw deal after another, and they are short on real friends beyond their students. But they really do talk like friends to each other.

3. *The Big Bang Theory* manages to capture the great joy and misery, the arrogance and the anxiety, of high-level nerd friendship in conversation that's unrealistically filled with unwitting one-liners. We learn the difference between the genuinely *theoretical physicist* who, to an extraordinary extent, gets away with thinking of himself as pure mind and so is relentlessly self-obsessed yet rarely lonely, and the merely *experimental physicist*, who is dragged down by his constant awareness of his not-so-good body and its needs and seems always to be awkwardly out of place.

Honorable mention: *Community* and *Parenthood* (which is much better than *Modern Family*).

The Last *Friday Night Lights*

I've delayed my promised post on the final episode of the instant classic TV show *Friday Night Lights* in order to give you time to view it.

High school football is one of the few areas of life free from both political correctness (or identity politics) and the materialistic rigors of productivity. Merit rules—merit defined in terms of the heart and skills of a warrior. So a show about small-town football is the perfect place to display what it means to be stuck with virtue today:

1. This episode in particular was about *family*—both "natural" (or biological) families and families formed by necessity and circumstances. The team, for example, is a family.

2. The episode (and the show as a whole) is very hard on Dillon—the small Texas town, the place. The evil oligarchs who really run the town decided to consolidate the two football teams (of the two high schools) into one incredibly well-funded and talent-laden team. Those evildoers gave no thought, of course, to the effect of the consolidation on unfortunate young men for whom the team is the only good and redeeming thing in their lives. They offered the coach (Eric Taylor) the job of coaching that team.

3. In an earlier season, they had fired him as coach of the Dillon Panthers (a school with a rich tradition of football success and enthusiastic boosters), despite falling just short of winning the state championship. He was given, instead, the seemingly impossible task of building a new team at underclass East Dillon High, where he had virtually no resources. It takes the coach just two years to develop greatness out of almost nothing. Not surprisingly, he says he's more proud of that team than any other. (And, although he has the class not to say it, he's hugely proud of the job he's done there—success that's made him a national legend and got him an offer as head coach from a major college.)

4. The coach turns down the super-team job in large part because it's about destroying the family that is his East Dillon team. It's no challenge to win "state" with all the new advantages. Any decent coach could do it, and he is proud of having done it without them. He also chooses for his biological family—especially his wife.

5. The coach leaves Dillon (because the evildoers have left him nothing there). He follows his wife to Philadelphia, where she can fulfill her personal ambition as a counselor at an elite college. It's pretty clear, immediately, that Philly and college are more her kind of places. And, we see the

coach relishing the challenge of rebuilding an urban Philly team. He's confident that his talent and virtue will display their transformative powers once again. He's not limited in a way by the small-town horizon.

6. We learn that anyone (or almost anyone) with heart and brains has to get out of Dillon. The most intelligent and talented players (mostly the quarterbacks) do, and they too flourish, eventually, wherever they end up. There has been, it's impossible not to notice, a brain drain from our small towns, due to globalization, economies of scale, and all that. The only thing left for a *man* to do for a living, it seems, is to be a mechanic or a teacher or a football coach (or maybe be in law enforcement). The only way to display one's moral and intellectual excellence is as teacher and coach: But the town leaders—themselves very short on talent and virtue—don't even begin to appreciate such excellence in the coach and his wife. (The grateful students and players do, but only to some extent.) We also see, of course, that for most of the players the experience of the team and "state" (and the coach) will be the highlight of their lives. Nothing they do thereafter will engage and challenge them as well as whole human beings.

7. The show is, most of all, about the aristocracy of talent and virtue, about people who have been given extraordinary gifts and can do great good wherever they happen to be. The coach is a man who chooses his words carefully. He speaks nobly and occasionally piously, and, when appropriate, with anger and a very restrained affection. His speech is as unvulgar as a coach—a leader of warriors—could conceivably be. He has class; he knows who he is and what he's supposed to do. He's more pagan than Christian; he's almost a Stoic who doesn't read books; some synthesis of Stoic and Spartan. He's the very opposite of a racist; the players know he relates to them according to their capabilities and circumstances, and what's noble and good—and what's vicious and contemptible—about players and people in general has nothing to do with race. The coach has a bit of a problem with women, insofar as he has little to do with students who aren't on the team, and like all manly men he's overprotective of his daughter. (His wife wonderfully compensates for his shortcomings in this area.) But he rather easily comes to appreciate that there's that rare woman with the talent and heart to coach a football team. And he and his wife, who, of course, have their "issues," have a marriage that's all about sharing the social responsibilities of personal excellence.

The Emmys (*Friday Night Lights, Mad Men,* etc.)

1. So the best news from the Emmys is that *Friday Night Lights* won two key awards—for writing and for lead actor (Kyle Chandler as the coach)—in the category of drama. Because this show (which, in my view, was the best on TV last year) is off the air, I've been reluctant to post on it. But now people will be rushing to buy the DVDs. I urge you to watch the virtually perfect last episode in order to be able to get maximum benefit out of my next post.

2. *Mad Men* has now won Outstanding Drama Series every year it's been on the air. It's a fine show that continues to get better, with the intensifying focus on Don Draper, that singularly self-made man, trying to get a handle on the mess that is his life.

3. The coach and Don are both blessed with huge talent that could flourish anywhere. But just thinking about *Mad Men* a bit leads anyone who cares about the moral drama that is any particular human life to appreciate that the coach is a totally credible model of admirable human excellence, while Don is a fascinating literary contrivance that's more a social psychological statement than an actual guy.

4. *Mad Men* suggests that in the techno-consumerist—yet still sexist and elitist—world of the 1960s, it's impossible to be a real man, someone who has control over his life and avoids self-pity and self-indulgence by knowing who he is and what he's supposed to do. But the coach is a real man with all the Stoic qualities; as a natural aristocrat he's not blinded by small-town prejudices and oligarchic conventions (and so the opposite of a racist and almost the opposite of a sexist). At the end of the show, we see that he's going to do as well in Philadelphia as he did in Dillon, TX.

5. *Mad Men* and *Friday Night Lights* would both deserve Oscars if they were movies, inasmuch as both are superior to what we can see in the theaters.

6. *Modern Family* won the comedy awards. It is a cheerful and somewhat edifying show, but it just isn't very funny. If you want excellent family shows (that end up being more funny in more subtle ways), watch *Parenthood* and *Men of a Certain Age.*

7. Jim Parsons got a second straight Emmy for his portrayal of the nerdy theoretical physicist on *The Big Bang Theory.* The show as a whole isn't getting noticed. But it's also one of the best-written shows on TV. Feminists should be upset that the women scientists on the show are being

ignored. Sheldon's scientist-girlfriend is funnier than Sheldon, and it should enlighten us all to think about such a brilliant and self-confident woman who's oblivious to her bodily appearance while being so candid about her bodily needs. It's Amy who delivers the laughs on their virtual (computer-screen) and real dates; Sheldon is pretty much the straight man.

8. I have to admit I didn't see many of the shows in such categories as "reality competition program." *The Daily Show* always wins and always deserves to in the variety show category; sadly it doesn't have any credible competition these days.

Never Let Me Go—Part 1:
The Souls of Donor-Clones: Love, Death,
and Personal Identity in *Never Let Me Go*

Never Let Me Go is one of the most thoughtful pieces of science fiction ever. The film (2010), directed by Mark Romanek, is based on the novel (2005) by Kazuo Ishiguro. It's hard to see how the film, although it doesn't capture everything about the book, could have been a better adaptation. It is a labor of love full of wisdom, and it certainly deserves a much wider audience and better critical reception. What I'm going to say is based on both the film and the novel, but I'm moved to write it by having just seen the film.

The story is about human clones raised at an English boarding school (not that different from the one you see in Harry Potter) as sources of organs for others. They've been created as donors and, in this alternative version of twentieth-century history, they're indispensable for perpetuating medical science's achievement in pushing the average human lifespan beyond one hundred years. They aren't taught any of the skills required to make a living. They won't need them. They'll die as young adults, and their productivity depends only on their health. So the school is particularly strict when it comes to prohibiting smoking, but otherwise quite easygoing. (Just like residential schools these days!)

Certainly there's little point in encouraging chastity as a virtue. The donor clones won't become (and don't have!) parents, and the one physical difference we can see between them and "normals" is that they're incapable of reproducing. But they aren't encouraged to lose themselves in mindless orgies or random one-night stands, as people are in *The Brave New World*. Nor is their self-consciousness dulled by a mood enhancing drugs, such as the one people use in *The Brave New World*. They soon enough connect something like sexual exclusivity with personal love on their own, and that's neither encouraged nor discouraged. Freed from social and biological necessity yet fully self-conscious, they enjoy what we might regard as an unrealistically high level of sexual freedom.

The donor-clones' sexual lives are unregulated, because there's no need to regulate them for them to perform their social function. So they show us what human life might be like if we continue down to the end of the road of detaching sex from reproduction. It won't be a world full of unobsessive enjoyment; jealousy and intimacy will remain, but it will also be a melancholic world of displaced or undirected and misunderstood longing. Sex separated from reproduction remains haunted by death and the personal longings associated by reproduction.

The clones in school are close to regular kids, having all the virtues and vices of highly self-conscious and relational (and so, polymorphously erotic) persons. It seems, at first, that they're very short on the various human longings for personal greatness or even political freedom, but the undirected anger—sometimes literally howling—of one of the boys shows that he knows he's been deprived of a purpose to channel his spiritedness. (He manages to take a kind of perverse pride—when half-dead—in being a particularly hardy and so productive donor.)

The girls know they've been deprived of being and having children. They especially long for parents, and they sometimes obsessively search for the persons on whom they were modeled. (One girl pages through porn magazines looking for a woman with her body.) They are haunted by the truth that they've been modeled on "trash" to be less than trash, to be, in fact, less than slaves (who, even in our South, couldn't be used in this way). They know well enough they live in a world in which no one can care for them but themselves, but that doesn't mean they live without personal love. The donor-clones care about their "status" or personal significance in each other's eyes, but they're imperfectly but genuinely resigned to the fact that they have no status—and so no recognition of who they really are—with anyone else.

It's not clear for most of the film why they're educated not only to read but also to create art and poetry in an environment where they can culti-vate personal attachments as social beings. We eventually learn that this is the first and last school devoted to the ethical raising of spare-part chil-dren. Their "guardians" wanted to prove that clones have souls too. As unique and irreplaceable persons displaying their inward lives, those guardians hoped to show that human clones can't be regarded as resources to be exploited—mutilated and eventually killed—for the bene-fit of others.

One of the clones asks with indignant entitlement why they can't have souls. There's no reason at all, it turns out. From the point of view of our science, we have two controversial claims here: The first is that all persons have souls (or personal identities that distinguish them from each other and all the other animals), and that clones—manufactured persons—would have souls, too. Our scientific sophisticates, of course, don't believe in the real existence of souls, and they're often excited about the prospect of the cloning of human beings as more evidence for nothing being special or deeply personal about any of us. Cloning will show that what we imagined the Creator does, we can do for ourselves. Our religious believers fear cloning too much. If human beings are successfully cloned, the clones will be just like us, full of irreducibly mysterious and wonderful individuality. They'll be more evidence still of the presence of God in the world through beings made in his image. The human beings made by men won't really be fully under their control and, as copies of natural beings, they won't really be their products. Almost everyone, the film shows us, overrates the onto-logical and theological significance of cloning.

Never Let Me Go—Part 2:
Special Education and Natural Rights

The boarding school we see might be regarded as a privileged moment in the history of donor-clones. Their strangely benevolent guardians gave themselves the tricky task of raising them as "special" in two ways. They had to be educated not to rebel against the special function they've been given, meaning that they're taught to be afraid to escape into the world outside and to accept who they are. That means they can't be told too much, too soon, about what their special function is. But they're also, of course, educated to be special in the sense of unique and irreplaceable persons, who are made for more than for serving some social function. There's no question of the donor-clones rebelling successfully against the fate or end they've been given but, badly educated, they would become needlessly anxious or agitated and so both needlessly miserable and unable to perform their social function well. In some basic ways, they're educated the way we all are.

Every film ever made about little kids in English boarding schools has the "subtext" of homelessness and abandonment; they all want to go home. The cloned kids, it's true, don't have memories of some particular home, but they still have the human longings for home—for even "regression to the womb" they never experienced—and so to live decently have to find out slowly how radically homeless they are. We're reminded by this of the educational process of "turning around" in the cave or comprehensive process of political socialization described in Plato's *Republic*. The cloned kids are certainly liberated from the comfortable illusions of tradition, culture, country, and family, and they're not even offered the solace of religion.

Those two views of "being special" that guide the donor-clones' education are, of course, incompatible, and one would soon enough have to give way to the other. So the school was closed as a failed experiment of misguided reformers, and the social utility—the benefit to other free persons—of the special function trumped the intensely personal or inward. We learn, from this extreme case, that it's always monstrous to educate persons merely to be part of some whole, and that it's equally monstrous to deny persons some satisfaction of their social desires to be parts of natural human wholes—beginning with the family.

This special school's guardians were different from those in Plato's *Republic* in not consistently preparing children for the task in service to their society for which they are fitted. But the idea of justice in Socrates' city depended on a thorough examination of each child to determine what he or she is best at by nature. The donor-clones, in fact, are much more than mere bodies, and so not best fit by nature for the function they've been given. The political decision was made to take no real interest in who they really are.

Nature, it would seem, disappears as a standard when it comes to clones; their purpose is given to them, not by God or nature, but by those who created them. The children are done a monstrous injustice by a human standard willfully trumping the natural (or divine) one, by willful blindness to what we can see with our own eyes about others. We Americans would readily say that these kids are being denied their inalienable natural rights. They are, by nature, free persons, and so they are radically different from the domestic animals we legitimately breed for destruction. Their "nature"—or who or what they are—was not, in fact, determined by those who made them.

In the *Republic*, we have to add, citizens are socialized to be of loving, friendly service to their fellow citizens. But the clones, of course, aren't citizens, and those they serve are socialized not to be their friends. The clones aren't even made to improve the quality of the English citizenry, because the English don't think of themselves as citizens either. They are, instead, for the indefinite perpetuation of free persons who refuse to think of themselves as parts of any whole greater than themselves. The clones are made to be bodies used to keep other bodies alive as long as possible.

The clones aren't nobly serving some common good. If there were some such good, they would be excluded from it as non-citizens. But there is, in a highly individualistic and high-tech time, no such good. There's no public view of what citizens share as beings with souls. That's one reason we've increasingly become all about keeping bodies alive right now as long as possible, as if their perpetuation is the point of all existence. Each of us knows we're not nothing, but we know nothing certain beyond non-nonexistence that we share with others. Regarding even our own bodies as our property, it would be hard for us not to regard bodies we make for our benefit as our property—no matter what claims they make for themselves.

There was a rumor among the clones that the real purpose of the gallery of their art and poetry was to provide evidence for their capacity for personal love. Clones who could prove they were in love—in the tradition-al, monogamous, intimate, personal sense—might qualify for a deferral for a few years from becoming donors. The clones, of course, were capa-ble of such love (despite being unable to have children), but it turns out that the rumor was untrue and nobody in power cared.

So, the effort at ethical education failed. The undeniable evidence that clones could be fine artists and poets (unlike even the chimps and the dol-phins) was ignored. Cloning didn't stop, but their "humane" education did. The schools became factories, where the clones, apparently, were treated as brutally as agri-business chickens. To abandon the production of spare-part clones, after all, would be to abandon medical progress and return to a dark time of incurable diseases, terrible suffering, and early death. This "alternative history" is better than the real history of the twentieth-century, during which millions and millions of people were slaughtered for no real or worthy purpose at all, people clearly not made to be History fod-der or fatherland fodder or ideology fodder.

The good news is that the new factory schools probably prepared the cloned kids better for the special function for which they were made; the bad is that the persons, as Aristotle says, can't become who they are by nature without social habituation or cultivation. The evidence that clones have souls, we learn, withered away. The privileged moment of enlightened donor-clones could only be for a moment, because it seemed to do nobody any good for them to be open to the truth about love and death.

We might have a moment's chill here as we think about what's going to happen as biotechnology eradicates the distinction between procreation and manufacturing. If we morph into conscious robots capable of manu-facturing other conscious robots, as the transhumanists predict, why wouldn't all the robots be regarded by the other robots as resources to be used? We won't believe that all robots are created equal, and we don't real-ly believe that robots, even if conscious in some sense, will be capable of personal love. But the manufactured clones have real bodies, and even a body that includes artificial parts is still a body. We aren't now—contrary to what our scientists sometimes suggest—and will never be conscious machines, although it is the idea of conscious machines that drives the pro-duction of clones for spare parts. We will never become simply manufac-tured beings, even if we perversely deny ourselves the joys of procreation.

Never Let Me Go—Part 3:
The Promise of Indefinite Longevity

The donor-clones seemed indispensable to fulfill the promise of what we call regenerative medicine. We can live as indefinitely long as classic cars. Every part can be replaced or regenerated, even the heart. The exception is the brain, which is clearly irreplaceable, but maybe, if properly maintained, it can be kept from deteriorating. Regenerative medicine at this point is mainly about therapies to restore the functioning of the organs we already have, and so spare parts don't seem as important as they once did. But that doesn't mean we'll not need them at all, which is why we're still working on developing artificial organs, and why we still need kidneys from live human beings to have some people around for as long as possible. Even with regenerative medicine combined with genetic therapies (that, for example, take out diseases), we know we won't live forever. It's just that we won't experience ourselves as having to die at any particular time, as no longer determined or shaped or haunted by the necessity of death. Death will no longer be viewed as inevitable, but as an accident to be prudently avoided. So, Socrates' courage on the day of his trial—a reflection of the wisdom he acquired through learning how to die—would have seemed like self-destructive anger if the regenerative doctor had just promised him another seventy years. In thinking about the progressive logic of the science that needs the parts of donor-clones, we think about the real ontological difference that might concern us. The huge difference is between those shaped by the real promise of indefinite longevity, and those condemned to an early death. It's easy to see that the latter will usually live more admirable and truthful lives, while admitting that it's probably unreasonable to choose death if science can offer each of us a way out.

The philosopher of the future who teaches us to live well with the indefinite longevity, that's not to be confused with immortality, has a huge job. He's not going to have much of an audience if he shouts the truth about the donor-clones, for example. We can now say that all men are created equal because they're all self-conscious and equally mortal. But our scientific progress is now based on our refusal to be defined by our morality, and that includes our refusal to be moved by the thought that the difference between living fifty and five hundred years is nothing in light of eternity.

The philosophers of the past taught something like people are really angry because they know how contingent and ephemeral personal existence is. But they have a real compensation in personal love, which gives personal significance to particular lives. It's love that's the main evidence that we're somehow more than merely biological beings, or just like the insignificant members of the other species. And we love because we're open to the truth about who we are, and that includes an openness to the real existence of other "whos" in a world full of "whats." It's easy to show that the quest for indefinite longevity is at the expense of distortion and destruction of the various relational dimensions of who we are. It's bad for love by detaching love from the reality of shared responsibilities in, for example, marriage and the family. But the promise is, to the extent we're unmoved by death, we won't need love to live well. And we won't be moved by anger and hatred either. So religion and politics, the two big sources of angry personal destruction, will just wither away. It's easy to respond that people might be more angry than ever. Death, seeming almost completely unnecessary and so almost completely accidental, would demand our constant attention as we fend off the various risk factors that threaten us, and our beings will be objectively more secure and subjectively more contingent than ever. The resulting "howl of existentialism"—or inarticulate rage—might generate all kinds of tyrannical policies aiming to free us from our personal contingency.

We can also see, of course, why so many people serious about souls, rights, and human dignity dig in against even cloning or manufacturing embryos to be destroyed in pursuit of the progress of medical science. The bodies of human persons can't ever be regarded as just another natural resource. Our bodies are indispensable parts of personal identity, sources of what makes personal life worth living. It's love that limits our anger at having bodies, at being stuck with existences that elude our control. The world defined by "rational control" would be completely unerotic and so eerily empty. Reflecting on the impulse behind spare-parts cloning shows us why that world is impossible for us to make and undesirable for us to pursue, at least too single-mindedly.

Never Let Me Go—Part 4:
A Female Philosopher-Clone

A renegade teacher tells the students at the school straight out, much ear-lier than they were supposed to know, what their purpose in life is, claim-ing that knowing what one's life is for is the only way to live decently. Unlike the free persons of Britain, she tells the cloned kids, they won't be able to choose for themselves how to live, to work in a supermarket or move to America in search of fame and fortune. Their unprecedented social determination contributes to free persons' unprecedented determi-nation to live as they please for a long, long time.

The clones we see do live as decently as people in their circumstances could live; they display the virtues appropriate to their real situation. But their decency doesn't come, as it did for British servants in aristocratic times, from finding honor in serving great men. Ishiguro also wrote the psychological masterpiece *The Remains of the Day*, which is about the crippling disillusionment experienced by a loyal, capable, and rather eru-dite servant coming to learn that the aristocrat he serves is a self-indul-gent appeaser of Hitler.

The clones' servitude is particularly touching because it's so free of illusions and disillusionment; both master and slave, in this case, have to live with the fact of naked exploitation. The cloned persons are deeply detached from the persons they were made for. So they are much more free than the servants of old to live for themselves as relational beings, for what they really know and love about persons. They are allowed, sort of accidentally, the best possible life available to them, arguably one better than the free persons they were made for.

The film ends with the central character—a cloned woman (Kathy H.)—sharing her hard-won wisdom. She's spent most of her life reading and daydreaming to a romantic tune ("Never Let Me Go"), full of what she imagined was unrequited love. (She eventually finds out it was requited, soon before the man who, so to speak, always loved her makes his final donation.) Her period of donation was deferred by volunteering to be a "carer," a clone assigned with caring for clones in "the recovery center" as donors—sometimes for a third or fourth time. Non-clones have to not know clones well enough to care for them. But clones still need care (as do we are all)—both physical and emotional—to stay alive as long as possible and so to be put to maximum possible use. Kathy found work more enjoyable than not and rather Stoically but sensitively, she did what she could to ease the suffering of the doomed. She was able to identify, to a limited extent, with people like her whom she didn't know well enough to love. That's not to say, of course, that her caring was exactly voluntary.

Unproductive personal love is no cause for deferral, but giving care that enhances the performance of the donor's function is. Nature, in effect, gives members of our species a deferral from early death to be caring moms and dads, without whom our species would have no future. Kathy's denied that natural deferral, but the one given her by her makers was judged to be almost as indispensable. Kathy, in fact, took a perverse pride in caring well enough that her donors did better or gave more donations than most, while remaining unusually unagitated about what was happening to them. She was assisting "the state" in its murderous tyranny, but she was also helping the donors live as long and as happily as possible.

A clone that dies as a result of his or her final donation is said to "complete." That, of course, makes a kind of sense. A complete life, even Aristotle says, is one in which one has fulfilled one's proper function in the most excellent way possible. A being without a function, Aristotle adds, is a good-for-nothing, and he encourages us to believe that it would make no sense to say only human beings are free in that negative way. Aristotle denies that there's such a being as a free person who can live without a purpose or even with a purpose that's merely a "preference."

The clone's life ends because he or she has fulfilled as well as possible the function he or she has been given—not by nature, as Aristotle would say, but by other men. In that sense, a citizen has led a complete life when he dies in battle after years of service to his country. And contemporary Darwinians are about restoring the idea of a complete life by nature; we should think in terms of doing our duty as social beings by falling in love, having kids, raising them properly, and then accepting nature's impersonal intention that each of us step aside—disappear as persons or particular beings—for the good of the species.

From a Darwinian view, in fact, the clone's life completes relatively early because he or she has done a kind of manmade or conscious and volitional duty to the species. Other lives last longer, because they make their contribution to the species in the slower, more purely natural way. But at some rather definite point those lives are superfluous, too. In either case, the idea of completion is a pitiless affront to the real longing of persons to stay around. Whether the function we allegedly complete comes from other persons or nature or our country, we know it's not our own. Free persons, if given the choice, would rather live incompletely or for an indefinitely long time. For the Darwinian, as for the Aristotelian, one piece of evidence for the goodness of nature is that it doesn't offer us that choice. So today's best Darwinians deny that indefinite longevity is possible, because the indefinite complexity of nature guarantees its triumph over all our efforts to thwart her mission to take out each and every one of us. Given the techno-choice against death, no Darwinian or Aristotelian doctrine about our true function as social or political animals could possibly cause us, the Darwinian has to admit, to choose for death or natural completeness. The truth is that we don't know how much conscious and volitional—or personal—evolution can supplant impersonal evolution, but there's no denying that there's been a wonderful amount of success already.

Still, it turns out, as Kathy says, that everyone loves and everyone dies. Everyone "completes" and nobody in love ever has enough time. So those who "complete" (about to die) and those who are genuinely self-conscious (or possess self-knowledge) don't really believe that that experience of completion is some kind of decisive compensation for personal extinction. We persons don't leave consciousness for good with our deepest thought being "my work here is done." I know I wasn't here mainly to work, and I'd rather stay, for example, to love my children than merely "live on" in a not really personal way, in them and their fading memories.

The idea of completion is based on purposes that are less than personal. And so the difference between a relatively short life and a relatively long one is insignificant, although at any particular moment we'd rather have more time. That's the main reason why it's so monstrous, we can see, for the personal donor to be killed just to keep some persons around a bit longer.

But Kathy knows she's being harmed less than those who made her think. The free persons of Britain don't think they have some function that completes their lives; they work to escape the imperatives of completion altogether. It turns out that personal love is the main reason to wish for—but not one that can be the source of—some kind of significant "deferral" from one's natural destiny. Every genuinely self-conscious person knows himself (or herself) to be a momentary speck between the two abysses of eternity in this world—a speck of infinite value because of who he or she is as a knower or a lover.

Everyone dies, no conscious life ever really completes, and there's no escaping from the incompletely requited longings connected with who we are and whom we love. It's understandable why the free persons of Britain work so hard to escape completion. To the extent escape really seems possible through our own progressive, scientific efforts, who can deny that we might well exploit unto death those we don't really know and love?

Still, the undeluded awareness of Kathy, the "carer," that those who created her don't care for her at all (she's in the very opposite situation of just about anyone who has parents or who has believed in the personal Creator) doesn't morph into anger. Her compensations are her real knowledge that their injustice can't get them what they think they want, and her real gratitude for the life she's been given (and not really by them).

There seems to be almost no place for religion in this story. Had there been a lot of real Christians in England, surely there would have been big resistance—a pro-life moment—clamoring for justice for the clones. But personal freedom—in some respects at least a Christian inheritance—had become freedom from any dependence on the loving judgment of a personal God. The guardians who devised the special education to display the souls of the donor-clones were, in fact, moved by the Christian thought that every person is unique and irreplaceable. Their "humane" intention disappeared with the closing of their school. And so too, it would seem, did any evidence—at least satisfactory to skeptics—for the proposition that the clones are real persons too.

Both the book and film do show us, however, that people are given souls or the capability for inward lives and personal love. They also show us the monstrous futility of trying to do for ourselves as free persons what the Christian God promised us. Finally, they show us that, while philosophy is, in a way, learning how to die, it can't really show us that free, loving persons are ever really reconciled with the idea that a complete human life is necessarily a mortal one. Our longings point beyond our biological being, and both the donor-clones and the free persons of England seem cruelly deprived of any faith in a personal Creator. Nothing they experience through the progress of science is evidence of his nonexistence. Quite the opposite.

Preliminary Thoughts on Technology, the Family, and *Super 8*

Super 8 is the only movie I've seen this year that's worth thinking about. I haven't, of course, seen that many. Posts on movies now in theaters on blogs by rank amateurs have their limitations. Here's one: I only saw the film once, a couple of weeks ago. I have talked about it some, including with the guys on the blog *Postmodern Conservative*.

The movie contains parts of lots of movies about home, coming-of-age, family, friendship, ETs, technology, and, maybe most of all, being homesick and at home.

It might be considered as a kind of suck-up by Abrams to Spielberg, but it's more than that. Abrams (see the TV show *Lost*) is more philosophical than Spielberg.

The first thing that struck me is how realistic the town is. At first glance, there's little more depressing than a Midwestern mill town (in Ohio—but it was actually filmed in Weirton, WV). But the town is actually quite beautiful. There are the surrounding hills, of course. But there are also all sorts of modest, quirky, charming houses from various decades—and the run-down but still functioning pre-Wal-Mart downtown. There is, of course, nothing gentrified about it, but it's a safe, decent, interesting place.

We have nostalgia for the town—and the year of 1979—because at that time families were clearly functional and caring enough. The movie has a lot of *Stand by Me* in it—friends marginalized at school being transformed by an improbable, dangerous adventure. But in this case, the kids aren't alone. Two of them have sad, screwed-up single dads who don't pay their only children much real attention. But those two dads stand up for their kids in a heroic way before the film's end.

Not only that, we get the impression that a typical family in the town is a big, screaming mess crammed into a small house. The parents in the house we see are smart, loving, and as attentive as they can be. Their kids are admirably self-reliant despite living on top of each other. They're happy. A kid stuck alone in a big house with a single parent is lonely and pitiful.

The movie has generally been viewed as anti-technology. But that's not so; it evaluates technological change according to the standards of child development and family life.

So, the film is pro-train, fairly pro-mill (meaning steel mill), and, of course, pro-Super 8. The Super 8 camera is technology that sparks the kids' creativity without keeping them stuck in their rooms. The kids are out and about in their filmmaking adventures—relatively but not completely unsupervised in the safe streets (until the Air Force vs. the ET thing breaks out) of town.

Soon enough after 1979, kids would be stuck in their rooms with the Internet and their virtual friends—wasting their creativity on their Facebook pages and all kind of computer-based games. Digital cameras too easily seem to make artists of us all. The year of the small-town Super 8 was a privileged moment in the history of technology—perhaps better for children and families than what came before and what came after.

Even though the techno-highpoint of the film is the spectacular destruction of a huge train—with metal spewing in all directions (but, more than miraculously, not even injuring the kids or killing the guy driving the truck the train collided with), the point is carefully made that such train accidents are exceedingly rare. Not only that, the sensitive-kid protagonist especially enjoys building trains, and it's a sign of the manipulative ruthlessness of the fat-kid filmmaker that he asks his loyal and sensitive friend to blow up one of his model trains to improve the film. I could go on, but let's just say that the film embraces the oft-articulated conclusion that trains are technology on an appropriately human scale, machines worthy of men.

The mill looms large and stark in the film. It, on one level, ruins the town aesthetically. The action of the film is initiated by the sensitive kid's mom being struck dead by a big piece of metal while working at the mill. Still, the film actually opens with a sign that brags about how safe the mill is—no accidents in over two years. Mills are no more routinely destructive than trains.

The mill allows both men and women to work close to home. It seems like a decent place to work, work worthy of men (in the gender-unspecific sense). In 1979, the mill is open and we're nostalgic for it. Once it closes, what do people do to earn a decent living?

In such a town, the only other professions worthy of men, it would seem, are high-school teaching (and coaching) and law enforcement. The mill surely pays better, for one thing, and there's no need to go to college or leave home to find work as long as it's flourishing.

Another good thing about the film is that the sheriff and his deputy are portrayed as men of courage and integrity who know what they're doing—real leaders. The high-school biology teacher is a rather heroic misunderstood genius who communicates telepathically with an ET—and so a tireless and courageous spokesperson for ET rights.

The Way

This serious and thoughtful—and maybe great—film is quite the labor of love. It's a film about broken families and broken lives made by the father-and-son team of Martin Sheen and Emilio Estevez. "The way" is the Christian pilgrimage of walking the Camino de Santiago or the Way of St. James to the Cathedral of Santiago de Compostela in Galicia, Spain. The long and tough walk begins in the French Pyrenees, covers hundreds of miles, and usually takes a month or more. It's one of the oldest of the Christian pilgrimages.

Even today, the film emphasizes, it's quite common and highly appropriate that the pilgrimage be made alone.

Today, however, few seem to make it in search of God. In post-Christian Europe, few who make it are believers. The pilgrims we see are nonetheless searchers in some sense. They're dissatisfied with living freely in the midst of prosperity. They're not poor; their journey is funded by credit cards, and they can readily take advantage of all the creature comforts available along the way. But their lives are impoverished nonetheless; they're angry and lonely and deprived in some way of personal love. They're evidence against the proposition that if you give people comfort and security they won't need religion—or a deeply personal, spiritual, and searching dimension to their existence—anymore. The film can be taken to support the proposition that even ordinary, affluent people these days still have souls.

The American—the Sheen character—is angry and despondent after hearing of the accidental death of his young son early on they boy's walk along the Camino de Santiago. He decides to take the journey himself. He was, in his pride and complacency, estranged from the life of his only son. The son—played by Estevez—wanted to see places for himself, and, because his is no ordinary life, he's positioned to drop everything to be a searcher. He tells his dad that a life is not chosen, but lived. A corny line, to be sure; still, it's adeptly directed against the conceit that life is nothing but a menu of choice.

The son—a man in pursuit of a Ph.D. out of genuine intellectual curiosity—decides to drop his pursuit of that credential in order really to wonder. He spends his life wandering—without even a cell phone (his dad complains he's the only person left in the world without one)—in search of we don't know what. But we do know he dies early on "the way." His dad's journey is to come to know his son in death as he did not know him in life. The film ends with the dad—a successful "eye doctor"—leaving everything behind to wander the world alone to come to see for himself.

The dad is a lapsed Catholic (like some Walker Percy character); he says time and again he's not much of a religious man. He refuses to pray with a priest when he hears about his son's death; however, a priest on the way does give him a rosary, and he admits later he puts it to good use. He does make the sign of the cross at the Mass for Pilgrims at the end of the way. But he also follows the advice of a gypsy father to go beyond the cathedral to the sea to do his full duty to his son, and the gypsy says that religion has nothing to do with what he owes his son.

The wisdom of the gypsy patriarch—Ishmael—is of the sacredness of family and tribe, bonds that have been promiscuously violated and broken in our individualistic time. It's not that those bonds oppose religion, necessarily, but they're not to be displaced by it either. Ishmael says, as a matter of fact, that he has two thousand close friends.

Love, Death, and *50/50* (the Movie)

50/50 is a pretty profound movie. It's also as perfectly cast as *Moneyball*, apparently because they were both cast by the same person.

Moneyball, of course, is about the attempt to impose rational control on a children's game, on not leaving the outcome of the baseball season to chance. Players are like cards. If properly counted, a game of chance becomes a game mastered by human calculation.

But the big game of chance, of course, is any particular human life. Each of us, we really know, exists for a moment between two abysses. Who knows how long his particular moment will last? From a certain view, each of us is an absolutely contingent accident in a universe absolutely indifferent to personal existence. It's not just here today, gone tomorrow. Each of us has no certainty about even getting to tomorrow.

50/50 is about a particularly risk-averse young man (of twenty-seven) in sophisticated, hip Seattle. He attends scrupulously to those risk factors that might extinguish his existence. He's all about the right diet and exercise. He won't even drive because he's seen the fatality statistics for drivers. He was raised by a smothering mom, and he's never told a girl he loves her. He's never even been to Canada! And of course he can't stand being late.

So, he's done what he can to exert rational control over his being, to make his personal existence as uncontingent as possible.

Due to an exceedingly rare genetic mutation, he gets cancer, nonetheless. He doesn't get a death sentence, though. He knows from Googling that he has a 50/50 chance of survival. If he were at Vegas, his friend remarks, he'd have the best odds around. But can people live well while being reminded so insistently about how chancy one's personal future is? The man who's been avoiding facing risks is now smacked in the face with his fate as a kind of toss of the coin.

The doctor who diagnoses him won't talk to him about his chances or even try to help him deal with them. He's not that kind of specialist.

He's sent to a therapist—a specialist in comforting him, in keeping him in a good mood. Her techniques fail her, until she falls in love with him as a whole person.

At a certain point, he tells the therapist that he's come to terms with dying. We all die, he tells her; you too will die. She regards this truth telling as pathological or alienating, but she lacks the words to talk him out of it.

Unfortunately, his serenity doesn't last, precisely because he's reminded that his impending death isn't certain. His chemo having failed to arrest the cancer, his only choice is to have a very high-risk operation that might well kill him, but could also conceivably cure him. The operation gets the job done in the decisive respect, and he's very lucky to get to live.

Along the way, he's reconciled with his caregiving mom and his father with Alzheimer's (both of whom he'd been avoiding), learns about deep or true friendship (this is the best bromance movie ever) from his buddy who, with all his faults, sticks with him, and gains enough knowledge about personal love to finally give his heart like a man to a woman (the therapist, of course). His personal being becomes a lot less contingent as he becomes less obsessed with risk, and more confident about who he is as a relational being. He stops trying to subject his personal existence to rational control.

This uplifting account neglects what the movie tells us about how little our society offers us in terms of living well with our mortality, so we're more death-haunted and experience ourselves as more contingent than ever. The dying, we see in various ways, creep us out more than ever. Real loyalty is rare; even the best of friends is somewhat unreliable. This poor guy ends up taking a bus home from chemo! He has quite the minimal support group; he has no tradition or community or extended family or church or God to rely upon for unconditional love and to make sense out of what he really knows. His mom turns out to be good enough, but she's all the real family he has. His friend (unlike his first girlfriend) turns out to be good enough, but that's because, despite his vulgarity and all that (he's a Seth Rogen character), he's way better than the typical good friend these days.

So, one view is that in a free and prosperous and enlightened society the need for religion would wither away, because people would readily find happiness on their own. Another view, of course, is that in such a society death would come to seem more accidental and so more terrible than ever, and people would be increasingly deprived of compensations for their contingency and their mortality.

"The Show": Emo Reflections on *Moneyball*

So I saw *Moneyball*. It's a fine movie. Brad Pitt has exceeded Robert Redford in his capacity to convey brooding and ironic depth—while adding envy, resentment, and parental love.

Jonah Hill is becoming more and more like Bill Murray, in one respect: he also always seems to play himself, and that's always more than good enough. He's close to the same guy he was in *Get Him to the Greek*, and that mixture of an endearing kind of shy integrity and nerdy enthusiasm fits equally well in both films.

Philip Seymour Hoffman had the toughest role as the no-nonsense manager who just wants to do his job.

The film is the tale of the underdog only in a way. Billy Beane (the Pitt character) is a general manager frustrated because, as a coach at a small-market (Oakland) team, his budget is a small fraction of the Yankee budget. His team makes the playoffs nonetheless, and his reward is for other, richer teams to seduce away his best players with lucrative offers. It's terrible that baseball success is that determined by team budget, the thought is.

Billy—a real smart guy who turned down a full scholarship to Stanford to sign a baseball contract—counters money with science. He brings in Peter Brand (the Hill character)—a Yale economics grad with an obsession with baseball statistics—to choose bargain players neglected by other teams for reasons having nothing to do with the actual winning of games. He's going to take advantage of what Brand calls the "epidemic failure" to understand the real causes of victory and defeat in the game.

Now, Brand doesn't invent the statistical model that drives the innovative player selection. That was done in a book by the hyper-nerd and horribly socially maladjusted Billy James. But no team had ever applied the method consistently, because they all were in the thrall of the apparently wrong romantic premise that you can't reduce the personal art of the sport to an impersonal science. It turns out that the scouts, with all their experience, have no idea what they're doing when it comes to selecting players.

The statistics that govern the rebuilding of the team are amazingly simple. Players are chosen pretty much for their knack for getting on base. Stuff like fielding turns out to make little difference. Counting the team's collective capacity to get on base turns out to be like counting cards in blackjack. It won't determine the outcome of a particular hand or game, but it's a method pretty much guaranteed to get results over a whole season (like over a whole night at the table).

This victory for the little guy is not a victory for players. They're treated like cards, traded or not according to the results of printouts. Even Brand complains that fans won't understand why an all-star is being traded in the middle of the season, but Beane doesn't care. His goal is winning, and it turns out that's all the fans end up caring about. It turns out that the scientifically detached general manager (who won't travel with the players for fear of getting attached to them) can gain rational control over the game. The owner of the Red Sox is impressed enough with the success of Beane's small-budget team that he offers him the largest contract ever for a general manager to come to Boston. He's worth it!

Beane doesn't come to Boston. But the Red Sox had already hired James anyway, and the statistical method governed the selection of the 2004 team that won the World Series—the one that broke the curse of the Bambino. Science defeated superstition!!

The film, thank God, is nowhere that simple. Baseball is saved from science, to some extent. Beane is quite superstitious; he doesn't watch Oakland games for fear of jinxing the team. The team wins twenty games in a row, but the truth is no science would have predicted that! That streak has the mark of irreducible randomness about it. Beane decides to go ahead and watch part of the 20th game in that streak when he finds out the A's are up 11–0. Incredibly improbably, the other team actually catches up and the score is 11–11. There's something to the superstition!? Well, no. A miraculous or at least somewhat improbable homer wins the game for the A's 12–11, and that victory is just as good as a game won 11–0.

In any case, Beane recognizes, baseball isn't about the regular season. People don't really remember a team unless it wins its final game (in the World Series). And there just aren't enough playoff games for the science to work. The outcome of the key part of the season is pretty random. The scientifically constructed A's are taken out by the Twins in the first round of the playoffs.

We also learn from Beane that he is quite ambivalent about being romantic about baseball. His own life story has filled him with "issues." He turned down the Stanford scholarship because scouts told him that he had all the skills required to be a baseball star. But—due it seems to some deficiency in character more than talent—he never made it as a player. The romantic dream of becoming a legend—a role model of personal excellence—didn't become real for him.

Scouts, it turns out, don't *know* how the career of any of their recruits will play out, and Beane blames them for not being scientific enough to *know*. But even the statistical science of baseball can't predict with any great degree of reliability the fate of any particular career. The science depends on aggregate results. Beane seeks rational control out of resentment, and even out of envy for those with both the character and talent to be stars.

Billy's shy, emo daughter, at his urging, sings a moving version of the song "The Show." It's an emo tune that was featured prominently in the emo classic *Juno*. It came out in 2008, and so the key role it plays in the film is strikingly anachronistic. Billy, the dad, seems unduly moved by it. Listening to it, apparently, kept him from taking the Red Sox's incredible offer—just so he could continue to play a big role in his daughter's life. He chose to be a dad, a man. He chose, not exactly romantically, for real life.

Baseball is a child's game, we learn, that some men get to play until they're forty and a few can stay involved in longer as managers, general managers, and so forth. "The Show," of course, is the name all professional baseball players give to the majors.

Billy's daughter changes the concluding words of the song to "You're a loser dad. Just enjoy the show." Only a loser would try to gain rational control over a child's game.

Race, Class, and Gender in *The Help*

Well, this is the first time ever that I've taken the "cultural studies" approach of featuring the themes of race, class, and gender in talking about a work of art. I'm, of course, against the "politically correct" tendency to reduce literary/artistic analysis to that trinity. And I'm especially "uncomfortable" with the word gender, not being sure that it refers to anything real. I know what "sex" is, both as an activity and as way of categorizing human beings (and even other animals) into two groups. But I'm not sure what gender is. I'm told it's a social construction, but surely male and female can't be completely detached from a natural foundation.

What's fascinating about this movie is its subtle approach to race, class, and gender. Class, I will explain, is not just about the ruling class being oppressive. It turns out that there's also "class," in the sense of people being raised well or for being responsible. To be "classy" is to display extraordinarily admirable manners and morals. This film is much harder on the middle class than it is on the remnant of Mississippi's aristocratic class. And it's the aristocratic class and the class of servants that ally to overthrow the pretensions of middle-class racist tyranny.

Let me begin what has to be a project of several posts with some fairly random observations:

1. *The Help* is one of the most thought-provoking movies in a long time. It's based on a best-selling book that I'm ashamed to admit I haven't read all the way through. That put me at a big disadvantage in the theater. I went to an afternoon show with my wife (who had read it), and the theater was packed with women's reading groups that had loved the book. The consensus was that the long film was faithful to the book, but only to a point. Much was left out. That's easy to believe, because the film was packed with fascinating characters, each of whom seemed insufficiently fleshed out. I've peeked a bit at the book, just to confirm some of my suspicions about the movie. But, as usual, I'm basically letting the movie stand on its own.

2. In terms of visual detail, this has to be one of the best movies ever made. You're convinced that this is exactly what Jackson, Mississippi was like in 1963. The middle-class parts of that city were pretty much like the rest of the country, except for three significant details. Every middle-class family had African-American "help," a maid who was lot more than a mere maid. So, the white women, like their more aristocratic ancestors, didn't

have to work. And there was extreme racial segregation; segregation that was, you might say, still in the process of being perfected.

3. The middle-class white women are so horrible you start to feel sorry for them. Their lives are pointless. Their aesthetically unimpressive houses are run and their children are raised by "the help." Their unerotic, boring husbands have little interest in them. They don't work themselves and have no ambition to work. Their lives are consumed by obsession with trivial pursuits—bridge clubs and stuff like that—and petty distinctions. Theirs is not aristocratic leisure, and their lives are creepily devoid of personal love and proper pride. The film has the appropriate moments when nature gets her revenge for their self-denial, but their response is usually more blind anger than tears of recognition. Surely the evildoing ugliness of these female, middle-class lives is exaggerated, and the two most prominent of these women in the film are presented as extreme cases. What drives the movie, more than anything else, is animosity against their kind.

3. The one pleasure of these white women, it seems, is tyrannizing over the woman who actually provides work and love in their homes. They are utterly repulsed by physical contact with blacks, and their concern with hygiene (reflected in an intensifying effort to make sure the races use separate bathrooms) is really a desire to have no emotional connection with those over whom they rule without limits. Still, they turn their children over to "the help," and let their hired women lavish loving affection on the their kids as if they were their own. What's especially striking is the utter lack of gratitude of the white women for what they have, for all the help they have received.

4. The white, middle-class women's (as one of the black women says) "godless" coldness was not peculiar to Mississippi. They remind us TV fans of Betty Draper on *Mad Men*, who also coldly dismissed the black woman she had hired to take care of her children over some imagined affront. But in New York, after all, there was no legal segregation, and African-Americans were fully protected by the law. They were eligible for government benefits. So, the godless coldness of early Sixties segregation made the lives of "the help" particularly precarious; they were almost completely subject to the whim of tyrants—tyrants who had no real class at all.

5. The situation of "the help" in Mississippi was in some ways more unbearable than ever. Their material situation was not horrible. As long as they worked, they ate; they had their own very modest homes, and so forth. It's not like they were being worked to death as slaves sometimes were.

What is worse is the whites' indifference to their very being, their utter insensitivity to who they are as particular beings.

6. The upside of middle-class life is that people work for themselves, the downside is that the relations among employer and employee become more all about the cash at the expense of any sense of personal responsibility or affection. Life in middle-class Mississippi was all about the downside in the absence of the upside. There's little evidence among the middle-class white women of the aristocratic virtue of generosity or magnanimity or the Christian virtue of charity, especially when it comes to "the help."

7. We sometimes read that the relations between the races were easier and more familiar in the South than in the North, because the lives of blacks and whites were intertwined. Whatever partial truth there was to that observation, the middle-class whites of Jackson were working hard to make it completely untrue. They wanted to believe that they only owed the help cash, and very little of it, much less than they would be worth under any impartially individualistic or "capitalistic" system.

8. There was amazingly little freedom of speech in Mississippi at this time. We learn that speaking against segregation was actually a crime, and nobody (even the two admirable, privileged, smart young white people) was doing it. And the blacks, of course, had to be more cautious than ever, as the whites emotionally distanced themselves from any concern for and so any indulgence toward them. "No sassying" became the increasingly insistent motto of survival, because it was increasingly the case that one slip meant not just being fired, but being basically unemployable.

9. The least we can say is that the federal government was way too slow in intervening in Mississippi, because things weren't getting better "on their own."

The Help—Part 2: Eugenia

My first post dealt with the film's display of the middle-class racist tyranny, mainly of women, in Jackson, Mississippi in 1963. My opinion is that what you see in the movie is a true and neglected feature of the horrible history of slavery and segregation in our country. But I can't help thinking that the middle-class white women are shown to be worse than they really were. (They were plenty bad, and their lives were objectively repulsive and monstrously unjust. It's just that even really screwed-up people usually have their good sides, too.)

This is because the point of view of the movie comes less from the stories told by "the help" than by the young white woman who collects them into a bestseller. This woman came from an old and prosperous southern family. She didn't live in some middle-class housing development, but in what is probably an antebellum mansion with lots of land out in the country. She is very smart, ambitious, and believes she is destined to write very important articles and books. It's clear that her family is rich enough that she's never really worked and doesn't have to work.

Her mother, like almost all mothers, wants her to get married, worries that's she's a lesbian and all that, but isn't obsessed in some Jane Austen way about how her daughter is going to get by all alone. Her daughter gets a kind of joke job with the Jackson paper writing an advice column on doing household chores. She, of course, has never done any, and so she has to ask "the help" for answers to the various practical questions. She never has and never will do any manual labor. Hers is basically aristocratic leisure in the sense that it's not true that she's been frittering her time away. She's working on her soul, in her way, and on ways to display her great individuality and singular enlightenment. She prides herself, with good reason, in not sharing the prejudices of her time and place: she's no racist and she's no Christian.

This young woman's name is Eugenia (aka "Skeeter"), which, of course, means well-born. She's well born in the sense that she's born into a good family—a family, as her mom says, that's been distinguished over time by its courage. She's also well born in the sense that she's been blessed by nature with extraordinary verbal/literary talent and at least somewhat extraordinary insight. So, like girls of her class, she goes to Old Miss, but doesn't get lost in the social life as much as she does in books.

On her shelf, we see *To Kill a Mockingbird* and Richard Wright's *Native Son*. Probably neither book was assigned in a literature class at the state university of Mississippi at that time. From *To a Kill a Mockingbird* she absorbed the admirable devotion to duty of the Southern Stoic lawyer Atticus Finch, who has the class to generously give his time and even risk his life for the rule of law and on behalf of a most noble and most unfortunate black servant. From *Native Son*, she discovers the anger of the oppressed and marginalized black person in our country, the neglected black perspective. She's thinks of herself as some combination of Atticus with literary ambition based on an insight that goes beyond the limitations of her class.

That comparison is not quite fair to Atticus, who risked a lot more and managed to stay home and continue to do his duty to his family and community rather than flee to New York, where anti-racist, Stoic, classy, literary southern ladies and gentleman were and will always be all the rage. That comparison is also not quite fair to Skeeter. She was also motivated by personal love.

Eugenia wasn't—or thought she wasn't (the actress Emma Stone, after all, is quite beautiful)—good looking. The boys told her she was ugly, and she wasn't invited to the big dances. The black woman who raised her (with the impressive name Constantine) told her both not to whine and that she was born for greatness. Eugenia both loved and idolized Constantine more than her parents. And she was clearly raised well, to be a genuine aristocrat, a person distinguished by her excellence. (A big and wonderful theme of the movie is how "the help," in general, raised less-than-beautiful white girls to value their personal significance, to help them be who they were born to be.) The love between Eugenia and Constantine—between two quite remarkable women—wasn't the kind that would diminish all that much when the white woman assumes the responsibilities of an adult member of her class.

Not only that, Eugenia's whole family genuinely loved Constantine and her family, including Constantine's beautiful, highly educated daughter. The members of the two races really did have an easy and familiar relationship, and so Eugenia's family allowed Constantine to keep working when very old, when her service was more trouble than it was worth. Skeeter's mom had one horrible day, when she gave into "peer pressure" (the whole DAR and its petty-tyrannical leader were at her house) and banished Constantine and her daughter from her house for what seemed to be a moment of insolence. The mom almost immediately regretted her cold act, tried to right it more than once, even sending her son to Chicago to bring Constantine "home." But Constantine still tragically died of a broken heart, and Skeeter's mom and dad did what they could to banish what happened from their memory. But the mom couldn't do the impossible; she was consumed with guilt and broke down when she finally told Skeeter the truth. The mom said her family's courage skipped her generation, because she had given in to the requirements of the conventions of being a beauty queen, a DAR favorite, etc. (Skeeter, of course, couldn't, given her lack of conventional beauty, ever have been tempted that way.) And she was extremely proud of her daughter's liberating and loving book, and even of her rising beyond the limits of her place in the direction of the big city.

Skeeter knows that the horrible betrayal of love here isn't just her mom's. When she comes home after college, she asks about the absent Constantine, but not *all that* insistently. She knows she too should have done more to look after her. When thinking about the betrayal here, remember that there really was lots of love, and these aristocrats did, for the most part, take responsibility for and were grateful (although not nearly grateful enough) for those that helped them live the way they pleased. Skeeter had the class to know that Constantine had been all about her in a way she had loved, but insufficiently appreciated. Her mom did too; even admitting that her own view was distorted by jealousy of the influence Constantine had had on her own daughter.

Skeeter's contempt for the middle-class women for not appreciating the perspective of "the help" is justified but excessive. For one thing, these women were her friends, and they did what they could to integrate her into their circle, set her up with suitable men, work on her appearance, and curb her weird and dangerous excesses. In thinking about the one-sided friendship between Skeeter and these women, I have to admit that I exaggerated their coldness myself in the first post. They lacked her education, her brains, and her opportunities. They, unlike Skeeter, didn't have what it takes to go it alone, and so they were stuck with living conventional—which means, among other things, racist—lives.

Not only did these middle-class women lack any insight into the black perspective, they weren't in any position to take on the aristocratic perspective. They weren't quite in a position to view a particular black woman with Skeeter's level of love and admiration. Skeeter was a bit short on gratitude again when she exaggerated their middle-class or conventional vices, and she wasn't big on seeing the selfishness of her contempt for them. Still, she was right to ally with "the help" in a literary effort to discredit them, to bring them down.

Rambling Rose and RIFF

Yesterday was the second and final day of the Rome (Georgia) International Film Festival.

I'm sad to say I had to miss almost all of it. But the final event—a showing of the film *Rambling Rose* followed by a discussion with the film's director, Martha Coolidge—was quite something.

Coolidge's strengths as a director are meticulous attention to the intention of the screenwriter, a sharp sense of place, and wonderful casting. Her other signature movie is the also underrated *Valley Girl*—one of the best mocks of the spirit of the Sixties ever (thanks to a very funny and strangely touching performance by Sonny Bono) and what might well still remain Nicolas Cage's most striking and manly performance. *Valley Girl* and *Rambling Rose* both present real men, real women, and real families both flourishing in and transcending the peculiar conventions of distinctively American times and places.

Rambling Rose has a few flaws—including its cornpone and quite unnecessary introduction and conclusion—that cause it to fall short of greatness.

But its virtues begin with one of Robert Duvall's (our best actor at his best) most memorable and subtle performances. We see the Christian Duvall in *Tender Mercies* (maybe *the* outstanding American film) and *The Apostle* (a bit over-the-top but very deep). *Rambling Rose* gives us the pagan or Stoic Duvall, who presents nearly the full range of the greatness and misery of our classically literary South.

Atticus Finch is a somewhat one-dimensional lonely Stoic patriarch (or dad), and the Gregory Peck portrayal is noble but boring. The Duvall character—Daddy Hillyer—is fully of irony and wit and chivalry and classical allusions without literary pretensions. But he is still flawed, and his equally sort-of-philosophic literary (historian) wife (played by Diane Ladd)—in touch with the source of the creative energy of the universe and full of the protective love of the mother of us all—has to save him from being seduced by the eugenic cruelty of modern science. Her fierce defense of her (adopted) daughter (and fellow orphan) reminded him to think and feel like a father.

It turns out a complete family needs both manly honor and courage and unflinching responsibility and the feminine realism that flows from personal love and so justice rightly understood. It's amazing the extent to which this movie celebrates marital fidelity and familial duty, the reconciliation of magnanimity and justice, and the transformation of "base love" into "higher [but still intensely personal] love" without any explicit debt to Christianity.

Rambling Rose also includes two of the best acted and most edifying sex scenes ever filmed. Rose, the hyper-promiscuous teenage live-in hired help played wonderfully by Laura Dern, both fails in her aggressive seduction of the Duvall character (he fends her off, he proclaims, the way the Persians weren't allowed to pass at Thermopylae) and is seduced by the clinically curious oldest son—the most brilliant of their children, his mother explains, but with "an evil streak." This movie, to say the least, is hard on uninhibited curiosity and the clinical view of human sexuality. (The physician from the North is quite the evildoing Progressive—I'll have to explain later.)

The children in this movie, I could go on, are probably meant to remind us, at first, of Scout and Jem from *To Kill a Mockingbird*, but they are much more interesting and far more realistic.

I have to cut this off: The script for this movie was written by Calder Willingham and based on the book he wrote of the same name. Willingham contributed to the screenplays of more of the AFI's top hundred films than any other author and was also quite a successful and almost-great novelist. He grew up in Rome, GA, and *Rambling Rose* is semi-autobiographical. For financial reasons, the filming was done in the Wilmington, NC area, but it's a tribute to the director that everything looks as if it could be Rome, GA in 1935.

It's a Wonderful Life(style)

1. Being too lazy or full of Christmas reverie to think up my own post, I'll just say something about the interesting recent comments of our own James Poulos.

2. It's now clear that I'll have to see *Avatar*, just to be against it in an informed way. My original strategy was to skip it. There are two movies out this Christmas season that are destined to make $200 million or more. *Avatar*, of course, has to take that in to break even. *The Blind Side*, meanwhile, is really making the huge bucks. I wanted to display my virtue by only seeing movies about real people with real problems and displaying real virtues and not ones that techno-collapse the distinction between flesh and blood persons and video game characters.

3. But now, I know that *Avatar* deals with the big themes of post-humanity, biotechnology, the rule of scientific experts, the nature of the divine, the oneness of nature, and all that. It does so in what seems to be a boring and unrealistic way, or as yet another pantheistic lullaby designed to divert our sophisticates from who they really are and what they are really supposed to be doing. The whole psychology and "spirituality" of the movie is so obviously dumber than anything preached at the Grace Evangelical Church of the family we see in *The Blind Side*. I'm still stuck with taking it seriously for a moment to show I'm genuinely interested in science, bioethics, the techno-future, and all that (which I am). So I pledge to sit through three hours of animated characters who don't correspond to beings we can really know and love (unlike those, say, in *King of the Hill*). (Believe me, I'll be getting to this only after seeing every holiday movie that might actually be good—including the funny, nihilistic (again!) one by the Coen brothers and the one that has Jeff Bridges being grizzly yet lovable.)

4. I've actually increased my knowledge of *The Blind Side* by reading the book. The film is pretty much as faithful as a film can be, and the book is unexpectedly deep pop sociology. The movie isn't perfectly faithful, though. It adds, for example, a rather cloying scene of the black football player sitting alone at the Thanksgiving dinner table and drawing in the members of his white adopted family. Generally, the main weakness of the film is to sentimentalize this tough, cagey guy and his family life a bit. The book is more realistic in portraying the messy details of family life and doing what's required to have every member of the family flourish. It's also

about the fact that major cause of success and failure in our free country is the quality of your parents. The mom in the book works hard to re-socialize their adopted black son from the projects as a rich, preppy evangelical, and with uneven but real success. With money comes responsibility, and the point of money is to live a virtuous life that isn't reducible to a lifestyle. Charitable responsibility is about a lot more than giving money to charities.

The dad in the book also displays quite singular forms of virtue. His huge wealth is pretty unstable, and he works hard to hide that fact from families and friends. (It's dependent in part on the ability of Taco Bell to keep its menu up to date with the increasingly tasteful sophistication of even quite ordinary Americans. He says in both the book and the movie that the quesadilla saved his ass.) He manages not to be consumed by entrepreneurial, workaholic anxiety, but to find plenty of time for family, friends, the unfortunate, God, and just fun. Our "Whole Foods," increasingly organic bourgeois bohemians can learn a lot from him. We certainly learn from the movie that the only real God is a personal, loving God, and that sports are the closest thing we have in our country to a genuine meritocracy (from which something like 80 percent of the poor blacks who could dominate are still excluded by what seem like forces beyond their comprehension and control).

5. The virtue described in James's lifestyle post is mighty lame by comparison. Imagine taking pride in sacrificing that big screen TV to have enough money to eat organic meat! Organic meat, no doubt, is getting cheaper all the time (I haven't checked this out myself), but I also hear they're almost giving those big screens away this year. And so, many a lucky "cosmopolitan" family might not have to make that hard choice (unless having a small screen is a perverse sign of status).

Up in the Air

Up in the Air seems, at first, to exaggerate in one character the modern tendency to confuse virtual or placeless, unencumbered life with real life to defend love, family, and all that from techno-capitalist tendencies to empty lives of meaning. Baggage, we hear in a self-help presentation by that character (Clooney), is more trouble than it's worth. Chastened by love, however, he later corrects himself by telling his relative balking at marriage that life without personal baggage can't be sustained, even if life, deep down, is pointless and we all die alone. A woman, of course, would never confuse virtual life with real life, although a clever and beautiful woman can enjoy both. Airports and Hiltons are horrible places that you wouldn't want to spend much time in, but they're pretty convenient if you only use them once in a while to get where you're going. They aren't meant, of course, to be homes. It's ironic that corporations these days inspire our loyalty and sense of belonging by giving us miles and points and stuff, while at the same time employing experts that employ heartless techniques to fire those with decades of service. Who can deny that we live in a time when genuine personal loyalty is weaker than ever?

But people who live more on the virtual side are prettier, smarter, and more fit and healthy than those stuck in places like small towns in northern Minnesota. The Clooney character finds himself all alone at film's end, and that's sad. Still, ennobled by what he's learned through his various experiences displayed in the film, nobody should believe—given how rich, handsome, smart, charming, and even sensitive he is—that he's going to have to stay that way long. If he does decide (fat chance!) to return to northern Minnesota, the women will be swooning all over him. And another character shows us it's pretty stupid for a brilliant businesswoman to uproot herself and take a job unworthy of her talents to be with a boy who said he loved her.

The movie seems to be about balance, but surely in a way that doesn't challenge its intended audience. It flatters the bourgeois bohemian pretension that it's possible for people like me to have it all.

Up the Book

I'm continuing my project of reading the books on which the still linger-ing Holiday movies are based. Walter Kirn's *Up in the Air* is very different from and much funnier than the movie. The book's narrator (the Clooney character in the movie) gives a rather urbane and quite sustained semi-agrarian commentary on the sad and ridiculous excesses of our techno-vir-tual displaced society.

For example: "In truth, I just don't care much about money. We always had enough when I grew up, and then one day, when my father went bust, we didn't. Not a lot changed. The house and car were paid for, we never ate out, and we always shopped garage sales for everything but major appli-ances, which my father knew how to repair. We threw a few more garage sales. It's like that in Minnesota, outside the cities. A town finds a certain level in its spending and almost everyone clusters around the mean so that no one has to feel bad if bad luck comes." (So that's the more egalitarian—rural but not usually agrarian—America for which Dr. Pat Deneen and oth-ers want us, with some very good reasons, to have nostalgia.)

On his failed attempt to impress a girl with Route 66 America: "I failed. Nothing there. That America was finished. Too many movies had turned the deserts to sets. The all-night coffee shops served Egg Beaters. And everywhere, from dustiest Nebraska to swampiest Louisiana, folks were expecting us, the road-trip pilgrims … The real America had left the ground and we'd spent the summer circling a ruin. Not even that. An imi-tation ruin." (So it seems to me that a real new Tocqueville from France—and not Bernard-Henri Lévy—would have noticed stuff like that.)

Finally, a genuinely unfashionable confession: "The radio is turned to Christian rock. Christian rock is a private vice of mine; it's as well-pro-duced as the real thing, but more melodic, with audible, rhymed lyrics. The artists have real talent, and they're devoted." I'm up for anyone—especial-ly someone living the virtual life—who sees real talent and devotion in the best efforts of our evangelicals to share their faith.

Fake Chastity and Made-up Religion

That's Countess Sophya's (Mrs. Tolstoy's) objection to the "Tolstoyan" movement that had grown up around her husband with his encouragement. In *The Last Station*, we see that Sophya understands her husband's great novels better than his ideological disciples. We also see that those novels (and the old genius himself) stand somewhere in between Sophya's selfish obsession with personal love and the Tolstoyan (and Tolstoy's own) political principles—directed as they are toward a kind of selfless or disembodied love of the people or humanity as a whole. The novelist says that love is the only answer, but without being as clear as he should be (or while being very conflicted) about what love is. Women, we learn, are more realistic and less puritanical than men, and the cure for ideological fanaticism in some young men is the loving seduction of a good woman.

One reason *War and Peace* is so realistic, we also learn, is that Mrs. Tolstoy constantly reminded her husband of what a man or woman would really do or say in this or that situation. So, this movie shows us what's wrong with even the seemingly noble intentions of ideologues, as well as the crucial and perplexing distinction between the personal profundity of great literature and the silly and dangerous utopian literary politics of even many great authors. We also learn that evildoing ideologues especially want to win control over the moment of death—purging it of wives and priests and anything else that would compromise a kind of fake Socratic nobility.

Tolstoy, we're charmed to discover, was no Socrates. He, for one thing, actually loved and liked and was endlessly aroused in all sorts of way by his wife (who gave him thirteen children and apparently forty-eight less-than-serene years). We leave the theater with a renewed appreciation for the highest purpose of private property. This movie deserves to win almost as many awards as *Crazy Heart* and, if I were an Oscar tyrant, I would give the best actress award to Helen Mirren.

Finally Saw *The Book of Eli*

1. The best Christian movie ever made remains *Tender Mercies*. But *The Book of Eli* is well worth thinking about by Christians.

2. James Ceaser was right to have observed that the brilliant and (comparatively speaking) erudite tyrant, played or overplayed by Gary Oldman, wanted the Bible for its rhetorical power. Its words are weapons, he says, to control the weak and desperate. Those words will mercifully alleviate his ruthless cruelty. If he can do some persuasive talking he can do less killing while indefinitely expanding his power over people. But I'm confused, I have to say, because when was the last time a tyrant actually used the words of the Bible in that way? They sure weren't the words of the twentieth-century tyrants. And the words of the Koran are a somewhat different kind of weapon. There's also some sense that the tyrant was deceiving himself about why he wanted those words. The longing in his eyes when he thought he was finally about to read them seems to be more about freeing himself from the tyrannical impulses dominating his soul. That, of course, was a genuinely Christian moment. At that point, not to give too much away, he learns he should have been nicer to his wife.

3. Of course, Denzel Washington does his usual great job, and his character is a nice variant on how amazing grace transforms the blind. That he received a revelation that gave his life purpose, an indispensable purpose, is presented as both real and moving. He knows he will complete his mission and can't be stopped by any or all forces. That does kind of muck up the battle scenes, where he does all manner of precision killing that can't be explained naturally. We know in advance—because he says so—that he's getting out of that house alive, despite the fact that the tyrant's little army has enough firepower to level it many times over. And only the hand of God explains why it doesn't occur to someone to just shoot him in the head.

4. The Bible ends up in the hands of a little band of intellectuals closeted on Alcatraz working to preserve all the books and music essential to human civilization. I like the emphasis that the future of civilization depends on books or that renewal will occur a lot, lot quicker with them. But it was deflating to see the Bible placed on the shelf as one essential book among many, right there next to the Koran and so forth. It's not clear whether or not the Bible is *the* book for us all, although there are several special reasons why it's the only book for Eli/Denzel.

5. The Bible, we learn, came a lot closer to disappearing entirely than the other essential books, because there was a concerted effort after the catastrophe to destroy every copy. Nobody was out to get, say, Shakespeare. It seems that the big war was blamed on the Bible, but it just isn't explained why.

6. Why did God empower a man to preserve the *King James Version* of the Bible in particular? Attention is called to that fact more than once.

7. The details of the war are a little too politically correct for me. It seems to have been a nuclear exchange that knocked a huge hole in the ozone layer. It was direct exposure to the sun that did most of the destruction of life. Virtually all vegetation disappeared. And anyone who didn't get underground and stay there for a year died. Lots of people were blinded. Still, the people around thirty years later seem pretty healthy all things considered, even though most or all of them apparently have never eaten their vegetables. Cats, dogs, birds, and mice managed to survive. And although water is extremely scarce, there seems to be plenty of gas for the motorized vehicles that are miraculously still running. In general, the movie, although arresting and profound in some ways, isn't really distinguished by exacting attention to detail. It's above my pay grade to figure it all out, but a lot more care was given to symbolism—Biblical and otherwise—and nods to many other films.

One more Eli point: The movie is actually quite Christian on what it means *to see*. It's quite possible for the blind to see in the most important way without the sense of sight. Biological eyes aren't that precious; smell and touch can compensate. (The movie attentively shows us that people with eyes don't really know how to smell—or touch.) Before the catastrophe, Eli says, people had too much and didn't know what was precious. The Christian point explored is what it really means to be wounded.

Eli Is a Christian Movie. And That's Good and True

I got an email criticizing me for not talking up *Eli* as representing the truth that is Christian theology. Good point, actually. Here's my feeble memory of what the movie's unfashionable but genuinely illuminating teachings are along those lines:

1. Each of us has free will and a personal destiny. No situation genuinely deprives us of all choice.

2. Prayer is, first of all, about gratitude for what we've been given. Maybe the main failing of the modern, high-tech world is that people had much more than enough but less gratitude than ever and so wasted much that was good. People forgot how and why to pray.

3. It's almost easier to pray when you've been given just enough and so you can see more clearly what's genuinely indispensable or precious. (Eli here reminds us of Solzhenitsyn in the Gulag.)

4. What we've been given that's most precious is God, family, and friends. Life without any of those is the closest experience we have to hell. Without those, we become worse than the other animals—cannibals, for example.

5. We should do more for others than for ourselves. Eli read that in the Bible but was so mission-driven that he forgot to live it. But then, he willingly surrendered the pleasure of reading the Bible to save a friend, a beautiful woman to whom he was not physically attracted. And his friend (Solara, the source of light) learned that, of course, not from the Bible, but from her love of her loving and sacrificial mother.

6. We will all be judged for what we do.

7. God is personal, cares about persons, and is incessantly active in the world. Creation wasn't some one-time thing at some point in the past as, say, Locke or the Big Bangers teach.

Individualism on TV Today: Larry David, Jerry Seinfeld, and Charlie Harper [Sheen]

Once again I find inspiration from one of my former students for a post. Here's his *Facebook* request: "I'm interested to hear your thoughts on the 'Palestinian Chicken' episode of *Curb Your Enthusiasm*."

Well, it was pretty lame, and *CYE* has clearly "jumped the shark." That show has always oscillated between comedic brilliance and cringe-inducing stupidity, and the latter tendency predominates now. One reason is Larry is just too much to take separated from the womanly realism (and something approaching love) of his wife Cheryl.

It turns out that the Palestinian place has the best chicken around. So, Larry doesn't hesitate to eat there, although he knows that almost all of its customers hate Jews and Israel. He becomes, in a way, a hero to the customers after they watch him try to make Funkhauser (a more spirited and loyal Jew) take off his yarmulke before entering the restaurant. Larry "hooks up" with a passionate Palestinian woman who calls him oppressor and occupier and stuff while having very aggressive sex with him. Funkhauser overhears one of their sessions and asks Larry how he could submit to that verbal degradation. He simply responds that he doesn't care because it's the best sex ever.

The Palestinian chicken people decide to open a second location next to Larry and his friends' favorite Jewish deli. All of Larry's friends show up to demonstrate against this inappropriate and insensitive act. All of the Palestinians are just as angrily demonstrating for their cause. Larry comes by and just can't decide whether to go with his friends (and his religious heritage) or his Palestinian sexual partner and the delicious Palestinian chicken.

If there's an ironic lesson, it is this: Becoming emotionally apathetic and self-centered enough to be most in touch with your ordinary desires is the key to overcoming the animosity that separates peoples, religions, nations, etc. But it's not really a lesson, because everyone on the show is more admirable (more loyal, courageous, loving, sensitive) than Larry. Unless you're for peace at any price, you can't be for a world in which we would be so lacking in real passion or indifferent to the suffering of others.

What *Curb Your Enthusiasm* and *Seinfeld* (and in a different way *Two and a Half Men*) mock is the insipid self-centeredness of Americans in the midst of prosperity. It goes without saying that these shows get laughs through exaggeration of real tendencies.

Alexis de Tocqueville, more than a century and a half ago, named this drift toward apathetic withdrawal into oneself *individualism*—which he displayed as a disease of the heart. But Tocqueville, probably mistakenly, thought that individualism would have its natural limits; he was worried that we would stop being concerned citizens, but it never occurred to him that we'd stop being parents and children. He assumed that people would remain passionate enough to reproduce.

But Larry on *Curb Your Enthusiasm*, Jerry (and George) on *Seinfeld*, and Charlie on *Two and a Half Men* are all, clearly, emotionally unfit to reproduce. They're specimens that Darwin would have a hard time explaining. And these shows, through exaggeration, help to explain the "birth dearth" among sophisticated Americans today, a democratic problem that Tocqueville didn't predict.

Back to the Imaginary Future:
Comments on Carl Sagan's *Contact* (with ETs)

The Big Think's *Age of Engagement* is advertising a showing of Carl Sagan's hugely influential film *Contact*. The film will be shown, appropriately enough, as an excellent example of how popularizing scientists influence the portrayal of "aliens" (or ETs) in film.

From the perspective of serious scientists, the most credible recent film presentation of extraterrestrial life is *Contact*, based on the novel of the same name by physicist Carl Sagan. Sagan, of course, was the most famous and successful popularizing scientist of our time. His book *Cosmos* sold more copies in America than any other scientific book, and the television series based on it was equally successful. He appeared as an expert on all of the important television shows and wrote a regular column for *Parade*. He was an articulate and often penetrating defender of the dominant scientific view of our species, our planet, and the cosmos, and he made clear in accessible language the moral and political implications of that view.

Much of Sagan's writing is unabashed scientific propaganda in support of the search for extraterrestrial intelligence. The possibility of intelligent extraterrestrial life especially animated his curiosity. He was distressed by the American government's lack of interest in pursuing such fundamental knowledge, observing that "every civilization in human history has devoted some of its resources to investigating deep questions about the Universe, and it is hard to think of a deeper one than whether we are alone."

To mobilize public opinion on behalf of this research Sagan talked up the likely technological and moral benefits of contact with beings more advanced than we are: Their wisdom might well save us, he argued, and it is most unlikely that they would use their weapons to destroy us.

The film *Contact*, written by Sagan and his wife, appeals (more than the book does) to the religious dimension of the search for extraterrestrial intelligence. It presents the comforting picture of advanced beings watching over us and gradually and benevolently intervening in our affairs. Through this contact, otherwise unknowable secrets about the nature of the cosmos are revealed to a human being. The revelation somehow brings inspiration to a world searching for meaning to replace discredited biblical religion.

But Sagan uses the image of the biblical God to promote his scientific view that whatever extraterrestrial intelligence we might contact would have "uncompromisingly benign" intentions. He assumes that our planet is technically the most backward in the galaxy; one more backward still would have no radio astronomy and so no way of contacting others. Our fears about extraterrestrial contact, he says, are simply evidence of our own "guilty conscience" about human history. They make no sense in terms of understanding a society more advanced than ours.

As further evidence that we have nothing to fear from extraterrestrial civilizations, Sagan observes: "The vast distances that separate the stars are providential. Beings and worlds are quarantined from one another. The quarantine is lifted only for those with sufficient self-knowledge and judgment to have traveled from star to star." Yet he also warns repeatedly that there is no scientific evidence for natural or divine providence or for the existence of extraterrestrial civilizations; any appeal to providence is "a failure of nerve" before the truth about the "indifference" of the universe.

But both technology and morality, Sagan says, clearly evolve. Human conflict and injustice are rooted in "the deep, ancient reptilian part of the brain"; human history is the movement away from reptilian behavior and toward living scientifically and cooperatively, from pure body to pure mind. With time, all forms of intelligent life become less passionate and violent, or more benignly godlike. The only glitch in the process is that moral evolution sometimes lags behind technological development, as is the case now on earth, raising the prospect of technological self-destruction. Extraterrestrials, he says, may aid us in moral evolution, saving us from ourselves.

There is nothing self-evident about this conclusion, however. Human technology and morality are rooted in specific features of our human nature and our earthly environment. We have trouble living well with the fact of death, in part because our bodies are frail and vulnerable but also because we are conscious of our bodily limitations. We experience ourselves as individuals. Our personal morality is rooted in the facts that we reproduce sexually and that our young take a long time to become independent. And our passions are a complex mixture of self-consciousness, sociality, and bodily impulse—of death, love, and sex. It is far from clear that extraterrestrials would share many of our experiences or could tell us much about how to live well with them.

Perhaps they could show us technological means to overcome some of the present limitations of being human. Although neither they nor we could become immortal—no life or even the cosmos itself will exist in its present form forever—we might learn how to postpone death indefinitely and make accidental death less likely.

But would that be moral progress? Would we be happier as a result? So far, the increase in human security through technology has not freed human beings from fear. Instead, human life has become more fearful; as death comes to seem less necessary and more accidental, individuals have more to lose. In any case, we usually identify spiritual progress with living well with death, not overcoming it through science.

Given the connection between love and death in human experience, wouldn't pushing back death lead to a reduction in love? Would our alien teachers understand how fundamental and precious love is for human beings? Love is a compensation, and for many, at least, a more than adequate compensation, for death.

Sagan does not confront these questions in *Contact*. His advanced extraterrestrials are loving beings, and they make their human visitor aware of how little she has loved, or made genuine contact with, her fellow human beings. There is even the suggestion that all intelligent beings experience cosmic loneliness or alienation, and so all need each other. But it is unclear how the extraterrestrials live with their mortality, and their love seems disembodied. They are too angelic, or passionless, to be seen as flawed mortals. They are unrealistically benign and so quite boring.

J. Edgar

I'm finally getting around to talking about recent films. Two that had great promise but ultimately disappoint are *J. Edgar* and *The Descendants*.

They both address the questions of virtue—particularly manliness and generosity—that have had my attention.

J. Edgar is about the founder of the FBI. Any analysis of the film should be, in part, about its historical accuracy. Mine won't be, because I don't know enough. But I will say up front that there's no clear evidence that Hoover was gay, wore dresses on occasion, routinely blackmailed presidents, or was lacking in personal courage. Insofar as the film has a point of view, it is about the manly director—Clint Eastwood—accepting those pieces of conventional wisdom masquerading as unvarnished truth for granted.

In *Gran Torino*, Eastwood takes a deeply flawed character and turns him into a kind of Christ figure—offering up his life unarmed to save his friends. The one thing that hero was never short on was courage and a kind of plainspoken integrity.

The character in *J. Edgar* is most obviously a blackmailing, paranoid liar obsessed hypocritically with the morality of others. We learn he was secretly gay, had a complicated (but perhaps not overtly sexual) relationship with his classy top aide and constant companion, had issues with his mother, put on at least one dress, denied the existence of organized crime, blackmailed every new president to enhance his power, was a master at taking credit for the courageous and heroic actions of his agents, was an effective publicity-hog in general, was obsessed unreasonably with the internal Communist threat, was severely judgmental and creepily investigative when it came to the personal lives of JFK and MLK, and had a uncannily loyal secretary.

The film mentions, so to speak, that Hoover demanded and usually got the highest level of professionalism from his agents and was a relentless path-breaker when it came to employing the latest techniques in fighting crime. It was probably a good and certainly an effective thing, for example, to have pushed to make kidnapping a federal offense, whatever the murky details of the Lindbergh kidnapping in particular. But the film doesn't dwell on those accomplishments.

The film focuses on Hoover's shortcomings when it came to personal virtues without really wondering—much less explaining—how it was that such a deeply flawed man could have built such an impressive and mostly admirable institution. There's a lot truthful to be said about Hoover's abuse of unaccountable power and how strangely pathetic and rather dangerous he had gotten late in life, but that can't be the whole story.

Overall, the film is psychologically lame. It doesn't give us a sense of the whole man—real or fictional. So it's mostly long and boring—one damn incident after another.

I don't think it's Eastwood's point that Hoover's closeted gayness was the cause of all his secretive and dishonorable excesses. Nor do I think he wants it to be his point that Hoover's gayness was caused by his overbearing mother and virtually absent father. But someone looking for psychological explanations could easily rush to those judgments. The film mostly seems lacking in more astute and generous judgments.

The fact might be that there's nothing so wrong with a public figure—a role model—wanting to keep his private life private. Certainly MLK and JFK wanted to do that, and we don't think we really see who they were when we focus on their womanizing. Certainly we blame Hoover for that kind of focus on our heroes' lives. (Our judgment concerning Hoover's hypocrisy should be limited, though, by the lack of evidence that he was casually promiscuous.)

Hoover can't be called wrong for keeping the sexual component of his relationship with Tolson (if there was one) to himself. He certainly was very open about that deep friendship between two remarkable men. The high points of the film suggest the delight—mostly conversational delight—two kindred spirits took in each other.

The Descendants: Love, Family, and Paradise

The Descendants is the most critically acclaimed film in the theaters right now. I'm not sure I know quite why. But one reason is the excellent track record of its director, Alexander Payne. His *About Schmidt* and *Sideways* are genuine classics.

The Descendants follows in their footsteps insofar as it is about an emotionally stunted man who goes on a kind of misbegotten but still personally revealing road trip and gets somewhat less self-absorbed and more open to a genuine relationship with a woman. For *Schmidt*, that woman is his dead wife, from whom he had been alienated or isolated for years, and the same is true for Clooney character in *The Descendants*. We see, of course, that those relationships are sadly incomplete because they're so one-sided. In *Sideways*, the screwed-up guy might have a real future with a living woman.

The Paul Giamatti and Jack Nicholson characters in the earlier movies are full of quirks that (especially in the Giamatti case, of course) suggest painful cluelessness, and they are neither handsome nor charming. They live on the lonely margin of society. They have very little going for them, and it's easy to know why they're sad sacks.

The Clooney character, by contrast, is rich, well connected, strikingly handsome and in perfect shape, eloquent and charming, has two beautiful and smart daughters, and, with the exception of his wife being on life support and later dead, seems to have everything going for him. It's a lot less clear what's wrong with him. Whatever it is was there well before his wife's fatal accident.

Clooney, the actor, lacks the nuance or range of the great Giamatti and Nicholson. His character, in fact, is most reminiscent of the guy he plays in *Up in the Air*. Both characters are somewhat sophisticated and hyper-presentable, successful, and very short on deep, relational feeling. And both films seem to suffer from the failure to let the viewer in on the cause of the character's flat-souled detachment or displacement in the midst of prosperity.

It might be, in the case of *The Descendants*, that the point is that we're wrong to look for a social or relational cause. Some people just have a kind of "heart disease" by nature. If that is the film's point, then it might be a little better than most of the critics who praise it think.

The film opens with the Clooney character (Matt King) complaining that Hawaii only seems to be paradise because people are screwed up there too. Because people are born to trouble everywhere, there's trouble in paradise too. The Hawaii we see is, in fact, as close to paradise as there is in this world. The weather's always perfect, the natural beauty is quite incredible, and people seem to have plenty of everything with little work. At first, the point seems to be that paradise isn't all it's cracked up to be because even or especially there people are still stuck with love—or the lack thereof—and death.

But Matt's negative judgment is conditioned, in large part, by the fact that he's particularly screwed up. He's stingy or the opposite of generous.

He's the descendant of Hawaiian royalty and missionaries, and his family inherited lots of land and money. Many of his feckless relatives spit away their fortunes, and their lives are somewhat dissolute. But they also seem to be more about family and friends, and they enjoy life in paradise for what it is, which isn't everything.

The Clooney character says he and his family live only on his income as a lawyer; he leaves his inheritance alone. He says he wants to give his children enough, but not too much.

The truth is Matt doesn't give his family much at all, much less than he easily could. He admits he's only the "back-up" parent; his wife has raised the daughters. He is so neglectful of her that he's unaware she's hopelessly in love with another man. He resolves to become a real husband only after the accident that puts her in a coma. We have reason to doubt that he would have followed through if she had really gotten better.

It seems he's thrown himself into his work, but it's not like his work as a real-estate lawyer seems so absorbing. He's stingy with his money, his time, and his affections, and so he doesn't really know or take responsibility for his wife, his daughters, his extended family, or his wife's friends.

Matt is a descendant of the founders of Hawaii. But he doesn't look Hawaiian, can't speak the language, and doesn't hang out with the indigenous people (or even his extended family). He's inherited the means to live like an aristocrat, but without taking responsibility for who he is as a Hawaiian. He is, on behalf of his extended family, the trustee for 25,000 prime acres that they apparently will have to sell or probably soon lose. The decision of a large majority of the family members is to sell at a comparatively modest but still huge price to Hawaiian developers, developers they know and think they can trust.

Matt, apparently as an act of a more expansive Hawaiian responsibility, decides to override to the vote of the family and continue to keep the land undeveloped. If we look carefully, we can see that this decision comes from a curiously isolated, unaffectionate guy. His relatives really need the money, and Hawaiians could use the jobs. The family may lose the land anyway. And we also notice an element of revenge—the guy his wife had the affair with will be out big commissions.

Matt's decision is an apparently noble or selfless but also passive-aggressive move that may tear his extended family—the descendants—apart with nasty litigation. Surely a man's responsibility is first of all to his family, to those he really knows and loves. It doesn't really seem that he chooses, as an aristocrat properly understood, for the Hawaiian *people*.

Matt does "grow" some on his road trip with his daughters to confront the man his wife loved. He does show his love for his girls; the back-up parent steps up to the plate in a crisis. His rather unjustified anger toward his wife is replaced by loving understanding.

The film ends with the girls and dad very passively and silently watching TV and eating ice cream. It's a family moment, to be sure, but they're all alone and not getting on with their lives. We don't have much evidence that Matt's heart has been enlarged all that much; there are definite natural limits to his capacity for knowing and loving other persons.

If that's the film message, then its intention as a movie about a dispossessed or displaced aristocrat has a kind of psychological subtlety that puts it up there with *About Schmidt* and *Sideways*, even if the characters and the performances aren't as good. Aristotle says stinginess is incurable, and there's a lot of truth in that exaggeration.

The Classy Grammys

The *Grammys* turned out to be one of the classiest and most entertaining award shows ever. Certainly the show blew away the Super Bowl on both fronts. Even the commercials paid their audience the compliment of being clever, genuinely witty, and even musically sophisticated.

Compared to, say, the Oscars or even the Golden Globes, the Grammys display little personal vanity, fashionable "Hollywood" political correctness, or drama detached from the artistry being honored. There's a lot that could be said about the general high level of performances and deep respect shown for the American tradition of popular music.

So let me just mention seven moments that particularly moved me, keeping in mind that I'm a pretty tone-deaf, musically illiterate, out-of-touch, old white guy from the sticks.

1. LL Cool J was a classy host. He displayed who he is without calling attention to himself. He was dressed for the occasion as a gentleman of style. He also led the nation in prayer for a lost member of the family of American popular music—Whitney Houston. The prayer, simple and personal (beginning with "Heavenly father"), in its way showed something about what unites our African-American and our Country popular music— the two sources of most of our soulful music excellence today.

2. Adele! I have to admit I've been suffering from Adele illiteracy, despite hearing my students sing her praises. I don't listen to a radio station that features today's hits. But her soaring, singular, incredibly strong voice is a once-in-a-generation thing, and so are her songs—based on deeply felt personal emotion. She holds nothing back. Her performance was absolutely unadorned or ungimmicky. She does nothing to call attention to her physical appearance. She's classy because she doesn't identify herself with being working class (who can't be charmed by her being so unpretentiously comfortable with her "common" accent?) but with experiences that transcend class and all that. She is, with all due respect, the sort of opposite of Lady Gaga (who's all about making vaguely but insistently political *statements*), and the opposite of Taylor Swift (I hate to be mean, but Taylor can't really sing). Adele's songs aren't so clever lyrically, but the music and her performances are (to speak English English for a moment) authentically *brilliant*. The best commercial, I think, was the Target one featuring the African-American kids singing the Adele song on the school bus—showing that her music, to make a corny but true point, overcomes

the barriers of race and class and all that. It's just a great bleepin' (to sort of quote Adele) song.

3. The Beach Boys singing "Good Vibrations." There's a lot mean that could be said here about mixing them up with the musically undistinguished Maroon 5. And the actual performance was a bit of mess, barely a shadow of one of the most memorable American recordings ever. Seeing and hearing the old Boys in their present condition was a bit sad. But a classic, one of our best pop recordings ever, was being honored, as was the troubled genius Brian Wilson. And the God, family, and deeply-felt romantic love orientation of the Beach Boys fit in perfectly for the evening.

4. The only insistently political statement of the evening was the opening song by Bruce Springsteen. I don't think it is one of Bruce's better songs, and the lyrics didn't really resonate with me, at least. But it's still always a treat to see the band, even without Clarence.

5. The tribute to Glen Campbell, who, suffering from Alzheimer's, is in the midst of his last tour. His own performance was, in its way, tough without being defiant. The audience's overwhelming reception of it was both an authentic and a classy appreciation of a famous but underrated (and path-breaking) performer. The Band Perry's fine performance of Campbell's "Gentle on My Mind" reminded me, of course, that nothing these days touches country at its best. It also reminded me of the old Glen Campbell show, which was itself a consistently classy, if short-lived, display of a moment in one of our country's musical peaks—when the music of the Sixties sort of merged with country (as in The Band and the later Johnny Cash).

6. Jennifer Hudson and Carrie Underwood. An African-American and a country product of *American Idol* turned out to be among our most intelligent and sensitive (not to mention hugely talented) popular singers. Hudson did justice to the Whitney Houston classic without quite the same voice through the simplicity of the arrangement. And who would have thought Carrie Underwood and Tony Bennett?

7. Paul McCartney—with a ballad and a Beatles medley. It's not that he's as good as he used to be as a performer. We were reminded that he just has a very good nature or was born with class.

Country Rules!

I've been asked whether I should reconsider my recent praise of *American Idol* as an admirably and characteristically American mixture of wisdom and consent.

Although I can't really speak as an authority (having missed several shows), I can see that a revision is in order. The judges—by becoming uniformly uncritical—didn't provide the requisite wisdom. And so, the will of the American people wasn't as informed as it might have been.

That's not to say I don't like the two finalists. Both Scotty and Lauren have voices beautiful and true, and they have poise and judgment far beyond their teenage years.

I'm also sort of happy that they're both country singers. The best popular American music comes out of Nashville these days—certainly it's distinguished by its high level of professionalism and its attention to the virtues associated with family, place, country, and God.

Scotty has become a master of projecting such a country image and of really playing to his audience. His interplay with Lady Gaga (whom I also admire for her talent and self-control) was classic. She gave him the true criticism that he should be more conscious about singing directly into the microphone, given the softness of his deep voice. She said something vaguely naughty (but not nearly as naughty as it might have been) about how he should think of the microphone. He pretended, in effect, to blush and kissed the prominent cross around his neck (I didn't realize Baptists did that sort of thing). He then went on to sing a goofy version of "Youngblood" (a song about being shamelessly on the make—the inane lyrics for that reason among many should have embarrassed him more than the Lady). Scotty's mainstream manipulations have, in fact, been pretty shameless, and the judges have allowed him to get away with one "safe choice" after another in his performances. I really don't mean to criticize this uncannily mature young man. He will certainly be a country star; maybe he'll be president. But Simon wouldn't have put up with his approach to what's supposed to be a singing contest.

Lauren actually has a better voice than Scotty. She is what she appears to be—a very nice, pretty cheerleader from a good family in semi-rural Georgia with a wonderful gift. Scotty always plays (and probably is) the perfect gentleman. Lauren hasn't been a particularly gracious winner, and she's had meltdowns at the prospect of being eliminated (although let me add that her southern manners are usually impeccable). Her performances aren't particularly innovative or cutting-edge; she's not all that literate musically. Again, I'm not being critical; I'm just describing a kid. Lauren's hometown of Rossville, GA is about sixty miles from where I'm sitting, and, if I had voted, I would have been tempted to vote for her both as the local favorite and maybe the most lovable or huggable of the contestants. One more point: she's not a kid when it comes to song choice. She knows who she is and what she can do well.

Both Lauren and Scotty have usually sung mainstream country hits; but, as far I know, never "classic country." Scotty, for example, hasn't turned to Hank Williams (or Hank Jr.) or Waylon or Willie or Johnny Cash or Merle Haggard, etc. He didn't even sing "Ghost Riders in the Sky," which would have fit his voice perfectly. That's because the best country is about sinning, suffering and redemption, and he's not seasoned enough or deprived enough to have suffered or even sinned much. He still has to grow into being a real country singer.

These two "cornpone country kids"—an unfriendly characterization I wouldn't choose myself—have astutely defeated three rock performers of arguably superior ability, imagination, and musical literacy. They are the jazzy Casey, the "give metal a chance" James, and the classic rocker Haley. Simon would have talked them up more effectively and precisely for their more able "signature" performances, and he would have challenged Scotty and Lauren to ascend to their level or be eliminated. Haley, in particular, hung on way beyond anyone's expectations—delivering memorably growly performances of three genuine classics—"Rhiannon," "Benny and the Jets," and "The House of the Rising Sun." And she got around to showing us—with his very competent, understated guitar accompaniment on her Zeppelin extravaganza—that she got her musical sophistication from her great-guy rocker dad. Simon would have told America pretty emphatically last week to keep her around, and that might have made a difference.

Again, let me say that I really like the two finalists, and they displayed their extraordinary merit week after week. They were models of consistency and even "authenticity." But they weren't pushed to be, as they say, all that they can be. The judges didn't judge. For Steven Tyler, everything and everyone is beautiful. This manner of indiscriminate praising, which I thought, early on, was the mark of a gentleman, just became lame. The other two weren't any better.

Of course, Haley's problem might simply have been that, by going the classic rock route, she was appealing to a demographic that probably doesn't vote in big numbers early and often. One of the problems of the consent feature of the show is that you get to vote as often as you can as long as the lines are open. That certainly is bias in favor of the opinion of teenage girls, and that has to help "Scotty the body."

One more point, the smashing victory of *country* over *rock* (even classic rock) is more evidence to defend my proposition that *American Idol* is a conservative reality show.

Happiness

So Here's What I Think about Happiness—Part 1

BIG THINK has done the big service of presenting many, many excellent and expert views on what happiness is and how to be happy. We increasingly think that this is the kind of self-help advice we need the most. Eventually, I'll get around to commenting on some of those expert opinions, but I want to begin by putting the "happiness issue" in context. It will take several posts to do so.

Few experts really doubt that the modern West is in the process of transforming the whole world. That's what globalization really is. And few doubt the superiority of the modern West when it comes to wealth, power, freedom, and even justice. But our relativists have a good reason for still denying that the modern West is *really* superior: Modern progress, we often hear, has been at the cost of virtue and happiness. The whole modern, technological effort has been to produce a world where we can feel good without having to *be* good. The result, our critics claim, is that people are wealthier, more powerful and more free, but less virtuous and less happy than ever. Our critics say that the modern, technological effort is, most deeply, a perverse exercise in futility.

It's easy to see that the modern West has been anxiously dissatisfied with itself for quite some time. According to the late-nineteenth-century philosopher Friedrich Nietzsche, modern technology provides the *how*—the means by which we might pursue happiness—but at the expense of killing God, meaning all sources of the human *why* or purpose or idealism. The truth, Nietzsche claimed, is that if people have the *why* they can live with almost any *how*. The great anti-communist dissident Aleksandr

Solzhenitsyn, for example, was clearly happy in the Gulag, and the philosopher/novelist Walker Percy noticed that Mother Teresa of Calcutta was happier than sophisticated Americans in the midst of abundance.

That doesn't mean, of course, that poverty is the secret to happiness. And Nietzsche exaggerates the indifference of even most purposeful people to the *how*. Studies show that, in most cases, an increase in material well-being makes most people happier for a while. But, at a certain point (something like $30,000 a year), there's no further correlation between money and happiness.

Not having any money at all—extreme or grinding material deprivation—really does make most people miserable. But there's a definite limit to the effectiveness of money in buying happiness. In the most technologically advanced countries today, the ones in which most people live in abundance, there's little to no connection between experiences of happiness and income level.

Aristotle still seems to be right, in saying that money is only good if you know what to do with it. It's good if it helps us ascend from mere subsistence for some kind of flourishing worthy of our pride and our love.

The early modern philosophers, such as John Locke—the philosopher who's the key to America—thought that the full point of human life is to escape from our miserable natural condition in search of happiness. As our Declaration of Independence says, we have life and liberty in order to pursue happiness. But Locke and the Declaration give us very little guidance on what happiness is.

For centuries, apparently, the *how* has been on the rise, but our certainty or confidence about the *why* on the decline. We're tempted to observe that this clash of opposing trends has kept our level of happiness steady. All our effort—and all the wealth, power, and freedom it has produced—may have made us neither more nor less happy. The percentage of Americans describing themselves as happy has remained the same for the past fifty years.

To be fair to Locke, he didn't think that the liberated pursuit of happiness would actually make us happy. The pursuit—and not happiness itself—is what distinguishes the free human being. The possibility of enduring happiness is the illusion that keeps us moving. We're spurred on by the incessant uneasiness that inevitably reappears after each ephemeral enjoyment.

Modern people, as David Brooks wrote, are on "paradise drive," animated by vague visions of a tranquil future where we'll be delivered from the anxieties that keep us from ever enjoying the present. The irony of Locke is that he taught us that we should employ our individual freedom to make ourselves happy, but he knew our futile pursuit would end only in death. The paradise at the end of the modern drive always eludes us.

Happiness—Part 2: Can We Make Ourselves Happy?

The modern world may have been inaugurated with the thought that we can and should make ourselves happy in this world. No longer should we be, as St. Augustine wrote, happy in hope for God's gracious deliverance from our otherwise inescapable misery. Our new goal is to work to change our environment and ourselves with happiness in mind.

Certainly the premodern thinkers—such as Plato and Aristotle, the Stoics, and the early Christians—were, in some ways, too pessimistic about the good we can do for ourselves.

Aristotle says that only a mature person can give us sound moral and political guidance. That's because he's been chastened by experience. He's undeluded about what's really possible, and he's habituated to enjoy living well with the tough challenges and pleasurable compensations (such as friendship) of being a "composite" being, stuck between being like the other animals and being some god.

Machiavelli, the first modern philosopher, tells us to reject such prudence as lazy timidity. He privileges the perspective of the audacious and impetuous young man, ready to use his freedom to go where no man has gone before. People need to start getting industrious and acquisitive—to start thinking effectively and sweating profusely—in pursuit of those satisfactions that nature and tradition arbitrarily or, as we will prove, unnecessarily deny us.

But the thought that happiness can be our invention might have produced a novel form of unhappiness: We can't help but think our unhappiness is our fault, and that we're commanded constantly to try to do something about it.

So we live increasingly less well with the ennobling responsibilities and intractable dissatisfactions of being merely human. The modern world, according to the contemporary secular social theorist Christopher Lasch in *The Revolt of the Elites*, is most of all in futile rebellion against "the ancient religious insight that the only way to achieve happiness is to accept limitations in the spirit of gratitude and contrition." We are, Lasch goes on, in rebellion against "the central paradox of religious faith: the secret of happiness lies in renouncing the right to be happy."

From this view, it's because modern thinkers regard gratitude and contrition as based on illusions that they locate happiness someplace in the future.

The Reagan Centennial (Or Happiness—Part 3: A Happy President)

Ronald Reagan would have been 100 on February 6. If they had a cure for Alzheimer's, he would have made it. Health-obsessed Americans today (disproportionally sophisticated liberals) should at least look to Reagan for longevity tips. He was one of our more vigorous presidents, despite the fact that he was easily the oldest.

All presidents have their strengths and weaknesses. But when remembering a great man, it's only right to focus on what is good and great. And I'm beginning to think about how to remember Reagan.

Reagan was a happy, confident president, confident in himself and confident in the goodness of his country and its devotion to liberty. In that respect, he was a lot like FDR, whom he often said he admired. Even JFK, by comparison, had emotional "issues," which were reflected in his disordered personal life and even in his indecisiveness as president.

Both Reagan and FDR were first elected by "negative landslides." The country had lost confidence in and people thought they were feeling the incompetence of the incumbents who were defeated for reelection. Hoover and Carter. Carter even gave his famous "malaise" speech—where he said the country as a whole was suffering from "a crisis in confidence." Carter, some observed, projected his personal "issues" on all Americans. Both FDR and Reagan restored confidence in the country and confidence in the president.

Reagan and FDR were both reelected by "positive" or affirming landslides. Everyone thinks they know that the 1936 Roosevelt victory was a popular vindication of the reforms or "regime change" called the New Deal. For Reagan, his 1984 mandate was surely more personal, insofar as it didn't extend to Congress.

Reagan's victory, as he himself said, was not about rolling back the New Deal. But it was a repudiation of the progressive view that the true narrative of American greatness is toward bigger and better government. That repudiation, in my opinion, stuck, and Obama hasn't overcome it. His progressivism was repudiated in the midterm election, and the likelihood of him rolling to a landslide victory in 2012 is very slim. Our current president does share with Reagan some moments of soaring rhetorical eloquence and personal class.

Reagan showed that a president could be "active" and "positive" on behalf of personal liberty. His signature thought domestically was all about the liberation of the energies of the American individual through lower taxes.

Reagan was also active and positive in opposition to the big, monstrous government that was "the evil empire" that was the Soviet Union. No one can deny that he reinvigorated the American military and aggressively opposed communism throughout the world—in Afghanistan, against the Sandinistas, etc., etc.—without actually getting American troops in a significant war. No one can doubt that his confidence and his prudence were key reasons for the deterioration to the point of destruction of Soviet confidence under his watch. We now know it was really, really prudent (contrary to what the experts were saying at the time) for our president to be so judgmental about evil that animated our enemy.

Happiness—Part 4: Another Happy President (Jefferson the Christian Epicurean)!

The author of the Declaration of Independence and surely our most "intellectual" president, Thomas Jefferson, wrote that we have life and liberty for the pursuit of happiness. In his private letters, Jefferson carefully distinguished between the modern, individualistic life devoted to the pursuit of happiness and happiness itself. He found in human beings two sources of happiness.

The first flows from the human mind and was most perfectly described by the philosopher Epicurus.

The second flows from the "instinct" or "moral sense" nature gives us as social animals. The moral doctrine that corresponds to that sense was most perfectly described by Jesus.

Because we are neither pure minds nor merely instinct-driven animals, neither Epicurus nor Jesus, by himself, is enough. That's why Jefferson actually described himself as a Christian Epicurean.

Jefferson explained that the Epicurean philosophers found happiness through their unflinching acceptance of the truth of atheistic materialism, and so in their capacity to live truthfully beyond hope and fear—the twin sources of the miserable restlessness specific to self-conscious mortals. That's the restlessness, of course, that's been intensified in the modern, middle-class, techno-energized world.

The philosopher has (as they say on *Seinfeld*) "serenity now" because he knows that there's no hope that human beings can escape their natural mortality (which they, of course, share with the other animals). He also knows that it's unreasonable to fear death. We know nothing of being dead, and it doesn't make sense to fear what we can't know.

The Epicurean even knows that self-conscious mortality is the condition of philosophizing, of the intellectual pleasure given to members of our species alone of seeing things as they really are. That happy combination of serenity and pleasure comes from the philosopher, as Socrates first said, learning how to die. He (or she) learns to get over the ridiculous self-obsession that flows from unreasonable hopes and fears. (Transhumanists take note.)

So why can't we all just be Epicureans? According to Jefferson, that kind of intellectual liberation will never be available to most people. It

requires considerable leisure, extraordinary education, and rare intellectual abilities.

Epicureans are also selfish; they're short on real emotional attachments to most people. They tend to limit their circle of concern to their
philosopher-friends. Charity or even compassion that leads to social or
personal service are not virtues often found among the more intellectually detached.

Socrates, we remember, wasn't much of a family man. A species full
of Epicureans wouldn't have much of a future.

That's why Jefferson turned to Jesus.

Happiness—Part 5: Jefferson, Jesus, and Darwin

The author of our Declaration, Thomas Jefferson, carefully distinguished in private letters between the modern life devoted to the pursuit
of happiness and happiness itself. He says that Epicurean philosophers
found happiness through their serene recognition of the truth of atheistic materialism, and so in their capacity to live truthfully beyond hope
and fear—the twin sources of the miserable restlessness of the Lockean
individual.

That happy philosopher, for Jefferson, is a very rare and most fortunate human occurrence. Even in times of Enlightenment his way of life
would not be possible for most people.

Ordinary people, Jefferson observes, are guided by nature to happiness
through a "moral sense," an instinct that caused them to find pleasure in
virtuously benefiting their fellow human beings in society. If there were no
natural connection between happiness and the performance of social duty,
then we would be absurdly unfit by nature for the social lives we must live.
The benevolent principles that correspond to our natural moral sense,
Jefferson claimed, were most perfectly expressed by Jesus. Following his
natural teaching is the way to human happiness

To see Jesus as more than the model natural being—as God—is to
muck up true morality with ridiculous mystifications, not to mention false
hopes and fears. That's why Jefferson engaged in the project of
editing/shortening the New Testament with his knowledge of natural
morality in mind. It's *his* Jesus he's recommending to us.

The ordinary moral person achieves happiness by following the biological or basically bodily instinct we've been given. Instincts—like mus-
cles—are strengthened through exercise, through habituation. Being good
is acting on one's social instinct to do good.

Such moral sense is distorted and even diminished, Jefferson claims,
by reading moral philosophy—which, for Jefferson, is pretty much hypo-
critical moralism. On this front, Jefferson hated Plato and the Platonists the
most, and the Stoics only somewhat less. Epicurus he ranks higher than all
the other the philosophers for being upfront on the fact of the incompati-
bility between philosophy and morality.

The view that the natural moral sense is the source of human happiness came to Jefferson through the Scottish Enlightenment. Thinkers such
as Adam Smith aimed to soften or socialize Locke's individualism through

the cultivation of moral sentiments. That sentimental Enlightenment went on to decisively influence the optimism of Darwin.

Darwin concluded that our species is not, in the most important sense, different from the others. The successful intention of nature is that all the animals have enjoyable or happy lives. And it's our basically unconscious determination by nature that should give us confidence that our existence is good. Darwin held that reason is a tool that serves our social instincts, so that human beings would progress morally as they progressed intellectually.

The Epicurean Jefferson wouldn't have made that connection between moral and intellectual progress. He didn't think that the mind exists to serve the body of the social animal. He thought, instead, that there was deep tension between what's best for the liberated philosopher or scientist—the being who is, so to speak, pure mind—and what's best for the social animal. It wouldn't have surprised Jefferson to have seen social instincts atrophying in the direction of apathetic indifference in our enlightened or pop scientific time.

We do have to admit there's a lot of truth to what Darwin says about the natural foundation of human happiness. The Lockean or individualistic or libertarian view is that happiness is subjective; what it is varies from free individual to free individual.

But there's a lot less variation, the sociobiologist E. O. Wilson says, than it first appears. For most human beings—most social animals—happiness is something like the opposite of loneliness. For the most part, studies show that married people are happier than single people, people from large families are happier than people from small families, and people with lots of close friends are happier than people with just a few.

Happiness also correlates strongly with faithful involvement in religious communities, active participation in political life, and worthwhile work with others. Happiness usually depends on really developing the attachments—a non-Darwinian would say the personal love—that come from doing what social animals do. No study confirms the individualistic thoughts that love is for suckers or hell is other people.

Wilson adds, quite realistically, that there are a few people who want to be left alone. And what's usually true, Jefferson remind us, isn't true for Epicureans such as himself. Jefferson, I think, wouldn't have thought that Darwin explains it all. I would add, you won't be surprised to know, that Darwin and Darwinians can't even explain what's most happily personal about love.

Happiness—Part 6: Why Americans These Days Are the Most Anxious People Ever

This expert explains why in a very detailed and most plausible way. Here's one taste:

> Is the United States more prone to higher levels of anxiety than other nations? Put simply, we are. Perhaps the most puzzling statistics are the ones that reveal that we're significantly more anxious than countries in the developing world, many of which report only a fraction of the diagnosable cases of anxiety that we do. One of the reasons for this is that the people in many of these third-world nations are more accustomed to dealing with uncertainty and unpredictability. I talk about this a fair amount in the book, but lack of control is really the archenemy of anxiety. It's its biggest trigger. [Sugarman, "'Nerve': Why Is America So Anxious?," *Salon*, March 20, 2011.]

So people in "less developed" nations have lives that are actually more uncertain and unpredictable; what happens to them is actually beyond their rational control. But they're used to it. We actually have more control over our lives. We can deal more effectively with, and know a lot more about, the various "risk factors"—nature itself, of course, is the most daunting risk factor.

Our lives actually are more predictable and secure than lives have ever been; we have less reason than ever, for example, to be anxious about a child dying. But it seems parents are more nervous than ever. Accidental death after all is still possible at any time, and we can and we do more than ever in response to that perception of contingency with our prudent calculations.

Is it true that the more "rational control" we have, the more anxious we are? Maybe that's because each of us is stuck with knowing how much the very future of one's own being is in one's own hands. We're stuck with being control freaks, always calculating—nervously or anxiously—about our personal security.

We're the people least likely to relax and let God or nature take its course. That fact, like most facts about social transformation, is both good and bad. But who can deny that it does anxiously rob us of the happiness or contentment we can enjoy right now. Is it harder than ever to be happily in love with or in the moment? We do spend big money trying to compensate for our anxiety with self-help programs that promise serenity now. I'll talk about the drugs later.

So it's not so much the actual lack of control, but obsessing over lack of control, that's the cause of anxiety.

We might be looking forward to a future with people blessed by technology with indefinite longevity obsessing over their lack of immortality. Death, having become much less obviously necessary and much more seemingly accidental, might consume our lives. We'll knock ourselves out like never before in accident-avoidance strategies—maybe spending our lives in lead houses communicating with our virtual (and so non-threatening) friends with the most advanced forms of social media.

But we'll still be worried about that asteroid that might pulverize our planet at any time, not to mention our lingering inability to stabilize the climate (against nature's capricious intention) in the most person-friendly form. And we'll still know that every particular being in this world has to go sometime. We're not going to bring the whole cosmos under our rational control.

Being Middle Class
(Or an Introduction to the Pursuit of Happiness)

Before talking more about happiness, I need to say something about the middle-class way of life we almost all live. To be middle-class is to be a free being who works. An unfriendly way of describing "being in the middle" might come from some Marxist: We're free like aristocrats to work like slaves. But that extreme claim would hardly be true to our experiences, which aren't so bad.

I'm a proudly middle-class guy. Every way of life has its limitations, though. And that's why every society—especially every modern society—needs a counterculture. (This post, obviously, is also an elaboration on the theme of the transition from natural to personal evolution.)

We Americans do talk a lot about the need for a counterculture. That talk comes from both the left and the right, from anyone who thinks that our freedom and dignity depends on understanding ourselves as more than middle-class or "bourgeois" beings, more than free beings who work.

The middle-class being—the being with interests and nothing more—can't sustain his freedom indefinitely, much less display the most sublime or soulful or deeply erotic dimensions of human longing.

Being middle-class (and nothing more) seems to generate two understandings of our freedom. The first we typically call "autonomy." We are free and dignified insofar as we don't live according to nature, but according to the law or standards we make for ourselves. Nature provides no guidance for particular persons because nature is indifferent to personal existence.

A world that does justice to *me* is not a natural one, and I have the duty to see the dignity in all beings—like me—who live personally or not merely naturally. We free beings transform our natural environment with personal significance or dignity in mind. In a certain sense, each of us is born free. In another, each of us has to work to make him or herself free.

People don't quite make themselves out of nothing; the fact of personal freedom is, in truth, a mysterious gift. But we're on our own to secure ourselves against the forces—beginning with natural forces—out to obliterate each of us. Our natural gift, in truth, is quite an ambiguous one; the other animals seem happy with their merely natural existences.

Meanwhile, we are more about the pursuit of happiness than happiness or enjoyment themselves. Our lives, insofar as they are free or not natural, are all about a restless seeking or searching that ends only in death. To be free is not to be happy. Happiness, as the philosopher Kant explains, is for mere animals, not dignified beings like ourselves.

The second understanding of our freedom we find in our power or "productivity." It's in our ability to be productive that we find our most measurable or secure evidence of our freedom.

Autonomy is unempirical, uncertain, too much an empty self-assertion or merely "identity politics." Productivity is the most reliable source of middle-class dignity. It's evidence that I really work—or not just fool around. Nobody, we think, has the right not to work. Productivity provides the best evidence that our claims for freedom aren't merely vanity.

Autonomy and productivity are both standards based on the view that freedom is personal or anti-natural. They're both opposed to the animal in us, and so the necessities connected with birth, sex, and death. An autonomous woman, as our Supreme Court has explained, is one who refuses to be defined by the natural, social, species-based necessity (and, of course, tribal necessity) of reproduction.

So autonomy and productivity are both unerotic and opposed to the limits to our freedom generated by erotic longing. Bourgeois sex, for example, is safe sex—or highly calculated sex. And bourgeois sex is the one-night stand, which doesn't compromise either autonomy or productivity or turn the pursuit of happiness into happiness itself.

As Tocqueville pointed out, of course, bourgeois sex (which used to be relaxed enough to at least reliably generate children) at least used to be at the foundation of the domestic tranquility of the American family, on which middle-class men ungratefully relied to maximize their productivity.

But that view of the family, we now know, unjustly privileged the productivity of men and compromised the autonomy of women and, to a lesser extent, men. Middle-class sex, the good news might be, is emphatically not what the other mammals do on the Discovery Channel. Free beings aren't simply doing what comes naturally.

The uncertainty of autonomy causes it to be subordinated to productivity. The autonomous woman free (against the letter of the Hippocratic Oath) to subject herself to cosmetic surgery—or turn herself into a patient for reasons having nothing to do with health—to improve her appearance (especially to look younger) usually does so to enhance her productivity, to turn herself into a more marketable commodity. She aims to avoid the undignified loneliness that is so readily suffered by the unproductive (especially the unproductive elderly) in a middle-class society.

And the professor, we will increasingly find, also will find it harder and harder not to do what's required to maximize his productivity—measured both in scholarly output and indices of student satisfaction. He soon, we can speculate, won't even be able to say that he, as an autonomous being, has a right to bad (and so unproductive) moods as clues to the truth about his very being. There's no reason a middle-class administrator will acknowledge that he (or she, of course) can't call his most productive (because good) moods his true ones, even if they are artificially or pharmacologically generated.

The Secret to Marital Happiness: Don't Have Kids or Have Lots of Them

That's the conclusion of of *When Baby Make Three* by W. Bradford Wilcox and Elizabeth Marquardt.

The discovery that being married without children is one path to happiness vindicated the feminists, the liberationists, the authentic followers of Simone de Beauvoir. Authentic people live for themselves; they refuse to be breeders; their lives are fulfilled without giving in to some biological inclination shared with the other animals.

But this line of thinking easily leads to this conclusion: Why get or stay married at all? Marriages without children may be happier, but they also end more often in divorce. The philosopher Nietzsche observed that one great error of the modern, liberal West is the sentimental, unempirical thought that love, by itself, will keep us together.

Having kids does tend to keep marriages together. And if you're going to go that route, the more the happier. Four or more kids seems, in a significant number of cases, to be the key here.

The authors speculate on why that's true:

> What accounts for the surprisingly higher levels of marital bliss among parents of large families, given the obvious financial, practical, and emotional challenges of raising a large family in contemporary America? This finding seems to be largely a "selection" story, in which particular types of couples end up having large numbers of children, remain married to one another, and also enjoy cultural, social, and relational strengths that more than offset the challenges of parenting a large family. In this case, the Survey of Marital Generosity suggests that fathers and mothers of large families are partly happier because they find more meaning in life, receive more support from friends who share their faith, and have a stronger religious faith than their peers with smaller families.
>
> Take religious attendance. Figure A2 shows that the parents of large families are about twice as likely to attend church, synagogue, or mosque on a weekly basis or more often. It is certainly possible that having a large family can bring some people to their knees! But it is also likely that highly religious

men and women feel called by God or encouraged by their religious networks of friends and family members to have large
families.

Are these people happier because they're more generous, more relational,
more purposeful, and/or more religious? Do they have larger families
because they're more religious—or feel called by God or their fellow
believers to be fruitful and multiply? Or are they more religious because
they have lots of kids—and so need and want the support and encouragement of a "church family"?

We do know, of course, that maybe the big reason America doesn't suffer from anything like the birth dearth of many other highly developed and
prosperous countries is the fecundity of our observant religious believers.
When I think big family, I immediately think of the Mormons, the orthodox Jews, the evangelicals of various kinds, and more traditionalist
Catholics. I also think homeschoolers.

Now the study's authors do add that we don't know for certain who's
happy. The study relies on people's self-reporting. It could be, they mention in passing, that people who have the most invested in kids have to
believe they're happy in their choices to get through the day. They're stuck
with the kids, like or not.

Why are those who have just a kid or two or three—those who practice moderation, it would seem—less happy that the extremists in both
directions?

Here are a few highly speculative observations:

1. People with a kid or two are robbed of happiness by excessive
parental paranoia. If you have lots of kids, you have to relax more than a
bit in each particular case.

2. That paranoia might have a Darwinian explanation: If your point in
life is to get your genes to the next generation, then the one-kid strategy is
highly risky. If you have ten kids, then success is pretty much guaranteed.

3. The people who have no kids and the people who have lots of them
are made happy by lives that have a kind of integrity. Either you're all
about personal autonomy or you're all about family. Either you're the free
individual described by Locke or Beauvoir or you're the social, reproductive animal described by Darwin.

4. Attempting to balance being an autonomous individual and a social
animal produces a kind of incoherence that leads to misery. You're
constantly confused and being pushed in different directions. You can't

even explain to people who you are. That's doubtlessly part of the misery in the midst of prosperity of which Americans, Tocqueville observed, are perversely so proud.

5. But all we have here, after all, are statistically significant but not overwhelming tendencies. I'm happily married and only have one kid. I admit, however, to having been overwhelmed with Darwinian relief when my daughter had my grandson.

Praising the Puritans

There's little less fashionable today than praising the Puritans, especially for their egalitarian political idealism, their promotion of genuinely humane and liberating learning, and their capacity for enjoyment and human happiness. Praising the Puritans is especially difficult for us because even most of our Protestants have abandoned them. When a European calls us Puritanical we don't say, "Yes, thanks a lot, you're right." Instead, we either deny it, saying we're way beyond those days. Or we admit it, saying that, "yes, we should be less capitalistic, less repressed, and more free thinking, just like you." But the truth is that the Puritans remain the chief source of the American difference—our ability to live freely and prosperously without unduly slighting the longings of our souls. It's the Puritans' idealism that made and even makes Americans civilized.

Tocqueville's *Democracy in America* almost begins by showing us how much our democracy owes the Puritans. He calls attention to two quite different English foundings, two quite different displays of democratic freedom—the one in the South and the other in the North. "Gold seekers," "restless and turbulent spirits," and solitary adventurers founded Virginia to get rich quick. They were England's "lower classes," people "without resources" or virtuous habits, people incapable of being animated by "noble thought" or some "immaterial scheme." They had no sense of home and no sense of having the paternalistic, magnanimous responsibilities of class. They weren't even ennobled by any bourgeois devotion to the virtue of worthwhile work well done. They, like the middle-class Americans Tocqueville elsewhere describes, loved money, but, unlike the properly middle class, they weren't at all devoted to the just principle that it should be the reward of one's own honest industry. The Virginians were in every crucial respect uncivilized (*Democracy in America* [*DA*] I. 1.2; all other references to and quotes about the founding in Virginia and New England—including the Puritans—are from this section unless otherwise noted).

So the Virginians readily accepted the introduction of slavery—or extreme stratification based on the introduction of a separate class of men who work and do nothing but—into the colony. That racist institution further contributed to their combination of "ignorance" and "haughtiness," enervating their minds and heightening their propensity to dishonor work. It diverted them further from useful activity.

The English of Virginia, Tocqueville wants us to see, had all of the vices but none of the virtues of hereditary aristocrats, as well as, of course, all the vices but none of the virtues of the American middle class. Their laziness was uncompensated for—as Tocqueville reports, aristocratic leisure sometimes was—by souls soaring above ordinary vulgarity in the direction of immaterial ideals. Everything ignoble about modern liberty in America Tocqueville, in effect, traces to the South's founding in Virginia.

He goes on to tell us that the Puritans established colonies without lords or masters—without, in fact, economic classes. They weren't out to get rich or even improve their economic condition; they were in no way driven by material necessity. They "belonged to the well-to-do-classes of the mother country" and would have been better off in the most obvious ways staying home. Their lives were structured by resources and by morality; they came to America as family men, bringing their wives and children. They were models of social virtue. They were also extremely educated men—on the cutting edge, in many ways, of European enlightenment. They were, Tocqueville observes, animated by "a purely intellectual need." They aimed "to make an idea triumph" in this world.

The Puritans were, in fact, singularly distinguished by the nobility of their idealistic, intellectual goal. They willingly exposed themselves to "the inevitable miseries of exile" to live and pray freely as they believed God intended. Those called "the pilgrims," Tocqueville observes, were that way because their "austere principles" caused them to be called Puritans. Their pure standards—their excessive claims for freedom from the alleged corruption of bodily need and pleasure—caused them to be insufferable to all the governments and societies now in existence. The Puritans always seem to others to be "enemies of pleasures" (*DA* II 1.19).

Puritan principles could become real only in a new world carved out of the wilderness, where they were the founders of "a great people" of God. They had no choice, they thought, but to be "pious adventurers," combining the spirits of religion, morality, family, and education with something like the restlessness that drove other "small troop[s] of adventurers going to seek fortune beyond the seas." Unlike the Americans Tocqueville observed himself, their restlessness led them to their true home and didn't leave them isolated or disoriented.

The first Americans of the North chose exile in America not for prosperity or physical liberty, but to satisfy an intellectual need that had nothing to do with their bodies. The Virginians, by contrast, were extremely moved by singularly materialistic, if not criminal, pursuits. (Most colonies,

Tocqueville notices, originate in the lawless greed characteristic of pirates.) But that's not to say the men of New England thought of themselves as too good or too pure for this world.

All of the democratic political freedoms that we Americans often trace to the social contract theory of the philosopher Locke were adopted by the Puritans "without discussion and in fact." Being clearly derived from biblical principle, they didn't depend on or exist merely in the speculative dialogue of the philosophers. Even the Americans Tocqueville saw for himself in his visit understood that accepting some religious dogma "without discussion" turns out to be an indispensable foundation of the effective exercise of political freedom.

Because the Puritan conception of political freedom wasn't based on the apolitical, selfish, rights-obsessed, and duty-negligent Lockean individual, it both not only demanded virtuous civic participation but also connected political freedom with the creature's charitable duty to the unfortunate. It set a high or virtuous standard for political competence and incorruptibility, and it didn't seem to need to rely on institutions with teeth in them to restrain the spirit of faction and boundless ambition of leaders.

Whatever Puritan government was, it was not another name for a band of robbers, just as Puritan freedom could never be confused with another name for nothing less to lose. The Virginians' view of freedom was finally merely useful or materialistic; it is the liberty of beings with interests and nothing more. The Puritans distinguished themselves by their "beautiful definition of freedom," "a civil, a moral, a federal liberty," "a liberty for that only which is just and good." That's the liberty for which it makes sense "to stand with the hazard of your very lives." Only if liberty is beautiful or for the displays of the most admirable and virtuous human characteristics can it really be worth the courageous risk of life.

The citizens of New England took care of the poor, maintained the highways, kept careful records and registries, secured law and order, and, most of all, provided public education for everyone—through high school when possible. The justification of universal education was that everyone should be able to read the Bible to know the truth about God and his duties to Him for himself. Nobody should be deceived by having to rely on the word of others; they had the democratic or Cartesian distrust of authority without the paralyzing and disorienting rejection of all authority (*DA* II 1.1) That egalitarian religious understanding, of course, was the source of the American popular enlightenment that had so many practical benefits.

Middle-class Americans, Tocqueville explains, later achieved a universal level of mediocre literacy that served as what was required for making money for oneself. For the middle class, education's justification was wholly practical or applied, and not at all for the cultivation of the mind or soul. But it's the Puritans who provided us the genuinely ennobling justification for universal education. For them, democratic education is liberal education, for discovering the liberating truth about who we are. The degrading theory that universal education must be primarily technical education dissolves for us Americans once we remember that the democratic view that education is for everyone has two justifications—one directed toward the body and the other toward the soul.

Tocqueville's Puritans, we might even add, were more for democratic liberal education than Tocqueville himself. He recommended the study of the Greek and Roman authors in their original language for the few Americans with the talent and passion to pursue literary careers and so to assume responsibility for the ennobling of democratic language. Most Americans, he thought, would just become dangerously dissatisfied with the banality of their industrious middle-class routine if infused with such aristocratic longing (*DA* II 1.15). But the Puritans believed that the soul's longings exist in us all and deserved to be educated in every case.

"Puritan civilization in North America," Marilynne Robinson observes in her collection of essays *The Death of Adam*, "quickly achieved unprecedented levels of literacy, longevity, and mass prosperity, or happiness, as it was called in those days." What's good for the soul, the Puritans showed, can also be good for the body, and the spirit of religion is what reconciles the pursuit of prosperity and human happiness (as opposed to the endlessly restless pursuit of happiness Locke described). It's most instructive to see the early Americans "seeking with an almost equal ardor material wealth and moral satisfactions." Just as it's instructive to see the marvelous combination of "the spirit of religion" with "the spirit of freedom." In this respect, the Puritans look less like extremists than evidence of the fact that, as Tocqueville says, "the human heart is vaster than one supposes; it can at once contain a taste for the goods of earth and a love of those of Heaven" (*DA* II 2.15).

Both the North and the South—New England and Virginia—began with extreme views of what human liberty is. Neither Tocqueville could affirm as what's "true and just," although both have elements of truth and justice. The Americans, with their subtle and unprecedented statesmanship, haven't found it necessary to choose, as Tocqueville says people are often stuck with doing, between the excesses of one extreme or another. America at its political best is a compromise between colonial North and South, between New England and Virginia, between meddlesome, intrusive idealists and vulgarly self-indulgent and morally indifferent pirates.

The Puritans can be criticized as hyper-moralistic despots in some ways, but the Virginians were amoral despots in others. For the Virginian, in effect, every man is the despot, and his point of living is to make himself wealthy and powerful, even at the expense of others. That view, truth to tell, is even present in the Lockeanism of our Founding Virginians, who regarded every man as a sovereign who consents to government only for his personal convenience. And it's the individualism or emotional solitude that is the product of that Lockeanism that paves the way to the soft despotism he feared far more than any Puritan excess. The American religious, political, and localist ways of combating individualism, Tocqueville makes it quite clear, are our most fortunate Puritanical legacies, ones indispensable for combating individualism.

We see this spirit of compromise in our Declaration and Constitution, in which the influence of the Virginians Jefferson and Madison was as much as prudent statesmen as principled theorists. The theoretical core of the Declaration is all about inalienable rights and not about the personal God of the Bible. "Nature's God" is a past-tense Creator, and the guidance he provides men now is questionable, insofar as they institute government and many other inventions to move as far away from being governed by nature as possible. But thanks to the insistence of members of Congress who were more under the influence of Christian Calvinism than, say, Jefferson and Franklin, God also became, near the Declaration's end, providential and judgmental, or present-tense and personal.

Probably the most nuanced or balanced judgment on the significance of our Declaration comes from R. L. Bruckberger in *Images of America* (1959). Bruckberger, another of our friendly French critics, took what Tocqueville said about our Puritans about as seriously as anyone, and maybe surpassed Tocqueville in seeing more clearly the connection between the Puritans and the Calvinist believers who helped to shape our founding documents. "The greatest luck of all for the Declaration," Bruckberger explains, "was precisely the divergence and the compromise between the Puritan tradition and what Jefferson wrote." A "strictly Puritan" Declaration, of course, "would probably not have managed to avoid an aftertaste of theocracy and religious fanaticism." But if it had "been written from the standpoint of the ... philosophy of that day, it would have been a-religious, if not actually offensive to Christians."

The Declaration as a whole, Bruckberger concludes, might even be viewed "as a more profound accomplishment," one of "the great masterpieces of art, in which luck is strangely fused with genius." The combination of American Lockeanism and American Puritanism/Calvinism produced something like an accidental American Thomism. It's that fact that led the American Catholic John Courtney Murray in *We Hold These Truths* (1960) to praise our political Fathers for "building better than they knew," although even Murray didn't acknowledge properly the Puritan contribution to what our political Fathers built. Arguably the Declaration as compromise is better guidance for Americans than the intentions of either of the parties to the compromise.

God is personal, but that fact supports rather than negates the equal right to freedom all human beings have. Properly understood, in Tocqueville's eyes, that understanding of equality unites the teaching of Jesus and the teaching of Locke, while both Locke and Jesus distance religious idealism from the requirements of good government. But it's still the idealism of Jesus that turns equality into more than a principle of calculation or self-interested consent, into a beautiful idea or an undeniable moral proposition that leads us to do good even at the risk of our lives.

Now more than ever is the time for our statesmen, legislators, and enlightened writers to talk up the Puritans in the name of the most sublime faculties, those with which we can be happy as human beings. The justice of the middle-class American, as Tocqueville says, is that nobody is above or below being a being with interests—someone who is free and who works for himself (*DA* II 2.8). But the Christians provide the indispensable addition that each of us is more than a being with interests, and so each of us shares in a kind of greatness the aristocrats reserved only for themselves. So each of us was made to enjoy civilization and liberal education and the leisurely, social, conversational contemplation of who we are under God. Truth to tell, we're much more repressed and unhappy these days than the Puritans ever were, at least at their best.

It's fashionable today to identify our Puritanical legacy chiefly with the moralism of our "religious right" and so to identify it with illiberal and prejudiced fundamentalism. We tend to contrast that moralism with leftism defined as the mixture of moral libertarianism and egalitarian political progressivism that characterizes our liberalism. That contrast is most misleading. Most of our enduring egalitarian, "leftist" (if you want) criticisms of individualistic indifference both personal and political, Tocqueville and Robinson show us, comes from the Puritans. To the extent that we remain egalitarian idealists and believe that our liberty is for doing good for all our fellow citizens and creatures we remain Puritanical.

So our Calvinism, contrary to Weber, is most deeply less about our spirit of capitalism than one of our main ways of curbing its selfish excesses. Our religion, as Tocqueville observes, saves us from degrading self-absorption and for the free and dignified performance of our common moral duties (*DA* II 1.5). The spirit of political liberty—the ennobling activity of citizens—depends, the Puritans taught us, on the spirit of religion. And they also showed that egalitarian citizenship depends on the truth that each of us is more than merely a citizen.

Christianity

Fat for Jesus

I don't know if this is such an appropriate post for Sunday morning. A study from Northwestern shows that people who regularly attend religious services are 50 percent more likely to become obese.

Several years ago I read an interesting book by a French literary figure on his recent travels through America. He reported on the whole-life consumer orientation of an evangelical megachurch. The exercise class was called "Fit for Jesus." I have to admit I was less amused than repulsed. Does that name mean that Jesus doesn't love fat girls, that you have to be fit to enter the Kingdom of Heaven? Are the Pearly Gates only so wide? Is "the path" really *that* narrow?

So, I have to admit I'm strangely reassured by this study. Not that being obese is a responsible lifestyle option, even if it is one that I have chosen. But people who really believe in the living and giving God, it would seem, can relax a bit about their waistlines. They know they're going to stay around even if they die a bit younger than they might if they more rigorously avoided refined carbs, exercised scientifically, attended obsessively to risk factors, and so forth. They certainly don't think that they have to knock themselves out trying to stay around until biotechnology is able to turn us all into immortal robots (who, if Mr. Kurzweil is right, will somehow get to continue to have virtual or disembodied sex).

People who go to church usually don't believe that their salvation is in their own hands, and that being itself is extinguished if and when they die. They aren't so anxious that they can't enjoy some pie.

The article is right about church suppers in the sticks. I've been to hundreds of them, and they are very old-fashioned in being about lots of food that studies show is bad for you. Plus, there's no portion control, and as you enjoy fellowship with other believers you're tempted to go back for seconds and thirds.

The article is right too, that enhanced health consciousness is making and will continue to make the "potluck" menus more sensible.

Avoiding obesity, nonetheless, is not really a good reason not to go to church with your kids.

The Megachurch and God's Love

BIG THINK has displayed a taste of the astute social commentary of Robert Putnam—the man who was so worried that so many Americans were bowling alone.

The success of the megachurch, Putnam explains, should be integrated into business models, combining, as it does, impressive overall size with consumer-centered niches that provide senses of community or belonging.

Those churches, to be sure, combine Christian belief with contemporary culture in ways attractive to the young. So they often seem, from the perspective of more traditional Christianity, to be aesthetically challenged. But, "contemporary Christian" music is hugely popular, outselling most of its secular rivals.

From even contemporary standards, that success can't be attributed to the actual quality of the music. As Hank said to Bobby on *King of the Hill* (after dragging Bobby home from his adventure with a "Christian rock" band), "Son, you're not making Christianity better, you're making rock and roll worse." It's something about the words, far more than the music, that's attractive to the young. The young, as the megachurch pastor Rick Warren wrote, are all about "purpose-driven" lives, and they hunger to combine purpose with personal love.

Putnam's expectation is that the megachurches will continue to become more market friendly by abandoning "hard right" politics. There's probably some truth in that unfriendly or even self-righteous observation, but surely churches lose their effectiveness if they become too market sensitive. As Tocqueville explains, religion in America does our people good only as a countercultural force, one that gives people, and especially the young, a point of view by which to resist being fashionable—to resist being carried along by libertarian narcissism and impersonal public opinion. Anyone with eyes to see knows that America's genuine counterculture today is found among observant religious believers.

If it weren't for those believers, for example, we really would have a birth dearth. They're the ones having the kids who are so important for securing our future—for example, for saving Social Security and Medicare.

Not only that, they're the source of the under-noticed and underrated American virtue of charity. The film *The Blind Side* displayed American charity—or loving service to others out of love of God—in a way that moved more Americans than the fuzzy pantheism of *Avatar* ever could. The Taco Bell tycoon and his wife were raised above the vulgarity (and racist exclusivism) of the southern, suburban McMansion by the Biblical view that every human creature is unique and irreplaceable and infinitely lovable.

Putnam has the opinion that being against abortion or being pro-life is "hard right" and so unattractive to the young. But surely anyone filled with personal love—beginning with the personal God—has to be pro-life, every life. And studies really do show that young people these days are more pro-life than their parents. Rick Warren, in my opinion, stung our president more than any of his other critics in the 2008 campaign when he got him to say that it was "above my pay grade" to wonder whether the unborn have rights.

A Joyful Christmas to All

I was at a local Christmas party last night. There I met a most admirable young man with six beautiful and happy children and a seventh on the way. He makes his living as a boutique metal worker (cupolas and such), and he's obviously a fine craftsman and an able entrepreneur. Not only that, he's quite the connoisseur of fine beer and wine and quite widely read. He speaks with the eloquent sophistication—not often found among cosmopolitan sophisticates—of someone with justifiable confidence that he knows what he's talking about. He's a Republican out of personal self-reliance; he has no idea why any responsible person would need or want more than catastrophic health insurance. His knowledge of theology shamed me; he mentioned author after author I had heard of but not read. He and a couple of the other men present had a sophisticated and politely contentious conversation about Calvinism and Covenant Theology. He reported that he and his boss talked theology almost every day over lunch, and that his boss, although a good and knowledgeable Christian, had distressing antinomian tendencies due to his neglect of the moral law of the Old Testament.

This guy told me calmly and almost as an aside that, because he's not a Roman Catholic, he and his family don't celebrate Christmas. His kids call Santa a stupid fat man. He, of course, is all for Christmas parties, but the thinks the birth of the Lord should be remembered every Lord's day. The Catholics, he explained, were really good at converting pagans by appropriating their seasonal festivals for Christian purposes. But December 25 signifies, in truth, nothing properly Christian.

Our country's first Christians, the Puritans, also were against Christmas as nothing more than an invention of popery. And I've said time and again, following Tocqueville, that we Americans wouldn't be much without the enduring influence of our Puritan tradition.

Our Founders tended to slight Christmas as nothing more than an English tradition that deserves to fade away in republican America. It's only a slight exaggeration to say Christmas almost disappeared from our country in the wake of the revolution.

Christmas, contrary to our Founders' hopes and expectations, still reminds us that we're more than Calvinists or enlightened, principled Deists or even some combination of the two.

Christmas survived in our country as a part of English history and belief that couldn't quite be extinguished. And, thank God, John Wesley was all for the celebration of Christmas, as were our Lutheran and Catholic immigrants. Christmas really caught on among the slaves brought over from Africa, who saw that it was all about personal liberation. Maybe the best Christmas hymns written in America were African-American spirituals—such as "Mary Had a Baby" and "Go Tell It on the Mountain"—rooted in both deep human longings and the earthy reality of what happened on Christmas day.

The England of the carols—primarily medieval and Catholic and aristocratic and certainly pre-Calvinist England—had it right that Christmas ought to be a joyful festival. It was the successor of the pagan festivals, but still something new, because the news was so much more unambiguously good than anything the pagans ever heard. Surely Tocqueville was right that the Christian message about the equal freedom of us all—a gift of our Creator—is our most precious inheritance from aristocratic centuries, and that Jesus Christ had to come to earth for us really to hear that message or have it become part of ourselves.

I could go on and talk about the most depressing thing America can do and has done to Christmas is to make it less joyful, to domesticate or banalize it, to turn it into "Happy Holidays" that are neither pagan nor Christian. But it's easy to exaggerate these criticisms. Christmas remains more Christian in America than we often know.

A joyful Christmas to all …

Lovely, Glorious, Beautiful Christmas

1. Somebody around BIG THINK should say something about Christmas. I know that's a divider—not a uniter—topic. Not everyone is a Christian.

2. Some Christians, like our founding Puritans, believed Christmas—especially its timing—is basically pagan, and they're not totally wrong. Many American Protestants remained, at best, ambivalent about the conspicuous celebration of Christmas until the dawn of the twentieth century. They figured out, among other things, that an end-of-year shopping surge had or could become indispensable for American prosperity.

3. Not only that, not everyone who calls himself or herself a Christian these days believes that God really became man to die for our sins. They tend to say Christmas is about generic views of hope and joy and peace, while discouraging real thought about what or whom to hope for.

4. So we've had, for a while, the Holiday Season, during which we say "Happy Holidays." We unite on Thanksgiving and New Year's, and then agree to disagree on what holidays there are (and what their point is) in between. "Happy Holidays" is really a depressing thing to say, as if we didn't love and respect each other enough to specify exactly what's worth celebrating and why. "Happy Holidays" turns the jolly season into a series of meaningless diversions. Two very impressive Jewish public intellectuals ended their emails to me this morning with "Merry Christmas," and I return the favor by specifying their holy days and my hope for their happiness on them as appropriate.

5. If we were really Christians, we'd start to figure out that we should do more, if not all, of our carol singing, partying, giving, and such between Christmas and Epiphany. The celebration should be the Twelve Days of Christmas. We shouldn't "Go tell it on the Mountain" until Jesus Christ is actually born. Songs about sleighs, winter wonderlands, Santa, Christmas being white, Christmas being blue, and so forth are, of course, welcome any time during the season.

6. My reform would make the Christmas season a lot less long, while not completely scuttling the amorphous "Holiday Season." Not only that, restoring the custom of a present for each of Christmas's twelve days would surely stimulate the economy in these tough times.

7. My title, of course, is from the classic uniter-not-a-divider movie, *A Christmas Story*, which is a wholly secular tale about an unreligious but

quite unelitist, unatheistic family in a seemingly unreligious, proto-rust belt town. As the president explains to us, when such ordinary folks don't focus on God, they turn their attention to guns. That's why Ralphie·is so obsessed he's willing to risk shooting his eye out to get the Red Ryder rifle. "Every kid, at the back of his mind, vaguely but insistently believes that he will be struck blind before his twenty-first birthday. And then they'll [parents, teachers, and other authority figures] be sorry."

I Wonder as I Wander

It falls to me on BIG THINK to say something good and true about Christmas. Here's a sign that we see in front lawns all across Rome/Floyd County, GA: "Christmas is a Birthday!" And it is!

Well, everyone knows that Jesus wasn't really born on December 25. But there's no particular reason that birthdays have to be exact. We're not remembering the date, we're remembering something unique, irreplaceable, something most worthy of our wonder that happened one day. More wonderful than the stars or the cosmos as a whole is the beginning of a particular life of a man or woman on earth.

A Christmas carol of Appalachian origin captures a lot about what's singularly wonderful about what happened the first Christmas day:

> *I wonder as I wander out under the sky / How Jesus the Saviour*
> *did come for to die / For poor on'ry people like you and like I /*
> *I wonder as I wander out under the sky*

There's nothing worse than subjecting poetry—especially beautiful songs—to analysis. But here's a few words on each of the three lines:

1. To be human is to wonder and wander. The being who wonders can't be fully at home in the cosmos the scientists can otherwise, perhaps, perfectly describe. There's nothing more wonderful than the being who wanders (and knows it) "under the sky." So, even Jesus was quite literally born "on the road."

2. He was born, for one thing, on the road to death. Why would Jesus "come for to die?" Unlike the rest of us, he didn't have to die. What does it mean to wonder about God as a loving, relational person who would chose to die to save us from death? What does it mean to wonder about God who wandered with us for a while?

3. And why would he choose to die for poor, ornery people? Why are distinctions based on wealth, status, and intelligence of no importance to the Savior? We want to say that haunting songs about our homelessness here and our longing to be at home somewhere else were fine for the Appalachian people or the oppressed slaves. We want to say we can be fully at home these days as free and prosperous and sophisticated techno-people, and so we don't need such illusions anymore. But the truth is that we're in crucial ways more homeless and so more poor and ordinary or uncertain of our true significance than ever—even if we have lots of money and cool stuff.

4. "I'll be home for Christmas" makes us more weepy—unreasonably weepy—than ever, because we don't give a moment of proper wonder to the true cause of our wandering.

5. Only if we wonder about why we wander can we be as at home as we can be with the good things and the good people of this world.

Thanksgiving, the Puritans, and St. Augustine

Thanksgiving is the holiday that brings us all together, whether or not we're Christians and whether or not we're American citizens.

It's the first holiday of the Holiday Season that begins around now and lasts until New Year.

We're so sure that saying "Merry Christmas" is intolerant and dogmatic that we're all about "Happy Holidays"—an exceedingly vague and non-judgmental phrase. It's a phrase that seemingly couldn't offend or inspire anyone. Still, it's the one that now manages to invigorate the commercial stimulus package that is the jolly season.

But nobody's so politically correct as to be offended by "Happy Thanksgiving."

From a merely historical point of view, maybe we should be more sensitive. After all, the original Thanksgiving was about the Christian European imperialists giving thanks for the initial success of their project to impose their idea of how people should live on this continent—even or especially at the expense of the way of life of the indigenous people. Maybe it's also about the indigenous people being suckered into choosing not to wipe the imperialists out while they easily could.

Still, there's something really good about that Puritanical idea: All people are equal under God. All are to participate equally in the political community. Everyone is to be liberally educated. Everyone is to have time for leisurely reflection. And nobody is above or below having to work for his or her daily bread.

Right now, I'm teaching St. Augustine's *The City of God*. The evangelical atheists on BIG THINK will no doubt accuse me of "cherry picking" what's good—meaning, most readily acceptable to us all—about that book for our edification.

But isn't it in the spirit of Thanksgiving for us to come together in thanks for what we've been given, including given by our great tradition of philosophers and theologians? I'm going to talk about perhaps the original Christian source about what we owe the Puritans.

St. Augustine explains that the philosophers had different views about how we should live. Some of them, such as Plato and the Platonists, thought that the best way of life was contemplation—meaning the way of life of the philosopher. Others, such as some Stoics, located it in action—meaning that philosophy is most of all a moral code for gentlemen and political leaders. And finally: Some had the more nuanced view that the best life is a mixture of contemplation and action; here my students are reminded of Aristotle's *Nicomachean Ethics*.

Augustine says there's some merit in all these answers, and some lives might well be devoted mainly to contemplation and others mainly to action. Thoughtful reflection is a natural human good, one that's good for us all. And so, no human life should be without leisure.

Leisure, of course, is to be distinguished from empty-headed diversion. The philosophers were wrong to not believe that leisure—free thought—is a duty for us all. Socrates was wrong, or at least gave the wrong impression, when he said most of us are stuck living in a "cave" of manufactured belief or are slaves to our political socialization or, for that matter, to natural compulsions beyond our control and comprehension.

Nobody who's devoted his life to action—the politician or the entrepreneur—should use the necessity of action as an excuse for running away from what he or she can't help but know about himself or herself. Nobody should try to lose himself in action or diversion. Businessmen shouldn't be so busy that their lives are some mixture of rodent-like restlessness and aimless recreation.

Part of the truth we should have the leisure to affirm, of course, is the many ways we should be grateful for what we've been given. We don't know spit about who we are unless we are, at least at times, filled with gratitude. That's why our leisure should be social or relational. Thanksgiving is for us all, and we never celebrate it by going it alone.

The philosopher, meanwhile, is not wrong on what genuinely human leisure is. Study in the broadest sense is one of the most pleasurable and worthy human pursuits. But even the philosopher should be moved by "the compulsion of charity" to act in service to others.

What's wrong with Socrates is that he lacked charity or personal love. Even Socrates was so lost in seemingly impersonal ideas that he lost himself, even he was about denying the deep or full truth about who he is. A charitable Socrates would have actually come closer to genuine self-knowledge. So Thanksgiving is, in part, about taking time personally to feed the poor.

It's easy and true to say that charity is a virtue that doesn't have a natural or self-evident foundation. The love we have for unique and irreplaceable and infinitely valuable other persons is rooted, Christians say, in love of God. Charity isn't empathy; it's much more personal and requires much more of each of us. Charity, first of all, means being of personal service for those who are emotionally impoverished by loneliness.

Augustine also says that sinful man hates the equality of all human beings under God. The sin here is our proud desire to willfully impose ourselves on others—to dominate them. The characteristic human sin is to perversely think of oneself as God, to act as a god in relation to other men. It's surely possible to know *that* truth about personal equality without belief in the personal God of the Bible.

The Christian, Augustine adds, has the duty to obey the law and act as a good citizen wherever he or she lives. Even such dutiful Christians were hated by the best Roman citizens. That's because they have to dissent from the civil religion of their particular city. They refused to accept the degrading belief that we're all deep down merely citizens, that the gods, in effect, want us to be "city fodder," that we're basically replaceable parts of some political whole. It's the Christians who paid the price for being so insistent that each of us is more than a citizen, more than a part of some whole greater than ourselves. And certainly that personal truth has stayed with us even or especially in our skeptical time.

Despite all the tyrannical political missteps by Christian leaders (including those by the Puritans), it's the Christians who gave us the idea that everyone is free from natural and political domination to be, as we say, a person, a being with his or her own conscience or irreducibly inward life and with a unique personal destiny. And that's why everyone needs and deserves a liberal education.

On Thanksgiving we can give thanks for the truth we all share about who we are. Thanksgiving is neither Christmas nor the Fourth of July.

Some Postmodern and Conservative Reflections About Nature and Our White Christmas

1. So this was the first significantly white Christmas in Georgia during my thirty-one years here. If I were a libertarian "conservative," I would add: Some global warming! But we postmodern conservatives would never say that. We are skeptical both about Al Gore's inconvenient truth and all that and about those who are "knee-jerkish" skeptical about all such Greenish claims. It snows around here once in a great while, and Christmas is bound to take a hit a couple of times each century.

2. We postmodern conservatives are prudent environmentalists. That is, we're anthropocentric environmentalists. We view nature from the point of view of what's best for the flourishing of human life.

3. No doubt nature would cheer if our species were to disappear. We're the species capable of trashing the planet to satisfy our superfluous or unnecessary desires. That's one of the big differences, of course, between us and the dolphins. It's not one that does us proud.

4. But we add that there aren't any dolphin presidents, princes, poets, priests, philosophers, physicists, or plumbers either. Maybe it's worth it that nature take a hit from a species able to display such diverse forms of great individuality.

5. Members of our species—some, of course, way more than others— are ticked off at the nature that's indifferent to the existence of particular individuals or persons. More than ever, particular people these days are saying nature is out to kill me, and I must to do something about it. Self-obsessed people living a very long time (far beyond the time required to do their whole duty to their species) and having fewer and fewer children couldn't possibly be good for nature.

6. Or maybe they are; today's individuals, more than ever, have trouble thinking beyond their own beings or of themselves as part of a whole greater than themselves. They think they know they aren't really just or even mainly part of nature, after all. According to Aleksandr Solzhenitsyn, sophisticated particular people these days tend to believe that when they are extinguished (by nature), being itself is extinguished. So maybe our individualism or personalism is, from the big-picture view, a form of human or species extinctionism.

7. There are popularizing physicists, such as Carl Sagan and very

recently Stephen Hawking, who tell us to make our sacred cause—now that God is dead and all that—the perpetuation of the species. They warn us that our species may only have a comparatively short time left on this planet—maybe only hundreds of thousands of years or even less. So we better get moving diversifying our existence throughout the whole cosmos. But who cares about the future of the species? Certainly not nature, and not a personal God. A Christian, I think, would doubt that we should regard indefinite species perpetuation as particularly important or as our job. Each of us, the truth is, exists for a moment between two abysses (as Pascal and Tocqueville write), and there's nothing we can really do about that (without God's gracious help, at least).

Our Greatest Living Political Philosopher

According to the French philosopher Pierre Manent, the nation is the modern form of the ancient *polis*, a particular place where people can and should find a political home. The nation is a body with definite territorial limits; customs, traditions, and political institutions; and a form fitted for beings like us with bodies and minds, eros and will—hardwired, so to speak, for living together in the truth, and experiencing the joys and responsibilities we share in common.

For Manent, who is among one of the most endangered of species, a French Catholic intellectual, the modern nation, at its best, is based on the realistic observations that each of us is a citizen, but more than a citizen. The city of God and the city of man are both places in which we can feel at home, if not quite fully at home.

Manent doesn't see the fundamental tension of the West as between city and man, meaning either between *citizen* and *philosopher* or *citizen* and *Christian*. That Socratic or Platonic tension is alleviated at least by the observation that each of us is more than both citizen and philosopher, but none of us is exempted either from being a citizen or from living well in light of what we really know.

The deeper tension Manent sees is between *magnanimity* (or proud claims of self-sufficiency, a greatness that deserves the highest recognition from others) and *humility* (our anxious awareness of our flaws, debts, and limitations, which we couldn't possibly overcome by our own efforts). The magnanimous man overrates his personal significance, of course, just as the humble man underrates his.

This dialectic between magnanimity and humility still exists, Manent suggests, even in Alexis de Tocqueville's democratic man, who, in one moment, proudly says nobody is better than he is and, in the next, impotently admits he's no better than anyone else.

That democratic man oscillates between two attitudes: I'm so significant that I can reasonably demand that the whole world exist for me; and I'm so insignificant that I have no point of view to resist the impersonal forces that surround me. Both the magnanimity and the humility of the free and democratic individual are too exaggerated, too unreal, to be sustainable.

What's left for free individuals displaced from the properly social and relational senses of magnanimity and humility? Hatred! Hatred of the body as an arbitrary and invincible limit to one's freedom. Why is that? The modern individual knows, or thinks he knows, that he is not his body. To be free, to be autonomous, is not to be determined by bodily need and instinct.

As our Supreme Court explained in *Planned Parenthood v. Casey*, to be an autonomous and dignified individual—the free being described by our Constitution—is to be mysteriously freed from being saddled by one's body, one's biology. A woman is free not to be a woman, not be a reproductive machine for her species or her country or her family. Furthermore, we all have a mega-right: "At the heart of liberty is the right to define one's own concept of existence, of meaning, of the universe, and of the mystery of human life."

This sort of free individual hates to be embodied, to be located in any physical or psychological place in particular. Manent regards that as the reason why today's Europeans are in the thrall of post-familial, post-political, and post-religious fantasies. The family, the nation, and the church are all institutions that come into being because we are free and rational beings with bodies.

Without bodies, we'd be free from personal love and personal death, we wouldn't have to defend ourselves against our enemies, we would have to generate biological replacements—children—to take over when we die. We have no reason to have kids or go to church or serve in our nation's armed forces.

The fundamental fact of Europe today is the *birth dearth*. Not having kids is, of course, bad for the species, although by some lights it might be better for the environment if our hateful species would just wither away. Not having kids, of course, is also bad for national security. And part of Europe's awakening from its vacation from history in fantasyland is its slow but real coming to terms with that *fact*.

Manent certainly gives Americans reasons to cherish our differences. We are, despite our reputation, less radically individualistic than Europeans these days, more likely to think of ourselves as citizens and creatures and parents and children. And it's our citizen-creatures who are proudly open to being citizen-soldiers, who stand up when Lee Greenwood sings. And we even have "unprotected" sex often enough that we have just enough kids to give our nation, so far, a plausible future—although it may be not actually be enough to save Social Security and Medicare over the long term.

The truth is that Manent gives us hope. Fantasies end, reality smacks us in the face, politics and God both have futures, although only God knows in what form.

Why Our Constitution's Silence on God Shouldn't Be Confused with Atheism (Especially by Atheists)

Given the increasingly complacently atheistic tone of many of the BIG THINKERS, I thought I'd introduce some realism about our Constitution's silence on God. My position will be, of course, somewhere between the "Christian nation" view of some dogmatic evangelical thinkers (such as those who don't think a Mormon is fit to be president) and the "Godless republic" view of some dogmatic evangelical atheists who claim to revel in the daylight of disbelief.

I think our Constitution's silence on God is one of our Framers' debts to the philosopher John Locke. Certainly our Constitution treats people as individuals—or not as members of classes, races, genders, or religions. In that respect, we have a classless citizenry, although far, of course, from a classless society. But Locke himself, as I will explain, would have thought of our Constitution's silence of God as a Christian contribution to human self-understanding.

Locke celebrates that breakthrough in egalitarian self-understanding that came with the Christians, the understanding that comes with the dis-covering of personal inwardness or subjectivity. So, while I think Locke was no Christian (unless you want to call a Socinian or anti-Trinitarian a Christian), he thought of himself as providing arguments and evidence for the fundamental Christian insight into personal reality. Christianity estab-lished the principle of the limitation of government by personal freedom. Locke thought that, with his discovery of personal identity, he could prove that individuals are both less and more than citizens. They consent to gov-ernment to protect their interests as self-consciously needy and vulnerable beings with bodies without surrendering their freedom for conscientious self-determination in pursuit of happiness.

For Locke, as for the Christians, both the individual and the church are autonomous—or free from political coercion to determine the truth about the free being's duties to his or her personal Creator. Locke could defend that conclusion, let me emphasize, without believing that most of what any particular church taught is true. He was highly doubtful that there is a living and giving personal God on which free beings could rely for love and security, and he taught individuals not to trust primarily in God, but in themselves. But he wasn't so doubtful about personal freedom as, from a natural view, a mystery that left room for belief in a Creator.

Consider that our Christians and our Lockeans—inspired by the idea that the free individual or person—ally against the classical republicans insofar as they think of people as basically citizens or part of a political community (or city fodder). Our Christians and our Lockeans agree that the emphatically Catholic Chesterton is right that America is a home for the homeless—a place for citizens who think of themselves as so equally unique and irreplaceable that they are far from merely citizens. In America, the homeless can be as at home as the homeless can be in any political community, precisely because that community does not compel them to deny what they really can know about themselves.

Christians, St. Augustine said, were often hated because they, on behalf of both the truth and their faith, had to dissent from the religious legislation of their political communities. They refused, like Socrates, to either believe in or worship the gods of their cities. From the classical, political view, the Christians actually seemed liked atheists. In our country, our Christians and our Lockeans have tended to ally against the classical republican idea of civil theology or, as Lincoln once put it, political religion.

The most noble and truthful Lockean interpretation of the Constitution of 1787's silence on God is that it's anti-civil theological. It can be criticized for not placing our country "under God," or for liberating political will from divine limits—for turning man into God. Or it can be praised for limiting the realm of political will, for freeing creatures and Creator from political domination for being who they truly are. Our Constitution, from the latter view, presupposes that the Christian view of the person and the God in whose image he or she is made is true. Our political leaders have always been free to express their faith in God, but not to turn it into legislation. For Christians, as John Courtney Murray says, American freedom is freedom for the church as an organized social entity with autonomous moral weight, and Locke, finally, wouldn't think of disagreeing.

God, for Locke, may well exist. Opinions about our duties to our Creator, as Madison, the most purely Lockean of our Founders thought, are a personal or private matter. God is not to be put to degrading political use, and so "civil theology" is not to direct or inhibit the natural—and inevitably social—human inclination toward theological concern.

Why Do We Deny That It's Our Nature to Die?

Dr. Craig Bowron has done as much as anyone to explain why we're all about exaggerating what medical science and the coming biotechnology can possibly do to extend particular lives. On average, we're living longer than ever, but that's not because much of anyone is getting into three digits. And we're much less accepting of the thought that death necessarily completes every natural life. Although we, on one level, think that it's a mark of sophistication to say that Darwinian naturalism explains it all, we're less on board with the Darwinian thought that nature intends each of us to be replaced. Each of us has a hard time thinking of himself or herself as a biological being.

One reason, Dr. Bowron explains, is that move from the farm to the city has removed the fact of natural death from our lives:

> Another factor in our denial of death has more to do with changing demographics than advances in medical science. Our nation's mass exodus away from the land and an agricultural existence and toward a more urban lifestyle means that we've antiseptically left death and the natural world behind us. At the beginning of the Civil War, 80 percent of Americans lived in rural areas and 20 percent lived in urban ones. By 1920, with the Industrial Revolution in full swing, the ratio was around 50-50; as of 2010, 80 percent of Americans live in urban areas.
>
> For most of us living with sidewalks and street lamps, death has become a rarely witnessed, foreign event. The most up-close death my urban-raised children have experienced is the occasional walleye being reeled toward doom on a family fishing trip or a neighborhood squirrel sentenced to death-by-Firestone. The chicken most people eat comes in plastic wrap, not at the end of a swinging cleaver. The farmers I take care of aren't in any more of a hurry to die than my city-dwelling patients, but when death comes, they are familiar with it. They've seen it, smelled it, and had it under their fingernails. A dying cow is not the same as a person nearing death, but living off the land strengthens one's understanding that all living things eventually die. [Bowron, "Our Unrealistic

Attitudes about Death, Through a Doctor's Eyes," *Washington Post*, February 17, 2012.]

Another reason is that our mobility, our productivity (based, in part, on all able-bodied adults having become wage earners), and our affluence have both made it possible and often made it necessary that the young not live with the old. The "multigenerational home" has almost disappeared:

> Mass urbanization hasn't been the only thing to alienate us from the circle of life. Rising affluence has allowed us to isolate senescence. Before nursing homes, assisted-living centers and in-home nurses, grandparents, their children and their grandchildren were often living under the same roof, where everyone's struggles were plain to see. In 1850, 70 percent of white elderly adults lived with their children. By 1950, 21 percent of the overall population lived in multigenerational homes, and today that figure is only 16 percent. Sequestering our elderly keeps most of us from knowing what it's like to grow old.

It's not like we intentionally banished the old from our lives because they bring us down by bringing death to mind. But it really has become true that the young do know less and less about being old and less and less about death and dying. They don't have the experiences that would cause them to be realistic about death. I'm not saying death isn't bad; it's just that it's not the worst thing. And, of course, it's the least avoidable thing. (Plenty of Americans pretty much avoid taxes.)

It's true, of course, that each unique and irreplaceable person is more than a biological being. But it's equally true that each person is a biological being, who gains a good deal of his or her freedom and dignity by living well (meaning, to begin with, living truthfully) as a being born to die. Who can deny an urbanized, techno-sophisticated population is singularly alienated—although, of course, necessarily far from completely alienated—from the natural facts and the accompanying natural longings and passions that flow from birth and death?

We're the animals burdened and elevated by knowing the truth about our biological destinies. And we torture the old, as Dr. Bowron says, when we resist biological death too much. We degrade the young when we get them to buy into biotechnological fantasies about the possibility or goodness of liberation from the distinctive joys, miseries, and personal destinies of who we are by nature.

Nature, Personal Death, and Other Ash Wednesday Reflections

The question of my last post: "Why do we deny that it's our nature to die?" The answer from many of my threaders: "We aren't merely or even essentially natural beings!" Human beings are free to overcome their natures and achieve immortality through biotechnology. The truth of evolution is not that we're slaves to an impersonal natural process beyond our control. Evolution can become conscious and volitional, and we can assume control over our personal destinies. Particular conscious lives are no longer hopelessly haunted by inevitable death. These are the times when we have reason to hope for immortality or at least indefinite longevity. I can be happy in hope if I have reason to believe that I won't necessarily die at any particular time.

Today, for Christians, is Ash Wednesday. We're reminded that we come from and end up ashes and dust. Each conscious human life, as Pascal said, is a moment between two abysses. Or, as that very emo band Kansas sang, all we are, after that moment, is dust in the wind. A couple of the threaders agree that a true Darwinian would agree concerning that natural insignificance of any particular person's existence. Nature—all there is, in truth—is the very opposite of being all about me.

Both the Christians and Kansas don't remind us of the fact of being ashes to ashes in the spirit of joyful or resigned or serene acceptance. The ancient philosophers and the Buddhists, in different ways, advised people to get over themselves and come to terms with their personal insignificance. It's possible, through intellectual discipline, to learn how to die, meaning to learn to be okay with your momentary, insignificant existence. So, the Epicureans (and don't forget that Thomas Jefferson and many other modern thinkers thought they were, deep down, Epicureans) wrote about a kind of serenity that comes when you truthfully get over your hopes and fears about your personal fate. That kind of serene acceptance was characteristic of the recent tough-minded death of the deeply atheistic Christopher Hitchens. It was also, we read, characteristic of Socrates, who taught that it was unreasonable either to fear death or hope for personal immortality.

The Christians say that the self-denial characteristic of Hitchens and Socrates is itself self-deception. Our longings to be more than merely biological beings define who we are all the way down. Each of us is a person—a conscious, relational, willful being essentially different from members of all the other species that we know about. So, we can't help but and quite rightly regard biological death as the terrible and random extinction of personal significance. And each of us can't help but only be happy in hope for personal salvation—a hope that some other person without our biological limitations can do for me what I so clearly can't do for myself. It is a deeply Christian thought that we can only be happy in hope. Ash Wednesday, of course, begins the season that's the prelude to Easter.

Almost all the readers of BIG THINK believe that the Christian hope is ridiculous, a fundamentalist fantasy that's been vanquished by the enlightenment of modern science. But there's no denying that the transhumanists—to whom I pay the high compliment of having thought through the technological or "rational control" impulse of modern science—have just as personal an aversion to biological death, to being nothing, over the long run, but dust in the wind. The transhumanist slogan is sort of the opposite of serenity now.

Is the transhumanist hope really more reasonable than the Christian one? Immortality through biotechnology, I think, is clearly impossible; particular conscious beings can never achieve for themselves the perfect invulnerability of complete disembodiment. Even if our bodies become indistinguishable from other machines, no machine lasts forever.

Indefinite longevity is hardly the same as immortality. In light of eternity, as St. Augustine wrote, does it really matter all that much whether each of us lives fifty or five hundred years? The latter is obviously much better than the former, because life is good. But eventually each of us is still dust in the wind without help we can't provide for ourselves.

Virtues and Politics

Courage?

One virtue BIG THINK has not been big on is *courage*. That might be a problem. According to Aristotle, courage is not only the first of the virtues, but all the other virtues participate in it. His opinion is much more reasonable, I think, than those who attempt to root all virtue in empathy.

To be courageous is to live well with danger. We all have to do that! Doesn't all virtue require not being enslaved to fear, being ready to risk everything for the right cause or principle or person or place?

People who praise being an entrepreneur often talk up risk-taking. But what they usually mean isn't even quite courage at all. The risk is that someone might end up poor. They don't often mean risking total oblivion—as did the pioneers and explorers and even inventors of the past. (The praise of the courage of Steve Jobs in the face of his untimely death—praise which may be just—has nothing to do with his job.)

Someone might say courage has become irrelevant. Those days in which most people have to risk their lives for their country or their religion or their cause or the truth or even their children are pretty much over. We're even suspicious of causes that lead people to risk lives—either their own or those of others. We think we're better off to the extent that John Lennon's imagining becomes real, and there's nothing to kill or fight for.

We tend even to think that people were crazy when they thought that there was anything higher than protecting the lives and liberty of the people around right now.

The truth is that we need some courage, at least, to just keep our heads. Each human life is pretty darn insecure, and we have to have some virtue not to be obsessed with our personal contingency, not to be obsessed with avoiding every conceivable risk factor. So we still have to be courageous to live with the facts of both the possibility of accidental death and the necessity of eventual death. Courage will always be required to live and especially to act well in light of what we really know.

The view that courage might become obsolete is promulgated by some transhumanists. If we free our beings from contingency by bringing them under our rational control, then all the virtues, beginning with courage, that flow from being moved by death will wither away.

The possibility of the coming *Singularity* works against courage. Courage makes sense as a way of displaying my nobility or my virtuous transcendence of my biological limitations through fearless action if I'm going to die anyway fairly soon. But if my death need not necessarily come at any particular time, arguably all courage becomes recklessness.

Anyone who really expects to live until the *Singularity* has every reason to be as risk-averse as possible. That person expects to transcend his biological limitations in a much more definitive way. The courageous man who dies in battle proves to us that he was more than a mere body; nonetheless, there's no denying he's now a dead body and nothing more (at least without faith). We're fooling ourselves, perhaps, if we think that the memory of his life can really compensate for its real absence now.

The all-volunteer army also works against courage. The so-called Greatest Generation was filled with men who often rather routinely displayed courage in a war well worth fighting. Now, we neither demand nor expect that citizens be soldiers. And President Bush the elder was the last commander-in-chief who had honorably and courageously served his country.

With the disappearance of the widespread expectation of courage, we become less grateful for those who still deploy their courage to protect us. The members of the various special forces, for example, have lives that have become so countercultural or incomprehensible that we rarely take them into account.

It's true that country music still displays the citizen-soldier for our admiration, just as it takes more seriously than most of us the thought that we achieve significance by thinking of ourselves as parts of wholes greater than ourselves. Most country singers are very careful to thank God and the military, and some make them both the point of their performances.

Next time, I'll discuss some thoughts on courage by the controversial philosopher of manliness Harvey Mansfield.

The Art of Manliness
(Or the Latest Self-Help Program)

I promised I would do a post based on what we can learn about courage from the philosopher of manliness Harvey Mansfield.

It turns out that there's a very sophisticated and entertaining website devoted to manliness as a kind of self-help program. And who can deny that many of our problems and miseries these days can be traced to a lack of manliness? There's even a book full of "manvotionals" entitled *Meditations on Manliness*. That, of course, is a very evocative title, reminding of us of the meditations of one of the manliest of philosophers, the Stoic philosopher-emperor Marcus Aurelius.

Manliness, Mansfield tells us in his book with that title, refers to the "spirited" (thumotic) part of the soul that Plato was very careful to distinguish from the soul's rational and desiring parts.

The fact of manliness is one reason we can turn to Plato to remember that we're not minds or bodies or even a mixture of the two. We human beings are some third entity that refuses to be reduced to either mind or body.

Because we're manly, we demand and we prove that we're more than mere bodies and more than mere minds. We insist on displaying and being recognized for our personal significance.

Manliness allows us to be courageous, in the basic sense of not being governed by fear. It also leads us toward the confidence that we know who we are and what we're supposed to do.

Manliness leads us in the direction of nobility insofar as it keeps us from being governed by our bodily desires. It also leads us in the direction of fanaticism or "decisionism" insofar as it keeps us from being governed by reason. Mansfield is almost too careful to tell us that manliness can be either be good or bad, depending on the cause it serves.

That's why the authors of *The Art of Manliness* are so careful to want us to admire the fictional Atticus Finch, who clearly employed his manliness to be governed by reason and a virtuous determination to be of personal service to others.

The website gives us six fine "life lessons" to be learned from Atticus. We learn that Atticus is governed by a sort of inner fortress that makes him worthy of ruling himself and others. Not to do his duty is to defile himself by not acting on the basis of what he really knows. If he doesn't truthfully rule himself or assume personal responsibility, then he knows he has no right to rule others, to be a representative in the legislature or even tell his children what to do.

That fortress is manliness in the service of reason. It is characteristic of all men who have real class. Atticus tells Scout not to use the "n-word" in referring to black people because it's "common." Atticus has a point of view by which to rise above the moral and intellectual tyranny of the majority.

People worthy of ruling—who know who they are and what they're supposed to do—are to be distinguished from common people, people lacking in class. One thing *To Kill a Mockingbird* does not do is show that ordinary people are capable of ruling themselves, of controlling their spiritedness with reason.

What we really see is that Atticus *is* a Stoic. The original Atticus was the best friend of the best of the Stoic philosophers—Cicero. The philosopher-physician-novelist Walker Percy wrote in his great essay "Stoicism in the South" that the leading southerners both before and after the big war thought of themselves as Stoics, as Roman patricians reading Great philosophers, as disciples of Epictetus and especially Marcus Aurelius. Percy says that Atticus is based on the very best of the southern gentlemen who really existed.

Their virtues were magnanimity and generosity—both of which lead them to take responsibility for their communities. And, of course, as the website explains, they weren't short on physical and moral courage.

I'm all for a Stoic self-help program, and even a school of psychology built on Stoic science. That's not to say the Stoics are right about everything. It's just that they're strong where we're weak.

Let me add quickly that a rational, spirited, confident, and admirable Stoic can be a woman. The Stoic in Walker Percy's first and best novel, *The Moviegoer,* is Aunt Emily.

The brilliant and highly responsible Stoic poet who raised Walker Percy, William Alexander Percy, was gay and lacking in the typical martial virtues (although not at all in courage). I tend to think, actually, that Will Percy was the most coherent and deepest of the southern Stoics. Walker Percy would have been nothing without being able to define himself in relation to "Uncle Will."

Odd Observations about Darwin and American Education

1. So the American understanding of science as technology—the modern understanding that flows from Bacon, Descartes, and that Cartesian Locke—contradicts the official view of our sophisticates that Darwin teaches the whole truth about nature and who we are. For the Darwinian, our species is, in the decisive respect, just like the others. Each member of the species exists to serve the species, and our happiness comes from doing our duty to the species as social mammals—basically by pair bonding, reproducing, raising the young, and then dying (or stepping aside for our replacements as nature requires). My ultimate point in life is to successfully spread my genes. And so it's naturally been the case that parents have found meaning by living on through their children, knowing that they continue to exist, for a while, in the grateful memories of their children.

2. As some Darwinians (such as Larry Arnhart, Francis Fukuyama, and James Q. Wilson) have correctly noticed, this account of who we are is basically conservative. It promotes family values—including such insights as people who come from large families are generally happier (because they're living more according to nature) than people who come from small ones. And it's natural for members of a social and vulnerable species such as ours to form tribes (or political communities) and to find happiness in loyal social and communal service. Religion also is natural as a way of enhancing social bonding and communal loyalty. Human beings are happier, as we say in the South say today, when they have family, political, and church homes. (Religion, from a Darwinian view, becomes perverse when it becomes too personal or too much about one's own significance or too much about unnatural, otherworldly hopes and fears.)

3. Thoughtful Darwinians call movements for personal liberationism—such that those that were initiated or radicalized by the spirit of the 1960s—a "Great Disruption" bound to be overcome by the impersonal imperatives of who we are by nature. Thoughtful Darwinians, such as Steve Rhoads, also call attention to the perverse and misery-producing consequences of denying the natural differences between men and women or detaching marriage from the biological duty to raise children or reducing marriage and parenting to a mere lifestyle option. The "Great Disruption," from an American view, began with the "strange" or

innovative views on marriage and family found in Locke. The history of the family in our country might well suggest that the disruption continues to get greater, and it's not that clear what kind of definitive brake nature will eventually have on it.

4. These days, Darwinianism can function as a kind of self-help program, one that almost always fails. We are at home in nature, the story goes, like the other animals. Our experiences of personal alienation from nature and from social life are illusions. We can and should be satisfied with the social happiness a beneficent nature makes possible for us. Darwinian enlightenment can at least mitigate our narcissism and existentialism. Nature is all there is; nature isn't all about me, and so my life will be all screwed up if I mistakenly think it's all about me. Like in all self-help programs, my happiness remains the goal. I can't be happy if I'm too detached from nature, and so I should listen to Darwin about what my natural desires are telling me to do.

5. For some Darwinian conservatives, this natural, impersonal enlightenment functions something like Socratic philosophy or Epicureanism or even Buddhism in freeing us from the self-indulgent and often cruel self-obsession that comes from thinking we're more than we really are. But Socrates or Epicurus or Buddha are not, of course, Darwinian role models. Darwinian conservatism reconciles scientific enlightenment with "family values." Socrates was afraid that philosophy would wreck the morality that supports indispensable social duty. In his own case, it made him an uncaring husband and dad and a very ambivalent and not-so-activist citizen. Darwin was confident that the natural "moral sense" would strengthen with human reason over time. The Darwinian conservative thought is that Socrates, these days, would know that he should spend more quality time with the wife and kids.

6. Thomas Jefferson, for one, thought that the truth about the moral sense was taught by Jesus. And he said, in effect, that he was a follower of both Epicurus and Jesus. The philosopher told the truth about who we are as thinkers or beings with minds, and the gentle moralist added the truth about who we are as beings with bodies fitted by nature for society. Jefferson never tried to reconcile the two teachings, and he even said that the moral sense was messed up by philosophy. Jefferson's Jesus was the one found in his very expurgated version of the Bible, one without our Lord and Savior's claims of extraordinary personal significance both for Him and for each of us.

7. Actually, it's not clear how this Jesus' teaching about generalized

benevolence would inspire, say, the stern sacrifices often required of parents—not to mention patriots or even real Christians. Jesus, of course, was less of a family man than even Socrates, and He privileged following Him over family values for everyone. Jefferson apparently had enough confidence in our natural sociality to worry—but not all that much—about the effect that enlightened rational calculation would have on our indispensable natural loyalties and duties. He did take the side of the farm against the city for basically moral reasons, although he also imagined the possibility of lots of something like philosopher-farmers (without explicitly mentioning slavery).

8. The evidence that scientific enlightenment has been good for the instinctual moral sense of members of our social species is more negative than not. We can see today, for example, Americans are divided into Darwin affirmers and Darwin deniers, and the former are generally thought to be more sophisticated and enlightened. But Darwinians, I think, have a very hard time explaining their own sophisticated behavior. Despite being very healthy animals living in a favorable environment, they're not having enough babies to keep the species going. They clearly aren't finding enough solace in thoughts of their inevitable replacement. They live more personally than socially or communally and are lonely and anxious as a result. They provide plenty of evidence that they aren't satisfied with the Darwinian account of who they are by nature; they can't help but think a lot more personally about who they are.

9. Meanwhile, the Darwin deniers—mainly religiously observant Christians—are living more as Darwin would predict. They're having lots of babies, raising them responsibly, and are less edgy about the prospects of getting old and getting dead. Someone might say that those, through faith in a personal and active Creator, who have confidence that their personal identity and significance aren't merely biological are more able to relax and enjoy what nature offers them. And they might be more likely to think that nature, being created, must basically be good. They don't have to rebel against impersonal nature to secure their personal beings.

10. It's a shame, of course, that we tend to be divided into two groups of extremists when it comes to Darwin. Religious believers, of course, often mistakenly deprive themselves of the resources of Darwinian conservatism. There's more natural support for their personal devotions than they know, and scientific enlightenment is much less a threat to how they live than either they or their enemies believe. We are more than biological beings, but we are also biological beings. And grace, Christians used to believe, completes nature, but doesn't negate it.

11. Darwinians, of course, need to abandon their dogma that the impersonal evolution can explain everything about who we are. They can dismiss our alienation from nature as an illusion, but they can't explain where the illusion came from or why it's so powerfully shaped the modern world. The most open-minded scientists, such as E. O. Wilson, distinguish between natural evolution and the conscious and volitional evolution produced by members of our species alone. And, as I will explain, that personal evolution isn't about serving purposes nature has given to all the species.

12. That conscious and volitional evolution is very unnatural is clear in Wilson's ecological obsession; he's perhaps (rightly) really spooked by the fact that the future of nature is in our personal hands. Even if we could, as the transhumanists hope, escape our dependence on nature, we would be depriving ourselves of all sorts of sources of wonder, love, happiness, and beauty. It's already clear it's not so good for the natural capability for love or happiness given to conscious, social mammals to separate sex from reproduction, for example.

13. It's obvious that any thoughtful Darwinian would demand that Darwinian evolution not be taught as a complete account of who we are in our schools. Such impersonal accounts, as Socrates would have predicted, are bad for the species, because they're bad for families, countries, and churches. That doesn't mean that natural science shouldn't be taught the way scientists think best. But Darwinism shouldn't be taught as a comprehensive scientific ideology in the manner of the "new atheists."

14. The real objection to such comprehensive accounts is that nobody has proven they're true, and they contradict what we can see with our own eyes about who we are. The new atheists—such as Dawkins and Dennett—are well below the pay grade of great philosophers, theologians, and scientists, and they incoherently or with a kind of contemptible sentimentality defend the worldview of impersonal science from a personal perspective. Dennett, for example, is about maintaining our devotion to equal person dignity as a conscious fiction, as if people could be deeply moved by or devoted to an account of who they are that they know, through science, is untrue.

15. One scientific proposition is that a species smart enough to come up with a comprehensive, impersonal theory of evolution would be one that would produce all sorts of behavior that would make it untrue. It's between hard and impossible for a conscious being to devote himself or herself to the species. The effort by Carl Sagan and other scientists to make species perpetuation our sacred cause by diversifying ourselves on many

planets fell flat. It's somewhat natural for human beings to think of themselves as parts of something greater than themselves. Aleksandr
Solzhenitsyn, for one, said that our inability to do so these days is the cause
of our irresponsibility and the pathetic misery of our personal isolation.
But everyone knows that the species—unlike God or country or family—
is something less than oneself, and so devotion to God and country have to
be understood as good for their own sakes, as the bottom line. They are
unrealistically devalued by Darwinian explanations. Those explanations
account for part, but not the best parts, of the relevant phenomena.

Václav Havel's Dissident Criticism

The most powerful, courageous, penetrating, and eloquent dissident opponents of Communist tyranny were Aleksandr Solzhenitsyn and the Czech
philosopher-playwright-president Václav Havel (1936–2011). We forget
that their criticism was directed, in a friendly way, toward the West, too.
Here's a penetrating excerpt from Havel's 1984 speech "Politics and
Conscience":

> Or the question about socialism and capitalism! I have to
> admit that it gives me a sense of emerging from the depths of
> the last century. It seems to me that these thoroughly ideologi-
> cal and often semantically confused categories have long since
> been beside the point. The question is wholly other, deeper and
> equally relevant to all: whether we shall, by whatever means,
> succeed in reconstituting the natural world as the true terrain of
> politics, rehabilitating the personal experience of human beings
> as the initial measure of things, placing morality above politics
> and responsibility above our desires, in making human commu-
> nity meaningful, in returning content to human speech, in
> reconstituting, as the focus of all social action, the autonomous,
> integral, and dignified human "I," responsible for ourselves
> because we are bound to something higher, and capable of sac-
> rificing something, in extreme cases even everything, of his
> banal, prosperous private life—that "rule of everydayness," as
> Jan Patocka used to say—for the sake of that which gives life
> meaning. It really is not all that important whether, by accident
> of domicile, we confront a Western manager or an Eastern
> bureaucrat in this very modest and yet globally crucial struggle
> against the momentum of impersonal power.

And here's some basic analysis:

1. Surrendering to the rule of everydayness means giving in to the
impersonal forces that surround you—public opinion, fashion, ideology,
and technology.

2. Everydayness is what characterizes the banal, prosperous private
life that's not constituted by the courageous sacrifice that makes possible
the assumption of personal responsibility.

3. Everydayness is characteristic of the "I" without any real content,

and so without the capacity to speak with meaning about the dignified purposes of human life.

4. Courage is required for every dimension of genuine human autonomy and dignity.

5. But courage is especially required for genuinely truthful human thought. And moral courage—the willingness to risk everything in the service of personal responsibility—is indispensable for intellectual courage.

6. Without courage, Havel elsewhere writes, "nothing is worth anything." Whenever a human being identifies morality with expediency or what's required to sustain his decent, prosperous private life, he always, "in the depths of his spirit … feels that nothing matters."

7. What the Czech and Slovak dissidents had to offer the "free world," what the world not dominated by Communist ideology used to call itself, is, in Havel's words, "the idea that a price must be paid for truth, the idea of truth as a moral value." The dissidents risked everything for the truth against the impersonal lie of ideology.

8. The dissidents—such as Solzhenitsyn, Havel, and Patocka—had, as Havel said, "a relatively higher degree of inner emancipation" than human beings ordinarily experience—certainly more than we Americans, with doubtless a few exceptions—do these days.

9. In President Havel's address to Congress in 1990, he concluded by giving an American example of the inner emancipation required to assume truthful human responsibility. Thomas Jefferson's words in the Declaration of Independence concerning the foundation of government in consent "were a simple and important act of the human spirit."

10. Those words were an *act*, because they were the foundation for the Americans' courageous dissident resistance in 1776 and, in the best cases, even today.

11. As Havel says, "What gave meaning to the act … was the fact that the author backed it up with his life. It was not just his words, but his deeds as well."

12. Here's something else Havel says the Czechs and Slovak dissidents knew: "The inability to risk … even life itself to save what gives it meaning and a human dimension leads not only to the loss of meaning but the loss of life as well."

13. As Solzhenitsyn and Havel both reminded us Americans, beings who are too attached to their material well-being can't even defend their bodies, much less their souls.

14. By the "natural world," Havel means the community constituted by our common awareness we can't help but have that causes us to transcend the domain of interests—our awareness of the more-than-biological significance of what we think and do. It is our common awareness of the irreducible phenomenon of conscience—or conscientious responsibility.

15. It is that common awareness that is the foundation of a real *polis* constituted by proud, responsible, active citizens.

16. Part of that natural awareness is that we surrender our freedom when we mistake ourselves for God, when we believe that the power of science is simply for the satisfaction of our unlimited and undirected desires.

17. We act irresponsibly when we claim to be guided by the Marxian utopian vision of "heaven on earth." That world, Havel explains, would be without evil and suffering. It would be a world without criminals. But it would also be a world without dignified "I's" and personal responsibility. Marxism, transhumanism and so forth are impossible and uncourageous dreams.

18. Responsibility, Havel told Congress, is finally to "the order of Being, where all our actions are indelibly recorded and where, and only where, they will be judged."

19. We really can't help but know, Havel explains elsewhere, that "we touch eternity in a strange way," and that "the world is more than a cluster of improbable accidents."

Alexis de Tocqueville's Relevance Today

Tocqueville (in *Democracy in America*) called the effect of democracy on the heart individualism, meaning apathetic withdrawal from larger communities into a narrow circle of friends and family. Democracy, or devotion to the equal significance of everyone, undermines the particular attachments that hold together family members, members of a particular class, citizens, and even creatures.

We democrats believe that love sucks, because it turns us into suckers. Our intention, to enhance our safety and secure our rights, is to have all our connections with other persons be governed by calculation and consent. Otherwise, we'll surrender to their rule of others, be subject to their control. The American democrat brags, with his moral doctrine of self-interest rightly understood, that he is so emotionally free that he never allows his heart to trump his mind or clear calculation about his interests. Have you noticed that Americans think and talk like such libertarians more than ever these days?

We democrats resist losing ourselves or thinking of ourselves as parts of personal wholes—of families, friendships, countries, personal religions, and so forth. And we certainly, in the name of freedom and equality, refuse to submit to personal authority—to politicians, priests, poets, philosophers, professors, and so forth. For us, there's no difference between authority and authoritarianism.

The danger, Tocqueville thought, was that our personal isolation would make us too anxious and lonely. Our assertion of freedom is based on the good news that no one is better than *me*. But the corresponding bad news is that I'm no better than anyone else. So, I have no point of view that trumps the pressures from the huge impersonal forces that surround me.

In my flight from personal authority, I end up submitting to impersonal forces: to public opinion (which comes from no one in particular), to popular science (promulgated by people who begin sentences not with "I think" but "studies show"), to technology, and to History. There's no denying, as Tocqueville says, that impersonal forces explain more and more—and personal choice less and less—about what happens in democratic times. Have you noticed that, despite all that talk about being creative, people are more conformist and fashion-conscious than ever these days? And I can't count the number of experts who've noticed that technology increasingly owns us, and not the other way around. Pop scientific experts, of course, have become our self-help gurus—replacing, for example, the wisdom of our elders and men of the cloth.

Apathetic withdrawal leads to self-surrender. The culmination of self-surrender, Tocqueville feared, would be schoolmarmish, soft administrative despotism, surrender to a providential authority that would take the burden of our personal futures, of being beings totally on our own in a hostile environment, off our hands. Insofar as we can say that being human is all about being personally responsible for one's own destiny, the culmination of individualism is a kind of lapse into apathetic subhumanity. You have to admit that the various features of the "nanny state" are most attractive to the most isolated or lonely Americans: single parents, old folks cut off from their families, the completely dispossessed poor, and so forth.

For me, the good news is that Tocqueville underestimated how radically individualistic apathetic withdrawal would be. And so he didn't understand that individualism would make soft despotism unsustainable over the long term. The future of human liberty is not as threatened by democratic excesses as he sometimes feared.

Tocqueville thought that the self-centered individual would lose all concern with past and future. But he didn't think he would actually stop thinking of himself as a being to be replaced. The American man he described is very unerotic and not much of a family guy, but he still manages to have a wife and kids. Their constant presence in his little house manages to arouse some real love in him. Tocqueville assumed that we'd remain social enough to be parents and children. His worry was the disappearance of active citizens, not the disappearance of children.

But maybe the biggest issue concerning the sustainability of liberal democracies today has to with people becoming so emotionally withdrawn or so self-centered that they quite consciously refuse to think of themselves as beings to be replaced. As Tocqueville would have appreciated, demographic sustainability is not *that* big of an issue in our country yet because of the social, Darwinian behavior of our observant (and often Darwin-denying) religious believers. But in most places in the West (and Japan etc.) we can see that people, on average, are living longer and longer and having fewer and fewer children. There's a birth dearth; people aren't being replaced in adequate numbers, and society is aging in a rather depressing way (if you think about it).

The Family and the American Idea of Liberty

A shortcoming of Lockean liberalism, the kind of liberty to which the Founders were primarily devoted, is its tendency to undermine the stability of the family over time.

As the nation's elites become more devoted to such principled individualism, the family weakens. Well before the Progressives, Tocqueville noted the many factors that would exact a toll on the kind of devotion that produces lots of well-raised children: self-obsessive, petty materialism; the restless anxiety that accompanies democratic affluence; the theoretical denial that we're anything more than ephemeral, biological beings; and doubt that human beings share moral or social goods in common—doubt that we really are, deep down, social and relational beings.

The modern democrat generally has more and more trouble, as he becomes both more principled and more narcissistic, thinking beyond his own, personal being toward generating biological replacements or finding loving personal compensation for his own natural finitude in his family, children, and personal accomplishments. From its beginning in 1776, one dimension of the nation's heritage is the thought of the Lockean individual in the state of nature that being starts and ends with *me*. If I don't endure, nothing endures.

That's not to deny that modern, democratic liberty has in some ways improved family life. As Alexis de Tocqueville said in *Democracy in America*, the disappearance of cold aristocratic formalities has been good for love in America, maybe especially for the friendship of the father with both son and daughter. Because everyone is free to marry the one he or she loves, there is less excuse than ever for the dangerous liaisons that inevitably accompany being stuck with marrying for money or property or social standing. Who can also deny that thinking of women more consistently as free, consenting individuals has done wonders in the eradication of unjust "double standards," making us much more attentive to the various dimensions of spousal abuse, undermining arbitrary and otherwise excessive reliance on "gender roles" in excluding women from the worlds of work and politics, and even in leading fathers to share the ordinary duties of parenthood?

In general, we should follow Tocqueville in resisting the temptation to romanticize what was better about even the recent past by making our nostalgia so selective that we forget the human misery and injustice people endured then and which we should be grateful not to have to endure now. Lockean progress, we have to admit, has in many ways been real progress. But that progress has not proven beneficial in every way, and it has not delivered personal benefits without imposing personal costs.

These thoughts are meant, as they say, to nuance the conservative narrative today. In many ways, things are both better and worse than ever today, thanks to principled individualism. It's not some alien "progressive movement"—operating against the intentions of our Founders—that's responsible for what ails us in our anxious time. America is in crucial respects more individualistic than ever today, and we have unprecedented benefits and unprecedented challenges as a result.

The Deconstruction of Marriage?

Our BIG THINKING friend Robert de Neufville is right to notice public opinion trending in favor of same-sex marriage. And so, it seems reasonable for him to predict that it will become legal everywhere in our country eventually.

Particularly telling is the absence of opposition to same-sex marriage among the young. The young are, if anything, more opposed to abortion than their parents, and certainly aren't about, for the most part, the unlimited right to choose against unborn life. I will explain why in another post. In the case of same-sex marriage, the "liberty" issue is disconnected from the "life" issue. When that's the case, the prevailing opinion seems to be, let people do what they want. The young also are sometimes admirably moved by the imperative of overcoming the history of oppression of gays in our country.

People who remain opposed to same-sex marriage really feel put upon when they're told that they have no reason for their belief, that they're moved by nothing but unreasonable animosity toward gays. But for most of recorded history, marriage was tied to the biological imperative of reproduction. So, the sophisticated Greeks of Athens, who not only accepted but celebrated homosexual sex, thought same-sex marriage was an oxymoron. Socrates (probably not a homosexual) got married and had kids, apparently, because the law commanded it. He did his duty to his country, but he didn't seem to have much personal fulfillment at home. For sophisticated Greeks, the duty of marriage had little to do with either love or sexual enjoyment. It was about the family and the country (the city). (We could even add here that Walt Whitman, America's most singular and civic-minded poet, wrote movingly and obviously about homoerotic themes without seeking any public status for being gay.)

Many religiously observant people simply have a different and not unreasonable understanding of marriage than the one that seems to be prevailing today. They connect marriage to a lifelong, sacred personal relationship that involves sexual fidelity and an openness to children. They use judgmental words like chastity and adultery and regard divorce as an evil to be avoided at almost all costs. They think that the institution of marriage is built on the biological difference between men and women, and they join the Darwinians in thinking that the main point of any social animal is to generate replacements and raise them right.

A very strong constitutional argument against the right to same-sex marriage, of course, is that none of the Framers of our Constitution recognized it. Many of our leading Framers knew that the denial of rights to black slaves was contrary to nature, and our Constitution's compromises on slavery were with an anti-slavery intention. Some of them, at least, were somewhat aware that it was unjust to exclude women from public and business life. But we can comb their writings all we want and fail to come up with any concern with gay rights. That doesn't mean that Jefferson or Franklin or Paine were full of animosity toward gays.

Not only that, the Framers recognized that the individualism of the national Constitution was limited. Indispensable social institutions were to be encouraged and regulated by the states, and the Bill of Rights, originally, was not meant to apply to state law. They really didn't think the social institution of marriage could be understood properly as a voluntary contract consented to by any two or more individuals for any purpose they chose. They, for the most part, were all about the individualistic philosophy of John Locke. But one point of the Constitution's federalism was to keep Lockean principles in a kind of "Locke box," so that they didn't end up distorting every feature of human life.

Today, our Supreme Court asserts that the single word "liberty" in the Fourteenth Amendment's Due Process Clause gives the national courts jurisdiction over every feature of state and local law. The Supreme Court has also said (see *Lawrence v. Texas*) that our Framers meant to give the word "liberty" no definite, enduring content. It is a weapon to be used by every generation of Americans to achieve progressively more liberty or autonomy. It's on that basis the Court might say that same-sex marriage didn't used to be a right, but it's become one now. We can wonder, of course, why judges are especially well equipped to know when a right becomes a right, or whether the Framers regard "liberty" as a weapon and nothing more.

On this basis, sophisticates have come to regard laws connecting marriage with the natural differences between the sexes as equivalent to laws (segregation) that required the separation of the races. Beginning with *Romer v. Evans,* our courts have begun to rely on the dissenting opinion of Justice Harlan as decisive here. "The law regards man as man" or does not distinguish among individuals according to some class-based categorization such as race, gender, religion, or sexual orientation. And it's true, after all, that our Constitution of 1787 mentions neither black nor white, man nor woman, Christian nor Jew, gay nor straight. This liberation of individuals from degrading categorization, the argument goes, includes from the natural categories man and woman, as well as any based on the natural or at least unchosen fact of sexual orientation.

One irony here, of course, is the Court, when it comes to race, has never quite acknowledged that Harlan's dissent is correct. That's because it would seem to outlaw all race-based distinctions in the law, including, of course, affirmative action aiming at diversity (as opposed to racial justice). But affirmative action based on sexual orientation is not an issue.

The general thought is that the idea of marriage between a man and a woman has to be supplanted with the idea of a marriage between autonomous individuals, who are free to choose how to put together their intimate lives. That redefinition fits with the way marriage has been reconfigured, in general, in a Lockean direction over the last few generations. Divorce has been much easier, adultery less stigmatized, and the connection between marriage and children has become progressively more attenuated. We're more okay than ever with unmarried women having children, and married people not having them.

Having said all this, we might remember that many of the benefits and privileges connected with marriage seem to presuppose child-rearing. Why should two married people without children be allowed places on each other's insurance? They are both equally individuals. They both are productive beings. Shouldn't each have his or her own job and his or her own insurance? In our high-tech time, there isn't enough to do at home to justify anyone having the right to stay at home without children.

And, as some gay activists say, by what right does the law seem to privilege marital over non-marital relationships? The Court, after all, seems to say that all intimate choices deserve equal respect. Won't same-sex marriage result in the increasing stigmatization of gays who choose not to marry? Doesn't sexual equality demand that government stop the moralizing of affirming marriage—including, by implication, marital sex—as somewhat more legitimate than other lifestyle choices?

So, doesn't the Lockean logic of our time point in the direction, as Ron Paul and other libertarians say, of concluding that the only way to properly protect individual liberty is for government to get out of the marriage business altogether? There might still be laws that protect and affirm parenthood, but there's no reason to privilege married over unmarried parents. Those laws, of course, would be beneficial for gays who raise kids too, and they would have nothing to do with who is and who is not gay. Marriage could still remain as a private or religious matter, with the contents of any social contract freely chosen without government interference.

One way to avoid this consistent conclusion, of course, is to retain the thought that marriage laws are to be chosen by the people, and they're not to be too rigorously subjected to the abstract logic of rights. So it might make all the difference, for the real future of both same-sex marriage and marriage itself, whether same-sex marriage is voted in by legislatures or commanded by a judicial determination of what liberty is these days. For that reason, I'm puzzled by Robert's indifference to how the change he considers more or less inevitable is made.

Tocqueville on Aristocratic Indians and Southerners

The last chapter of the first volume of *Democracy in America* by Alexis de Tocqueville is about the then-present and probable future of the three races that inhabited our country at the time. Tocqueville identifies them by color—the reds, the whites, and the blacks. That is, the Indians or Native Americans, the Europeans and the descendants of Europeans who emigrated to America, and the descendants of the Africans who were brought to America as slaves (and who, of course, mostly remained slaves themselves).

It turns out that each race—each color—represents the three ways of life that existed in America and, from a certain view, the three ways of life possible for human beings. Americans, it turns out, are both more and less than middle-class democrats.

The blacks—the African-Americans—are slaves. They aren't free and are compelled to work. That is, work for others.

The whites—the dominant class in America—are members of the middle class. They're free, and that's the good news. The bad news is that they have to work. They have to work for themselves in order to survive and prosper.

They're middle-class because they're free like aristocrats to work like slaves. They think of themselves as beings with interests; nobody is above or below being self-interested or responsible for one's own material needs.

The reds—the Indians or indigenous Americans—Tocqueville describes as aristocrats. For us, it's not so obvious why Indians belong in the same category as the hereditary aristocrats of Europe. But Tocqueville explains that the Indians—really, the Indian men—pride themselves in not devoting themselves slavishly to manual labor, to, say, agriculture. They, like the European aristocrats, think of themselves as free from work so that they might pursue nobler activities: hunting, fighting, and giving speeches about hunting and fighting. And so, they regard the way of life of the middle class as unendurable drudgery. They often pride themselves in believing that they would rather die than surrender their way of life. They really did display plenty of evidence that their lives were defined more by courage and honor than by fear. Because they knew how to die well, they thought they also knew how to live well.

At a certain point in this chapter, Tocqueville's analysis takes an unexpected turn. He says that the southern slave owners—the ruling class in the

South—are also aristocrats. That is, they are far more like the Indians than like their fellow Europeans in the North. They, like the Indians, prided themselves as being free from the drudgery of manual labor so that they're free for nobler activities, activities in which they could display their distinctively human virtues—courage above all. Like the Indians, they were all about hunting and fighting and giving speeches about hunting and fighting—which they called politics. They thought, like the Indian, that merely being concerned with one's interests is slavish.

If we think about it, we actually have more evidence than Tocqueville ever did that the South is the most aristocratic part of our country. We learn from southern writers from William Faulkner through Walker Percy that southern leaders took their bearings from the Stoics, especially the philosopher-emperor Marcus Aurelius. They modeled their lives on the great Greeks and Romans and understood themselves as possessing the paternalistic virtues of aristocratic rulers devoted to assuming honorable responsibility for their communities. (Think Atticus Finch in *To Kill a Mockingbird*.) But the magnanimity of the Stoic attorney who courageously protected blacks from redneck, lynch-mob lawlessness can't really be confused with justice. That's why so many southern gentlemen were stunned when the blacks they thought of as under their protection started "insolently" to demand their rights. Most of those gentlemen were way too slow to see that segregation was always a violation of the spirit of our individualistic law and a sin against the Christian principle of the equality of all human beings under God.

We also know, of course, that our armed forces have always been disproportionately southern. Southerners have always been more devoted to hunting and fighting. There are all sorts of studies that show, for better and worse, that the South remains, even today, the most honor-obsessed and violent (as well as most well mannered) part of our country. It also remains the most spiritual part of the country; genuine or soulful religious belief, Tocqueville reminds us, is an aristocratic inheritance.

Our president has mocked the rural South for its desperate attachment to God and guns. To be fair, he should have added something about the southerner's proud attachment to his country—reflected, of course, in his country music. There's a lot to be said for the man who proudly believes that it's his God-given duty to fight to defend the place that secures his freedom and stands up with tears in his eyes when he hears Lee Greenwood sing. It's southerners and those with southern envy who are particularly moved by tunes that remind us that every citizen must also be a warrior.

But much of Tocqueville's analysis of the Indians and southern aristocrats focuses on their weakness and injustice. The honorable superiority of
aristocrats, he shows us, is largely (but not completely) imaginary. The
Indians styled themselves as above the need to work, but they were all too
easily corrupted by the temptation of European luxuries. They fatally compromised themselves by attempting to acquire those unnecessary goods
without engaging in productive labor. The Indians could have preserved
their way of life much longer had they minimized their contact with
European, middle-class civilization. The southern master, in turn, was corrupted by an excessive attachment to luxuries imported from the North or
from Europe. His aristocratic agrarianism made him too subject to the
manufacturing of cities that were not his own. The rulers of the South—
those who dominated the political class and the legislatures—were not the
self-sufficient yeoman farmers of Jefferson's poetic imagination.

The Indian who thought that he could benefit from the fruits of
European technology without engaging in technological activities himself
was actually unjust. Why should anyone have the benefits of work without
working? And by making himself unnecessarily vulnerable to the superior
power of European military technology, he made his real defeat on the battlefield all too easy. The southerner, of course, did exactly the same thing.
The showdown between honor and high technology on the battlefield—
both the Civil War and the Indian Wars showed—usually results in the victory of the side with more real power. Both the Indian's and the southerner's imaginary superiority was overwhelmed by the economic and military
might that was produced by all the real work done by the northern
Europeans.

The injustice of the southerner was, of course, much greater than that
of the Indian, because he demanded all the luxury of high civilization without working. He depended on the labor of slaves. And his slavery was
much worse—much more monstrously dehumanizing—that that of the
ancient Greeks and Romans. In the ancient world, the slaves came from
countries that lost the last war. Slaves were kept in line through fear, but
there was no attempt to destroy their spiritual or intellectual freedom.
That's because everyone knew that slavery was the result of bad luck.
Being a slave said nothing about your nature or who you really were. In the
ancient world, there were philosopher-slaves, such as the Stoic Epictetus,
just as there were a couple of philosopher-emperors.

Only with the influence of Christianity, Tocqueville explains, did
human beings come to see that slavery is fundamentally unjust. And so,

slavery disappeared among the Europeans. It reemerged among the Americans, who contained it to members of one particular race in an attempt to minimize its injustice. It was unjust—contrary to God and nature—to enslave anyone but dark-skinned people of Africa. Even many of the southerners at the time of the Founding knew that the slavery of blacks was unjust. But that theoretical conclusion contradicted their aristocratic practice (think Jefferson), and it came to have less and less influence among leading southerners.

The southerners, Tocqueville shows, came to believe that members of one race were slaves by nature. They used racist materialism to account for their aristocratic pride. Modern racism is a monstrous mixture of modern materialism and ancient honor, and it justified unprecedented injustice. The southerners, in effect, tried to make their theory true by engaging in what Tocqueville calls spiritual despotism; they tried to deprive their black slaves of their natural freedom by reducing them to merely material beings. They attempted to enslave not only their bodies but their souls.

The proud and fearful fantasies of the southern imagination—based in part on the horrible injustice of racist slavery—fatally weakened the South. Tocqueville could already see that the South was a lost cause. The North—where everyone worked—was becoming increasingly more productive than the South where, in a way, nobody worked that hard. Neither master nor slave was properly motivated to be all that productive—the master was too proud, and the slave lacked the incentive that comes from working for oneself.

The southerners, Tocqueville added, knew that their cause was lost. They didn't surrender that cause, in part, out of honorable contempt for being merely middle-class—the same contempt that motivated many of the Indians. But they were also afraid of what would happen if they freed the slaves. They couldn't help having various natural intimations of the immensity of their injustice, but they really didn't think that emancipation was a real option. Their whole way of life would be ruined, and God knows what the blacks, in a way quite justly, would do to them in revenge if given their freedom. The southerners, in truth, thought they were engaged not only in an honorable defense of their way of life, but a fearful defense of their very lives.

So, Tocqueville allows us to feel more than a little sympathy for the plight of the southerner of 1830. He even says that their desperation was so deep that they couldn't bear to speak of it. A war between the states or regions, if it came, would be fueled partly by southern desperation and maybe even more by southern aristocratic indignation. The southerners were enraged at the relative decline of their place in the Union. Tocqueville leaves us with the impression that honorable and violent men would eventually believe that they had no alternative but to fight, and that they would probably fight hard and well—if somewhat unreasonably—and lose. (Lee was a great and honorable general, but he was too enamored with the glory of victory through frontal assaults on the enemy; the South was too short on men and guns for that strategy to succeed over the long term.)

Tocqueville's basic prediction was of the disappearance of the way of life of the Indian and the southerner. The middle-class, productive way of life of the northerner would increasingly dominate everywhere. It would do so in the name of both justice and power, but it would also do so at a cost. The cost would not only be in diversity, that is, of genuine multiculturalism or multiple ways of life. The cost would also be in terms of diversity of manifestations of genuine human greatness or extraordinary individuality.

The cost would also be in terms of knowledge of how to live happily and virtuously with what we can't help but really know. Democratic individuals, Tocqueville observes, are particularly disoriented or rather clueless in terms of knowing who they are and what they're supposed to do. They can't experience themselves as merely beings with interests, but they have no point of view by which to discover who else they might be. Aristocrats, by comparison, "know their place" or their humanly worthy purpose. Tocqueville also observes that because they are, in that sense, more spiritual, aristocrats believe that they can afford to be less calculating and more spontaneous; they're less about the pursuit of happiness and more about its enjoyment. The truth is that aristocrats (both the Indians and the southerners) are both more and less deluded than the middle-class Americans who have put them pretty much out of action.

Let NPR Be NPR (By Not Being PR)

Here's an article that explains well why Congress should get the national government out of the radio and TV business. A taste:

> NPR's [National Public Radio] defenders would respond indignantly to this argument by proclaiming that NPR is the nation's highest form of *journalism*, that it's utterly *nonpartisan* and *unbiased*, unlike those low-brow partisans Rush and O'Reilly, and that terrible calamities will befall Americans, especially poor and rural folks, if NPR is taken off the federal dole.
>
> Unfortunately, these claims become harder and harder to justify, especially in the wake of conservative muckraker James O'Keefe's video showing NPR's top fundraiser, Ron Schiller, sucking up to what he thought were two wealthy donors affiliated with the Muslim Brotherhood. Schiller casually berated Jews (especially ones who own media companies), the Tea Party, evangelical Christians, and Republicans.
>
> But even leaving that sting video aside, evidence that NPR leans leftward is not hard to find. Take NPR itself, for example. The host of its own "On the Media" show, Bob Garfield, recently confessed: "If you were to somehow poll the political orientation of everybody in the NPR news organization and at all of the member stations, you would find an overwhelmingly progressive, liberal crowd." [Scott Walter, "Save NPR by defunding it," *Philanthropy Daily*, March 17, 2011.]

The problem, of course, is explaining why a Congress elected by the Tea Party, evangelical Christians, and Republicans should fund a media outlet that not only disagrees with them, but also has contempt for them as stupid and immoral. That's especially true, of course, in a time of potentially crippling public debt.

Some might say the Right has its Beck and Limbaugh, and the other side needs its advocates to have a fair-and-balanced media. That's surely true.

Beck and Limbaugh have gotten rich through their ratings. It's a sad commentary, you might add, that the truth, justice, and excellence of NPR should have to survive on such a commercial basis! But NPR could, in truth, easily get by both without commercials and without government.

Nobody denies the quality of NPR's viewers—their education and wealth. The government-only pays are a very small part of NPR's bills even now. And, as the outlet that reinforces the opinions of the comfortable, left-leaning establishment, it could reasonably ask its affluent listeners to pony up just a bit more to have their self-esteem raised by expertly presented supportive information and analysis.

Then NPR could be what it really wants to be without having to worry about catering to a Congress (and indirectly an American public) it doesn't even like or respect.

You could also add that NPR made sense when there was just a limited number of channels and stations and no internet, no satellite radio, etc., etc. There's a media niche for every manner of opinion and taste now, and they can be very accessible at a very low cost.

The House vote to de-fund was pretty much straight party line. That could mean the Republicans are partisan and the Democrats are nonpartisan defenders of the public good. Or it could be the difference between fiscal conservatives and big spenders. Or it could be that NPR is not so nonpartisan. Not that there's anything wrong with that.

Why I'm Not a Libertarian

1. The genuinely realistic postmodern conservatism, from one view, is somewhere in between the Front Porch or agrarian/traditionalist and Libertarian *extremes*. That true but precarious position, as Ralph Hancock has shown us so eloquently, eludes theoretical articulation. For most practical purposes, as I tried to add, it points in the direction of compromise.

2. So we postmodern conservatives are somewhat concerned about the excessive libertarianism of the *Tea Party* candidates in the various Republican primaries. If I could have voted in the Republican primary in Kentucky, for example, I would have voted for "the other guy." That is, I wouldn't have voted for the theoretical (libertarian) ophthalmologist Dr. Rand Paul.

3. Dr. Paul suggested, both imprudently and falsely, that *The Civil Rights Act of 1964* is unconstitutional. That libertarian stand discredited the presidential candidacy of Goldwater (who later on revealed to us how libertarian he really was) by making it too easy to dismiss him as an extremist who preferred abstract liberty to the decency of racial equality and justice.

4. In general, tutored by TV's Professor Beck, we're hearing that true conservatives should regard the New Deal etc. as unconstitutional. It's become fashionable to harp on the Progressive narrative from Woodrow Wilson to Lyndon Johnson as the key to what has derailed our country. The implication is that our Court abdicated its responsibility by not declaring the regulatory administrative state unconstitutional.

5. Maybe we should remember, to begin with, that *The Civil Right Act of 1964* was a legislative accomplishment. And its intention was to extend the colorblind spirit of the original Constitution to areas that could reasonably be regulated by government. It was the one time our national government interpreted the Constitution correctly with respect to race. It was the mean between the segregation that preceded it and the affirmative action that succeeded it. It was better than *Brown* in both its intention and its outcome. Of course, an error was made insofar as its constitutionality was thought to flow from the Commerce Clause instead of flowing from the broad powers granted Congress by the Fourteenth Amendment in pursuit of the destruction of the racist regimes of the states. But that misplaced justification, remember, was thought to be necessary in response to what almost everyone now regards as erroneous Court decisions.

6. More generally, it's a libertarian error to believe that we can look to the Court to protect us from the excesses of the regulatory state. And the truth is that it's a matter of prudence to know what those excesses are. No candidate is going to get elected campaigning against the constitutionality of *Social Security* and *Medicare*. The real debate is over how to make them demographically sustainable, and even on that score it'll be really hard to tell the truth.

7. The "Progressive erosion of our freedom" narrative oddly seems to jump these days from LBJ to Obama. None of the presidents in between those two very liberal Democrats fit the Progressive mold, and their successes and failures have to be viewed according to a different model. And when I think about the Sixties, I can't help but remember that devotion to Civil Rights was one thing really good about LBJ, and someone might say that he played a significant part in creating a country that elected an African-American president.

8. The general presumption of liberty doctrine found in *Lawrence* and loved by libertarians such as Randy Barnett is very flawed, insofar as it is a guide for judicial review. The Court (as the first Justice Harlan said in the neglected moderate dissent in *Lochner*) usually should give the benefit of the doubt to the law, as is appropriate in a democracy where principles have to be compromised prudently in the face of complicated and often unprecedented situations.

9. Remember that Randy is both pro-*Lochner* and pro-*Roe*. In my view he's 0 for 2.

Said vs. Knew?

1. Our Founders built better than they said. Is that because no theory can comprehend great practice? Or because there's no theory adequate to the truth about who we are? Perhaps it is both cases, to some extent.

2. But some Founders built worse than they said. (Like those behind the French Revolution or even relatively non-sociopathic Communist tyrants such as Castro.)

3. Tocqueville (and Brownson and Burke) distinguishes between the two categories in a very clear way: The Americans (and English) had a long experience of self-government and their leaders thought like statesmen more than theorists. The French intellectuals—excluded under the enlightened, despotic monarchy from public life—were in the thrall of irresponsible "literary politics," some combination of abstract theory and poetic romanticism. Some Americans—such as Mr. Jefferson—were more attracted to French literary politics than others. So Mr. Jefferson was far superior as a theorist to Mr. Adams, but Mr. Adams was the more realistic statesman (who saw right through the French from the beginning). Perhaps Rousseau was a superior theorist to Burke, but ... just as perhaps Alexandre Kojève was a superior theorist to Raymond Aron, but ...

4. The deepest theoretical current of our Founding is Lockean, and our Constitution and our Declaration are more Lockean than anything else. But ...

5. The Declaration was a statesmanlike legislative compromise between the "past tense" God of Locke (and his penurious state of nature as a replacement for *Genesis* etc.) and the living God of the Christians. Nature's God morphed into being also the God of the Bible, producing a kind of accidental Thomism. The result was better than either of our two highly principled Foundings—the Puritan or the Jeffersonian—while incorporating much of what was best about both. Something like that could be said about the emergence of the exact language of the religion clauses of the First Amendment. The individualistic and implicitly anti-ecclesiastical right of conscience became "the free exercise of religion"—for participation in an organized body of thought and action under God. And it was Madison the statesman—not the theorist of, say, *The Memorial and Remonstrance*—who was all for the compromise.

6. So it's not so mysterious why the Founding practice was better than the theory of the leading Founders (from a theoretical point of view). Still, we still seem to need a theory that justifies those great legislative

compromises, because the history of the country, from one view, is the erosion of the compromises in the name of high Lockean principle (see, once again, *Lawrence* v. *Texas* and the general emergence of the presumption of liberty doctrine). The big objection to the jurisprudence beginning with *Roe* is that it makes prudent legislative compromise impossible.

7. We Americans, as Tocqueville says, are much better than what we say when we talk the basically Lockean moral theory of self-interest rightly understood. But a problem is, he adds, that what we say does, over time, tend to transform who we are. For Locke (and for *Lawrence*) words seem most of all to be weapons in the service of the progress of individual liberation over time. There is surely a disjunction in Locke between what he says and what he knows (on the state of nature, just to begin with), but that's because he does really think that words aren't meant to correspond to some enduring truth about who we are. Our leading Founders, we can't deny, were to varying degrees aware of that Lockean purpose for words.

8. It goes without saying that, for me, Thomism is a kind of rough way of saying that we need to restore the personal logos of the Christians, to recover the ways we are open to God and personal reality generally by nature. That theory would include a lot of Augustine. It is, as Walker Percy says, to some extent these days about putting back together what's true about European existentialism with what's true about Anglo-American empiricism.

9. Our task is about putting back together what's true about Pascal, what's true about Locke, what's true about Darwin, what's true about Aristotle's proud and responsible political science, and what's true about premodern or "receptive" natural science as found in Aristotle and Thomas—which includes a proper appreciation of both wonder and love. Such a "postmodern realism" could never be articulated in a theory like the one found in Rawls's big book.

Went to a Tea Party

So, I was a guest on the local Tea Party radio program yesterday. I disagreed with the tea partisans about everything—mainly to provoke discussion but also because I'm not exactly their kind of conservative. We parted on good terms, but with them being a bit stunned by my recalcitrance. They also immediately invited me for more. Next time, they'll be even be better prepared with facts and arguments to set me straight.

But it was refreshing to see ordinary citizens so concerned—and so self-educated—about basic constitutional issues. According to Alexis de Tocqueville (who is, I hope you've figured out, an authority for me on just about everything), the vice of modern democracy is *Individualism*. He doesn't mean of course the "rugged individualism" or John Wayne or even the entrepreneurial individualism praised by our Randian libertarians. He means apathetic withdrawal into a small circle of friends and family, a withdrawal based on the mistaken judgment that, in general, love and hate are more trouble than they're worth. Individualism is a kind of "heart disease" that turns active citizens into passive dependants, a disease that can morph democratic self-government into a kind of despotism.

Individualism is what's mocked through exaggeration on *Curb Your Enthusiasm* and *Seinfeld*, and more seriously or ponderously in Jonathan Franzen's novel *Freedom*.

Here's an example of our radio conversation: Tea Party guy wants me to agree that the Department of Education is unconstitutional, and that's because our Founders intended education to be controlled by the states and localities, to be responsive to the will of active citizens and not pointy-headed experts.

My response is that the Department is not unconstitutional. Most of the leverage the Department has over the states is in the form of grants, which the states and localities are free to refuse. And, in any case, education has kind of emerged as a right of citizens, and the Fourteenth Amendment has plausibly been construed in a way to limit the discretion of the states over whether and how to provide access to at least primary education. But I do agree that there ought to be more local control, and much of what's wrong with education in our country has to do with perverse professionalization, expert bureaucratization, needlessly meddlesome accreditation, and the oxymoron "schools of education." Citizens should work through their legislators state and national to reverse those pernicious trends.

Tea Party Guy: That means the real problem is the Sixteenth Amendment, which gives the national government too much easy access to too much money through the income tax on individuals. We need to repeal that amendment and explicitly deny the national government the power to tax incomes—that is, to tax productivity. We should have a genuinely Fair Tax or taxes—taxes on consumption, which don't affect productivity.

Me: Aren't taxes on consumption regressive? The average guy has to spend virtually all his income on consumption—on stuff he and his family needs. The rich guy can afford to shield most of his income from a consumption tax.

Tea Party Guy no. 1: Our scheme includes a way to deal within that issue through redistributing consumption revenue to those stuck with paying too a high percentage of their gross incomes for this tax.

Tea Party Guy no. 2: Life is unfair, and it's just immoral and counterproductive to tax productivity, etc.

I could easily go on. But it is surely refreshing, you all must agree, to see ordinary citizens revisiting *First Principles*.

There Ain't No Fascists (Worth Ranting About) in America These Days

My fellow BIG THINK blogger, Mark Seddon, has written that Glenn Beck is "Goebbels" or a Fascist or Nazi rousing the masses up in a dangerous, murderous way. Palin and the Tea Party and so forth are all Fascists! If we don't wake up, freedom and decency may not have much of a future. America today, apparently, is like the final days of the Weimar Republic.

I admit Beck's show is pretty extreme and bordering on bizarre. American labor unions aren't characteristically socialist or Communist these days. Not everyone who uses "social justice" in a sentence is an evildoer. And FDR and Woodrow Wilson weren't all bad, etc.

But all my experiences with the Tea Party are of reasonable men and women genuinely concerned about the future of liberty in their country. They're much more hyper-individualists than anything else, and they believe their opponents are the Fascists.

Palin, for what it's worth, I view at this point as a sideshow who's "jumped the shark" and remains enabled by the "mainstream media" who want to create the impression that she *is* the Republican Party. The goal: if people have to choose between Obama and her, then many will hold their noses and stick with the president. The mainstream media is all too aware she's the candidate who performs most poorly against Obama in the polls. But most Republicans no longer seriously consider her as a presidential alternative in 2012, for that reason and many others.

Beck, in a fairly strange way, and some Tea Party experts, with scholarly support, call the president a progressive and progressives Fascists. Their evidence comes from the 1930s and 1940s, when many progressive thinkers rejected the idea that individuals exist for themselves and have infinite value. They should be regarded instead as merely parts of the State or as expendable fodder for the production of some glorious classless society in the Historical future. From this view, Stalin and Hitler were equally progressives, and the many intellectuals seduced by communism were basically progressive Fascists. From this view, all totalitarianism—whether allegedly of the left or the right—is Fascism. And we have to add that it was the progressives of the early twentieth century who were so in favor of various eugenics schemes that everyone now agrees were shameful offenses against human dignity.

I agree that President Obama can't be identified with this Fascist form of progressivism. Whatever he is, he's not a Fascist. But neither are the Tea Partiers nor Palin nor even Beck (whom I'm not endorsing in any way). Our Republic is not about to be overthrown by Fascism of either the left or the right.

My conclusion is that Beck is wrong to call Democrats these days Fascists. But too many Democrats are wrong in calling Republicans or Tea Partiers these days Fascists. There should be a moratorium on the label Fascist (when referring to our fellow Americans), because it really doesn't address the dangers we actually face these days. Remember, it was our president who so eloquently called for civility.

Being Progressive?

1. The Tea Partiers—and many other conservatives—distinguish between the view of our Founders (good) and that of the Progressives (bad). The Progressives (beginning around the turn of the twentieth century) have undermined the intention of our Founders, which was to protect individual freedom by permanently limiting government through a written Constitution.

2. Our Founders, from this conservative view, took their bearings from *human nature*—what's always true about members of our species. The Progressives think that we—and so society—change for the better over time. We are less products of nature than of *history*. We live at a more advanced point in History than that of our Founders, and so our devotion to their great accomplishments doesn't mean that it makes sense for us to uncritically follow their guidance. For the most part, conditions and people have changed for the better.

3. That means that, for Progressives, the history of our country should be understood as *evolution* toward *bigger* and *better government*. The New Deal was an improvement over what came before it; new social conditions made the welfare state necessary, possible, and beneficial. The same is true of the various reforms of the Sixties—from the Civil Rights legislation to LBJ's Great Society. And the same is true of the various reforms of President Obama and his Democratic Congress—especially the reform that uses the power of government to guarantee affordable health care for everyone.

4. What the *Progressives* call historical evolution, some conservatives call *The Road to Serfdom*. Americans have gradually surrendered their freedom to the *soft despotism* of a meddlesome nanny state. Obamacare really means government care at the expense of personal choice and responsibility.

5. It seems to me that the *Progressive* and (conservative) *anti-Progressive* narratives share common exaggerations. As a "public philosophy," Progressivism in America stalled out in America in about 1966, with public disenchantment with the obviously imprudent excesses of the Great Society. Around then, the Supreme Court abandoned its flirtations with the idea that our Constitution somehow includes "welfare rights." And around then, it became perfectly clear that FDR's 1944 allegedly new and improved list of security-based rights (guaranteed by government) was not going to catch on.

6. That doesn't mean we still haven't had plenty of Progressive intellectuals and all that since then. But their view hasn't dominated our political life. LBJ (until Obama) was our last Progressive president. Carter was just confused. Clinton abandoned his early Progressivism after his party was swamped in the election of 1994 (which of course has obvious similarities with the 2010 Republican landslide).

7. So President Obama's miscalculation, it would seem, was to think that he had a Progressive mandate. His victory in 2008 was essentially a "negative landslide." So was FDR's in 1932, you might say, but through Progressive reform he turned it into a hugely positive affirmation in 1936. But at this point nobody thinks Obama is going to win in that way in 2012. Even if he squeaks by (which is somewhere between possible and likely), the Republicans will retain control of Congress by a comfortable majority. It'll be no Progressive mandate.

I Would Raise Taxes to Fund a (Necessary) World War!

Robert De Neufville, my fellow BIG THINKER, has said I said I think raising taxes is never the right thing to do. His rhetorical strategy is to show all Republicans are nuts because they have that opinion. Obviously, big wars have to be funded with higher taxes. Then he makes "the move" to the position that it's dogmatic and cruel to believe that we couldn't save Medicare through higher taxes.

Now the line Robert quotes from me is one where I summarize the position of Michele Bachmann, who presented herself as the courageous defender of pure principles.

I even showed the absurd extreme to which she pushed that tax prin-ciple, causing poor Pawlenty to grovel in apology over some increase in a cigarette tax (or fee). Surely that tax was fairly insignificant. Not only that, if you're going to tax something, you might as well begin, for reasons too obvious to mention, with cigarettes.

Our friend Robert ignored both the *literary character* (which he must have noticed as a political theorist) and the *social scientific character* of my post.

I explained why debates preceding a caucus (and, in this case, in the immediate context of a straw poll) are likely to favor extremely principled and imprudent candidates. The audience of the debate is composed of voters who are generally more enthusiastic and ideological than even main-stream members of their party.

Not only that, a "yes, but" answer on the tax question would require more nuance than would be possible in the time allotted. So, that mischie-vous Byron York was playing with the candidates by asking them a ques-tion that he knew they would all have to answer in an "exceptionless" way. Of course, any Republican in power might accept a compromise that would include a dime of tax increases for every dollar of tax cuts. Even Reagan raised taxes, etc. The reason the Republicans weren't about compromising during the fake crisis of the debt ceiling was that they had the president where they wanted him. The point of our separation of powers system is to compel compromise out of necessity; it's not meant to get ambitious men and women to compromise when they don't have to.

I also was trying to explain, in my social scientific way, that the debate format favors *authentic* candidates—those who are perfectly comfortable because they really believe what they're saying. This time it favored Bachmann most of all, because her brand of authenticity resonates with so many of the likely caucus voters. But it also favored Santorum and Ron Paul. It wasn't so good for Romney, Huntsman, and Pawlenty. And although people tend to think Gingrich is authentic on the level of ideas, there's too obviously the problem of "his record," meaning his whole, messed-up life so far.

In 2008, you'll remember, the debate format favored the authentic McCain and Huckabee. (That is, the early, unscripted, "what the Huck," authentically evangelical Huckabee.)

Robert was employing a tried-and-true partisan tactic of attacking the relative extremism of the rhetoric of the campaign for the nomination of the other party. But when the audience shifts in the fall, the rhetoric inevitably shifts. (It might be the case that Bachmann is so darn authentic she can't make that move, but it's also very unlikely that she'll get the nomination.)

In any case, I do agree with the general Republican view that the idea that raising taxes could save Medicare, as it now exists, is an illusion. And that the president's attempt to move us in the direction of European social democracy through higher and more progressive taxation is fatally discredited—perhaps even in his own eyes. *Bigger government* through higher taxes can't cure what ails us now.

That's not to say that raising taxes is always wrong, of course. I thought I also made it clear that I thought that raising that debt ceiling is surely right for now, given how much of government spending now goes to paying off the debt. Surely my praise of Santorum for courageously calling attention to Bachmann's showboating was clear enough. Finally, I mentioned that Bachmann herself said that *tax* issues aren't like *life* issues. They're only about *money*! So my post, I thought, was a defense of a prudent, pro-growth, reform and (as little as possible) truncation of our present entitlement system.

"I Saw Americans Fighting"
(Or Our Secretary of Defense Wants Our NATO Allies to Start Acting Like Real Countries)

Mr. Gates has forcefully reminded our allies that, to be credible politically, they have to pay for their own defense. Here's a taste of the *New York Times* article on his fine speech:

> The United States accounts for about three-quarters of total military spending by all NATO countries, and it has in the past taken the lead in military operations and provided the bulk of the weapons and materiel. But in a post-Soviet world, there is growing resentment in Washington about NATO effectively paying for the defense of wealthy European nations.

Some conservatives opposed the election of President Obama on the grounds that he would make America more European. He would spend a lot more money on social welfare programs, and a lot less on defense. Both moves would endanger the future of our liberty, not to mention that of the Europeans who parasitically depend on us for protection.

Liberals respond, of course, spending more money on people's welfare and less on guns are signs of civilization's progress. Being more attached to God and guns, as our president said during the campaign, is nothing to be proud of. The world is evolving in a direction that will be less political and less about military force.

Some of our conservatives—not to mention European conservatives such as Pierre Manent and Roger Scruton—even think that Europe is in the thrall of a post-religious and post-political fantasy. Sophisticated Europeans believe the country or nation is withering away, but that would be news to the Chinese and even the Russians. They also think that self-government (as opposed to meddlesome, soft bureaucratic despotism) is possible without strong European nations, but human rights can't really be protected without definite political forms and loyal citizens.

The withering away of the family and religion in Europe might be the main cause of the birth dearth, which even the Europeans are finally coming to recognize clearly as a threat to national or civilizational security. In our country, we notice, there's a strong correlation between fertility and observant religious belief, and so our demographic "issues" aren't nearly as serious.

Admittedly, broad sketches of this kind are never completely accurate and admit of many exceptions. Some European governments are, in some ways, facing up to the debt and big, unsustainable government issues more candidly than we are. But still, exaggerations do highlight inconvenient truths.

Mr. Gates's complaint amounts to something like this: In order for Europe to be Europe, America has to be America—or pay a lot more for defense. You guys don't have to be nations in the full sense, because we're all that and more. We're not going to let you be parasites forever. If Obama's administration were all that European, our Secretary of Defense, surely, wouldn't be speaking so toughly and so realistically.

Sure, the Democrats Want to Tax the Rich.
(But They Also Think They're Entitled!)

This article calls attention to a fascinating inconsistency shared by our two parties (Brian Faler, "Ryan Says Rich Should Pay More as Sanders Defends Entitlements for the Wealthy," *Bloomberg*, May 31, 2011):

1. Republicans (particularly Paul Ryan) want to cut taxes for the rich. But they also want to means-test entitlements—such as Social Security and Medicare. That means the rich will pay less to the IRS, but get less (or ideally nothing) from those programs—because they don't need government's help to sustain themselves.

2. The Democrats (particularly the socialist Bernie Saunders) want to raise taxes on the rich—mainly to help pay for entitlement programs. But they also think the rich, like everyone else, are fully entitled to all the benefits available from those programs.

3. Republicans (meaning, in the extreme case, libertarians) think that taxing the rich is literally counterproductive. The less they pay, the more incentive they have to use their talents and resources in productive ways. The resulting prosperity benefits us all. There's also the libertarian thought that taxing productivity is unjust; free people deserve to keep what they earn through their industrious and rational exertions. What we have here, of course, is sometimes called *supply-side economics*—or, in a more unfriendly mode, *trickle-down economics.*

4. Democrats tend to believe that entitlements should be thought of as something all citizens deserve—or not as charity. "Means-testing" would undermine support for these programs in a variety of ways—but, first of all, through a misconception of what they are.

5. The Republicans, it's true enough, want to "demoralize" entitlements by viewing them as aid to the unfortunate. Then, they become something the individual should think of himself or herself as working not to need. The ideal of "entitlement," the problem is, leads us to think we have a responsibility to provide the program to everyone, no matter what we (meaning the government) can actually afford. Republicans don't want entitlement programs thought of as "rights," but as something, ideally, a free and prosperous society can minimize or get beyond.

6. The Democrats deny that taxing the rich is counterproductive. The Republicans say they forget that eroding the conditions that maximize

productivity guarantees the implosion of those programs we may actually need.

7. Let's conclude by wondering whether there's a certain kind of noble consistency in insisting that the rich pay more in taxes and not be entitled to government payments they don't even need.

Will (the Election of) 2012 Be Like 1996?

Looking to past elections to predict the outcome of one soon to come doesn't usually work that well. Back in October 2008, I looked to eight past elections to try to gain some perspective on what might happen in November. It turns out that sound historical comparisons can only be made after the election is over. At that point, of course, they can't be said to have predictive value.

In retrospect, 2008 seems most like—but of course nowhere near exactly like—1980. It was, first of all, a negative landslide—an emphatic rejection of the incumbent's and his party's incompetent and somewhat corrupt record. McCain, it's true, was not the incumbent, but the negative judgment was rendered against Republicans in general. McCain didn't say anything to suggest that he was less clueless than Bush concerning the economic meltdown.

Another comparison, of course, is between the men Obama and Reagan. In both cases, there was nervousness about the candidate being too extreme. In both cases, voters were reassured by competent and charming debate performances. A lot of voters said something like, "What the heck, let's give the new guy a chance. Look at all the ways the guy we have now has screwed up." The Iran hostage crisis, stagflation, whining about the national malaise, and all those other things Carter was blamed for weren't exactly like the said meltdown and the mishandling of the Iraq War, but there is a lot to the comparison.

To some extent, of course, 2008 was like 1932. FDR and the Democratic congressional candidates won a huge negative landslide against the perceived cluelessness of the incumbent about what to do about the Depression.

Progressives would like to think that 2012 will be like 1936. The "negative landslide" of 1932 was supplanted by a "positive landslide" in an unusually ideological election. Voters seemed to endorse the *New Deal* or progress based on bigger and better government.

But the Democrats also won big the congressional election of 1934, whereas 2010 was clearly a repudiation of the President's main addition to big government: Obamacare. Voters these days really don't think bigger government can cure what ails them. In that key sense, they're just not Progressives. It's true that they may not want smaller government either; that's why the Democrats are doing well by seeming to defend the status quo on Medicare. The election of 2012 isn't going to give the president a Progressive mandate, just as it won't give a Republican a mandate to implement the whole Ryan plan immediately. If the race were between Obama and Ryan, the key swing voters would choose reluctantly and without that much enthusiasm.

The fundamentally conservative nature of the voters—not wanting Progressive movement toward bigger government or libertarian progress toward smaller government—might mean that they're nervously happy with *divided government* or *gridlock*. The President, in this scenario, gets reelected, but the Republicans retain control of the House and maybe pick up the Senate (lots of vulnerable Democratic seats this time). This semi-conscious perception might be why the best and the brightest Republicans—like Mitch Daniels—aren't running in 2012. It is also probably why the swing voters might well go with Obama over the Republican candidate. It would be imprudent, their judgment might be, to give either party both of the political branches right now.

The 2012 election won't even be like Reagan's victory in 1984. The Gipper won by a huge landslide, but the victory was partly personal, partly ideological. The outcome was certainly a reward for the perception that, due to the president's influence, America was back both economically and as a force for good in the world. But it wasn't a mandate for that much change. The victory didn't extend to the Republicans coming anywhere near taking over the House. Still, Reagan's landslide was a very significant step in the transformation of America into a center-right—or not particularly Progressive—nation

As far as I can tell, Obama's margin in 2012, assuming a mediocre or better Republican opponent, will be less than the one he gained in 2008. He's won very few new converts, and a lot of moderates, independents, Obamacons, and downscale voters who gave him a chance now regret it, for a variety of reasons. In this respect, his situation is loosely like the one Bush faced in 2004, except (a big except) the President has a nine million vote margin to play with. Even Bush, remember, managed to get reelected by his people ratcheting up the turnout in key states. Obama probably won't be able to do that, simply because his get-out-the-vote effort was so remarkable (and so expensive) last time. It's hard to top a really effective effort.

A better comparison for 2012 is to 1996. The President became unpopular because of an ill-considered health care reform (HillaryCare and Obamacare—it's important not to forget, of course, the complications to this narrative coming from the latter actually passing). The result was his party took a thumping in the off-year election. But the president outwitted Republican congressional leaders who tried too much too fast—who over-estimated their own mandate. Instead of making 1996 an ideological con-test, the Republicans were stuck with the dull, inarticulate, "responsible" mere competence of Bob Dole, who was just too old.

But 1996, don't forget, was a time of quite extraordinary peace and prosperity, and the president found it is easy to take credit. He also responded to divided government with an ideological flexibility that led to ending welfare as we knew it. He and Speaker Gingrich were about to sit down and negotiate their way to entitlement reform we could have believed in, when the Monica Lewinsky scandal broke. (Is the Obama administra-tion overdue for a scandal? Yes, I know it won't be the president's sexual misdeeds this time.)

It remains to be seen how America will look on both the peace and the prosperity fronts in November 2012. A Republican victory is far from inconceivable, assuming the party fields a credible candidate.

I just saw a Republican comment that it looks like another Bob Dole year for our party. The truth is that Dole—who was an excellent sen-ator—is looking good compared to the Republican candidates in the race so far.

The Violent Death of Osama Bin Laden

I thought I'd offer some random observations:

First off, I agree with my fellow BIG THINKER Kris Broughton that it's most unreasonable to fear terrorist retaliation. That's not only because the odds are overwhelming that almost all of us will die some other way, but because our government has done a fine job of diminishing the capabilities of terrorists over the last decade. We should be more grateful than we are.

I have to admit that I was somewhat surprised by the intensity of the elation that came with the news that, in the words of our president, "Justice was done." Bin Laden had been marginalized for years, and his demise has little real strategic significance. But it is always good to be reminded of the highly competent and stunningly routine heroism of our special forces, and certainly America needed a victory. Justice was done, after all.

I actually am happy for our president that he was able to fulfill a campaign promise, just as I'm happy to be reminded that he's been serious about continuing President Bush's war against terrorists. As the full story unfolds, we'll be particularly impressed, I think, by the competence and resolution of CIA Director Panetta, General Petraeus, and Secretary of State Clinton. We were reminded that sometimes our commander-in-chief and his advisors have to act secretly and alone—while keeping Congress and our so-called allies (in this case, of course, Pakistan) in the dark. This was an act of war.

Without dealing with the specifics at this point, a debate is just beginning about the ways we acquired the crucial intelligence that produced this invigorating success. President Bush won't be completely vindicated, I suspect, but matters will turn out to be more complicated that many of his critics have supposed.

I really appreciate the facts that bin Laden needed just to be killed and his body disposed of immediately. Some trials are luxuries we can't afford. (Can I say he needed to be killed for something like the reason Nixon needed to be pardoned—to decisively put a national nightmare behind us?)

Happy (Belated) Constitution Day

A few years ago Senator Robert Byrd of West Virginia snuck through some legislation requiring that every college and university getting government aid (almost all of them) have some kind of Constitution Day celebration.

Someone might say it's unconstitutional to make them do that! But it is constitutional. Government can and does attach all kinds of conditions when it distributes what used to be the taxpayers' money. Although I don't think anyone is really watching, our provost here at Berry is worried enough to make sure we comply.

It's always awkward when Constitution Day falls on a Saturday or Sunday. No college is going to think the Constitution is important enough to cut into students' Saturday, what with football and all. (And a big point of the Constitution is that we have the right to reserve Sunday for the free exercise of religion.) So, this year the commemorations are occurring before or after the actual day.

It's worth noting that the rare college that doesn't take government money—such as Hillsdale in Michigan—is usually all about teaching the Constitution on a daily basis and so has Constitution Day stuff quite voluntarily. The usual criticism of such places is that they take the Framers' words too seriously or haven't adapted them to our times. Studies show that real *constitutional literacy* is very high at Hillsdale.

Compulsory educational Constitution Day activities have been, of course, a boondoggle for many professors. Most years I make some extra bucks giving a Constitution Day lecture somewhere. Last year, I spoke against unconstitutional judicial activism at Georgetown. This year, I'm giving a seminar to some of our country's top young Jewish thinkers in New York City on St. Augustine and war instead.

What does St. Augustine have to do with our Constitution? Here's what I'll work into the seminar: it's the Christian idea of the person that's the real foundation of limited government. People aren't merely citizens or parts of their countries, just as they're not merely parts of nature. Government is limited by the fact that each of us is free to be much more than a political being.

And our Constitution's silence on God (an unprecedented silence for such a document) is based on the Christian insight that the true God is to be distinguished from the fraudulent gods of the city and so true theology—the theology of the person—from degrading civil theology.

Because, as our Supreme Court once said, our Constitution presupposes a certain understanding of who "the Supreme Being" is, our Framers refused to use Him as a political tool. If you don't like that answer but like God, you can say instead our Constitution presupposes the Declaration of Independence, and the Declaration talks about the Creator.

Constitution Day actually has caught on a bit in these parts through the Tea Party. Those notorious partiers sponsored an ambitious and diverse event in the Forum in Rome, GA yesterday—on the actual Constitution Day. The event included all kinds of music, games, educational activities, and booths and stuff sponsored by local businesses. I would give you a report, but I didn't go. My impression is attendance was respectable—including lots of non-partiers—but maybe a little disappointing. One reason: the Rome Beer Festival was the same day. No, I didn't go to the beer festival either.

Here's a big difference between Constitution Day and the Fourth of July: On the Fourth, beer and patriotism are found at the same events.

Bored on the Fourth of July?

Well, I'm really not. But a lot of BIG THINKERS must be, because we have nary a post so far talking up *the American holiday*. So, *Happy Fourth of July*!

Today is the celebration not so much of independence (voted on July 2), but of the argument for it—*the Declaration of Independence*.

The Declaration is, of course, the argument for independence given by the united Americans against Britain. The argument is that the British government—especially the *king*—is tyrannizing us systematically and repeatedly violating our rights. But the Declaration is also an argument for the independence—for the equal freedom by nature—of every human person or creature or individual. Our government(s) will claim *sovereignty* by the consent of individuals who are sovereign by nature.

So, today we're celebrating by sharing our allegiance to truths we hold to be self-evident. We are, as G. K. Chesterton wrote, "a nation with the soul of a church." Churches are held together by common belief in particular dogmas. We're held together by common belief in the principles set forth, Chesterton wrote, with "dogmatic lucidity" in the Declaration.

The not-so-silent Calvin Coolidge wrote that those principles are restful because they're final. We believe that no progress can be made beyond them—just as we believe that our progress comes from more faithfully and consistently acting in accordance with them. The Fourth of July, in that light, should be a day of rest for the same reason every Sunday should be. We need to take a break from our incessant activity to remind ourselves of the foundation that makes our free and restless prosperity possible.

We can criticize the authors and signers of the Declaration for not acting in full accordance with their principles. Jefferson knew that all human beings—including those imported from Africa to be slaves—were created equal and had inalienable rights. But he didn't always act according to what he knew.

We remember that it was the Abolitionists, from the very beginning, who talked up more than other Americans the stirring words of the Declaration as the foundation of their liberationist cause; so did our first strong proponents of the rights of women. The southern slaveholders ended up openly denying the Declaration's truth, saying that Jefferson didn't know what he was talking about. It was in the context of the spilling of a huge amount of blood for a new birth of freedom that Lincoln rededicated us to the Declaration's proposition that all men are created equal.

Later, I will remind you that even on the level of principle our Declaration was a legislative compromise, with the result better than the theoretical intention of Jefferson the philosopher. So, I don't really think we should regard the principles of the Declaration as quite as restful or final as Biblical revelation—nor do I think our Founders would have wanted that. But I won't continue on *the Fourth of July*.

Change, the Elderly, and the Welfare State's Implosion

"The central issue," James Capretta writes, "in financing Social Security … is the long-term fertility rate." If it were reasonable to hope we could soon be anywhere close to returning to Baby Boom birthrates, there would be no talk today of entitlement reform. It goes without saying that people would rather keep what they now have, and that our politicians would be relieved to let them have it. Tea Party constitutionalism would have, at best, a very marginalized constituency.

The Lockean might begin to attempt to solve this problem by saying that the old should just become more productive, and so we need to push the retirement age (and, of course, eligibility age) back, way back. If the elderly are healthy, they should keep working. We can expect some of that, and responsible experts say many or most people might well be stuck working as long as they can. But there are obvious limits to that remedy.

A high-tech society is full of preferential options for the young; the old might be healthy, but they still often lack the mental agility required to keep up with all that techno-change. Even in my profession, college teaching, which isn't very hard and you don't have to be very smart to perform adequately in the classroom, there's plenty of complaining that the abolition of mandatory retirement is keeping the relatively ineffective and out-of-touch around at the expense of scholarly productivity and consumer (student) satisfaction. The aging, overpaid professorate is one of the most compelling arguments against tenure, one that will prevail soon enough in our techno-meritocracy.

If the old keep working, we'll figure out soon enough, it'll have to be in less productive and (much) lower-paid—not to mention more insecure—positions. We, after all, value the wisdom connected with age (being chastened by experience and all that) less than ever, and we're getting more skeptical of the thought that being old means being entitled.

Some of our Tea Partiers—especially those in my rural South—believe that the destruction of the welfare state will restore the situation that prevailed in most of our country's history of liberty: the elderly (like on *The Waltons*) will return to live in the homes of their children and grandchildren. I actually favor government programs that facilitate that happening, but again there are limits. A Lockean or techno-productive or displaced society has dispersed families throughout the country and world. The ties that produced extended families are weaker than ever; it seems less natural or normal for parents and their grown children to share the same place.

In most of our history, our health care system has been dependent on most caregiving being done voluntarily by women (like on *The Waltons*). But that isn't possible in most cases in a Lockean country where women have become productive individuals just like men, and where there are fewer young people to provide caregiving—either paid or voluntary—for the burgeoning number of elderly. Not only that, health care will remain far too costly for ordinary families to afford, and techno-progress by itself won't make it cheaper. We're getting better and better at keeping the old and frail around, but our wonderful success in sustaining their biological being often takes decades of expensive medical intervention. The good news is that we're gradually but steadily pushing back cancer and heart disease. The bad is the default form of dying is becoming Alzheimer's, which is a long, predictable, costly, caregiving-intensive process for which there is no cure. For young women compelled by duty or circumstances to care for an old parent with, say, Alzheimer's, there will seem to be less opportunity than ever to become a mom, and so the situation they face will be worse still for the generation to follow.

Locke himself rather coldly suggested that the only compelling tie parents will have on their grown children will be money. He wanted to free individuals up from the constraints of patriarchy; he didn't want parents to be able to rule—or order around—their grown children. He didn't want people relying on love—except the love for little children (who are temporarily incapable of taking care of themselves). If you're going to get old, which Locke was all in favor of, you'd better get rich, and our libertarians aren't wrong to say we should do what we can to encourage people to save for their own futures. Now, of course, the virtue that comes with that kind of self-reliance is coming back; pensions and even Social Security have become unreliable, but so too have 401(k)s, which can no longer be counted on to produce returns that beat inflation. The average person is less sure than ever that his money will last as long as he will, but he surely knows that he'll be stuck, nonetheless, largely with depending on his own money to live well.

The implosion of the welfare state, which is caused, most of all, by our aging society, doesn't look like a new birth of freedom for old persons. As we learn, say, from Socrates' musings in the *Republic*, there might be nothing tougher than being old and poor in a democracy, a "regime" or society which has no idea what old people are *for*. That's not to say that we're going to begin euthanizing them or even "rationing" them to early graves. We know they're free individuals or persons—they're not nothing—and so we're committed to helping them stay around as long as possible. To say the least, we don't know much about how they might have purposeful and prosperous lives in our increasingly individualistic world.

Christopher Hitchens on What's Most Obvious About 9/11

Hitchens always speaks his mind, and that's always good, even when he's not right. So, he's told us that God is not great and that, in fact, God ruins everything. He's the most resolute opponent of tyranny around, and, for him, God is a tyrant who animates tyrants.

I think he's wrong about God, but you have to hand it to Hitchens. He's an atheist who knows evil and evildoers when he sees them. That means he knows virtue and the virtuous—such as our courageous police and fire-fighters—when he sees them, too. For Hitchens, what seemed most obvi-ous to us initially about 9/11 was, in fact, what was most obvious—and so "the main point" we should remember this week:

> To the government and most of the people of the United States, it seemed that the country on 9/11 had been attacked in a particularly odious way (air piracy used to maximize civilian casualties) by a particularly odious group (a secretive and homicidal gang: part multinational corporation, part crime family) that was sworn to a medieval cult of death, a racist hatred of Jews, a religious frenzy against Hindus, Christians, Shia Muslims, and "unbelievers," and the restoration of a long-vanished and despotic empire. [Hitchens, "Simply Evil," *Slate*, September 5, 2011.]

That means the "desire to say that the 9/11 atrocities were in some way deserved, or made historically more explicable, by the many crimes of past American foreign policy" is "perverse"—or just doesn't square with what a rational person can see with his own eyes. It's the kind of blindness that comes with a willful denial of the truth.

The same goes, of course, for "the contemporary comments of the 'Reverends' Jerry Falwell and Pat Robertson" about 9/11 "being a punish-ment from heaven for American sinfulness."

For Hitchens, there are "left" (or theoretical/intellectual) and "right" (or theological) explanations for the suffering and death of ordinary Americans caused by the attacks that deny that our anger makes any sense. They are in his secular, morally responsible, republican, scientific, freedom-loving mind, "more or less identical" in not holding our enemies responsible for what they've done. So they are identical in denying the facts we can see with our own eyes.

Hitchens reminds us of the various fantastic accounts of the 9/11 events as some "U.S. or Jewish plot" circulate not only in the Muslim world but throughout the West. And it gives him a special pleasure to remind us of a book published by the American, Presbyterian Westminster/John Knox Press that claims that those events "were planned in order to furnish a pretext for intervention in the Middle East."

One of Hitchens's conclusions is that too many of our 9/11 celebrations will be all about dissing the anger that should be aroused by the truth of the obvious version of what happened:

> So, although the official tone of this month's pious commemorations will stress the victims and their families (to the pathetically masochistic extent of continuing to forbid much of the graphic footage of the actual atrocities, lest "feelings" and susceptibilities be wounded), it is quite probable that those who accept the conventional "narrative" are, at least globally, in a minority.

I'll have more to say about Hitchens's excellent, most empirical comments in another post. But for now: let our 9/11 remembrances begin with an acknowledgment of what really happened, and so with the anger that corresponds to genuine understanding.

More on 9/11

1. So the reason I wrote about it was to prepare for a talk I had to give today at Berry College on 9/11. I was looking for an approach that would be nothing like those of the other professors speaking. The "let's begin with being angry at evildoers" approach was, in fact, not echoed by the others.

2. They were all good talks, but they just didn't "resonate" with me. One was basically let's brush our 9/11 anger away with understanding the complex historical causes that would produce such acts, and let's acknowledge that all the religions of the world, despite their doctrinal differences, are all about peace. And so, the way to peace is interfaith dialogue that embraces diversity but culminates in a common prayer for peace.

3. I still have to begin with angry hostility toward those guys (and their multinational organization) who were out to murder us and wipe out, insofar as they could, the various achievements of the modern West on behalf of human liberty and dignity (not to mention who were all about wiping Israel off the map on a principle perhaps as anti-Semitic as Hitler's). They weren't about embracing diversity or difference or human rights or accepting any law that wasn't religious or any peace that wasn't on their tyrannical terms.

4. Another talk was about the danger to which we've succumbed of "demonizing" Islam as a whole. We've fallen into a complacent "us vs. them" mentality based upon an uninformed social construction of a simpleminded distinction between good and evil. This is basically the same thing that happened during the Cold War, with the social construction of us vs. the evildoing Communists. Now it goes without saying that any conflict will generate simpleminded chauvinism that can stigmatize some innocents along with the genuinely guilty. Still, the war against Al Qaeda has been based on the realistic perception of a genuine threat; one result of our realism is our pretty decisive victory in that war. The Communists, anyone who has read Solzhenitsyn or the Verona papers knows, were really, really evil—that is, really cruel, murderous, totalitarian enemies of who we are as free beings. I, of course, am all against "demonizing" Islam as whole, but so was even President Bush. So I remain convinced that we begin not with condemning "demonizing" but with the "demons," so to speak, the murderous tyrants who are really out to get us.

5. In my talk, I explained that it's right to begin with *anger*, but that should be followed by *anger management*. The first part of that therapy

was or should have been a kind of *self-confidence* based in the superiority of our way of life—including its deep capacity for personal virtues beginning with courage and its capacity for self-criticism and self-correction. Next should come the *gratitude* we should feel for those who did so well in protecting us from a second attack. Here we begin with the passengers of Flight 93 who refused to be victims and we end with the incredible ingenuity, competence, and devotion of those we loosely call *special forces*. Finally, there's *moderation*; we learned a lot over the last decade about what we can and should do and what we can't and shouldn't do in defense of our liberty and security.

George Will on the Emptiness of Our 9/11 Remembrance

I've gotten a couple of emails accusing me of hating Muslims. Well, I don't. I'm, of course, also aware of the many studies that show that Islamic believers in America are characteristically solid, loyal citizens—in many ways more admirable than most of us. Maybe that's something we should celebrate today: Our country is very good (not as good as it used to be, but that's a topic for another day) in assimilating people of a wide variety of faiths from all over the world. Lots of Islamic believers know of no religious reason for not embracing the American idea of political freedom—meaning freedom from an all-encompassing, tyrannical "law." And most Muslims throughout the world are disgusted by murderous fanatics acting in the name of Allah. Let me remind you that even President Bush was very careful to say that we weren't at war against Islam.

My own view is that we just don't know what to think or do in response to 9/11 today. George Will goes a long way toward explaining why:

> The depleted armed forces that have been fighting these wars [Afghanistan and Iraq] for a nation not conscripted into any notable inconvenience will eventually recuperate. For mostly oblivious civilians, the only recurring and most visible reminder of the post-Sept. 11 world is shoeless participation in the security theater at airports. It thus seems wildly incongruous that some Americans rushed to proclaim that 9/11 "changed everything."
>
> The dozen years between the fall of the Berlin Wall and that of the twin towers featured complacent, self-congratulatory speculation about "the end of history." The end, that is, of a grand politics of clashes about fundamental questions of social organization. By the time 9/11 awakened the nation from such reveries, some Americans seemed to be suffering "1930s envy," a longing for the vast drama of global conflict with a huge ideological enemy.
>
> Ten years from Sept. 11 national unity, usually a compensation for the rigors of war, has been a casualty of wars of

dubious choices. Ten years after 1941, and in more recent decades, the nation, having lost 400,000 in the unavoidable war that Pearl Harbor announced, preferred to remember more inspiriting dates, such as D-Day.

Today, for reasons having little to do with 9/11 and policy responses to it, the nation is more demoralized than at any time since the late 1970s, when, as now, feelings of impotence, vulnerability and decline were pervasive. Of all the sadness surrounding this anniversary, the most aching is the palpable and futile hope that commemoration can somehow help heal self-inflicted wounds. [George Will, "Sept. 11's Self-Inflicted Wounds," *Washington Post*, September 9, 2011.]

So, first of all, 9/11 didn't change everything. (Pearl Harbor did.) Ordinary Americans weren't inconvenienced at all by the resulting military conflict. The war against al-Qaeda was necessary and successful, but it was conducted mainly by Special Forces and with no involvement and little attention by ordinary citizens.

The war in Iraq now seems optional and botched. We should be grateful for those military volunteers who did as well as anyone could, but we don't much want to remember it.

Will is right that 9/11 did, in a way, explode the pretensions of *The End of History*: Modern liberal democracy had won! The defeat of *Communism* was the obliteration of the only credible rival ideology. All that's left to do is bring the rest of the world in line with a bunch of mop-up operations.

The argument of the Iraq War, given with some eloquence by President Bush in his Second Inaugural, was, as some have said, kind of "Leninist." Liberty and democracy are still destined to win, but the people in the Middle East need the push of our powerful help. It's increasingly clear that the result of our intervention might really be that we'll have less influence in that region than ever, and we may well have little control over even the future of Iraq and Afghanistan. Iran, meanwhile, just isn't scared of us at this point.

End-of-History theorist Francis Fukuyama opposed that Leninist war from an "organic" view. Democracy will win by movements that organically originate among various peoples themselves. Our military intervention can only muck the more-or-less inevitable up. That view, of course, also now seems naive.

We've had an Arab spring, and it's always encouraging to see tyrants deposed. But we don't know what's coming next in Libya, Egypt, and so forth. It may well not be regimes we can believe in or even work with, and our influence over their change will be pretty darn marginal.

So, maybe we do have 1930s (or 1940s or 1950s or even 1980s) envy. America powerfully defeated insane Western ideologies—*Communism* and *Fascism*. The conflicts were necessary; citizens were mobilized, and the victories enhanced—with plenty of good reason—our proud experience of personal and political liberty. *We* were the people free of the delusion that it was necessary to choose between one form of tyrannical, murderous ideological insanity or the other. And we were willing to fight—all of us, if need be—to save the whole world for personal freedom.

Now, we feel demoralized and impotent. The victory over Islamic fanaticism is very ambiguous and limited, and it's not a victory that inspires and should inspire the same kind of pride. It turns out history isn't over; our power and influence (and that of the West as a whole perhaps) is diminishing, and we can't even grasp—much less face up to—the unprecedented challenge of China's authoritarian, capitalist, imperial technophilia. (It turns out the Internet won't save us from that!)

Celebrity Studies—Part 1

Celebrity, in the most obvious sense, is the lowest form of fame. Being a celebrity is a sort of gift of public opinion, which is formed by no one in particular. And so, celebrity is as ephemeral as public opinion itself. Being a celebrity is like a gift in often being unearned and somewhat arbitrary. Although it's not as mysterious and unconditional as, say, the gift of grace, being a celebrity, despite all the marketing experts in the world, continues to elude rational control.

A celebrity isn't generally infamous, although they're often adulterers and have spent time in rehab. They can even spend time in rehab, like Tiger Woods, to be cured of the mega-adultery caused by sex addiction—a disorder that causes celebrities to have sex with lots of partners but not enjoy it. Sometimes they've even been convicted of crimes, and sometimes, as in the case of the "lovable goof" ex-governor and celebrity apprentice Rod Blagojevich, their convictions are only a matter of time. But it's almost impossible for a murderer or child molester or tax evader to become a celebrity simply by committing spectacular crimes.

It's pushing it to call the Unabomber a celebrity, although he turned out to be a pretty thoughtful guy. The same with the abortion clinic bomber Eric Rudolph, although he turned out to be a very resourceful guy. Bonnie and Clyde might have been celebrity murderers, but without any opportunity to cash in on their fame. Today, we have more trouble than ever in connecting being a celebrity with hiding out or being on the run. It's certainly pushing it to regard J. D. Salinger as having been a celebrity, although we can definitely say that he (inexplicably) passed up the opportunity to be a celebrity.

One definition of celebrity, of course, is being able to cash in on one's fame. Celebrities don't go on celebrity cruises or endorse products or make public appearances for free. The often somewhat mysterious ability to make so much for doing so little is the main reason sensible people envy celebrities. Our Founding philosopher, John Locke (who did what he could to live as a celebrity while he was alive) didn't actually say work was a good or noble thing, and so we can't help but look up to people who have either worked or lucked their way out of it. Besides, celebrities so clearly are better at using their money for real fun than uptight CEOs. And fun is more fun when it's noticed; the rank that celebrity provides cries out to be displayed through its privileges. The link between celebrities and their public is the one between exhibitionism and voyeurism, a pretty impersonal but nonetheless real expression of sociability.

Celebrities say they value their privacy, and many of them surely have too little of it. They wish, like we all do, to be seen and not seen at will. In an increasingly impersonal and disconnected world, most of us have too much privacy. Privacy or anonymity or insignificance may be the thing Americans work most hard to avoid. Studies show that the Americans most obsessed with the lives of celebrities are particularly unlikely to participate in civic life, but that may be because they're the Americans who are particularly unlikely to have easy access to significant forms of political participation. Many or most Americans record their deeds in both words and pictures on Facebook to give their puny lives significance to a not-so-select group of friends. The life of every celebrity appears to be a Facebook page writ large with too many "friends" to count, although even the biggest celebrities, it seems, are too anxious to dispense with Facebook, Twitter, YouTube, and so forth themselves. Anyone who believes that Britney Spears is washed up or played out has to deal with the fact that she just passed Ashton Kutcher as the American with the most Twitter followers.

Celebrity Studies—Part 2: Reality Shows and Virtue

Being a celebrity isn't necessarily connected to an extraordinary display of virtue or excellence in accomplishment. Well, that's not quite true—Paris Hilton and Sharon Osbourne are obviously quite savvy at manipulating the media to secure their celebrity status. Reality shows have connected celebrity to quite mundane accomplishments—like having lots of kids or losing lots of weight. Now, being *The Biggest Loser* is surely something about which to be proud, but it's hardly a great enough accomplishment to really gain the deep admiration of millions of Americans. All the biggest loser does, finally, is ascend (or, better, shrink) to normalcy from being a genuinely huge loser—a person who's self-indulgently become too fat to function or even to go on living.

The biggest loser remains the biggest loser in the sense that he or she needed outlandish incentives and mass encouragement to weigh about what most people weigh. And so, he or she doesn't really escape the excessive judgmentalism people have these days about the alleged vice of obesity. (Celebrities are more aware than the rest of us about the severity of that judgmentalism; they know that people demand that they use personal trainers and the latest artificial enhancements to make looking young, beautiful, and fit seem effortless. The one form of responsibility they unreservedly embrace is that it's irresponsible to let oneself go. I've read that no matter how messed up Charlie Sheen's personal life gets, he never misses a trip to the gym or a hair appointment.)

Similar observations could be made, of course, about those minor celebrities who succeed on the show *Celebrity Rehab*. Most Americans don't need expensive rehab to perform the ordinary responsibilities of life, although it's impossible not to admire those celebrities (from Heidi Fleiss to Rodney King) bold enough to actually get paid for displaying their (often failed) efforts at rehabilitation to millions. (The celebrity physician to the celebrities, Dr. Drew Pinsky, is obviously laughing all the way to the bank.) Some reality shows make celebrities out of people who are just stupid and borderline unsocialized, such as the aggressively inarticulate Guidos and Guidettes grinding their guts out at the Jersey Shore. It's hard to believe, but it's really true, that some people actually want to be like them! (It's also true, of course, that much of the attention given to the gullible, morally confused, and not-so-beautiful Guidette Snooki is not about envy or admiration; she, like some other "reality" celebrities, excites our moral sense by showing us that not only are celebrities not better than us, they're much worse than we ordinary decent folk).

That's not to say that reality shows of a kind don't create some of our more admirable celebrities. *American Idol*, the most successful of these shows, is an authentic singing competition. The finalists raked from obscurity really do have fine voices and work very hard and very intelligently to improve quickly as performing artists. The judging is an appropriately American mixture of wisdom and encouragement. The judges themselves are celebrities, but there's no pretense that any of them, except Simon Cowell, knows what he or she is talking about. Simon is the expert. The real judges, the millions and millions of Americans who vote, do in large measure take their cue from Simon, but not always. Without the popular check, Simon would become a tyrant. Without his wisdom, Americans would vote blindly for whomever they happen to like. It goes without saying that the process doesn't work perfectly in picking the best artist time and again. But it, much like the American system of government, works pretty well in reliably producing a competent, meritocratic result.

Celebrity Studies—Part 3: Role Models

Celebrities, generally speaking, are fairly irresponsible or selfish—out for themselves. They have less reason than we do not to be. They have rare opportunities to do whatever they want whenever they want. And not having been raised (as aristocrats once were) for their privileged lives, they usually aren't good at handling that freedom. Tiger Woods's escapades are legendary only in number. His was an exaggeration of the celebrity propensity to think of oneself in the moment and then buy oneself out of the consequences later. Tiger, of course, was known as that rare celebrity who gave equally intense time to both his game and his family. And his admirable personal focus, we thought, was reinforced by his Buddhism. But it turns out his life is just another example of celebrity freedom, one magnified by being an actual billionaire.

The only reason all men, promiscuous by nature, don't live like Tiger, some of our scientists tell us, is that they're constrained by the repressive conformity of bourgeois life. That repression makes sense for most of us, certainly, because we lack the wherewithal to live without it. Tiger, of course, was cashing in not only on golfing greatness but on his "role model" reputation, and it's almost sad to think that all his (surely fake) rehabbing and confessing might not work in getting him most of the latter back. But eventually it just might. At this point, Tiger remains a celebrity insofar as he remains a great golfer, and that will require more self-discipline than ever. The greatness that comes with talent and skillful self-discipline can make the dignity that comes with being ordinarily good superfluous.

The criticism of celebrities as negative "role models" is a staple of social conservatives. A generation ago (I use this example because I'm old) Vice President Dan Quayle criticized writers of the hit show *Murphy Brown* for allowing the lead character to have a baby out of wedlock. The character Murphy Brown, a celebrity TV journalist on the show, was, in fact, a role model for many ambitious American women. As socially conservative criticism Quayle's comments were flawed by the fact that Murphy Brown made a pro-life choice; she, to some extent, put her baby before her career, and certainly before her personal freedom. The real issue is that it's no big deal for a rich celebrity woman to have a baby on her own, but that's not the case for most women. A conservative would say that TV shouldn't promote the celebrity separation of parenting from marriage. A pro-choice critic might actually complain that it was too easy for Murphy to keep her productive and fulfilling way of life while not having an abortion. For ordinary aspiring career women, the choice is at least somewhat starker.

Either way, the problem is that if we look up to celebrities as role models, we might be persuaded to destroy our own lives by attempting to live as freely or irresponsibly as they do. And the "culture of celebrity" creates the impression that the only reason we must be more responsible is that we lack the freedom from necessity that celebrities enjoy. It also creates the impression that we're not allowed to rank a celebrity according to his or her moral fiber or admirable exercise of personal responsibility toward others (beyond, of course, not grossing us out by letting oneself go). That may be why, in fact, we generally allow celebrities to be trashier than ever, and why they bother less than ever to hide their trashiness from us. And their shamelessness—abetted by the shameless media that won't give them the space even to pretend to be moral exemplars—is one reason why very young people who are lost enough to be stuck with video searches for role models way too often look, talk, and act trashier than ever. (Saying more here would require beginning with Britney and Britney-types and the little girls who seem to be devoting their lives to being them).

Every judgmental observation of that kind admits of many edifying exceptions and nuanced qualifications, such as the relatively innocuous (so far) Taylor Swift among the mainstream teen-oriented performing celebrities and the pop Christian counterculture that attracts a significant segment of the young (especially, but not only, in my southern part of our country). It's true that even Taylor doesn't claim to be all about chastity, and too much of pop Christianity is more about emotion than habituation.

I can honestly say that I can't think of a young person I know who is obviously "going somewhere" who is more than amused or diverted by celebrities. Certainly the newly-minted professors who in their postmodern way are developing "celebrity theory" don't actually orient their personal lives around the persons they study. As far as I can tell, the intelligently artistic young used to take musical celebrities—such as Dylan or the Beatles or the Grateful Dead—more seriously than they do now. That may be—although there are throwback exceptions such as Bono and Springsteen (both well past their primes)—because musical celebrities don't take themselves as seriously as role models as they used to do.

And even (or especially) ordinary people know that when celebrities possess a singular artistic greatness, their lives are not for envy or imitation. Two of the most revered and beloved American celebrities were Elvis

Presley and Michael Jackson. Certainly their deaths plunged us into grief in a way rivaled only by the assassination of a president. Americans were "connected" to Elvis and Michael at least as much as they were to President Kennedy. But everyone knows that their lives were sad, screwed up, and self-destructive, and their young deaths were virtually suicides. Nobody models his or her family after Elvis's or Michael's. And everyone knows they used their great wealth to gratify extravagantly their bizarre personal fantasies. In Michael's case, everyone thinks they know (whether it's really true or not) that much of his wealth was consumed by buying his way out of criminal self-indulgence with children, and both of them, it seems, couldn't help but be degradingly, desperately addicted to drugs. We know somehow that the greatness of Michael and Elvis was inseparable from their misery, and their deaths filled us with love based on understanding—or maybe on the misunderstanding—that Michael and Elvis died for us.

Anyone would love to sing like Elvis or dance like Michael, and it's even fun to dress up like them. But hardly anyone would want to live or really be just like either of them. Still, Michael and Elvis, in their ways, were genuinely spiritual men. Elvis's big love, we know, was gospel music, which he kept rather personal or private. Michael was quite the humanitarian. And unlike, say, Lady Di, he put hundreds of millions of his own dollars where his mouth was. He certainly energized the "We are the World" impulse in millions, and that he managed to be both incorrigibly shy and completely unable to hide his heart from the world was genuinely moving.

Shifting, briefly, to a deeper version of celebrity greatness, we can all say we want to be troubled enough and spiritual enough to appreciate the music of Johnny Cash. But who would want to go through the hell of actually being Johnny Cash? (We can say the same, of course, about Charlie Parker and Thelonious Monk.) It's only when celebrity is detached from singular talent and some kind of greatness of soul that the "role model" problem emerges in a big way.

Celebrity greatness, being self-absorbed or irresponsible, is still easily distinguished from political greatness. Politicians (or, better, political leaders) either aren't or are more than celebrities. President Obama is quite the celebrity, but he's more than that. (Before he ran for president, it wasn't so clear he was more than that.) Bill Clinton, Al Gore, and Mike Huckabee are now merely celebrities. Sarah Palin, because the shameless media imposed the burdens of celebrity on her, was stuck with (and really enjoyed) skillfully making the transition from politician to celebrity. Being governor of Alaska was boring and paid poorly; becoming president was and will continue to be a most improbable long shot, but now she's rich and famous and commands the media's attention in all its dimensions. Palin, like Lady Di, is amazingly adept at linking her celebrity status to causes beyond herself, but increasingly the content of the cause seems secondary.

John Edwards was a slick celebrity lawyer who passed for a while as a politician; that's why we needed the *National Enquirer* to let us in on what he was up to all along. Political commentators, such as Rush Limbaugh, Glenn Beck, Jon Stewart, and Keith Olbermann are celebrities and nothing more; they're judged for their entertainment value. That's not to say they don't influence public opinion, but that they do so with blithe irresponsibility.

We doubt politicians really are more trustworthy than celebrities, but we demand that they be so. We expect them to behave more responsibly in their personal life (although the path-breaking Clinton narrowed the gap between celebrity and politician here), and we hold them accountable for what they actually do in power. The best way they have of being respected—or even being popular—is by being effective. It's amazing, in a media-driven, high-tech democracy, that more celebrities don't morph into politicians, and it's equally amazing that so many politicians perform badly or are so boring on television. Few politicians have what it takes to morph into celebrities. (The boys from Arkansas, Clinton and Huckabee, are much more quick, glib, and entertaining than just about all politicians, and it helps, of course, that Mike was trained as and excelled as a preacher and that Bill also remains fluent in "evangelical").

Celebrity Studies—Part 4: Celebrity and Democracy

Schwarzenegger is a rather singular example of an outstanding celebrity actor who became a genuinely responsible political leader. Some postmodern studies suggest that people voted for Arnold because they couldn't tell the difference between the real man and the invincible action hero from the movies. But everyone now knows no mere man who plays action heroes could keep California from tanking. Then there's the very singular case of Reagan—the bad actor who became a great president. Fred Thompson reminded us that most bad actors who look like presidents shy away from the arduous work required actually to be a political leader. (Note for the record that, although the overwhelming number of celebrities are Democrats, examples of celebrity statesmanship are usually Republican.)

Celebrities, of course, use the stage they've been given to express their political opinions (who wouldn't?!), and they are often irresponsibly quite self-righteous about the ignorance and corruption of those who run the government. As artists, they're especially contemptuous of Republicans, who are vulgarly obsessed with money and cater to "fundamentalist" and patriotic or anti-artistic, anti-liberationist opinion. But they're indulgent of Democrats who look down on folks in the heartland for desperately clinging to their guns and their God from the heights of celebrity affairs on the West Coast.

Celebrities characteristically engage in the silly "literary politics" that used to be reserved to poets and novelists and other more genuine bohemians. They usually aren't particularly well-educated and informed. They're even more easily seduced by conspiracy theories than ordinary people. We can turn, for example, to Charlie Sheen and Rosie O'Donnell to learn that 9/11 was really the secret plot of the American government. And celebrities love the sovereign disdain for the facts in pursuit of the conspiratorial "truth" that characterizes the engaging "narratives" of Michael Moore and Oliver Stone. Living in huge houses hanging off the sides of hills in the overpopulated and earthquake-prone California desert, they're especially concerned about the future of the planet, and they unreservedly admire the Al Gore who designed his account of an inconvenient (and very alarming) truth for their edification. Celebrities regularly display their pseudo-sophistication on Bill Maher's show, certain they're on the vanguard of moral and political enlightenment. None of this is to say that celebrities have much more impact on the outcome of elections than other very rich people. Celebrities, like philosophers in an unjust country, don't desire and aren't compelled to rule. It's only fair to add that many of the causes celebrities so generously fund to display their class have done much good for real people (as well as other species and nature as a whole).

All this celebrity stuff wouldn't have surprised the leading commentator on America and democracy's most genuine (or sympathetically but truthfully critical) friend, Alexis de Tocqueville. Tocqueville said democracy turns even art and literature into industries, and people turn to them less for profound truth and moral guidance than for relaxation or diversion from their stressful, productive, restless lives. That means, of course, that democratic people depend on the doings of celebrities for emotional relief, and that they usually don't have what it takes to esteem art and literature with the leisurely seriousness that the great works deserve. People who enjoy reading *People* and even *Entertainment Weekly* (including me) usually know that nothing crucial or authentically momentous is being displayed for them there. Those skillfully produced publications aim not to tax the mind or even enlarge the heart.

Many critics of democracy say that celebrities have replaced real greatness: true artists and true heroes. And Tocqueville observed that democracy causes us to doubt the reality of statesmen and heroes; profound and admirable personal greatness are too troubling and too dangerous as exceptions to our egalitarian rules. It's also true enough, as Tocqueville adds, that in an impersonal, egalitarian, bureaucratic, high tech, commercialized, commodified, centralized world, what outstanding individuals do is less important as a cause of change than "forces," such as technological development, the market, and public opinion. Due to the beneficial power of these forces, ordinary life is clearly more comfortable and secure and seemingly less heroic. We only need heroes, we often think, when modern life breaks down, and, even with the economic downturn and the continuing possibility of terrorism, we think we've figured out how to make it break down less and less often. For those whose heroes have always been cowboys, these are probably the worst of times in America. The Marines and Special Forces who heroically protect us every day think of themselves as more alienated from mainstream, self-indulgent, consumerist American culture than ever. Certainly the distance between them and the "culture of celebrity" continues to grow.

But we still know artistic greatness and artistic integrity when we see them. Even in the world of popular music, we admire the steadfast distance that separates Van Morrison, Joni Mitchell, and even Bob Dylan from various fashionable (including fashionably political) currents. (We also notice that they show us that the true artist needn't be neurotic nor die young.) We also notice the fall of Paul Simon and even Springsteen into the fashionable and politically correct world of celebrity. (To be fair to Springsteen, the longing remains to celebrate heroes, but once he left the real world of Jersey and Jungleland, he can't find them).

Not only that, but we still continue to recognize heroes for who they are and rank them above celebrities. That's why there persists a strong market for movies about the men who fought in World War II. And everything Clint Eastwood does shows us the moral ambiguity and deep nobility of heroic courage; no American, except celebrity critics and celebrity Academy Award voters, could be unmoved by *Gran Torino*. Americans remain both democratically open and nobly resistant to sophisticated deconstruction of our allegedly heroic Founding Fathers. We're repeatedly told that we ordinary people and especially ordinary celebrities these days are better than them; they were racist, sexist homophobes and we're not. But most Americans still know that their singular courage and foresight will always deserve our deep gratitude. For celebrity displays of patriotic gratitude, we, it's true, have to move from LA to Nashville, to, for example, the Zac Brown Band's appreciation of who has protected our right to eat chicken fried steak on a Friday night. But country music, everybody really knows, remains, despite its commercialization and standardization, the most impressive and probably most influential form of American mass market music.

Country fans and even country stars also know that higher than patriotism is religion, and they're more about thanking the Lord than even thanking our Founders. And for real spiritual guidance, most of our celebrities, we know well enough, are useless. Scientology has not caught on, and the New Agey, pseudo-Buddhist, astrological kind of stuff so popular among the West Coast stars interests more than engages us. There's no denying that *Avatar* was both loads of fun and an unrivaled techno-accomplishment. But to what extent did it achieve its celebrity creator's intention of turning lives around in the direction of the oneness of nature? Surely more Americans became different or better men and women as a result of the very personal Christian charity lovingly displayed by the Sandra Bullock character in *The Blind Side*. We know it's a telling sign of the superficiality and narcissism of "celebrity culture" that so few celebrities are serious Christians or orthodox Jews or Mormons or adhere to any faith that imposes a strong communal moral discipline on its members. For a while, we thought of Mel Gibson as a rather dazzling exception, but even his faith turned out to be too mixed up with celebrity vices to sustain our admiration.

All in all, I'm more sanguine than most celebrity theorists about Americans knowing well enough the limits of celebrity, while acknowledging that being stuck with celebrities is more a downside than not of democracy.

I Dig That Rock and Roll Music
(But What Does It Mean?)

Carl Scott is probably the blogworld's leading expert on the content of rock music (both words and music). He calls those words, once in a while, its ideological dimension.

Carl both is trained in political philosophy—especially Alexis de Tocqueville's *Democracy in America*—and actually knows and loves the music. Not only that, he seems to believe in God and America.

I have to admit I'm weak on the musical knowledge. For one reason, I'm tone-deaf or close to it. For another, I'm too old to be keeping up with the latest musical trends.

But I do like "classic rock." On my car radio (yes, I use the GPS but not the CD player), I rarely mess with National Public Radio. Instead, I listen to an excellent station that plays nothing but the classic tunes of the sixties, seventies, and eighties.

Here's Carl's very thoughtful and thought-provoking conclusion:

> While rock's primary ideological element thus is sexual/psychic-al libertarianism, its secondary element, I would argue, is a profound ambivalence about modernity. This often is expressed by opposition to corporate capitalism, but it runs much deeper. Fundamental to the best rock's "timeliness," I think, is its disappointment with or even despair over the materially well-provided-for modern life. How to best deal with the supposedly good contemporary life and the conformist temptation to resign ourselves to its satisfactions is one of its basic themes. This is why rock resonates in the enclaves of the prosperous around the globe while it never really catches on with impoverished populations, and a major reason why it came to be identified as a white thing in America. For our (rich and middle-class) generations, the best rock artists serve a similar purpose as the romantic poets did for earlier ones—as the rare souls who glimpse the full implications of modern rationalism for living, and whose art seeks to provide an aesthetic refuge and alternative ("Carl's Rock Songbook #17," *First Things*, August 30, 2011).

Rock music, at its founding (so to speak), really was about celebrating rocking and rolling against uptight middle-class conformity. That softened into the sexual revolution of the 1960s.

Rock has remained all for those two modes of sexual freedom, to some extent. But sexual liberation is boring these days, because almost everyone is liberated.

Rock has not been about "the working man." That's folk music. When Springsteen steps out to whine about Youngstown or embrace Woody Guthrie's message, he lets us know he's being more folky than rock. And Joan Baez had to change the words of *The Band*'s "The Night They Drove Old Dixie Down" to make it a working man's song—or not a noble display of rebellion against the first form of Yankee imperialism. Folk music has too often been Northern intellectuals with a very questionable political agenda singing about some imagined working man. To be fair, I wouldn't put Bruce in that category; early on, he was quite poetic about the working men he actually knew in New Jersey (and he celebrated their romantic longings with a power rarely found in rock).

If my memory serves (or has been enhanced by *Jersey Boys*), the working man's band in the early seventies was *The Four Seasons*, who didn't sing about the plight of the guy with the lunch pail. Who wants to party to *that*? I could go on to say something about the greatness of *Neil Diamond*, but that might not impress a BIG THINK audience.

Rock, after its anti-war phase, has been about images of liberation from middle-class productivity, for a kind of amorphous freedom. It's definitely not been about political revolution, just as it's not generally been about "social responsibility." It was sometimes about drugs, but more often has been about dissatisfaction with the limited satisfactions available to members of the white middle class (without employing the remedy of drugs). It's fairly rarely been about mocking being middle-class (even she's a small-town girl who's crazy about Elvis is basically the suburbs mocking the country), but usually it takes the misery (or displaced longings) of living with unprecedented freedom in the midst of prosperity all too seriously.

So the whining is usually ineffectual and readily commodified—a safe form of bohemianism, a Marxist (or libertarian!) might say—for our bourgeois world.

It might be significant that rock rarely follows Tocqueville in seeing being a citizen or being a creature or being a responsible parent as ways out of our lonely emptiness. It might be significant that *country music* often does.

Why doesn't he give more examples, you say? Because I might screw them up. I'll leave them to Carl.

The Tax Code and My Summer Vacation

So one of the guys at Panera Bread this morning asked my view on the *flat tax* or *fair tax* or whatever.

My response was that my objection to the present tax code is that rich guys pay a lower percentage of their income in taxes than I do.

Why is that? I use most of the money I get to buy stuff. I have very little left to tax shelter in one way or another. Not only that, I can't afford some fancy accountant to do my taxes for me. I'm on my own. Now my inability to save much might be attributed to my being lazy or wasteful, but those, in fact, are not the main reasons.

Rich guys only use a small percentage of their income to live. Most of the rest they can hide. And they have accountants and lawyers who are much better (because they make a lot more) than the ones employed by the government to help them. They officially pay a higher rate than me, but under the present tax code they have plenty of perfectly legal ways to keep what they have from being taxable.

Common sense tells me a genuinely loophole-less flat tax might even the playing field to my advantage. Common sense also tells me that Congress, which reaches majorities by building coalitions of diverse interests, will never come up with such a tax.

What really ticks me off about paying taxes is deductions. I should have a big, six-figure salary (given that I'm ranked among the top fifty political-theory professors in the country), but I don't. Contrary to what you're thinking, I'm not blaming my college for this. Not making the big bucks is one downside of living in the sticks.

Fortunately, I usually have modest sources of other income from writing, editing, speaking, and even blogging. On that income, I'm self-employed. So I have to pay the self-employment tax. That, combined with state and national income taxes, would make most of my extra income disappear. (The people who really get a raw deal under the present tax code aren't really people like me, but highly industrious middle-class people who are completely self-employed.)

Fortunately again, there are many deductions I can take, almost too many. Not only stuff like professional travel, but even, say, my books, journals, newspapers, and cable bill. Why cable bill? Because I've published and blogged on and made a buck or two talking and writing about TV, movies, etc. (as I hope you've noticed). Plus, they have *news* on TV.

Without the services of a fancy accountant, I have to figure out what these deductions are for myself. In many areas, it's just impossible to know where, under the law, I should draw the line. Politics is about everything! Why can't I deduct the expenses for every move I make and everything I read or see? (Surely you can hire an accountant, you might say. Well, my personal situation is pretty hard to get hold of for your average numbers person. And some people like to cut their own grass. Others like to do their own taxes. I'm in the latter category.)

This guy at Panera told me about a friend of his who writes mystery novels. She has them published at vanity presses, but she can still show they make a little money. Her next one will be about Norway. And so, she's figured out she can write off her trip there, which might mainly be a vacation (who knows?).

How can I write off my summer vacation(s), I asked myself? By blogging about them! So let me share the first of many stories about my summer vacation to the mountains of North Carolina.

Due to an Internet, midweek special, my wife and I were able to spend a couple of days at the historic Grove Park Inn in Asheville, NC. It's very classy; President Obama has stayed there twice. It's a little large and convention-oriented to be hyper-luxurious, but it's plenty luxurious for us.

One thing can't be denied: the Inn has a fabulous view from its elevated porch, one that includes a stunning golf course, forests, the quirky but riveting skyline of the city of Asheville, and the North Carolina mountains (which are more green and beautiful than the Rockies).

A lady next to me commented: "Well, the view's nice, but it would be better with a lake." It would, in fact, be better with a lake.

On the Tea Party Menace
(and the President's Strategy to Keep His Job)

Our BIG THINKING friend Robert de Neufville has outlined an important component of President's Obama's case for a second term.

Sure, the economy is tanking as well as the president's ratings, because he seems pretty clueless. (Just as, to be fair and balanced, President Bush came to seem pretty clueless on the tanking of our Iraq strategy.)

Not only that, studies show that American opinion is trending against *big government*. People increasingly don't buy into Obama's *progressive vision* that bigger and better government could possibly cure what ails us these days.

But it turns out, Robert claims, that the Republicans aren't really the shrink government party. That's because they're dominated by the Tea Party, which is, at heart, theocratic. The Tea Partiers want big, moralistic, intrusive, religious government. And most Americans, after all, don't want that! (They really don't!)

So the president's form of big government, being less intrusive, will be seen as preferable to the Tea Party form.

Robert is surely right that the Democrats will do well to campaign against the *Tea Party Menace*. He admits they will do so the way Republicans or the Right used to campaign against McGovernism or against the *Red Menace* of socialism or communism.

Most Americans, studies show, don't like and are suspicious of the Tea Party, partly as result of a relentless mainstream media attack on its character.

That means that many sophisticated Americans these days have roused themselves up to believe that anyone with opinions that are religious or conservative is in secret alliance with the Tea Party—at least fellow-travelers!

A member (well, probably more than one) of the faculty at my Berry College is talking about the threat of the Tea Party takeover of the college. As far as I know, no faculty member and no more than a couple dozen students or so have any affiliation with or total agreement with those partiers. But still …

I have admit that we can't dismiss the possibility that those gun-toting defenders of Second Amendment rights might be planning a takeover by force of arms. (That's a joke, son! They're very law-abiding folks!)

My serious point is that Robert mischaracterizes the partiers to some extent. It's true that they are disproportionally religious. And they trust candidates who display their Christianity in public.

But although they think, with a kind of misguided piety, that our Founding Fathers were more Christian than they really were, those partiers aren't theocrats at all.

Here's what they think: wherever the national government—especially bureaucrats and judges—goes, religion is chased away. So they want really small government so that they can live as they please.

All libertarians are for living as they please in the absence of government regulation. But it pleases the Tea Partiers, very often, to live self-sufficiently as Christians with big families. What's so bad about that?

A big issue for many of the partiers is home schooling. They don't want the government getting in the way of their decisions on how to educate their very own kids. I have to admit that even I (who didn't home school and would probably, on balance, always choose against it) am creeped out by the over-the-top hostility of our bureaucratized educational establishment to parents' right to make this kind of fundamental choice for themselves.

Not only that, the real problem with the Tea Party for Republicans is its highly principled hostility to our welfare state—the tendency to think that Medicare and Social Security are unconstitutional and that taxes on productivity (income taxes) are immoral. Bachmann gets her "street cred" with the partiers not so much from reading Christian authors as from claiming to study the economist Ludwig Von Mises (a brilliant and radically anti-statist thinker, the Founder of the highly accomplished "Austrian school" of economics). The real problem with the Tea Party will be the perception that its goal is to roll back the New Deal, instead of prudently reforming our entitlement programs (as most Americans want).

I have no idea whether Michele actually reads or understands Ludwig's tough books, and I don't agree with him on lots of things. Still, you have to admit: He's several pay grades higher than Friedman or Krugman or Reich.

Our Tea Partiers are really about thinking of the economic crisis of our time as an opportunity for a kind of new birth of freedom from government dependency. They are all about libertarian means for non-libertarian ends, for living, to repeat, as they please. Their religious intensity points away from big government, and that means all Americans opposed to big government have no reason not to ally with them. They're part of—not opposed to—the libertarian drift of our time.

The Political Case for America's Superiority

The Americans, as our English friend Chesterton observed with some ambivalence, are the seeming oxymoron, a creedal nation. We are, he memorably said, a nation with the soul of the church. America, he added, is all about the romance of the citizen and a home for the homeless everywhere. The American creed is that all human beings are created equal, because there's a personal center of significance in the universe that grants each of us significance. Everyone, in principle, can be a citizen of our country who accepts the dogmatic lucidity of that national faith.

That faith is about citizens, because it's the foundation of the way of life shared in our territorial home. It's a faith that the foundation of citizenship is not a merely national construction; we're at home with the thought that the nation is not the real source of the significance of citizens. And so, the true foundation of citizenship lies in the truth about the person and the relationship between being politically at home and our truest home. We've never shared the French view or even the view of the ancient polis that citizens are created out of nothing. Nor have we ever shared today's European view that the person must be detached from the citizen to display his true freedom.

The American view is that citizenship is only one part but a real part of whole human lives; the person experiences himself as both a political and transpolitical being. The romance of the citizen, for us, displays part of the truth about the equal significance we all share as unique and irreplaceable beings. (That means, as Chesterton learned, in part, from Lincoln, that our Declaration's faith is not merely or most deeply Lockean. There is a foundation for the significance of each particular person in nature itself, and that thought depends at least upon a distinctively Christian sort of Deism that was a product of the Declaration's legislative compromising of Lockean and Calvinist concerns.)

This view of America, which finds its home among conservative Americans today, is the best explanation of why America can be a nation without succumbing to nationalism, of why we are so comparatively adept in reconciling the particularity of the citizen with the universality of personal principle, of why History (with a capital H) never took firm, depersonalizing root here, of why the most Christian of Americans can be the best citizens, of why there are credible Christian and secular accounts of our founding principles that are in some respects in principle irreconcilable but nonetheless are readily compromisable, and of why we are so confident that the nation is the form by which democratic self-government can and should take root everywhere.

This view of America is arguably weakening in the face of the envy of our sophisticates of the purer or post-political morality of the Europeans, but its future may be if not certainly the last, arguably the best hope for the future of both the person and the citizen, the combination indispensable for self-government in our or any Christian or post-Christian time everywhere. America's persistent, political self-understanding of itself as a nation, as Charles Krauthammer pointed out in a somewhat different way recently, is the main reason why we continue to fund a huge military establishment capable of projecting our power and influence everywhere. The Europeans have chosen to have minimal military expenditures and increasingly reduced military capabilities. When they need airlifts, they turn to our Air Force, and they rely on our navy for keeping the open seas open. Much of Europe's relative de-politicization or de-nationalization is parasitic upon one nation in particular.

The Europeans can afford not to do everything required to defend themselves precisely because we choose not to be like them. For us (at least so far), the European life of excessive personal liberation in comfort and safety is decadence based on self-denial. If we choose to live like them, who, in fact, would protect us? We seem stuck with being a nation, and the Europeans, it seems to me, ought not only to praise our distinctiveness, but follow the advice of their conservative or national thinkers—such as Roger Scruton and Pierre Manent—and do what they can to imitate it.

I'm not endorsing any particular American intervention, but I do think the isolationism of the republicanism of our Front Porcher friends misunderstands who we are and our indispensable purpose in the world in our time. I also think it's more pagan than Christian, but that's a story for another time.

How and Why We Should Listen to the French

I've concluded that there's no better way to keynote this wonderful conference on the large and beneficial influence of French Catholic writers on
America than by giving a talk all about me—someone who's not at all
French, can't comfortably speak French, and is only ambiguously a writer.
There's no better way to assess the reach of this influence but to find it in
someone who's really not particularly French, not particularly literary, and
in truth pretty narrowly American.

Nobody's better situated than *me* to assess objectively the merits of
modern French Catholic writers. Because I've often used Alexis de
Tocqueville, Pierre Manent, Chantal Delsol, and other French, Catholic
political thinkers to call attention to the limitations of the theory of the
American founding, I've been accused of being anti-American. Not only
that, I've sort of figured out that Alexis de Tocqueville, author of the best
book on America, thought that the French Catholic Pascal taught the truth
about who we are, and that the psychology of Pascal more than the History
of Rousseau (or the ambiguously natural/Historical Locke) explains to us
best of all who we are. The best American Thomist, the philosopher-physician-novelist Walker Percy, agrees that the Americans, who really are
Cartesians who've never read a word of Descartes, need Pascal to understand that their legendary pursuit of happiness is mostly a diversion about
what they really can't help but know about themselves.

Our pursuits, as Tocqueville says, are feverish and often insane. Percy
adds, inspired by both Tocqueville and Pascal, that we're quite literally
deranged. We certainly can't explain our strange and wonderful human
behavior with our Lockean and Cartesian theory. Just beneath the happy
talk pragmatism of our pop Cartesian experts Tocqueville and Percy hear
the howl of existentialism, which is really, as Pascal explains, an expression of the misery of man without God. But Tocqueville and Percy also follow Pascal in not confusing restlessness with hopelessness. They see in the
restlessness of the Americans reason for a glimmer—or maybe much more
than a glimmer—of hope.

I plead guilty to being unduly influenced by French Catholic thought
and by Americans who have been particularly open to French Catholic influence, such as Percy but also the American Catholic agent for today's French
Catholic political thinkers in America, Dan Mahoney, and the American
Mormon Thomist dissident Straussian Francophile Ralph Hancock.

That doesn't mean I'm anti-American. One way I use to defend myself against that charge is, quite humbly, to compare myself with Socrates. Socrates must have been happy with Athens, as the Laws say in *The Crito*, because he never left that place. He was quite the stay-at-home. I, too, never leave America or at least our Hemisphere (rightly claimed as ours by President Monroe) except on business. I've never even had the European Vacation made famous by Chevy Chase.

Our friend Jim Ceaser is famous for unreservedly defending American foundationalism against our European critics. But he prances off to France every chance he gets. As a college professor, I've been blessed by living in abundance with very little real work, but I haven't used my leisure to be a voracious consumer of French culture, as our libertarians or bourgeois bohemians might have predicted. I'd admit freely to being influenced by alien currents of thought, but I use them to make our place better.

Tocqueville, everyone knows, wrote about the Americans for the benefit of the French, by showing the French that we're both better and worse than they are. When I write about the French, I think mostly about what's best for America. I certainly haven't made any big effort to get my work known in France. And in that lack of effort I've succeeded almost completely. There are various ways Americans today relate to French thought. The first, characteristic of many conservatives (such as the so-called West Coast Straussians and students of Fox Professor of Tea Party Studies Glenn Beck), is to proudly proclaim that we don't need any (to quote the unmatched eloquence of our vice president) foreign aid. American has a flawless Founding and was later messed up by the German influence on the Progressive Era and the French envy of the Obama Era.

One flaw in this account of our founding innocence of all things French or German, to begin with, is that our philosopher Locke was basically a Cartesian, and Descartes was French. Another is that Tocqueville really does understand ourselves better than we understand ourselves, showing us that our pragmatism and progressivism aren't really so much alien intrusions but indigenous expressions of the American, democratic mind.

The second American way of relating to French thought, characteristic of many liberals, amounts to French envy. We need to get less Puritanical and more French. That means we have to stop being sexually repressed, gun-toting, workaholic, religious nuts. We have to transform our greedy, brutal capitalism into a European social democracy so that we can switch over to that near oxymoron, the French work ethic. That means we'll have all the leisure we'll need to be appreciative enjoyers of French culture—for example, sitting for hours in cafes in squares graced by cathedrals that were built based on beliefs that no sensible person has anymore.

There's a second kind of French envy that's much less common: It is found among certain very admirable American traditionalist Catholics, many of whom are shaped in some measure by the after-virtue philosophy of Alasdair MacIntyre. Only the most individualistic currents of European thought, beginning with the Protestant dissenter Puritans, got to America. From the very beginning America lacked what it takes to have genuine political or spiritual community. And then America morphed into being the most imperial of the modern nation-states—out to dominate the world with its particularly brutal form of capitalism. Lately we've been unjustly invading countries to protect our oil and to make everyone become democratic individualists just like us. There's little to no hope for America. But Christendom—the way of life that existed in the Europe prior to the nation-state—might rise from the ruins of Europe. There's even hope, in Europe, in what's left of the Christian Democratic parties and in the universalistic, post-national aspirations of the EU.

There are some curious convergences in the trendy left and seemingly traditionalist forms of French envy, beginning with exaggerations—really, caricatures—of American individualism as it exists right now in our relatively unsophisticated heartland. But more important is willful ignorance of the fact that, by Tocqueville's standards, Europe is generally speaking much more individualistic than America right now. Individualism, remember, is, according to Tocqueville, a kind of heart disease, an emotional withdrawal into the confines of one's own puny self based on the mistaken judgment that both love and hate are more trouble than they're worth.

My view of Europe today isn't of course based on firsthand observation. I'm not that kind of social scientist. I've listened to the criticisms of Europe from the best French, Catholic political thinkers, beginning, of course, with Pierre Manent. These criticisms are *both* French and Catholic. According to Manent, the nation is the modern form of the ancient polis, the place where people can and should find a political home. The nation is a body, with definite territorial limits. It's a real place with customs, traditions, and political institutions.

Human beings, the Catholic adds, are more than citizens, though; they have another and higher home than their political one. That fact is represented by the universal church. But the universal church isn't meant to and can't really displace the particular nation. So today Europe is making two fundamental errors: It's abolishing the nation and denying that all particular nations exist under the universal church. Much of today's Europe is in the thrall, the emphatically French and Catholic man Manent explains, of a kind of post-political, post-familial, and post-religious fantasy. People have so withdrawn into themselves that they aren't even making enough babies to secure their political future. They hate their bodies, Manent shows us, because they've become so sure that they're nothing more than bodies. The *eros* of Europeans is less and less aroused and shaped by the familial, political, and spiritual responsibilities given to beings like us.

We can also learn much from Tocqueville or Manent or Beneton about the excesses of our individualism, about our inability to keep Locke in the Locke box, about the horror that is *Roe v. Wade* and the mean woman side of our feminism, and about the more narcissistic and laughably risk-averse elements of our creeping and sometimes creepy libertarianism. And as Orestes Brownson, the nineteenth-century American thinker most influenced by French, Catholic currents of thought first explained, the Americans—with their merely contractual understanding of the origin of political authority—never have had a proper theoretical understanding of the political or national virtues of loyalty and gratitude.

Still, Manent admits that, following the example and much of the analysis of Tocqueville, we are, comparatively speaking, better off because the family, the nation, and religious belief remain stronger here. Thanks mainly to our observant religious believers, we're still having enough babies to keep ourselves going. And we, more generally, are doing what it takes to defend ourselves politically. We even still think that the old and the disabled are mainly still the responsibility of particular families and not some impersonal state. Not only that, we still practice the virtue of charity as particular persons in big numbers and often on a grand scale.

We've read the studies, often written in the spirit of Tocqueville, that American conservative Christians are distinguished by their philanthropic generosity and their voluntary caregiving, and their churches, at their best at least, are attentive to the whole lives of particular persons. We learn from today's French Catholic writer, Chantal Delsol, that the virtues most slighted in our high-tech and exceedingly productive world are those displayed through caregiving, although it's caregiving far more than productivity that displays to us the depths about who we are. The Catholic principle of subsidiarity, while officially extolled everywhere in Europe today, is at least somewhat more alive, as Tocqueville explained, in the virtuous voluntary activity relatively prevalent in our country, in the virtue displayed, for example, in *The Blind Side.*

Intellectuals in Politics?

A professor of philosophy—Gary Gutting—opinionating for the *New York Times* invites us to think about the relationship between politicians and intellectuals. He says that politicians, to be credible, don't have to be intellectuals, but they have to have intellectual lives. They have to be consumers of what intellectuals (or experts) write in their journals—such as *Scientific American* and *The New York Review of Books*. He also recommends that the candidates have a debate that is basically a quiz on whether they know and can think about what intellectuals know—about history, policy, and such.

The professor also notices that the Republican candidates tend to take pride in being anti-intellectual. The exception, of course, is Newt Gingrich, Ph.D., who has done well in the debates by speaking with the authority of a professor on a great variety of issues. Newt, having not worked in politics and having spent his time hanging around a conservative think-tank for over a decade, seems to have taken on many of the trappings of an intellectual. Newt's lead in the polls might be evidence that even Republicans are much more open to intellectual leadership than the professor believes.

Our professor concludes by being excited, as are others, with the prospect of a race between two professor-candidates, our president and our former Speaker. That would make for some very interesting debates, no doubt. But you have to wonder whether (intellectually informed) skill in debating actually predicts outstanding or even competent presidential leadership. The prediction does work for Lincoln, but we remember he barely went to school and never hung out with intellectuals.

Our only Ph.D. president, Woodrow Wilson, made a strong, scholarly case for the presidential leadership being about visionary, idea-charged rhetoric. But it's easy to make the strong case that his misguided idealism—as haphazardly implemented in his second term—actually really screwed up the world. It's also easy to make the case—even to his liberal or Progressive supporters—that our current president's competence has not risen to anywhere near the level of his soaring campaign rhetoric. Someone might say our (law) professor-president came to office lacking the experience—and so the knowledge—required to know how to lead. Newt has the edge on President Obama in one way: he served for two decades in Congress, after failing to do what's required as a professor to get tenure. Those, however who worked closely with him as Speaker don't speak well of his organizational skills, and they say a lot about his general instability and his obsessive sense of self-importance. His "vision thing" helped the Republicans regain the House after a long absence and got him elected Speaker. He was, on balance, a forced-out failure as Speaker. The evidence is that he doesn't have the character and temperament, beginning with self-discipline, to be chief executive.

The professor defines the intellectual as someone who finds fulfillment and happiness in the life of the mind, someone who finds his (or her) natural home in the university. Gutting is such a purist that he complains that even the universities are being contaminated by corporatist and political concerns. He cites Plato's *Republic* to support his point.

In the *Republic,* Socrates distinguishes carefully between the philosopher and the intellectual (or sophist). The philosopher, the purist when it comes to his lifetime devotion to the truth about all things, doesn't want to rule, and he'd have to be forced to take an interest in political affairs. For the real philosopher, the questions are more obvious than the answers, and Socrates himself was famous for ending conversations with a confession that he remained too ignorant to know what to do. Socrates would not be a very ineffective policy advisor—lacking both the expertise and the motivation to tell the chief executive what he most needs to know. Socrates talks about the rule of philosopher-kings, but he has to distort who philosophers really are to make that possibility plausible. The philosopher-king is a wise man—not a seeker of wisdom like Socrates. He *knows* the idea of the good, what gives being its being-ness. Not only is he perfect when it comes to wisdom, he's a perfect ruler. He knows both what *is* and what *to do*. The professor is right to object that there's nobody real like that, and Socrates, of course, knew that too.

The intellectual, for Socrates, is the sophist, the person who employs his knowledge to gain wealth, power, and recognition. He may sometimes be idealistic enough to believe he can really improve the world. But usually he puts his knowledge at the service of a particular ruling group in his own interest (think the Newt who got big bucks to make a persuasive case for Freddie Mac).

The sophist is never as smart as he thinks he is, but he certainly is confident of his expertise. He really does know something, but he believes he knows everything. And usually he mistakes technical competence for the whole of wisdom, forgetting the irreducible moral component in human lives, the part that can't be captured by expertise. The explanatory theories of economists immediately come to mind here, as do Newt's (and others') various forms of techno-enthusiasm.

The famous sophist in the *Republic*, Thrasymachus, gets an unfairly bad rap. At a certain point in the conversation, Socrates even says that he and Thrasymachus have become friends. Here's why: a sophist would be indispensable for persuading people that philosophers should rule, for gentling them with tricky arguments that are far from wholly reasonable or in their true interests. The Republicans, we might want to say, often are spirited enough to see through the trickiness of sophists, although sometimes, of course, at the price of slighting what the experts really do know.

When thinking of intellectuals, I really think of experts: people who have an often high level of useful knowledge in economics, health care, public policy, and so forth. I don't completely trust these experts. I don't see them as animated by love of knowledge simply, but as more vain, fashionably elitist, and potentially more tyrannical than most of us. Being an intellectual is no guarantee of being either a person of character or a person who actually knows what it takes to rule well. Republicans know that an intellectual rarely has the interests of ordinary people primarily in mind.

That's not to say that political leaders shouldn't be avid consumers of what intellectuals know. But they should be careful to assess for themselves the significance of what their studies claim to show. All of us, in truth, should be all about being careful in that way. Surely the example of Newt shows at least that it's far from self-evident that the most intellectual candidate is the one with the character and competence required to lead. Let's hope the Republicans wake up to this fact fast.

Conservative Liberal Political Analysis Today

The controversial social analyst Charles Murray has written an important book (*Coming Apart*) on the unprecedented class divide in America today.

Before getting to what's going on right now, I'd thought I'd say something about Murray's general approach, which originated, as he suggests, in Alexis de Tocqueville's *Democracy in America*.

Tocqueville came to America to figure out why democracy—contrary to the fears of the recently dispossessed French aristocrats—could be so compatible with human decency and human liberty. The Frenchman discovered all sorts of features that made America exceptional—so exceptional, in fact, that it's not so clear Tocqueville thought the American solution could be exported elsewhere.

America democracy, we would say today, works so well because of "cultural capital" that may not be, strictly speaking, of democratic origin. Freedom depends on a high respect for morality and a high level of habitual moral behavior. Liberal political and economic institutions depend on a conservative foundation.

Murray says that the Americans have been regarded "as different, even peculiar, to people around the world" in at least nine ways. It goes without saying that my comments will be somewhat different from his. And I'll only have space in this post to discuss one feature of American exceptionalism: *industriousness*.

1. As Murray explains, Americans not only work hard, they understand work to define, in some large measure, who they are. Tocqueville said to be American is to be middle class, or somewhere in between being a servant and being an aristocrat. The Americans are free to work for themselves, but they must work for themselves. A life of leisure is not for them. They are free like aristocrats, they know, to work like slaves. Tocqueville explains that the Americans hate the theory of the permanent equality of property through government redistribution, just as they hate the idea of a permanent aristocracy. They think neither rich nor poor should be exempt from work, and they have trouble distinguishing the life of cultivated leisure from that of the bum.

2. In the history of our country, we can see an increasing premium being placed on productivity as the source of one's worth. Lives devoted to voluntary caregiving or religious prayer or philosophy become increasingly devalued. And Americans, of course, criticize both the European

aristocracy of the past and the European social democracy of the present as ways of letting too many people get by without working for a living. Europeans, such as Tocqueville himself, think of Americans as plagued by a rodent-like restlessness that keeps them from relaxing and enjoying life, even in the midst of prosperity. Americans admire the poor insofar as they are "the working poor," or trying hard not to be poor. They are somewhat repulsed by the content poor—such as the bohemians of old or the panhandler.

3. Murray wisely borrows from David Brooks in identifying today's American meritocratic elite as bourgeois bohemians. They know that pursuing the lifestyle options of the bohemians depend on being bourgeois— or earning the resources required to pick from our diverse society's lifestyle menu of choice. For the bourgeois bohemian, bourgeois trumps bohemian. The virtues required to be industrious and productive come first. One's bohemian pursuits shouldn't get in the way of getting to work on time and completely ready for action. That's why even our professors have become careerists tied to assessable, measurable standards of productivity. And that's why we no longer identify substance abuse as part of the deal when it comes to pursuing artistic excellence. Most readers of BIG THINK are bourgeois bohemians—not that there's anything wrong with that.

4. Murray is also alarmed that lower-middle-class Americans are losing the habits connected with work. He notices that "the norm" that "healthy men in the prime of their life are supposed to work" is eroding. The key indicator here is the number of men who say they just aren't available for work, who think they can define themselves in the absence of work, even when work is available.

5. Is it really true, as Murray claims, that we're now defined by two classes? The first is all about personal productivity, entrepreneurial ingenuity and so forth. It is less "aristocratic" or classy and laidback and more an "achievetron" meritocracy based on productivity than ever. The other class, meanwhile, is losing the virtue of industriousness or what's required to be middle class. Are Americans less united than ever by the shared virtue of industriousness? (I have to admit I'm not at all sure about that.)

I know that everything I'm saying is questionable and that Murray's analysis is way short of perfect, and I invite your criticism.

Our Two Tribes:
David Brooks Weighs in on Charles Murray

David Brooks has weighed in on Charles Murray's controversial (but undeniably engaging) *Coming Apart*. That's appropriate, of course, because Murray's description of our meritocratic elite depends so much on Brooks's earlier description of our bourgeois bohemians. Brooks's judgment on Murray: "I'll be shocked if there's another book that so compellingly describes the most important trends in American society."

Brooks is unparalleled as a summarizer and popularizer of social science. So, we do well to note what he finds especially noteworthy about Murray, with my spin added, of course.

1. The income gap between rich and poor is wider than ever.

2. But the word "class" doesn't describe that gap adequately. American is divided into two "social tribes," two comprehensive and segregated ways of life.

3. The "upper tribe" inhabits "an archipelago of affluent enclaves clustered around the coastal cities." Its members move, with their kind, from one enclave to another.

4. More important than the huge differences in income are "the big behavior gaps." They didn't exist, say, in 1963, when almost all men in both classes were in the labor force and almost all kids weren't "born outside marriage."

5. The behavior of the upper tribe is surprisingly "traditional." Its members have gotten over the flaky excesses of the Sixties' "Do your own thing," "free love," and that. Their residual radicalism is all talk. They are reliable spouses and parents. Their divorce rate is low. Their families are, as the experts say, bourgeois.

6. They understand that "bohemian" enjoyment depends on bourgeois habits, and so I'm surprised Brooks didn't say straight out that they're more bourgeois bohemian than ever. A Darwinian might add that they should be having more children. The members of our upper tribe don't seem all that erotic, but they're often all that entrepreneurial, innovative, and all those other Harvard Business School buzzwords.

7. The "upper tribe" is richer not because of hereditary privilege but because it is more productive than ever. It is a meritocratic tribe based on education and I.Q. Its members understand themselves, not without reason,

to deserve the money and status they have. That's why "liberal guilt" is becoming an oxymoron. And that's why our liberals are morphing into libertarians. (One characteristic of meritocracy, of course, is the vice of ingratitude.)

8. Even empathy—which is weaker than charity or paternalistic responsibility—depends on common experiences. And the tribes have fewer common experiences than ever.

9. Members of the lower tribe "are much less likely to get married, less likely to go to church, less likely to be active in their communities, more likely to watch TV excessively, more likely to be obese."

10. Someone might want to say that the upper tribe is smarter and fitter (or at least thinner) and the lower tribe stupider and fatter than ever.

11. That seems mean. But consider: the new meritocracy is based on education and I.Q. And the gap between whole-food eaters and fast-food eaters might be more pronounced than ever.

12. Certainly the members of the lower tribe seem to lack what it takes to be self-disciplined and productive social animals. Life, for them, seems more "disorganized" or anxious and insecure than ever. That's why they take refuge in the mindless diversion of TV, which is mainly for them.

13. They want to do better than they are; their values are far more bourgeois and traditionalist than their actual behavior.

14. The members of the lower tribe are disoriented and out of control. They're not displaying the healthy social behavior that Darwin attributed to members of our species, and that used to be displayed by all our classes.

15. Particularly telling, perhaps, is the declining role of the churches in socializing and regulating the moral behavior of the lower tribe.

16. Some conservatives say that this tribal divide is caused by the culture of dependency encouraged by our welfare state. I'm not that kind of conservative. I dismiss that explanation as anything approaching the main cause.

17. A Marxist would say that as capitalism develops—as the division of labor is globalized and otherwise perfected in the direction of productivity and efficiency—the gulf between the bourgeoisie who do mental labor and the proletariat who do physical (or at least un-mental, machine-like) labor becomes starker. The lives of the " petty bourgeoisie" (small property owners) are proletarianized. The safety nets—such as unions and churches and neighborhoods and even families—on which people have relied are eroded by the rigors of market competition. As a result, the lower tribe is deprived of the moral contents of life.

18. It goes without saying that the Marxist explanation is incomplete and very much exaggerated. But we can wonder whether it's completely untrue. A real Marxist would say that it's laughable to believe that there could be an enduring government remedy to our increasingly pronounced and demoralizing division into tribes.

19. I could go on and explain why Brooks's recommendation of compulsory national service wouldn't work as such a remedy, but I'm out of space, or at least patience.

Higher Education

Three Simple Suggestions for College Teachers

So the most honest and penetrating book I've read about American higher education in a long time is *Higher Education: How Colleges Are Wasting Our Money and Failing Our Kids—And What We Can Do About It* by Andrew Hacker and Claudia Dreifus. They're not even conservatives!

There's a lot to say. But let me begin with the first two of "three simple suggestions" they give in one place to improve teaching:

1. *Monitor laptops*. Why? "In almost all the classes we attended, at least half the screens displayed games of solitaire, reruns of sporting events, messages to friends." (Here it's easy to add playing with Facebook and other "social networks.") What those screens do is "keep the professor from being the center of attention." And they even stifle the bored student's imagination; surely it's more fun and better for the student just to "daydream."

I would add: laptops actually stifle real note-taking—an indispensable skill for really paying attention and so often for avoiding boredom. And they make questions and so forth less likely, because the student becomes more likely to be absorbed in his or her crutch, the computer.

I don't actually do this, but there's a strong argument for banning laptops from the classroom. At Berry College, thank God, most students don't bring their computers to class. (I could write a separate analysis on "texting" in class. I'm reluctant to do so only because I'm so guilty myself of texting during boring academic meetings—a virtual redundancy—at the expense of my daydreaming skills.) *In general—this is the truth—the less technology in the classroom the better.*

So it's not surprising that the second sensible suggestion is:

2. *Stop PowerPointing.* "If PowerPoint continues, students will spend their entire college careers in darkened rooms where their instructors cannot even see their expressions. Files of slides etch the day's outline in stone; new ideas can't be added, as they can on the chalkboard. If graphs or pictures are needed, they should be photocopied beforehand and handed out as the class starts."

Isn't that said well? I occasionally tell students that there are two beautiful things in this room—the great or at least most instructive text we are studying (the book which is never a textbook) and me. So why would I have you looking at a screen? Again, of course, the platitudes that find their way onto PowerPoint slides take the place of real note taking and provide multiple disincentives for really paying attention. That includes, of course, the instructor paying attention to the students. The compressed PowerPoint message almost always reduces something complicated to something simple, something to be memorized. (PowerPoint probably does have a role in teaching stuff like biology and accounting, but that's not for me to say.)

It's true that I've taken to giving outlines of the reading for the day—handed out, as recommended, as the class starts. There's both a cost and a benefit in doing that; perhaps it's my concession to the spirit of the PowerPoint Age.

How to Avoid Plagiarism
(and the Future of Higher Education and All That)

So the third suggestion of Hacker and Dreifus in *Higher Education* concerns avoiding *plagiarism*. Plagiarism is easier than ever these days—thanks to the abundant resources on the web. And the ingenuity of the plagiarist is typically a step or more ahead of the development of the software designed to thwart him (or her).

First off, don't tell students just to do a paper on something having something to do with the class. That kind of assignment makes it really clear you don't care that much what they do. And it both enables and comes close to excusing the web search for something, anything, to fulfill this vague and unhelpful assignment.

Ideally, our authors add, the paper assignment should be specifically tied to what's done day-to-day in class and incorporate and feature responses to the reading done for the class. That undermines the student's creativity, someone might say! But it actually liberates by focusing the student's imagination on the point or points of the class.

An imaginative and erudite instructor will so obviously structure a unique assignment for his class that a generic paper can't be found to fulfill it. A professor may not be able to prove (beyond a shadow ...) that it's plagiarized, but he (or she) can just give it a bad grade for not fulfilling the assignment.

In classes like political philosophy or constitutional law, research papers, in my opinion, aren't even appropriate assignments. Students are confronting tough texts (great books and opinions) for the first time. They need to read them for the first time in a direct and unmediated way. They need to experience firsthand the liberating greatness and unrivaled insight of Plato, for example, and they shouldn't be diverted from the real thing by (relatively) boring articles on Plato. They need to experience the true pleasure of reading. They ought to be reading to find out what's really true about who they are and what they're supposed to do. They ought to be animated by the thought that the author of this or that book that has stood the test of time can teach them all sorts of stuff they probably couldn't have figured out on their own.

For those (few) students who grow up to be scholars, there'll be time for the secondary stuff later. And those "budding scholars" especially need to be taught to be suspicious of relying on what the fashionable experts (and their abstract and convoluted theories) are saying. Those students who go to law school, of course, will know in advance that you can understand what the courts are doing best by working your way through the actual opinions, which are often much more subtle and fascinating (and screwed up) than what the experts think about them.

It wouldn't be hard for me to prove to you that one of the most important skills a student can pick up in college is how to read complicated books closely and comment accurately and intelligently on what he (or she) has read. That skill will influence in a big way, for example, how well he (or she) will speak and write for his or her whole life—on and off the job.

The widespread acquisition of that skill will also, of course, determine whether the busy and productive lives of today's young people will often be completed by reading "real" books for pleasure.

Also, in my opinion, professors should always assign more than one paper per class. Part of the evaluation of students should be their willingness to knock themselves out to correct their shortcomings.

Finally, if you do assign a research paper (as is sometimes appropriate), students must be required to do the paper in stages, with each stage carefully reviewed and graded. That, for one thing, makes plagiarism almost impossible. For another, it's true that most students need that help to connect research to writing.

All this advice, it goes without saying, is most likely to be followed by professors at relatively small colleges with relatively small classes.

Getting Technology Out of the Classroom?

The high-tech parents from Silicon Valley are now sending their kids to a school—the Waldorf School of the Peninsula—that sells itself as computer-free. Why? Because such technology is a distraction, turning attention away from reading, writing, numbers, talking, and thinking. It's certainly difficult to deny that computers inhibit "human interaction and attention spans." (Matt Richtel, "A Silicon Valley School That Doesn't Compute," *New York Times*, October 22, 2011.) So much more useful by far than iPads and Google are chalkboards, blackboards, bookshelves, No. 2 pencils, workbooks, and wooden desks.

Students, of course, really need to find better purposes for their hands than pounding on keyboards and clicking on various websites. So, they should spend time honing their knitting skills, with the simple but most useful goal of making socks. To synchronize body and brain, nothing's better than reciting verse while playing catch with beanbags.

The argument against this low-tech approach, of course, is that students have been brought up with computers, and they find them riveting. There's no way to hold their attention these days without them. Students lack the virtue or habituation to be approached "really" or personally—as opposed to indirectly or virtually.

But shouldn't school be about facilitating education by fighting against the indulgent excesses of any particular time and place? It's just not true that little kids or even college kids are so corrupted that they can't be approached anywhere but online. It's even true that they know they've been deprived of a lot in a society where everyone spends too much time in front of a screen. They long for better habits than our high-tech world automatically gives them; they long for the discipline that allows them really to learn for themselves with others.

Most students, of course, get computer literate at home. Everyone knows these days that being always online and compulsively Facebooking messes with your brain and makes you a less fit friend for real people. It's great to be attuned to popular culture in all its forms, but those who really understand it—and put it in its proper, ironic perspective—have read lots of real books with the care they deserve. Maybe it's true that much of what we really need to know can be found on Google, but Googling really doesn't let us in on who we are and what we're supposed to do with what we know.

It's since come to my attention that Waldorf Schools are infected by the pseudo-philosophical and sometimes nutty ideas of their founder. I have no idea how infected the Peninsula school is. If you go to the comment thread to the article, you can see the controversy, and you can see more by looking to the article linked in the first comment in the thread below.

I actually don't think anything described in the article on which this post is based is nutty. Much of what I'm saying is summed up by an eloquent comment in the *NYT* thread:

> We should not be so quick to flood grade school education with new technologies, simply because it's available or because we think it could give us an edge in global economic competition. Computers today are easy to learn to use at any age, quickly and effectively. But there are only a few short, critical years of early development in which to teach a child the basics of being human, how to love learning, and the best ways of working with others. There is no app for that, and there never will be.

Legendary Teachers

Another fine feature of *Higher Education* by Hacker and Dreifus is its sensitive and altogether unideological treatment of professors who become legends. Among the legends they mention, one is still alive and teaching (Michael Sandel of Harvard). The others are Allan Bloom (during his heyday at Cornell), Michael Harrington (who taught at New York's Queens College), and Conor Cruise O'Brien (in the 1960s at New York University).

There's one darling of conservatives (Bloom), a socialist (Harrington), and two quirkily somewhere in between (O'Brien and Sandel).

Such teachers aren't "interdisciplinary"; they soar beyond the confines of the disciplines. They have, our authors observe, "enough confidence in their own ideas to say what they believed, not what an academic discipline demanded."

The truth is that "Incredible, passionate, awesome teachers take the whole world as their oyster bed, even if their assertions aren't always backed by formulas or footnotes." These four "awesome teachers," I have to add, wrote as they taught, and each produced books that influenced the educated public, the world of ideas beyond the university. So they were viewed with considerable suspicion by the world of scholars. It's true that legendary teachers publish, but not primarily to contribute to the scholarly literature of some discipline.

"Needless to say," our authors go on, "there's a risk of ego trips, as well as misusing classrooms for a rostrum." I've had just enough firsthand experience with Sandel and Bloom to be certain that neither seemed to be plagued self-doubt or self-esteem "issues." Not only do such legendary teachers believe they have something of great significance to say, but what they have to say can transform the lives of students by helping them see who they are and what they're supposed to do. Such teachers, it goes without saying, are always enemies of relativism or proceduralism or reducing education to some measurable technique.

Legendary teachers are always in some sense *evangelical*, about spreading the good, truthful news. Bloom was an evangelist for *philosophy*, Harrington *socialism*, and Sandel *justice*. Legendary teachers are always *realists* (there's a real world out there we can know) and in some sense *moralists*.

The wonderfully accessible yet profoundly erudite books of Bloom and Harrington had a great influence on me.

I've written a fair amount on Bloom, but nothing on Harrington. But I was very moved by the honesty of Harrington's unjustly forgotten *The Politics at God's Funeral* (1983). Harrington, once a serious Catholic, wrote about his version of Pascal's wager. The Christian Pascal observed that we're miserable in the absence of God, and so we have nothing to lose by betting on the possibility that he really exists. But, Harrington claims, God is dead; belief is no longer possible these days. So his wager is that socialism can do in this world what God promised in the next, overcome our loneliness and alienation through the establishment of a completely satisfying egalitarian community. For Harrington, it's socialism or nothing—or at least being stuck with being lonely, alienated, and otherwise miserable.

As Marx first said in "On the Jewish Question," daily life experienced under capitalism provides plenty of support for Pascal's claim that we're pointless accidents—whimsical, weightless productivity machines—in an indifferent universe. And Tocqueville (in the best book on democracy and the best book on America) said that the most truthful democratic individual experience is existing mysteriously (and strangely and wonderfully) for a moment between two abysses.

Let's face it, there are plenty of good reasons—including, for example, the fall of communism and the impending implosion of our minimalist welfare state—why hardly anyone really believes in socialism in that evangelical a way anymore. But only an "awesome teacher" could have done so well in giving the most compelling case for socialism.

I don't have the time or space to deal adequately with Bloom's *The Closing of the American Mind* (1987) now. It's a book about almost everything and almost without footnotes. His message is that Pascal was wrong; we're not necessarily miserable without God. In a time when all serious morality has been discredited, relativism reigns supreme, and God or real belief is about dead, the alternatives are philosophy or nothing. And Bloom was as evangelical for philosophy as a way of life as Harrington was for socialism.

For me, thanks, in part, to thinking through the brilliant evangelical books of Harrington and Bloom, the bottom line is neither philosophy nor socialism. But I'm just as moved (I hope) as these awesome teachers by the challenge of Pascal.

My own beginning is that real belief—and the personal reasons for it—are far from dead. So Bloom and Harrington exaggerate the extent to which life in our world has been reduced to nothing, and people continue to live well not under socialism and without being primarily philosophers. But libertarians and other techno-enthusiasts beware: Good exaggerations are always instructive precisely because they contain much truth.

More Thoughts on Liberal Education Today

It's no secret that most of our colleges that give lip service to "liberal education" don't deliver it, and what they do teach exaggerates—not moderates—the undignified confusion of our time. They certainly don't give students the impression that there's much, if any, moral or humanistic "content" (versus "method"—such as critical thinking or analytical reasoning) that they need to know. And so they don't give students the impression that their education is about who they are and what they're supposed to do.

Not only that, but the permissive and indulgent atmosphere of our colleges extends adolescence far more than it serves as a bridge between being a playful child and assuming the serious responsibilities of an adult.

So, Charles Murray, in *Real Education*, seems on strong ground when he argues that we should declare the brick-and-mortar college obsolete for most purposes it now claims to serve. The students who go to college in pursuit of a technical career—the overwhelming majority of them—might be better served by a more focused and condensed education that would take much less than four years and wouldn't require "the residential experience."

Maybe we should abandon the pretense that the B.A. is the admission ticket to the world of most white-collar work. Students might actually be less confused if they were free from the fantasy that anything about college can give them a standard of freedom and dignity higher than productivity. Murray concludes that "liberal education"—including real precision in the use of language and real knowledge of what's required for moral choices—might be preserved for those most likely to assume positions of political, intellectual, and economic leadership in our country.

This sort of conclusion is unsatisfying if we believe that every human being has a soul worthy of being educated. Everyone, of course, has to live well with the responsibilities given to begetting and belonging beings open to the truth, including the personal truths of love and death.

Everyone should be productive, of course, but everyone is also more than a productive or entrepreneurial being.

Liberal Education and Entrepreneurship

I have to admit I've been warming up a bit to the out-there techno-optimism of Ray Kurzweil displayed so prominently on BIG THINK. He (like lots of people) has been called "The New Nostradamus," and I have to admit that I take some of his predictions—like literal immortality for particular persons in this world—about as seriously as I take those of the original Nostradamus.

But it is good to know about Kurzweil's somewhat plausible confidence that solar energy, aided by nanotechnology, may soon meet all our energy needs. That means that our concerns over "peak oil" and nuclear meltdowns might only be a passing phase in the progressive development of technology.

Kurzweil, I think, goes too far or displays his ignorance in calling techno-entrepreneurship liberal education.

It might be liberal education in this ironic sense; the only real freedom is freedom from nature. And the only real knowledge is power. So those who liberate us from nature through the generation of power are the most free and rational among us.

That might mean that Bill Gates and Mark Zuckerberg are the most liberally educated Americans. That fact—if it is a fact—should chasten professors of philosophy and the humanities and such who mistakenly dismiss them as pretty clueless nerds. Bill and Mark, our professor of liberal education claim, don't know anything about love and death or the beautiful and the good or true pride and genuine humility, etc. *The Social Network* should at least cause us to wonder about Bill and Mark's wisdom and virtue—and the wisdom and virtue of our techno-meritocrats in general these days.

Yes, I know, Bill is—in quantitative terms—the most generous man in the world. He would be the richest man in the world if he didn't give a huge amount of money away to his good causes. But trying to get by on $50 billion or so might not quite be heroic virtue. Bill is a good man, but he's no Socrates or Maimonides or St. Paul or Pascal or Shakespeare or Mozart or Mother Teresa, etc.

Yet, in Kurzweil's telling, the great techno-entrepreneurs should be our "role models" or exemplars of human excellence. And so there's no point in reading Socrates or Shakespeare closely and openly in the traditional spirit of liberal education, in order to learn who we are and what we're supposed to do as particular persons. Reading the great books and listening to Mozart are, in Kurzweil's world, nothing more than hobbies. The immortals of the future are going to need lots of hobbies.

Kurzweil says, of course, that we won't have to live well with death for long. All we have to do is stay alive long enough to be around when techno-immortality kicks in.

Love has to change. It'll be detached from birth, death, and embodiment in general. It'll become either somehow more intimate—pure consciousness hooking up with pure consciousness—or fade away. Either way, I'd rather be a live machine or conscious software than a dead Romeo!

Here's something I actually find challenging about Kurzweil's view of liberal education: if he's right, we don't need brick-and-mortar colleges any more. They only stick irresponsible kids in a kind of delayed adolescence earning meaningless credits and memorizing easily-googled information. Entrepreneurs—like Bill and Mark—don't care about degrees and often don't bother to get them.

There's something to admire about that anti-credentialist spiritedness. It used be that great poets and writers and such didn't aim to graduate from college. Now they get Ph.D.s in creative writing. There's no study that shows that novels and poems have gotten any better as a result.

And I agree professors have to make a better case that liberal education is about reading perennially relevant great books—written by minds and hearts even greater than Ray's. They have to explain patiently to Ray that self-knowledge—or being a truthful person—is about a lot more than information and power.

Great Books??

1. Let me highlight an argument against "Great Books" education that I read and heard lately in various places by the eminent Dr. Pat Deneen of Georgetown University and the *Front Porch Republic*.

2. First off, that education is relativistic. The student learns that certain books are great, but they disagree on God, morality, science, and all that. So the student has to judge which kind of greatness is most true and the best guidance on how to live. But said student also learns that he or she is much dumber than Plato, Thomas Aquinas, and Nietzsche. So how to judge? What right does insignificant me have to judge? This promiscuous appreciation for greatness, to say the least, is not an obvious cure for the moral impotence and confusion of our time.

3. This relativism is especially a problem, Patrick adds, in the best seller by Allan Bloom. There we get the strong impression that great thought has emptied the contents out of moral life—beginning with religion and the family. And because the Enlightenment isn't really touched by allegedly deep criticism by Maritain (and other neo-Thomists), T. S. Eliot, and so forth, there's no going back. So these days the choice is between being a philosopher and being nothing, but most people can't be philosophers. And philosophy is nothing more than living constantly in light of the finality of death and has no moral content beyond what's good for philosophy. Not only that, finally all the great books—the ones by the philosophers—agree on this philosophy or nothing thing. (Obviously I've given my own spin on this to get your attention.) Patrick goes too far in calling Bloom a relativist; he has a standard. But how helpful is it, really, in deciding how to live these days?

4. A lot of Great Books education is combined with a kind of uncritical deference to the philosophic wisdom of the American founders. But from the point of view of a professor at a Catholic university (Patrick's), don't we have to be judgmental about the efforts of, say, Machiavelli, Hobbes, and Locke not only to "tame" but to destroy Christianity (see the symposium on Strauss referenced below)? And don't we have to explain (employing the truth about who we are) why they failed, contrary to their intentions or at least hopes (say Patrick and I)? So don't we have to criticize our "political Fathers" for being so Lockean (says Patrick especially)? We can't quote Jefferson on "monkish ignorance and superstition" as if he were simply right or great or whatever! I would add, following the

example of the best American Catholic "public philosophers" John Courtney Murray and Orestes Brownson, that we should, as loyal Americans (we Porchers and REM fans are all about standing for the place where we live), actually explain why our Fathers built better than they knew—which means criticizing their thinking and affirming (most of) their practice with a theory that at least wasn't completely their own.

5. Patrick also says that a Catholic university should give "the pride of place" in teaching Augustine and Thomas Aquinas. Not only are they "our team," so to speak, but they teach much truth that can't be found in other great books. That means, it seems to me, rejecting the ancient vs. modern distinction as the key to understanding the West and even reason vs. revelation the way it is understood by many Great Books teachers.

6. We American Catholics or just we American realistic postmodern conservatives don't necessarily know that much about Maritain or Eliot, but we do know that our American Thomists Walker Percy and Flannery O'Connor know stuff that Jefferson certainly didn't.

7. Still, the polemic for teaching "Great Books" remains very valuable in pushing the teaching of "real books," as opposed to technical books, textbooks, or trendy books.

Some Introductory Thoughts on Great Books and America

1. The study of great books is usually contrasted with the use of text-books and other technical books. It is contrasted, in other words, with study of the studies that show us what we most need to know as productive beings in a free, middle-class society.

2. It's inevitable in our society that most people will think they don't have time to read such books. They'll even condemn, with some good sense, reading such books—like Plato's *Republic* or Shakespeare's *Tempest*—as a waste of valuable time. Courses that feature the serious study of such texts continue to become more rare.

3. When busy and productive people read, they often want to be entertained, and that means that books should read like movies. That's why they love John Grisham—whose charm disappears with careful or repeated reading. Or they want books to provide practical advice in a user-friendly form. The bestsellers are often self-help books—about achieving serenity or sexual satisfaction or a romantic connection now or how to avoid an audit or obesity.

4. Lots of people today want to read about celebrities, who are more psychologically accessible than great heroes. Celebrities reassuringly display the vices most of us might have if we had the money. (Good recent examples are Tiger Woods and Charlie Sheen. Admittedly, the cases of Elvis and Michael Jackson, bizarre people with singular talent, are more complicated.)

5. These observations may seem condescending (because they are). But they're not really critical. If you really are performing responsibly the duties given to you by middle-class life, there isn't that much time to read. (I, for example, have been told, with justice and on behalf of charity, that I think I have more time to read than I really do.)

6. Even the author of the greatest book written on America, Alexis de Tocqueville, didn't think most Americans should read the great books written by the Greeks and Romans. He even said there's no higher education in America, because there's no class of people freed from work for leisurely contemplation.

7. Tocqueville observed that democratic middle-class people aren't proud enough to believe that they're essentially more than beings who

work. So they don't regard philosophy, science, poetry, and theology as intrinsically pleasurable and choice-worthy pursuits. Science, for example, they think of as useful for making work easier and more productive and for making lives more secure and comfortable.

8. In an obvious way, Tocqueville seems to have been wrong to say there could be no higher education in a middle-class democracy. In *The Chronicle of Higher Education*, you can read that more young people than ever are in colleges and universities—the education we call higher—today.

9. But you can also read that a higher percentage than ever of students have basically technical majors—from pre-med to exercise science to marketing or public relations to turf management—than ever. They're reading boring but effective textbooks full of useful information reinforced in the class's PowerPoint presentations, doing very practical group projects (often in labs), and being challenged by detail-driven objective tests.

10. Much of what's left of the humanities seems based—in a postmodern way—on the allegedly candid self-awareness that what they teach is merely an assertion of personal identity.

11. Quantitative assessment dominates what's called higher education more than before. It's power or productivity that can be measured, and the people who come up with the measurements aren't poets or even rocket scientists (most often they're professors of education).

12. What about pure science or theoretical physics (as opposed to merely experimental physics)? I was reminded of the deep significance of that distinction from watching *The Big Bang Theory*. America has the cutting-edge programs! That's true, but there's a real dearth of actual American students benefiting from those programs. For a real multicultural experience, walk around some physics building at MIT.

Racism, Sexism, Classism and the Great Books

From my postmodern view, maybe *the chief purpose of higher education is to counter the dominant view of who we are—which is partly true and partly degrading prejudice—of our time.* Our tendency is to view human beings as free and productive—as autonomous individuals with interests. This means that we don't regard anyone as less than a being with interests—or as existing merely to serve others. We all have a right to look out for our own interests, and so to be treated as individuals and not merely as part of some larger whole. That means that it's not really news to any of us that racism, sexism, classism, and so forth are wrong, and we usually think that it's an affront to our dignity to be thought of as merely parents or citizens or creatures. We tend to be all about autonomy and self-definition.

But we're weak—often very weak—in thinking of people as more than productive or self-interested beings. We tend to think that human distinctions that can't be measured quantitatively aren't real, just as we tend to think that a true meritocracy is based on productivity. We tend to think that because the great authors of the great books of the past must have been racists, sexists, and classists and, of course, not as technologically advanced or as productive as we are, they have nothing real to say to us. So, our prejudice is to study them critically—or condescendingly—*as remnants of discredited prejudices.*

We also tend to think that words are weapons. They don't reflect reality but are ways of technically imposing ourselves on others and on nature. So, we too readily believe that even the greatest books of the past were really instruments of *domination.* Plato's *Dialogues* were really in support of Greek aristocracy and patriarchy, and *The Federalist* defends political institutions that would protect elitist property rights. When we read even a "great book," we ask, too complacently, whose interest was it written to serve? We are so certain about our superiority when it comes to productivity and justice, that we tend to think we know, before reading a word of Shakespeare, that there's nothing real to be learned from him about who we are.

Our prejudice, to be blunt, is that we believe that there's nothing real—nothing to be known—about love and death. We've just about forgotten that a rational being—a being with *logos*—is necessarily also an *erotic* being. We've forgotten how to *think* about whole human persons; we've forgotten how to think about the purposes or point of being human.

Whatever their shortcomings, the best authors of the past—and even, of course, the best authors of our time—aren't in the thrall of our prejudice that we're merely productive beings. They think love and virtue are real, and that we're stuck with both as self-conscious mortals in this world. They know a lot about us that we usually and quite wrongly think we don't need to know to live well.

Higher education is about the coming to terms with the full truth about who we are. And surely our deepest pedagogical prejudice, the one that keeps us from coming to terms with the true greatness and misery of being human, is that education can be reduced to technology or what's required for productivity and a polemic against residual racism, classicism, and sexism. For us, genuine higher education should begin with the thought that rational and erotic beings are more than productive and autonomous individuals, and the best books for us are those that show us most deeply and eloquently why that is.

Postmodernism *rightly understood* opens us to what's true for us in "premodern" thought, without dismissing what's both true and new in our great modern accomplishments.

Irresponsible Professors and Lonely Students

Students, professors used to think, needed both guidance and those models of human greatness that could help them discover who they are and what to do. One irony, of course, was that when professors offered such guidance, students didn't particularly need or want it. They often came to college with characters already formed, already habituated to the practice of moral virtue. In those days, the real experience of professors was often a kind of blithe irresponsibility that came with moral impotence. *They could say what they wanted without the fear of doing all that much harm*—or all that much good. In many cases, students thought, with good reason, that their professors were basically reinforcing what they already knew from more firsthand—or not merely bookish—communal experience.

Today's students, we can say, are often stuck with being searchers. They are—or might be—particularly open to the traditional claim of liberal education: we can find the answers to the questions concerning human identity through reading and talking about those books that take those questions seriously. By default, we might say, college is stuck with the job that religion—the Bible and churches—used to do.

They embrace, by default, the most radical versions of the modern idea of freedom—called *postmodern relativism* on the left and *libertarian non-preferentialism* on the right. Students, more than ever, are free to choose in all areas of their lives in college. They have almost *limitless freedom* in choosing what to study, and hardly anything moral or intellectual is required of them. What few requirements that are imposed on students are so broad and flexible as to point them in no particular direction at all. In the name of freedom and diversity, little goes on in college that gives them any guidance concerning who they are or what to choose.

Students, in fact, are often taught that what they do is both completely voluntary and utterly meaningless. They're even taught that their freedom to choose is close to unlimited and completely unreal. The human person has no real existence in the wholly impersonal nature described by our scientists. Students learn from neuroscientists that "the soul" must always be put in quotes, because it doesn't correspond to any material or chemical reality. From biologists they learn that what particular individuals or members of species do is insignificant or makes no real difference to the flourishing of our species, and the flourishing of species is the point of all natural reality.

Sometimes our students learn that, although the self or the "I" is really an illusion, it's one we can't live without. According to the scientist Daniel Dennett, belief in human dignity is indispensable for the flourishing of members of our species. So, we should embrace that belief in view of its beneficial social consequences.

But it's still the case that there's nothing real backing up any confidence we might have in personal importance, just as there's nothing real backing up our experiences of love or free will. We need to call true, our philosopher Richard Rorty explained, those illusions that make us feel free, comfortable, and secure. One way to do that, Rorty adds, is not to believe the scientists when they compare our personal experiences to some objective truth. By saying that "truth" must always appear in quotes, we avoid disparaging what we choose to believe by comparing it with some real standard.

Despite the best efforts of talented professors, students never really believe that the "I"—the reality of the person each of them sees in the mirror—doesn't exist. They can't really reduce what they think they know about themselves as particular beings with names and personal destinies to merely useful illusions.

So, the main effect of higher education today is to show each of them how really alone in a hostile environment he or she is.

There's no better way to convince someone of his or her utter isolation than to tell him that you—meaning your personal experiences—don't really exist, although it's okay if you pretend that you do. That's why from the point of view of profound outside observers—such as the great anticommunist dissident Aleksandr Solzhenitsyn—it's easy to hear the *howl of existentialism* just beneath the surface of our happy-talk pragmatism. Our students are so lonely, in part, because they don't think they have the words—but only howls of desperation—to describe truthfully who they are to others.

Despite all the therapeutic efforts to build inclusive and diverse communities, our colleges are often very lonely places. Because our highest educators believe they have no authority to rule the young, they've allowed our campuses, in many respects, to revert to a kind of state of nature, something like the war of all against all for the scarce resource of personal significance or dignity. There, as Tom Wolfe has described, the *strong and the beautiful* "hook up," the *weak and the ugly* are condemned to "sexile," *the clever* use their cunning to master the fraudulent arts of networking and teambuilding or to become trendy, marketable intellectuals, and *the timid and decent* are shown the vanity of their slavish moral illusions.

Administrators, meanwhile, look on with politically correct nonjudgmental cluelessness.

Students are stuck with using all means available to establish who they are through their success in manipulating and dominating others. They're also stuck, of course, with the challenge of distinguishing between how they "dress for success" and who they really are, between the self they construct to impress themselves upon others and the self that does all that constructing. So, no matter whether a student succeeds in establishing his or her importance in the eyes of others, he or she is stuck in some ways with being more lonely and undignified than ever.

All in all, it seems that today's student gets to college *more free* (in the sense of lost or empty or disoriented) than ever before, and the effect of college, in most cases, is to make him or her more lost still. It's still not true that the graduate ends up believing that freedom really is having nothing left to lose, because the personal self or soul and its longings is more exposed than ever.

The End of Tenure?
(Or the Collapse of Our Safety Nets—Part 1)

A questionable (but honest and penetrating) part of *Higher Education?* by Hacker and Dreifus is its assertive case against *tenure* for professors.

I have little doubt that tenure is toast. Its disappearance will be chronicled as part of the movement from *defined benefits* to *defined contribution* that's at the heart of the current transformation of our various safety nets. *Risk*, as I've said before, is being transferred from employer to employee. The argument for tenure has always been a combination of academic freedom and job security. Increasingly, we believe that claim for freedom is really an excuse for self-indulgence, and that sort of security is incompatible with the requirements of the increasingly competitive or productivity-oriented global marketplace.

The academic world is hardly exempt from the general pressure to become a meritocracy based on productivity. Productivity, of course, has to be measured. And so, professors, like everyone else, have to be held accountable. Tenured professors, the thought is, can't be held accountable. They can do what they please and not be fired.

As literally a grandfather, the end of tenure—like the transformation of Medicare into a defined contribution plan—won't affect me. In both cases, my safety nets are grandfathered in. The taxpayers will be stuck with my old-fashioned Medicare payments, and if my college ends tenure, it very likely won't do it for me. A combination of self-interest and facing up to our inevitable future probably should cause me to yawn when thinking about tenure's end.

Still, it's not clear to me that doing away with tenure will actually be an effective response to the authors' fairly just indictment of higher education in America today. "Our principal premise," they write, "is that higher education has lost track of its original and enduring purpose: to challenge the minds and imaginations of this nation's young people. ... Our campuses have become preserves for adult careers ... professors, administrators, and yes, presidents have used ostensible centers of learning to pursue their own interests and enjoyments."

I certainly agree that at too many colleges and universities undergraduate education has been sacrificed to pointless and idiosyncratic "research." And the research agendas of vain and mediocre scholars have too often driven what's taught even in introductory courses. Faculty members are too often evaluated by the quantity of publications, and the result is the silly and shameful proliferation of specialized journals nobody reads. Our authors challenge the dogma that research enhances teaching. In most cases, they show, the research imperative is at the expense of the attention and direction students most need. Both faculty members and administrators have used the support of research—and other questionable institutional amenities—to enjoy themselves at the expense of what should be the core educational mission.

Undergraduate teaching—teaching students what they really need to flourish as educated persons—needs to become the priority again. Why would doing away with tenure serve that goal?

The faculty member who devotes him or herself to teaching at an "unelite" place with a large teaching load is already sort of a sucker. Our authors admit that the market value of that faculty member declines over time. Such genuinely exemplary teaching is about impossible to measure. (Student evaluations don't really measure much.) The result, our authors admit, is that such dedicated senior professors are pretty much stuck where they are. They are, from a market view, overpaid, even as they also suffer from "salary compression." What they do well other places don't really prize. Those who want to move on have to publish—even at the expense of teaching.

But, you might say, at least these suckers can say they're appreciated where they are. Sometimes they are, of course. But we have to add that they're evaluated by administrators who so often are clueless about what good teaching is and by careerists quite willing to take shortcuts to pad their resumes to get ahead. (Our authors are really tough on the bloated salaries and general shortsightedness of our administrators.) They want a program they can sell, and that approach, to say the least, might not include a proper appreciation for a professor of philosophy known for his or her "tough love" and small but exciting and elevating classes.

It might well be true that doing away with tenure will give some lazy teachers the incentive to do better by causing them not to think of their jobs as entitlements. It would certainly inspire some senior professors to do more research. But my final thought is it would hardly support the freedom and dignity of the many devoted teachers we still have, despite it all.

More Wisdom from the Left? (This Time on Tenure)

Let's turn to an exaggerated account of the slide of our professors into the proletariat given by *The Nation*, our leading journal on the left. Let me repeat what I've said before, good exaggerations contain a lot of truth. And we conservatives often ally with leftists in a limited and selective way in our criticisms of what are sometimes called "the excesses of capitalism."

One way among many we conservatives differ from leftists is that we regard Marx's *Communist Manifesto* as an over-the-top and fairly misleading exaggeration of the bourgeois tendency to commodify everything people think and do. We certainly don't think the dominant contemporary tendency is to reduce the great mass of people—the proletariat—to the utter misery of being nothing more than cogs in a machine earning nothing more than subsistence wages. We conservatives remember what leftists often forget: Marx even knew he was exaggerating. He was trying to arouse the hate that would foment revolution.

But we conservatives also know, from writers such as Tocqueville, that modern democracy does have the middle-class tendency to erode all "values" that don't serve productivity (or technology). As Marx says, our bourgeois tendency really is to take the "halos" off beautiful and noble ways of life and evaluate them according to their cash value. It's in our time that women—in the name of their freedom and dignity—have become (and, a Marxist would say, are more or less stuck with becoming) "wage slaves" just like men. It's also in our time that professorial "autonomy"—based on the view that the truth and all that are intrinsically worthwhile—is eroding in the direction of measurable productivity. There's no denying that fewer and fewer students are majoring in "the liberal arts," and that the overwhelming majority of them are choosing technical, marketable majors.

Let me offer you one particularly intriguing (because far from completely true or completely false) taste from our leftist (Marxist) author:

> What we have seen instead over the past forty years, in addition to the raising of a reserve army of contingent labor, is a kind of administrative elephantiasis, an explosion in the number of people working at colleges and universities who aren't faculty, full-time or part-time, of any kind. From 1976 to 2001, the number of non-faculty professionals ballooned nearly 240 percent, growing more than three times as fast as

the faculty. Coaching staffs and salaries have grown without limit; athletic departments are virtually separate colleges within universities now, competing (successfully) with academics. The size of presidential salaries—more than $1 million in several dozen cases—has become notorious. Nor is it only the presidents; the next six most highly paid administrative officers at Yale averaged over $430,000 in 2007. As Gaye Tuchman explains in *Wannabe U* (2009), a case study in the sorrows of academic corporatization, deans, provosts and presidents are no longer professors who cycle through administrative duties and then return to teaching and research. Instead, they have become a separate stratum of managerial careerists, jumping from job to job and organization to organization like any other executive: isolated from the faculty and its values, loyal to an ethos of short-term expansion, and trading in the business blather of measurability, revenue streams, mission statements and the like. They do not have the long-term health of their institutions at heart. They want to pump up the stock price (i.e., *U.S. News and World Report* ranking) and move on to the next fat post.

There are two big points here about the reduction of the professors to members of the proletariat. First, more and more college teaching is being done by "contingents," by temporary faculty members being paid by the course. They are, in fact, being hired to generate credit hours (which have a price) and nothing more. In a sense, they contribute no "mental labor" at all to the running of the university; and so, given the oversupply of available bodies in their line of work, they are, in a way, being overpaid at subsistence. In fact they often get less than subsistence. Second, the running of universities is being done less by professors and more by bloated and highly paid cadres of bourgeois administrators. These "managerial careerists" are animated by "the business blather of measurability, revenue streams" and the nonacademic amenities that they believe are the key to attracting students (paying customers).

Professors often say that the reason college costs so much these days is the bloated administration. Administrators tend to say it's the underworked, overpaid, and endlessly vain tenured professors. There's doubtless some truth in both directions. But we conservative and leftist professors— serving our class interest—should defend tenure. In the best cases, our class interest is in the college or university that refuses to reduce education to productivity and keeps the halos, so to speak, on truth and beauty and all that.

I will discuss the leftist author's argument for tenure later. But let me close by reminding you that the above is an exaggeration; there are plenty of colleges and universities where these bourgeois tendencies aren't particularly strong. At those places the majority of credit hours tend to be generated by tenured professors.

Getting Back to Single-Sex Dorms

The movement for a generation or so has been toward a lifestyle of increasing freedom on our college campuses. That means "no rules" (beyond those connected with health and safety—no smoking and free condoms) and single-sex dorms. It also means dorms full of reckless drinking and "hooking up." (That is—hooking up for the strong and "sexile" for the weak. The latter can't go back to their rooms until given permission by their more attractive and successful roommates.)

Meanwhile, classes are easier than ever and students are studying less. Classes are also probably more boring—with the PowerPoint and all. Not to mention what I've said before—too many classes are taught by "contingents" or part-timers, and the incentives for faculty excellence are increasingly weighted toward research and away from teaching (even at four-year colleges). One fact I recently read is that the average American kid in college right now has a B plus average while studying no more than a couple of hours a day. I could go on to show it's amazing how few real books (versus textbooks) most college students read these days, often fewer than they read at home.

Another problem plaguing student life at liberal arts colleges is the widening gender gap, with over sixty percent of students now women. That fact artificially inflates the self-esteem of already vain and lazy men. It subjects women to a "competitive marketplace" far more rigorous than the natural selection described by Darwin. Everyone knows, of course, that women of college age are significantly more mature than men. They're much more about planning for marriage or at least enduring relationships. But the scarce resources of men-children aren't properly incentivized to attend to or even inquire about the grown-up woman's hopes and needs. So women, it seems to me, are much more stuck with hooking up at college than they would put up with in real life.

On balance, we can say that college is both really expensive and screws kids up. It doesn't prepare them at all for real-world responsibilities. And so, it would be easy to conclude that the brick-and-mortar college has outlived its usefulness unless it reforms—or gets over the illusions of liberation of the Sixties. Back to single-sex dorms is certainly a good start.

The college at which I teach—Berry College—is an exception to the general rule.

Conservative Education—Part 1

I'm spending the week speaking at and otherwise participating in the national honors program of the Intercollegiate Studies Institute (ISI)—a conservative educational foundation.

The students are spectacularly impressive. They come from many of our elite institutions, but also from various small colleges. With one exception, they're all undergraduates or new graduates. That exception is a young woman who was homeschooled, entered a state college at age fourteen, graduated at seventeen, and now is well on her way to a Ph.D. in a leading program in political theory at twenty. She was very disappointed with college because it was all about reading boring textbooks and too many students bragging about just getting by. She's now in love with really hard real books—by authors such as Plato, Aristotle, Tocqueville, St. Augustine, Pascal, Leo Strauss, Eric Voegelin, and many others—and she now has the time to indulge the heck out of her real passion while she is still very young.

Educational theorists will note that I didn't detect any hint of possible deficient socialization in her case. I did notice excellent manners, amazing self-confidence, a real love and respect for her family and friends, and a very rare ability to talk with people of all ages as her "peers." That means, of course, that she's singularly free from "peer pressure."

The first thing anyone would notice at this program is the very wide diversity of opinion among the professors present. It's even very hard to say why they all could be called conservative.

Perhaps none them are libertarian, though. One very erudite speaker quoted Marx's *Communist Manifesto* with approval on capitalism devaluing all forms of human excellence untethered to productivity, and he praised the achievement of Germany's Christian Democratic form of social democracy as a genuine and more humane alternative to capitalism and socialism. (I'm not saying I agree in either case. Marx knew he was exaggerating to foment revolution, and certainly it's clear enough that Christian democratic parties of Europe don't have much of future.)

Another very prominent professor here said that conservatives these days should oppose the emptiness of globalized or radically displaced techno-progressivism. He's an admirer of the virtue defended by the agrarian writer Wendell Berry. He's all about returning real power back to localities and even restoring the relative autonomy of local economies. It's also clear that he tends to vote Democratic (as does Berry). There's a strong faction of professors and students with him, and they will have none of the libertarianism that people so often mistakenly confuse with conservatism. They don't even think highly of our founding philosopher, John Locke, and they argue that the Anti-Federalists were often right about the danger of America becoming more of an empire devoted to selfish individualism than a republic.

At the same time, there are professors and students around who are big on defending the Lockean understanding of liberty that is behind our Declaration of Independence and Constitution. They oppose the kind of Progressivism that leads to big government, and they are at least fellow travelers with the Tea Partiers. But even these guys aren't libertarians; they also emphasize respect for the authority of our Founders and the indispensability of serious religion, devoted citizens, and strong families for sustaining our liberty. But they don't think we can or should go back to Berry's farm.

Conservative Education—Part 2: Music

Today at the ISI honors program we were graced with a beautiful presentation on liberty in American poetry and song. The classy and distinguished presenter asked the students to update what he said with examples from twenty-first-century popular songs.

Needless to say, there was a lot of attention paid to Lady Gaga. She's all about freedom defined as acceptance of being "born this way," as not being ashamed of and taking a certain pride in being what you're meant to be (given that God doesn't make mistakes). This might well be an encouraging message for gay kids. But that idea of freedom applied generally is really an affirmation of being determined. It lacks the dimension of self-improvement or striving toward perfection or overcoming natural challenges. There's a character in the film *The Last Days of Disco* who muses, "To thine own self be true? What if thine own self isn't so good?"

Another student called our attention to the indie band Arcade Fire's "The Suburbs," which he described as a somewhat positive exploration of the unprecedented freedom enjoyed by kids who grow up in the suburbs (far from completely positive, of course). I should know more about this very smart group than I do, given its victory over Lady Antebellum and Lady Gaga for the Grammy.

An older faculty member (not quite as old as *me*) reminded the young folks of the superior profundity of the music of the late 60s and early 70s. His example was Kris Kristofferson's "Me and Bobby McGee"—the version sung by Kristofferson himself and not the distortion by Janis Joplin. According to this astute professor, KK gets us in touch with the depths of modern nihilism, while finally rejecting it.

The point was made in passing several times during the session that if we want to hear about freedom as a virtue these days, we have to listen to *country music*. An audacious student got up to prove that point by singing parts of the Zac Brown hit that celebrates our freedom to eat chicken-fried steak on a Friday night (a freedom I myself have never exercised). More than half of these sophisticated (yet conservative) kids knew the lyrics and sang along. This seemingly simple song actually is about gratitude for the seemingly simple things in life—like the look in a baby's eyes that give us peace of mind that money can't buy. Who can deny that if we want to find worthy celebrations of American freedom these days, we have to look to the country?

Conservative Education—Part 3:
O Canada! O Canada!

Last night at the ISI honors program (after a long and luxurious dinner at a great restaurant), we actually had a speaker from *Canada*—a brilliant professor of political philosophy (who, with a beautiful, booming voice, is also an opera star). His topic was the view of America from Canada. (As usual, this post contains my reflections on this most instructive presentation—not so much a presentation of what the speaker actually said.)

Canada, from the nation's beginning, embodies conservative criticism of America's revolutionary tradition. The Tories who opposed our revolutionaries and remained loyal to the British government (the Loyalists) often went to Canada. And Canada's founding—authorized by an act of Parliament—was sort of the antithesis of a revolution.

The Canadians have traditionally been a lot less about individual liberty and more about humane order and good government. So, the stock Canadian criticism of America is that we're selfish, imperialist, chaotic individualists who aren't attentive to the details that make civilized social life possible. In Canada, the Royal Canadian Mounted Police went West before many settlers, ensuring that law and order would show up before the people who needed to be governed. Our West, of course, was pretty wild and lawless there for a while, which was good for John Ford and John Wayne. These days we can see that this line of Canadian criticism retains much truth; all we have to do is compare Toronto with any major American city.

George Grant, probably the best Canadian thinker, published the deservedly highly influential *Lament for a Nation* (1965). Grant lamented the disappearance of Canadian distinctiveness; his nation had become more or less Americanized. To be American, Grant thought, was to be technological, to be all about the mastery of nature for human convenience and the unlimited satisfaction of our material desires. All that was left to remind us of the Canadian and, more generally, pre-technological past were "intimations of deprival." We long for what we're missing, but we've lost even the words to express what's true about the goodness of human life and the goodness of being.

Grant's understanding of America as the most modern part of the modern world owed a lot to the German philosopher Martin Heidegger. Heidegger's polemic against reducing knowing and being to technology has had a huge influence on both the American left and right. Grant was also indebted to the great philosopher Leo Strauss, who once called the fundamental modern or technological impulse "the joyless quest for joy" (aka the pursuit of happiness). And Grant, finally, was indebted to the Russian/French thinker Alexandre Kojève, who wrote that the end of History is here and all that's left to do is work out the details of the universal and homogeneous (and so dehumanizing) state that's enveloping us all.

This kind of Canadian line of criticism of America has sometimes been called *Red* and *Tory*. (I realize I'm using *Red Tory* loosely—and the phrase has a somewhat different meaning in Canadian politics today.) It's *Red* because it's based on the thought that a decent nation has strong political institutions, and that among these is the national provision of medical care for everyone. The Canadian view is that the extreme economic inequality and the extreme insecurity of the unfortunate in our country are both most uncivilized.

But this criticism is also *Tory* because a decent society depends on strong traditions—encouraged by government—that support the family, churches, and the perpetuation of particular communities, including some social hierarchy. The *Red Tory* can't be confused with a Communist or even an American socialist.

The American *Libertarian*, we can say, is the opposite of *Red Tory* so understood. That means, of course, the Canadian conservative as described by Grant is not much like most American conservatives. An American *Red Tory* would be a kind of mixture of liberal/progressive on the economic front and a tough cultural conservative. It would be really hard to be such an American conservative—given that we fought so hard at different times in our history to defeat both the *Reds* and the *Tories*.

Canada has changed a lot since 1965, but I'll pass over that fact for now.

I'll conclude, instead, by telling you that our Canadian speaker concluded by emphasizing that Grant was wrong or at least a big-time exaggerator about America. It's far from the case that everything has been subordinated to technology here. A Canadian conservative can observe much about our country that is more conservative, even from a Canadian point of view, than Canadian life today. He called attention to the enduring strength of American religion, the admirable loyalty of the Americans to their Founders and their Constitution (and their corresponding willingness to die for the nation that secures their rights), and the constitutionalist foundation of much of our relatively intense political participation (yes, he did mention the Tea Party). In their devotion to the American tradition, American localism, and the duties of American citizenship, most members of the Tea Party can't be confused with libertarians (or, of course, Red Tories).

Conservative Education—Part 4: Does Charity Begin at Home? Or With the Saints? (Or What Do We Do in a World Where Our Heroes Have Become Entrepreneurs? And Not Even Cowboys?)

A couple of people have written me (doubtlessly Canadians) complaining that I distorted the thought of the great Canadian thinker George Grant. Grant, later in life, found inspiration in the French saint Simone Weil, who died in 1943 at thirty-four. Grant lost interest in the philosophers Strauss and Heidegger as soon as he came to the conclusion that they couldn't teach him what he most needed to know.

That's a good criticism. My response is that once Grant turned to Weil, he went beyond the confines of the Canadian tradition and even beyond the realm of political thought as it's generally understood.

Weil, it's claimed, died out of love—meaning a love of other persons out of love of God. She was one the twentieth century's geniuses—a philosopher, a mathematician, and a mystic. She was born in an agnostic Jewish family, had a couple of deeply personal revelations of God's love, became a deeper believer in at least most of what the Catholic Church teaches about the personal, loving, relational God and the human good, but may well have never been baptized a Catholic. She taught that most of the world's greatest religions taught much of the truth, but she wasn't for some kind of synthesis that incorporated all of them. That would reduce each of them to less than what it is; each religion, like each human person, has to be approached as a whole.

Weil was also for the spiritualization of work. When she wrote about the irreducible needs of the human soul, she meant both bodily needs and spiritual ones. She was a pacifist, but she fought (ineptly) on the republican side in the Spanish Civil War and in the French Resistance against Hitler. She felt so strongly both the joy of love and suffering of her fellow persons that she certainly neglected the needs of her body, but not out of some illusion that her body wasn't part of her.

What Grant took from Weil, above all, is that the highest virtue is charity. It is, in a way, a supernatural virtue. It flows not only from God's revelation, but also from a deep analysis of who each of us really is.

Weil's philosophy is strikingly original yet deeply Platonic—some say, including Grant, even gnostic. She thought that in order to create the world God had to make himself absent, but it's still the case that the largely chance-and-necessity world points beyond itself in the direction of its Creator. Even, geometry, she explained in a Platonic way, does this. Thinking of the world in terms of the incomplete absence of God should remind us of the great Christian mathematician/philosopher Pascal. But Weil, far more than Pascal, was really all about the love, all about charity. (Pascal was more about our miserable anxiety—or extreme personal contingency—in the absence of God. Pascal thought himself to death, Tocqueville observed, before he was forty; Weil died young for a somewhat different reason.)

As it happens, one of our speakers at the conference criticized our founding philosopher, John Locke, from the point of view of Weil. This guy is the laconic, bookish type—a graduate of the Great Books St. Johns College and a comparable Ph.D. program at the University of Chicago.

What's wrong with Locke, in his opinion, is that he tried to separate our natural experience of liberty from both justice and love. According to our Locke, our deepest experience isn't relational, which means it's selfish and lonely. The deepest form of poverty, Christian charity suggests, is loneliness. So, the foundation of our government doesn't do justice to either the true needs of the body or the more specifically spiritual needs of our soul. We can't learn about the spiritualization of work from Locke, and so for him work becomes something we can work ourselves out of through techno-progress. So we can say that the Americans became in some ways richer and in other ways poorer than ever.

A Lockean might respond, of course, that any attempt to politicize love and charity leads to tyranny. Charity is personal, not political. It might be good to have a civilization of love, which we don't. But there's no political route to that goal.

But the man inspired by Weil says that our political order might be more personal and so more local—or less techno-cosmopolitan and impersonal. Weil herself wrote a lot about the French need for roots in thinking about their social and political life after the Nazis are defeated. Her words inspired the tough or rather stoic existentialist Camus, but bored the French re-founder General Charles de Gaulle.

The least we can say in criticism of our time is that we're too rarely inspired by saints and heroes—by lives wholly devoted to charity or extraordinary courage—because we think that what motivated saints and heroes is some kind of dangerous insanity. But the real point of the study of Great Books is to keep the experience of saints and heroes—and philosophers and poets who could do justice to saints and heroes—alive in our techno-time.

Conservative Education—Part 5:
Growing Up from Libertarianism
(Or a Beginning of an Answer to George Will)

This conservative post has nothing to do with the ISI conference, but it does have to do with education.

All over the Internet, we find the conclusion that America is marked by creeping (and, in truth, sometimes creepy) libertarianism. That's because, our experts say, the unlimited and unregulated menu of choice that is the Internet is forming our young people. Consider the recent analysis by George Will on what he calls the nature of our regime.

But maybe we shouldn't give the young such pride of place in thinking about our future. For one thing, the young tend to get old and, if they're lucky, very old. We have an aging society oriented around the young. In the long run, that society is going to be less about preferential options for the young. After all, really old people seem to have all the time in the world to *vote*.

Not only that, the young will sometimes grow up. I just got an email from one of my smartest students ever. At Berry, he was all about economics and its libertarian values. I once asked in class whether anyone was a consistent Machiavellian: that is, all about using other people to satisfy his or her personal desires. This guy raised his hand. I had to tell him that if he were really a consistent Machiavellian, we'd never know it. Machiavelli says that the best users employ the language of religion and morality to sucker other people into doing what they want. The best libertarians (or libertines) are always closeted ones.

Open Machiavellians—such as many professors of economics, Randians, and such—are really bragging about their freedom, and nobody in his or her right mind would really believe them. I remember my bragging student being rather sad and even death-haunted, even with all the good things modern life and his own efforts had given him.

Here's what this young man just wrote me. It's worthy of your wonder, and I will display his words with only two comments. He's grown up well, and he actually got a lot out of his liberal and religious education at Berry College:

> I enjoyed the post you linked to [my BIG THINK post right
> before this one]. I think you might find I have mellowed a bit
> over the years. I'm not really the raging libertarian I once

thought myself to be. I think I may have mentioned that I accepted Christ when I was 24. At my core, I would still generally agree with Locke in that charity and love are properly placed on the personal level. But, I view it that way through the lens that God calls us as individuals to love and be charitable to one another. Too often, I think that the perspective becomes (at least for charity) the government is better positioned to be charitable. We then abdicate our personal responsibility by believing that the government will take care of that function for us.

I find that troubling since I think we grow as men and women through sacrifice. Charity is a form of sacrifice, but it can come at various levels. At the one end of the spectrum, there is the relational gift of one individual giving directly to another, which I think is particularly powerful because it is done face-to-face with an open acknowledgement of the dignity of the other person. I also personally believe that this level of charity is the most likely to inspire some form of personal responsibility on the recipient. And then somewhere towards the other end, you have the impersonal bureaucrat dispersing "charity" to an individual she will never see with money that is not hers. I think the former is a far better representation of what is expected of us and is closer to the type of sacrifice that refines us. That said, I do take a more Hayekian view around the need for minimum social safety nets in those cases where personal charity has failed.

There is a need for heroes and saints in the world today. They certainly would make better role models than the ones that society promotes. But, I think coupled with that there is a deep need to recognize evil and monsters in the world. In some ways, heroes and saints are best identified and admired when there is an open acknowledgement that their opposite exists and that we should fight against those opposites.

Well, one more comment: His chastened, limited devotion to liberty is based on the insight, made famous by Solzhenitsyn, that the line between good and evil goes through every human heart. That's the foundation of liberty I can believe in.

Is Higher Education Worth It?

The fascinating billionaire entrepreneur Peter Thiel (a Facebook guy, the PayPal guy, etc.) seems to be carrying the day against the educational establishment in answering this question negatively.

He's teamed up with Professor Charles Murray to make some fine points. I will of course make the points in my own way.

Higher education must be overpriced. The cost is rising several times faster than inflation. What is most of the money for? Needless amenities, bloated and self-indulgent administrations, and overpriced tenured professors.

A really bad way to start out in life is saddled with debts. Your options are limited, and you, of course, lack the freedom to take entrepreneurial risks. You're pretty much stuck with getting the highest paying job you can, that is, join the mediocre herd in some corporation or such.

If college is primarily about liberal education (or philosophy, literature, and such), then too many people are going. According to Murray, most people just don't have the IQs to think both abstractly and precisely enough to appreciate the finer points of language and logic. The so-called liberal education or "general education" students now receive is a kind of senseless torture. The efforts to "engage" the average guy are dumbing down such education in a way that makes it equally boring to the few who could benefit from it.

If education, in most cases, is about learning technical skills, to prepare people for the kinds of work available to most people in a high-tech, middle-class democracy, then why pay big money to study at a brick-and-mortar university? The person majoring in exercise science or public relations or beverage management or even elementary education could pick up what's needed in a couple of years. And most of what is needed, in such cases, could be delivered online.

It's difficult to say that, in most cases, the "residential experience" is actually good for students these days in terms of developing personal responsibility and the other features of moral virtue. The dorms are "state of nature," and lots of safe yet otherwise irresponsible sex is going on in a way that it just can't in real life. This is especially corrupting for both men and women in different ways at most liberal arts colleges. The gender imbalance makes men vain and silly (or vainer and sillier) and women are stuck with the rigors of the artificially competitive marketplace.

Classes are too easy; nobody flunks out anymore. Students are catered to like consumers. They don't have to do much for themselves—like cooking or cleaning.

Not only that: Students aren't becoming in any sense literate in ways that would benefit them as citizens, parents, and so forth. We've punted for the most part on cultural literacy and civic literacy and theological literacy and even personal finance literacy.

It's always been the case that many genuine geniuses haven't gotten much out of school. (Steve Jobs!) And those who are, in my opinion, the very best and deepest American authors of the twentieth century—such as Walker Percy or Flannery O'Connor or Shelby Foote or William Faulkner—didn't learn how to read and write in college. Percy majored in medicine, O'Connor boring, textbook sociology, and Foote and Faulkner dropped out. That's surely why Thiel is giving fellowships for such people to drop out. (Actually, that's not why he's giving them; he's creating the impression that the highest human type is the entrepreneur.)

Certainly professors have become too risk-averse and careerist, saddling themselves for no good reason with autonomy-sucks such as measurable learning outcomes and student evaluations. Professors, more than ever, are stuck with being agreeable and productive in depressingly conventional ways. One piece of good news is that they may be less absentminded; the bad news is that college is becoming progressively more technical and less philosophic or genuinely liberating.

In order to facilitate discussion, I'll leave the case in the other direction mostly for later. But one thing now: What makes Thiel more interesting than even Steve Jobs is his serious interest in the philosopher Leo Strauss, one of the most impressive thinkers of the twentieth century.

What interests Thiel about Strauss—who flourished in the very rigorous and aristocratic German educational system and received an old-fashioned German doctorate—is his candid and deep exploration of what's required for genuine human liberation. (A whole separate, pro-American post could be written on why Strauss was, nonetheless, a misfit in the German university system but flourished in ours.)

So, Thiel says that the Straussian issue is the libertarian issue. But for Strauss, liberation doesn't mean freedom to "do your own thing." It depends on a huge amount of education. Thiel is a pretty competent amateur Straussian, but his liberation level might be called fairly low from a certain view. He hasn't acquired, for example, the language skills, as far as

I can tell, required to read the premodern texts—Plato, Aristotle, and such—with the care required to liberate himself from modern prejudices.

Libertarianism is a prejudice that's especially strong these days. It's true enough that Jobs dropped out of college and invented lots of amazing "i" stuff. But he wasn't liberated the way a theoretical physicist is, and just about all of those physicists needed the discipline of a Ph.D. program to know what's really going on—naturally speaking.

The lack of such liberation may be one reason Thiel sometimes seems suckered by the promises of transhumanism. Hardly any Straussians are.

For Strauss, there's the still the higher kind of liberation of Socrates. (Who admittedly didn't have a Ph.D. and didn't publish.) But Socrates was no libertarian. He reminded us in most memorable and amusing ways of the self-indulgent and pretentious view of freedom that animates every permissive democracy (such as ours). That view of freedom is ugly in its self-forgetfulness, in its denial of the necessity that provides the foundation for human nobility and even philosophy.

In general, genuine liberation requires a huge amount of conventional discipline. And in addition to the habituation that comes from a society that takes tradition and tough-minded virtue seriously, there's the need for genuinely higher liberation, which, in the West, has usually found its home in universities. Our colleges and universities may be failing us, but that doesn't mean we don't need them.

Someone might also talk about Thiel's division of human beings into the "mob" and the liberated, which he learned from misunderstanding Strauss and Plato in a certain way.

What Is Higher Education?—Part 1

For most people who aren't geniuses, the college degree is an indispensable credential for entering the world of the middle-class professions. People who get college degrees make lots more money and turn out better in general. People who have the best brands of degrees—such as Harvard's—do much better still, and so it might be regarded as only fair that such degrees often cost more.

Although plumbers and auto mechanics are often underrated in terms of brains and income, we still have to say that, in a high-tech society, those who do "mental labor" tend always to be improving their position relative to those who do primarily physical labor or labor according to a routine developed by others.

That's why the top 20 percent of Americans, even with the economic downturn, still are, in many ways, doing better than ever. It's also why those in the genuinely middle, middle class—typically without college degrees—seem stuck with lives that are getting more vulnerable and more pathological.

Alexis de Tocqueville, in his hyper-prescient *Democracy in America*, actually said that he found no higher education in America (in the 1830s). He did find that primary education, in a completely unprecedented way, was available to everyone. Universal literacy is the foundation of a middle-class democracy. Everyone who needs to find a job and make money on his own needs those basic skills.

Someone might say that Tocqueville's observation isn't true at all when it comes to America today. Many or most Americans of college age are, in fact, in college of some kind now, and we call college higher education.

But by higher education Tocqueville meant leisurely and attentively reading the best books in their original languages, metaphysics and theology, and theoretical science. He meant the proud and disinterested pursuit of the truth characteristic of Archimedes, Pascal, Plato, Descartes, and Shakespeare. He meant an education that can't be reduced to an industry or even a technology.

He didn't mean textbooks, computerized programmed learning, PowerPoint, Scantron tests, group projects, experiential learning, technical skills, or even applied science. He didn't mean what college means for the overwhelming majority of American students now.

It's true that the choice of the technical college major is almost always preceded by a certain number of required courses. But that number is going down, and those courses seem to be more and more detached from the tradition of "liberal education" (or introduction to higher education rightly understood).

Increasingly, the core courses are evaluated according to the acquisition of skills, such as critical thinking, problem solving, effective communication, responsible decision-making, teamwork, and so forth, divorced from what used to be regarded as the content of higher education. The technical imperative that these "learning outcomes" be measurable is becoming more insistent. (I'm skipping over what's happened to the social sciences and humanities through political correctness and identity politics.)

It's far from an altogether bad thing that most American students think of college as a way of acquiring technical skills. They really do need them, after all. Everyone has always known that a life devoted to metaphysics, theology, literature (either reading or writing it), or theoretical physics has always been for the nerdy and uncannily gifted few. Those with such devotion often have a sterile contempt for those who employ scientific knowledge to improve the human condition, and that contempt is not only unproductive but unjust.

If all that's true (as I'm saying for the sake of argument), then surely the traditional and very expensive trappings of the brick-and-mortar residential college aren't the best or most efficient way of acquiring the requisite skills. That's why online, for-profit, and strip-mall methods of educational delivery are becoming more popular. It's why we were sympathetic when Rick Perry tried to employ all means necessary to drive down the cost of an Aggie degree.

So we return to Tocqueville's observation that universal American education, although the admirable and indispensable foundation of a free and prosperous middle-class democracy, isn't higher education.

Tocqueville adds, however, that the Americans were fortunate to have a second foundation for their egalitarian devotion to universal education: the Puritans.

The middle-class view is that we're all free beings with bodies, responsible for ourselves and especially for securing our own interests. The Puritan or more idealistic form of "all men are created equal" is that we're all also beings with souls. The Puritan devotion to universal education—which I will discuss soon—begins with the thought that each of us should be able to read the Bible for him or herself.

But for now, here's a paraphrase of one Facebook response I got to my original post: Is higher education worth it? To get a job—no. To discover "the good life" (through philosophy and such)—you can't put a price on *that*.

High-cost college is surely worth it if you discover a different and much better way of life than the one you would have lived without it. (It goes without saying that I'm not talking about a different and better way of making money.) But these days our colleges aren't all about *that*. If college were mainly about *that*, ironically, it would be a lot cheaper, if not as cheap as Governor Perry has in mind.

Still, in a country as free as ours, it will always be a misleading exaggeration to say that all education has become enslaved to the imperatives of productivity and technological innovation.

What Is Higher Education?—Part 2
Can It Teach Us How to Die?

The most recent issue of *Perspectives on Political Science* is mostly devoted to a symposium on the most able, thoughtful, and comprehensive book written on Plato in a very long time—Catherine Zuckert's *Plato's Philosophers*.

One of the contributors to the symposium, Robert Kraynak, asks, in effect, whether Zuckert is more than a mere scholar: "Is she a convinced Socratic or Platonist?"

Zuckert claims, as Kraynak reports, that the Socratic view of philosophy "has lessons and applicability for us today as we face the impersonal universe of modern science yet still need to know the human good for the purpose of leading a good and noble life." Socratic philosophy (at least as presented by and improved upon by Plato) is "the best philosophy," because "it alone answers the question 'Why philosophy?' in a way that stands independently of any cosmology, metaphysics, or scientific view of the natural universe."

"The crucial test," for Kraynak, "would be whether or not Socratic philosophy can make people happy in some reasonable sense, especially by overcoming the fear of death and cosmic insignificance . . . If Socrates provides the best answer for Zuckert, has she learned from him how to be happy in the crucial sense of overcoming the fear of death, or she still afraid of dying like the rest of us?"

It's that test, Kraynak explains, that shows us whether or "great scholarship and philosophical knowledge" actually do us any good.

Philosophy, according to Socrates, is most of all of learning how to die. If higher education did teach us how to live well with what we can't help but know about personal death, wouldn't it be priceless?

Modern philosophy—says Hobbes—reduces that fear to fear of a violent death and fear of punishment in hell after death. The first fear can be alleviated by good government and modern technology. The second fear can be alleviated by propaganda or "enlightenment" that shows there is, in fact, no hell.

Modern philosophy—says Descartes—also promises that through technology we can push death back, way back, perhaps extending indefinitely the life of every particular human being. If that happens, our lives will be less haunted by death, and we will be happier than maybe even Socrates himself.

A general modern hope or expectation is that with good government, prosperity, security, and technology, religion—the illusory hope we have about death—will fade away, as people become happy enough with what they really have in this world.

So, a modern hope—in a way—is that both the Socratic and the religious ways of getting over fear of death will become equally irrelevant. They were both based on illusions and didn't work that well anyway.

But maybe the modern hope was misguided. The twentieth century was characterized by existentialism, by the deep perception of the absurd insignificance of the freedom that characterizes each particular human life.

Existentialism isn't about fear, but anxiety. Sure, we fear death, but deeper than fear is anxiety about who each of us really is. When I disappear, being itself disappears (from my point of view)! And all I am is an utterly contingent accident existing for a moment between two abysses. The fact that, while I'm around, I have plenty of stuff and lots of creature comforts doesn't change *that*! And the fact that I die peacefully in my bed at a very old age doesn't change *that*!

Perhaps the most courageous person of the twentieth century—the anticommunist dissident and profound author Aleksandr Solzhenitsyn—observed that he heard just beneath the surface of the happy-talk pragmatism of the Americans the "howl" of existentialism, the loud inarticulate sound of utterly lonely insignificance. I hear that howl, in fact, just beneath the optimism the transhumanists have about the coming Singularity.

Here's a big educational question: Can Socratic philosophy teach us once again how to die? How to get over ourselves, our self-obsessions? However that question is answered—and leading experts disagree on the answer, isn't it at the core of higher education?

For Socrates, death is a necessity we can't change. Since we don't know whether it's better or worse than life, it's unreasonable to fear it.

This means that there are things worse than death. This explains why Socrates stood up for himself and his philosophizing before the city of Athens, even at the expense of his life. But what would Socrates have done that day if the regenerative-medicine physician had let him know the good news that everything could be replaced, and that he could be reasonably assured of seventy or more years beyond the seventy he'd already enjoyed?

What Is Higher Education—Part 3: Is It All about the Soul?

So far we've concluded, following Alexis de Tocqueville's *Democracy in America*, that most of what we call higher education is really technical education. It's the acquisition of indispensable skills for people in a middle-class democracy. That technical education at our brick-and-mortar colleges typically includes some "liberal education," but that part of college education is getting smaller and somewhat more vague and perfunctory. That's because we no longer know what the humanities are for, beyond sharpening basic skills in critical thinking, effective communication, and so forth. The sciences, as far as I can tell, are more confident and meritocratic than ever, the humanities more dazed and confused and so angry and suspicious of the "logocentrism" of meritocracy.

Tocqueville adds that identifying science with technology is basically a democratic prejudice. We tend to value science as useful for generating the power required to make us more comfortable, secure, and free from material drudgery. But the truth is that there's also pure science or theoretical science, which can be distinguished even from experimental science. (The importance of this distinction is one reason among many I admire TV's *The Big Bang Theory*—with the intellectual superiority of the theoretical Sheldon to the experimental Leonard always being displayed, although Leonard is a nicer guy with more normal human emotions.)

Tocqueville cautions democrats that if they neglect theory technological progress will eventually atrophy. We can see that, in fact, most of the best theoretical programs can be found in our country today, but a strikingly disproportionate percentage of the students and professors didn't grow up here. We know enough to spend the money, but we're not so good in raising and educating kids to become the most top-flight of scientists.

Tocqueville also mentions the need of any democracy for even more countercultural forms of higher education. He says those responsible for the literary life of any democracy—including ours—should study the best Greek and Roman authors in Greek and Latin. That's not because they were better than us in every respect; even Greek and Roman philosophers were distorted by aristocratic prejudices.

But the democratic tendency is to become so skeptical of the need of the soul that the very words that correspond to those needs will be emptied of meaning or just disappear. Democratic language will become more abstract and technical, using words like "input" when what is really meant is opinion. Language becomes less attuned to the personal longings of the being who loves, dies, and is open to truth about all things. Metaphysics, theology, poetry, and philosophy will lose ground without constant replenishment from the influence of authors who were all about the soul.

Tocqueville makes the elitist point that this sort of "classical education" shouldn't be for everyone in a democracy. For those stuck with middle-class, technical jobs, such an education would arouse passions for greatness that just can't be satisfied these days. An accountant full of classical learning would be dangerously discontent. But the author, of course, can "sublimate" his discontent through literary expression.

That's not to say that Tocqueville is so elitist that he doesn't think we all have souls with longings. It's just that most of us aren't going to be responsible for those keeping those longings alive in our language. Somebody might say that the reason our popular music is so full of anger these days is that our language is so impoverished. When you can't find the words to say what needs to be said, it's hard to express yourself rationally and moderately.

What Is Higher Education—Part 4:
Should We Be More Puritanical?

Tocqueville found two sources of the American devotion to universal education. The first is the universal literacy that is a requirement for a country where everyone works for himself. Being middle class is somewhere in between being an aristocrat and being a slave (or servant). The aristocrat is free not to work, to enjoy noble leisure by depending on the work of others. The slave is stuck with working for others and not for himself.

The good news is about being middle class is you're free to work for yourself. The bad, we might say, is that you're free like an aristocrat to work like a slave. As Marxists say, the overwhelming majority of people in capitalist countries are wage slaves. They're stuck with selling their time for money. Anybody who is free and has to work has pretty much has to know how to read and write, add and subtract, and so forth.

The other source of American devotion to universal education Tocqueville traces to the Puritans. The Christian belief is that we all have souls, and the Puritan belief in particular was that we all have a duty to read the Bible for ourselves. So serious were the Puritans about the idealistic egalitarianism of this religious belief, Tocqueville explains, that they turned it into a political idea. And so, our first Puritans were the most democratic people in the world up until that time. Most of our democratic political institutions, in fact, can be traced to the Puritans.

The Puritans, as Tocqueville described them, didn't have the aristocratic prejudice that liberal or genuinely liberating education was only for the few. They thought nobody was above work, and nobody was below leisurely contemplation about our true destiny. That's why the Puritans were so serious about preserving Sunday from work. Tocqueville thought that the Americans should remain at least Puritanical enough to preserve Sunday from the busyness of commerce and the mindlessness of the recreation industry.

It's true, as you all want to shout in unison, that the Puritans had their downside. They had, Tocqueville reminds us, ridiculous and tyrannical laws, as they tended to turn every sin into a crime. So severely serious was their egalitarian idealism that they were way too politically intrusive when it came to caring for souls, forgetting the great principle of religious liberty.

The great contemporary novelist, Marilynne Robinson (author of

Gilead and *Home*), is all about getting us to remember what's good about the Puritans as a way of recovering real civilization in our country.

Robinson reminds us that there was a revival of something like Puritan (or Calvinist) enthusiasm in the American East as a result of the Second Great Awakening. The radically egalitarian political idealism—particularly the insistent abolitionism—of this revived piety made these neo-Puritans (mainly Congregationalists) so hated in their native states that the Puritans once again had to become pilgrims. They relocated in the Middle West, where they started a good number of racially and gender integrated colleges (like Oberlin).

At these colleges, everyone did manual labor, including the faculty. That way, the educated class would be more useful, and there would be no economic barriers to higher education. The goal was to create the classless, humanely and spiritually educated world intended by the original Puritans. Those new colleges, Robinson claims, were real liberal arts colleges, where "the humanities in the very broad sense" were generously studied.

These colleges did not have what Tocqueville called the middle-class purpose of learning a trade or skill; they were educating beings with souls, who only incidentally had interests. Liberal education—beginning but not ending with the Bible—is a vehicle for liberation of every human being.

Liberal education, Robinson contends, was understood as liberating education by these new Puritans in a more immediate sense. They were often founded as stations on the underground railroad. They were structured "as centers of humane learning that would make their graduates and those influenced by them resistant to the spread of slavery."

The abolition of slavery was only one feature of this project for political liberation. Its aim was "near utopian," to reform American society "by practicing as well as pointing to standards of justice and freedom to which the nation had not yet risen." For them even more than the original Puritans, their religious enthusiasm was the source of boldly innovative egalitarian idealism—the theory and practice of "generous and transformational change of the whole of society," and not just "the suppression of slavery in the states of the South."

The Calvinist Puritans, Robinson claims, are the foundation of the humane, egalitarian left for much of the history of our country. Their idealism was indispensable for spurring the American Revolution; the theory of Locke was not generous enough to inspire the honorable risk of everything in pursuit of liberation for prejudice and patriarchy.

The theory of Locke also was not genuinely liberal enough to cause men to risk everything to abolish slavery; it made men (like Thomas Jefferson) anti-slavery far more in principle than in practice. Mr. Jefferson would not have thought much of integrated Oberlin, or the underground railroad, or providing support to the radical John Brown.

I'm no Puritan, and it could be Marilynne Robinson and Tocqueville aren't above exaggerating to make their case for the Puritans. Nonetheless, we should explore every source of higher education in our country.

David Brooks vs. Moral Individualism

David Brooks is better than he says in the *Social Animal*: He doesn't really submit himself to the authority of the latest studies in neuroscience, and he still takes his bearings from a combination of sociology and political philosophy.

Let me make that point by saying a couple of things about David's latest column (David Brooks, "If It Feels Right . . . ," *New York Times*, September 12, 2011).

The first thing to note is that Brooks said nothing about neuroscience or any other form of hard science—that is, in this case, scientific studies about our natural hardwiring.

Instead, we see that classic combination of sociology and philosophy. He begins with the latest sociological study on the moral opinions about young Americans, finding that they, more than ever, regard moral choice as a matter of individual preference and so not really moral at all.

Brooks also cites philosophic authorities—Allan Bloom and Alasdair MacIntyre—who are famous for their polemics against relativism or emotivism. Young people today, MacIntyre claims, live after virtue or in a world where there's no longer any common understanding of what being good or excellent is, and the result is, Bloom adds, that they have flat souls or lack the experiences and longings and even words that allow them to be more than competent conformists. Can we say that this sort of analysis and worry isn't found among the neuroscientists and evolutionary psychologists?

We have to add that Bloom's big authority on what Americans are like is Alexis de Tocqueville's *Democracy in America*, which might be called a masterful synthesis of sociology and philosophy. It's a book that was written in the 1830s, but its analysis, as Brooks surely knows, is truer now than when it was written. What the sociologists discovered Tocqueville predicted they would have discovered in a really democratic, libertarian time such as ours.

Brooks's analysis is basically the same as Tocqueville's, whom we might say is his silent authority. According to Tocqueville (and Brooks), American kids have become too anti-authoritarian. In Tocqueville's words, they have become Cartesians without ever having read a word of Descartes. The Cartesian method is doubt, and doubt is also the democratic method. The American democrats systematically, as the bumper sticker says, "question authority." They refuse to be governed by the words of other persons, because then they would unfreely and undemocratically be ruled by others. That's why American Cartesians never actually read a word of Descartes—they won't submit to the philosopher's authority or that of any person who would recommend his great works. (That last observation, almost all by itself, explains why American education is so one-dimensionally technical and otherwise screwed up today.)

The result is that the individual becomes locked up in himself—in his puny mind and his contracted heart. He (or she, obviously) becomes anxious and disoriented, and then passively impotent. The good democratic news is that nobody is better than me. The corresponding bad news is that I'm not better than anyone else. Another piece of bad news is that no solitary individual has the intellectual or emotional resources to create himself out of nothing. Not even God himself has to do that.

So the seemingly intellectually liberated or morally self-determining individual ends up, by rejecting personal authority, submitting to the impersonal forces that surround him. Democrats or American "Cartesians," Tocqueville, observes, tend to be governed by "fashion" or impersonal public opinion—opinion that comes from no one in particular. If we all submit equally to some impersonal force, then no offense has been committed against democracy. But the offense against personal liberty and genuine moral responsibility, Tocqueville shows, is profound and actually unprecedented.

That's the explanation of a sociological fact Brooks draws from the study: Young people today lack what it takes to resist rampant consumerism. (Tocqueville adds that democratic people also too readily defer to the impersonal authority of popularized science—the experts who rule us through the allegedly impersonal authority of their studies.)

So what's wrong with young people these days is that they don't have what it takes to think freely—or as freely as people can think. And they don't have the spirit of resistance required to act morally against the impersonal, degrading forces that surround them. As Tocqueville says, individualism culminates in apathetic passivity, in an indifference to the moral choices of others based on the perception that moral judgment is repressive cruelty. The individualist refuses to love or hate—believing that they're both more trouble than they're worth. (Think Seinfeld or Larry David for laughably extreme cases here.)

Brooks's article, after all, is really a polemic against the slacker libertarianism of young people today. There's no better or truer way to insult them than by saying your obsession with "negative freedom" is keeping you from thinking or acting freely. Let me just mention the names Ron Paul and Ayn Rand here just to increase the size of the group that will feel the insult.

It turns out, Brooks and Tocqueville add, that genuinely religiously observant Americans have, at least sometimes, a point of view by which consumerism can be resisted, as well as tradition in which moral responsibility has weight and makes sense. The same can be said, Tocqueville adds, for anyone with a sense of class.

Most of us, in our moral individualism, have no idea who we are or what we're supposed to do. And, in the crucial respects, neuroscience and evolutionary psychology don't offer us the help we need. All honor to David Brooks for reminding us of the indispensability of philosophy, religion, and personal authority.

Teaching, Research, and Me

It's surely appropriate that I follow up a post on my *summer vacation* with one on the two kinds of *work* of the college teacher. More than one person who read the previous post remarked that I was just reminding people that, for the college teacher, the phrase "summer vacation" is redundant.

People like me, they say with an unattractive mixture of envy and resentment, have the whole summer off. I respond: But I'm doing my cutting-edge *research*! Even my wife, who's usually loyal, says give me a break.

Here's a sad fact that doesn't apply to me so much right now (but did when I was paying preppy school tuition rather than home schooling): Faculty members who teach heavy loads during the regular year usually end up having to teach during the summer too.

That's for two reasons: Faculty members with the heaviest teaching loads have the lowest salaries. And they don't have time do the research required to get funding to have time to do research.

A faculty member who devotes his or her life primarily to teaching is, according any objective measure, a *sucker*.

The sensible goal is to get time to do research (and publish and all) and so to get a job where there's plenty of time to do research. Time spent teaching, from this entrepreneurial view, is time wasted.

As I've written before, a tenured faculty member who's all about the teaching is pretty much stuck where he or she is. Good teaching, despite the best efforts of many boring professors of education with minimal knowledge of statistics, is pretty much impossible to quantify, at least in most fields. And in any case: Teaching, in part, is about *fit* with the institution. It's not clear how much being an effective teacher one place transfers to another. Because sometimes it does and sometimes it doesn't, colleges don't want to take a chance on mere reputations when making hiring decisions, especially beyond the entry level. Nobody has less bargaining power than someone whose employer knows he or she ain't going anywhere no matter what. Tenure, from this view, is less about liberation than about being chained up.

In any case, college and university administrators are often not that interested in how the classroom teaching is going. Or at least they believe that professors are pretty much expendable and replaceable. College presidents and such are in fact much more expendable and replaceable than good professors of philosophy, but it's understandable why they usually don't think of themselves that way.

The only reason four-year colleges (which aren't about cutting-edge research) give time for and "count" faculty research appears to be a humane one. They want to give their faculty members some incentive and a fighting chance to be marketable. But in most cases, the professors' success in being researchers, although sometimes remarkable, doesn't usually rival what's done by those who have a lot more time. The good researchers at four-year colleges usually get the paternalistic recognition of making the all-star team in a weak league. It's assumed that if they were really good, they wouldn't be in that league. On the whole, a study could easily show they're not so good; the best and the brightest do gravitate to the big bucks and light workloads of the research institution.

The four-year college professor starts out behind and then is condemned to a world of (relative) drudgery that will cause him or her to get further and further behind. But there is another way of looking at the situation.

Now, according to Naomi Schaefer Riley, we have studies that show that teaching aids research. Most of these studies are about experimental science, and so I don't know and hardly care whether or not they're on the money. But the proposition is backed up by my own experience and common sense: You don't really know something until you explain it to the others.

In my own experience, every time I teach a book (and I only use real books, as opposed to textbooks), I reread it. And every time I read it, I see stuff I missed before. That really, really helps me in my research. That's because my so-called research is pretty much writing essays about "great books" (or at least really good books) and how they help us understand what's going on today. By teaching a book time and again, I'm constantly explaining to very young people how it applies to their lives.

Not only that, I've spent over 30 years teaching at a small college. So I've taught all sorts of courses out of my field, courses that aren't about anything I studied in graduate school. Those courses about are about stuff I should know to understand our country's political life—such as constitutional law. It turns out that I've never taught a course that hasn't resulted in some kind of publication and not helped out in articles and books apparently having nothing to do with the course.

I could go on here. But the moral is something like this. The idea of publication—at least in the social sciences and humanities—is controlled by the hyper-specialization of the research university. So, in my experience, too many professors at small colleges suffer from "self-esteem issues" that keep them from writing what they really know, from exploiting the superiority of their more comprehensive perspective.

I hate words like "interdisciplinary" because they're empty, overused, and usually dripping with vanity. But in a certain way, the superiority of the four-year college teacher comes from having no discipline. Everyone who really knows me knows I have no discipline. Just take a look at my office.

Berry College:
The Biggest and Almost the Most Beautiful Campus

Travel and Leisure has ranked the place where I teach eighth in the nation in terms of beauty. That's news, of course, to those who have the leisure to travel a lot, and we expect to be overwhelmed by such visitors soon.

I think we might be ranked too low. No. 5 Florida Southern, for example, is talked up for its buildings designed by Frank Lloyd Wright. I would say that they're more really interesting than truly beautiful. Certainly the natural surroundings of the foothills of Georgia are more pleasing than those of the interior of Florida, even with those random sinkhole lakes.

It's true we've had sinkholes too, but we generally fill them in. It's also true that the water in the big lake on Berry's campus disappeared more than once due to sinkholes. It's no longer a lake but a kind of science experiment displaying what grows in the bed of an ex-lake. So I may be writing out of bitterness here.

Berry is also, you can learn, the largest "contiguous" campus in America, with the 26,000 acres actually touching one another. I'm not sure what the larger non-contiguous campus is.

I do know that Berry has the best acre-to-student ratio in the country. We only have a little over 1,900 students. So well over ten acres is available for each student. It's easy to be alone at Berry, although it's hard to be lonely.

Another great thing about Berry is that the college is "private," and so not subject to the bureaucratic idiocies—such as misguided political correctness—characteristic of state schools. (It's true that we're more than a bit touched by such stuff by the necessity of being accredited. But no college can avoid that.) We're also not tied in any big way to the sinkholes that are the collapsing state budgets throughout the country.

We're "Christian in spirit" and have a chaplain, but we're not connected to any particular denomination. So we're not enmeshed in the factional squabbles and "doctrinal correctness" issues found at many colleges that are Christian in some more particular way.

Our curriculum is not particularly Christian at all. It's what you might find at similar four-year colleges, and faculty is not chosen for their religious beliefs (or, for that matter, for their lack thereof). Well, our range of majors is actually larger than most small colleges; we're great at animal science, for example.

Our student body—partly because we're in a very Christian part of the country and partly because our campus is dry—is free of fraternities and sororities, and actually has dorm visitation policies, and so forth—is probably mostly pretty seriously Christian, although there are more than a few student skeptics. There are lots of active student religious organizations. No one Christian denomination dominates, though.

These peculiar characteristics actually turn out to be good for intellectual freedom. At Berry, for example, it's actually possible to discuss in class whether Roe v. Wade was rightly decided. There'll be students on both sides, and none of them feels afraid to speak up.

Are Group Thinking and Group Learning Oxymorons?

Susan Cain has written a fine think-piece that praises some introversion as indispensable for creativity (Cain, "The Rise of the New Group Think," *New York Times*, January 13, 2012). To some great extent, Socrates and Jesus were solitary men. And the wisdom they shared with us couldn't have been captured in group reports or multi-authored articles.

Not only that, we live in a society that discourages, in so many ways, thinking for ourselves. We defer so readily to public opinion, fashion, and what the experts say and the studies show. Most studies that show stuff have a lot more than one author. Most books that change our lives have only one, and we don't live in a time when many are being written.

Just about every good play or novel or painting, of course, has its source in the vision of a single artist.

We also see, of course, that in the disciplines that require deep thought and personal interpretation (such as philosophy—especially political philosophy—and history), articles almost only have one author. Technical and scientific reports usually have more authors than they do pages.

If we want learning to be personal, personal thought has to be encouraged and rewarded. And persons, of course, have to be held personally responsible for both what they've learned and the ways in which they have expressed their thoughts.

In a class dealing with "real books" (such as ones written by Plato or Kant or Jane Austen or Pascal or Simone Weil), I find that the best students get less than ten percent of what's really going on, and "what's gotten" differs dramatically from student to student. If they had to produce a multi-authored paper, the result would be flattened out to what they can explain to each other. It goes without saying the good students would be particularly shy about expressing their most unconventional thoughts, especially ones that have to do with God, love, death, and such, to the other group members. They would also be shy about being too enthusiastic or "erotic" about what they've read to others who just didn't work as hard or care as much as they did. (All this is why I can't stand "peer review" as even a stage in evaluating student papers.)

It also goes without saying that the natural result is for good students to have quite different views on the truth and significance of what they've read—in part, due to what else they've read and their personal experiences.

How could they possibly write a conclusion based on some consensus that's more than a bunch of feel-good banalities?

Good students do, of course, learn from each other through conversation. Part of a great class is something like a Socratic dialogue—keeping in mind that the participant closest to Socrates (me) dominates the discussion in various ways. The community of learners doesn't mean that all the learners are equal in the ways relevant to actual learning.

In the end, the student paper should be a rather solitary, introverted effort, although not one so introverted that the author is not excited about the possibility that the truth can be shared in common. "Shared in common" in the Socratic sense is a long distance from groupthink or what's usually meant by collaborative learning.

Another problem with "group projects" as a learning tool is that our society already rewards being witty and fashionable and pleasing to others far too much. It also already rewards too much shirkers whose main talent is taking credit for the real work of others. Let sucking up be saved for the actual world of business. It's not a skill that should be rewarded by college credit.

Here's another problem: collaborative learning is also often an excuse for professorial laziness. Why read twenty papers when you can read five (written by groups of four)? The group dynamic also means that the papers will only be so good or so bad, and that means that the professor won't be taxed by a product that is too "outside the box" of what's expected.

If you ever sign up for a class that's a mixture of PowerPoint presentations based on some textbook followed up by group projects and presentations, immediately drop it and ask for your money back.

The philosopher Rousseau was against taking the idea of dispersing wisdom to everyone characteristic of the Enlightenment too seriously because the real goal of that approach is the production of a vain and pseudo-sophisticated herd of seemingly meritocratic techno-elitists. The philosopher—or the genuinely Enlightened person—is always a law unto himself. He's almost always not characterized by the ambiguous virtue of working well with others.

Harold Bloom, Dead Stuff, and the End of American Education

There are a lot of cool posts on BIG THINK today. Austin Allen's on stuff that the great literary critic Harold Bloom declared dead is a kind of an ironic appreciation. The "subtext" is that one of the critic's charms is that news of something's death from Bloom is typically greatly exaggerated.

I'm going to avoid that critical tendency by not following my instinct in posting on the death of Mitt Romney's campaign. Or by explaining why Newt Gingrich's campaign against our president would be DOA.

As an unapologetic digression, I will say what, in truth, Newt Gingrich should have said in his famous anti-CNN South Carolina moment of fake indignation: The mainstream elite media have made it impossible for decent men and women to run for president. That's why you're stuck with *me*.

Getting back to Harold, it's easy to observe that saying rock and roll died with the band The Band is an exaggeration. The Band may well have been the best band ever, but that's just to say that the rock genre, like every other, has rare peaks of genuine excellence. Philosophy didn't die with Socrates, the purest thinker of the West. Nothing in even Springsteen's storytelling approaches "The Night They Drove Old Dixie Down." But how many Canadian displays of the authentically Confederate point of view can we really expect? Given the close connection between The Band and Dylan, we might want to say that really classy and deep popular music died with Dylan. But Dylan is still alive and singing. His voice is shot but the spirit is still more than willing.

Harold also says, of course, that the Western canon and American education are dead. Again, both exaggerations, but ones I kind of like.

I can hardly wait until the idea of the Western canon dies. The whole idea, it seems to me, is that a bunch of sort-of sacred texts were imposed on Western civilization quite arbitrarily. Those books, it follows, are to be understood as tools of logocentric, patriarchal, phallocentric tyranny.

The idea of the Western canon disappears once we remember that the West is distinguished by making universal claims for truth through reason or philosophy and monotheistic revelation. The books weren't written just for the West, but for the cosmopolis that includes us all, or the City of God that includes us all.

Readers were passionate, attentive, and meticulous in the ways Bloom described when people read books because they thought they were the best way of knowing the truth that would set you free.

The key thing about Plato's *Republic* or the *Bible* or Shakespeare or Maimonides or Thomas Aquinas is whether or not what they say is really true. Answering that question requires, in each case, long and loving study. Thinking of such books and authors as merely part of some Western canon already discourages the reader from approaching the text on the terms set forth by the author.

The anti-canonical criticism of those books is usually in terms of their racism, sexism, classism, imperialism, and so forth. But those standards of criticism—on behalf of the free and dignified equality of all individuals—are quite Western.

Of course, we should read non-Western books in the same spirit we should read the so-called Western ones. Do they contain the truth that can set us free?

Killing the Western Canon as Western Canon is one ingredient among many of the revitalization of American education.

One reason, of course, that American education is not dead as a whole is that the unique diversity of American colleges and universities (meaning, to begin with, the huge number of private and religious institutions) makes it easy to find places here and there where the best books are read in the right spirit.

We might add, to placate the many atheists on BIG THINK, that Nietzsche thought that the most noteworthy achievement of the West so far is found in the statement "God is dead." Getting over that alleged insight, he thought, depended on getting over some of our most cherished Western prejudices.

What's Wrong with Teenagers?
(They Don't Have Any Moral Virtue)

Alison Gopnik explains convincingly that we haven't been concerned enough with our children's moral virtue—or acquiring the habits required to flourish as free and rational animals in a society such as ours ("What's Wrong With the Teenage Mind?," *Wall Street Journal*, January 28, 2012). Aristotle, of course, distinguished between moral virtue and intellectual virtue. Intellectual virtue is acquired through teaching, but it has little to do with the discipline required to choose well.

> In the past, to become a good gatherer or hunter, cook or caregiver, you would actually practice gathering, hunting, cooking and taking care of children all through middle childhood and early adolescence—tuning up just the prefrontal wiring you'd need as an adult. But you'd do all that under expert adult supervision and in the protected world of childhood, where the impact of your inevitable failures would be blunted. When the motivational juice of puberty arrived, you'd be ready to go after the real rewards, in the world outside, with new intensity and exuberance, but you'd also have the skill and control to do it effectively and reasonably safely.
>
> In contemporary life, the relationship between these two systems has changed dramatically. Puberty arrives earlier, and the motivational system kicks in earlier too.
>
> At the same time, contemporary children have very little experience with the kinds of tasks that they'll have to perform as grown-ups. Children have increasingly little chance to practice even basic skills like cooking and caregiving. Contemporary adolescents and pre-adolescents often don't do much of anything except go to school. Even the paper route and the baby-sitting job have largely disappeared.

Let me emphasize a few points.

There are now a huge number of years between puberty and living as a responsible adult. It used to be, not so long ago, that people got married around puberty, and sex was connected almost immediately with children and parental responsibility. Now, young people have well more than a decade, it seems, in which they're told to practice safe sex. You can do what you want, as long as it's consensual and disconnected from birthing and dying. The virtue of chastity, it seems, can't possibly be practiced for so long. Safe sex, of course, falls short of moral virtue, because it has little to do with our social natures as pair-bonding and reproducing animals.

In our high tech and individualistic society, children rarely have meaningful chores. They don't learn how to cook, because there just isn't much real cooking at home. If they do cook now and again, it's not as a routine and needed contribution to family life. Caregiving used to mainly be for the elderly—grandparents, etc.—living at home as part of the family. But parents today are too busy—both of them with careers and all—to devote themselves much to such voluntary caregiving, and so children are doing even less of it. Children are less likely to really know— much less care for—elderly members of the extended family, although there are typically more of them. They aren't learning the duties connected with love. In smaller families, of course, children are also doing a lot less caring for one another—again as a routine and needed contribution to family life.

Our kids aren't picking up—under expert adult supervision—the skills of family life. They aren't, as the author cleverly says, starting that kind of "internship" for life at an early age.

Kids are spending a very long time doing nothing much morally virtuous or of genuine social significance beyond going to school.

The author is surely right that this long period in school allows for more diversity in learning of "subjects." That doesn't mean school is harder than ever. Nobody believes that. And school—both high school and college—has surrendered its civilizing function, its inculcation of the principles of moral virtue or decent behavior, its responsibility to help students figure out who they are and what they're supposed to do. School, in other words, is more merely technical than ever.

Someone might say we should follow the example of the Amish or the Mormons and do what we can to get kids to marry and have their own kids young. The immediate objections: That would get in the way of their education! And it is an offense against their freedom as individuals!

All these generalizations are, of course, exaggerations. They apply most of all to the children of our increasingly meritocratic elite—the bourgeois bohemians. They apply a lot less to merely middle-class Americans, or to Americans living in the sticks.

At my Berry College, I recently talked to a hyper-admirable young lady who's working two jobs and earned big scholarships to pay every cent of her college expenses herself. Not only that, she's involved as a leader in every facet of college life and does all kinds of charitable stuff. She's also close to her five siblings, who do a lot to raise each other. She has the habits of Aristotle's morally virtuous person, while being intellectually virtuous too.

But she also reports that she and her brothers and sisters aren't so interested in having big families themselves. After all, who wants to be that worried about money all the time? Do we live in a time when we've figured out that virtue depended on necessities that are now so easy to avoid? Can that be good?

Liberal Education for the Twenty-First Century

So, my title is misleading. The basic content of and case for liberal education didn't change when we moved from one century to another. I'm not big on century analysis and even less on decade analysis (the Sixties!).

Liberal education is under attack these days in pretty predictable ways. It's irrelevant, unproductive, too expensive, excessively time-consuming, and even undermines the habits required to flourish in our high-tech society. All those criticisms have some merit but none of them is new. They all miss the point of liberal education.

Liberal education is certainly counter to our obsession with proving education is worth the time and money through measurable competencies and outcomes. If education is about the competencies required for today's world of work, then most of the liberal stuff can be jettisoned. A college education could be achieved more quickly and a lot more cheaply. Most competencies can be delivered and demonstrated online. And the only reason college takes a whole four years is that students are required to do more than demonstrate their competence.

When liberal education is defended as indispensable or even very useful for the world of work, its defenders end up looking pathetic.

The "effective communication" required for the business world isn't enhanced, it seems, by courses in literature. Professors of literature have gotten all theoretical, and nobody knows what they're talking about. Their communication may be profound, but it's hard to say it's effective in a way any productive employer can use. The study of foreign language is more dispensable than ever, because everywhere the language of business is English. Knowing some Mandarin in the manner of John Huntsman might be a useful adornment, but the effort put in, truth to tell, is not worth the "value added." Huntsman, a Mormon missionary, used the language to convert the Chinese. But for almost all business purposes, there's no need to think much about the souls of one's partners in profit. Even former Harvard president Larry Summers, who you'd expect to have some interest in culture, says don't waste your time on learning languages or working through tough texts from the past. Everything you need to know on the culture front can be Googled.

The same thing goes for "critical thinking" or "analytic reasoning." Once you regard these skills or competencies as divorced from any particular content (or culture or civilization or permanent human questions), then they can be just as easily—or better—learned through solving problems that arise in the business or engineering worlds. Philosophy is (or used to be) less about a method of reasoning than joyful discovery of the truth we can hold in common.

The "Socratic method," so to speak, was conversational, and its results hugely time-consuming and inconclusive. The conversation in the *Republic* takes fourteen hours, and when it's over it's unclear anyone knows what justice is. One thing the guys do end up agreeing on is that conversations of that importance deserve a whole lifetime. Who has that kind of time these days? (Well, things may change if the Singularity really comes.) But the truth remains that liberal education does deserve a whole lifetime, and anyone who doesn't have it is missing out.

A good clue at what is missed is described by the philosopher-novelist Walker Percy. He contrasts the old method of conversational psychiatry (often Freudian), which involved a huge number of expensive, talky sessions and got unreliable results, with the new drug-based psychiatry, which often gets fast and reliable results. The alleviation of symptoms, however, isn't the same as really knowing what's wrong with you. That's why Percy said you have a right to your anxiety as an indispensable clue to who you are. Anxiety, of course, can be prelude to wonder and the joy of shared discovery. You have the right not to be diverted in one way or another from knowing the truth about who you are. The old-fashioned doctor of the soul was far less about cure than about understanding.

Our competencies, unlike philosophy or theology or poetry, disconnect the method from the end, and that means they're disconnected from liberal education. We also learn from the *Republic* that the rhetorical method—disconnected from the end—is characteristic of sophists or technicians for hire. Some of my best friends are sophists, and marketing, management, public relations, (even) law, and so forth are all education for sophistry. There's nothing wrong with that! (One good criticism of Plato—made by many modern philosophers—is that he gave such useful, productive, and ambitious people an unfairly bad reputation.) But education for sophistry is not liberal education.

One way to defend liberal education is to distinguish properly between *labor* and *leisure* as two goods that should be characteristic of every human life. So, to bolster the case for the defense, I've uncovered—through Googling, of course—a classic essay by Mortimer Adler, "Labor, Leisure, and Liberal Education."

Liberal education is about nothing, Adler contends, but the thoughts and activities that fill up our leisure time. Liberal education is good for its own sake for the same reason that every human being—every person—is good for his or her own sake. I'll say a lot more about the strengths and limits of Adler's essay soon.

Let me close for now by dissing or at least qualifying another contemporary defense of liberal education: some claim liberal education should be about what's required to be a *productive citizen*. I've already said that the case that liberal education makes us more productive is weak. The case that it can contribute to citizenship is stronger. To be a citizen is to be a part of a particular place in the world with its own traditions, customs, understanding of justice, and both privileges and duties. A citizen needs to do a lot of untechnical reading unrelated to most work to experience himself or herself as properly at home. So, citizenship really does require "civic literacy," as long as that phrase is understood broadly enough. That education might be called liberal education insofar as it's required to be a free man and woman located in a particular, political place in the world.

Still, to be a citizen purely speaking is to be all about service to a country (or "city" in the Greek sense). Each of us knows that he or she is more than a productivity machine and more than a mere citizen. It's finding out who we are when we're not working for money or our country (or even our family) that liberal education is all about. In the pure sense, liberal education isn't about citizenship—although it far from abolishes the duties of citizenship, just as it as far from abolishes the duty to work.

Liberal Education vs. Killing Time

So, I've gotten too many enthusiastic and too many critical emails about my recent "Liberal Education" for the wrong reasons.

It was critical, of course, with the general approach to education these days. But it wasn't about "general education" in the sense of the courses any particular college requires for graduation. "Liberal education" could hardly be limited to general education. And general education necessarily addresses issues that have nothing to do with liberal education.

Socrates, remember, criticizes the sophists for taking money for teaching. It's true he didn't do that. I do that, although not nearly what my wisdom is worth.

The price of not taking money was certainly felt by Socrates' wife and kids, not to mention a country (city) that could have used a lot more of his effort and advice. On the work/leisure issue, Socrates had a kind of joke: he had no leisure for his family and country, because he was all about doing his duty to the god. His mission from god, remember, was to spend all his time finding someone wiser than himself, thereby proving the god wrong in the observation that no Athenian is wiser than Socrates. It's doubtful that the god meant that Socrates should spend all his time trying to refute a divine claim for wisdom.

And, of course, what Socrates called work, conversational inquiry in the marketplace—almost anyone else would call leisure—or shooting the bull. What Socrates called leisure was doing his financial, "quality time," and other duties to his friends, family, and country. It was what we call work. When we've finished our work, then it's time for leisure. But what we call leisure time Socrates viewed as for real work—a kind of work that's almost indistinguishable from play.

For Socrates, what is generally called leisure is the real work of life, which is also the most enjoyable human activity, the one that makes life worth living. Philosophy isn't restful or even exactly contemplative. It's what the philosopher Hobbes called "the lust of the mind" that's never fully satisfied, but is longer lasting and more satisfying than any lust of the body.

One meaning of Socrates calling himself a "gadfly" is acknowledging that he's, from one view, a parasite, living off the blood and treasure of the Athenians (especially his rich friends) while offering them nothing certain that they can really use.

So, "liberal education" isn't education for being Socrates, because

Socrates showed us clearly the disaster that would befall us if we all tried to be like him. One criticism of liberal education as it's often understood is that it creates a class of parasites who justify themselves with inconclusive claims about their singular wisdom and virtue. That criticism has always had a lot of merit, especially if liberal education is understood to be the whole of education.

From our view, what we might call the Socratic error was institution-alized for centuries into what Mortimer Adler called "the aristocratic error …, the error of dividing men into free men and slaves or workers, into a leisure class and a working class, instead of dividing the time of each human life into working time and leisure time" (from Adler's essay"Labor, Leisure, and Liberal Education").

Socrates himself actually does make that kind of division at one point. He says that every human art—such as medicine—is selfless or directed toward the object of the art. That's even true, in a way, of the philosopher or physicist, insofar as the thinker loses his or her puny self in the object of his thought or concern. But Socrates adds that everyone who practices a "selfless" art also practices the wage-earner's art, which is the same for all those who engage in the various selfless arts. Even doctors and philoso-phers, in real life, have bodies, and so are concerned about the size of their paychecks. Their concern here is no different from that of plumbers or police officers.

Socrates didn't properly defend either the necessity or the nobility of the wage-earner's art by practicing it himself. And so, we don't look to him for a true appreciation of the dignity of worthwhile work well done. We don't even look to him for a proper appreciation of the freedom and digni-ty of most human lives.

That's why, Adler explains, when we think about liberal education we have to think about the great advance of the last century or two. We think that everyone should work for a living, and that everyone should have some leisure time. Everyone, we can say more intentionally and truthfully, should have both the wage-earner's art and liberal education. High technol-ogy has, in our country, come fairly close to freeing all men and women from a life of nothing but drudgery. Almost no one need spend all his or her time earning a living.

To use Adler's words, "industrialists"—we might say entrepreneurs—"interested solely in productivity" regard "the man of leisure … as either a playboy or dilettante." That misunderstanding was useful when it was used to get those lazy aristocrats of old to work. But it degrades us all in a time when every man, to some extent, can be a man of leisure. Leisure time has to be more than free time. It's the time to display and enjoy much of what human freedom is truly for.

That doesn't mean, of course, being a playboy. Hugh Hefner has always impressed me as someone who has desperately but unsuccessfully—and all too seriously—spent his life trying to convince us that he's happy.

But there's a lot to be said for at least appearing to be a "dilettante"—or all about the joyful discovery of knowledge of all kinds. Maybe there's a lot more to be said for the professor not who's interdisciplinary (a tired, empty word) but who has no discipline at all. Well, that guy is no Socrates. But who is these days?

Let me close, for now, with Adler's "final word" on "the most infallible sign of a liberally educated man": "Aristotle said that the mark of a happy man is also the sure sign that he is liberally educated, namely, that you never find him trying to kill time."

Well, one more point: A Christian must ask—what about the virtue of charity? Well, Socrates was pretty weak on that front too. But even St. Augustine says charity shouldn't consume all our lives—open as we are to the strange and wonderful truth about who we are under God.

The Big Issues in Higher Education These Days

So, the final issue in my Public Policy class this semester is higher educa-tion. Here are some controversial propositions generated from papers I've just read from the class. I'm not saying they're all true, but they all are worth thinking about:

1. Too many people "survive college" and are getting diplomas these days.

2. Graduating from college has become incredibly easy if you shop around for easy courses and easy majors. Even if in many cases it's not so easy to get an A, it's also really easy not to flunk.

3. Math and natural science are fairly hard everywhere, and it's really possible to flunk. The answers in science and math are usually black-and-white or objectively true or false. So, it's impossible to bluff your way through calculus and advanced statistics. You have to both be smart and study hard to do well.

4. So, math and science are all about the fact-value distinction. Facts are real, values are "emotive." From their real view mathematicians and scientists look down on the self-indulgent BS (or more precisely, B.A.) artists.

5. Then there's the humanities and social science as they're usually taught. A student with a quite average ability in language and minimal effort can listen to lectures and know enough to write acceptable answers on exams.

6. But the truth is that students of such unexceptional ability—unless they're driven to "overachieve"—don't really understand the reading for the class. That's true, for example, of the boring but dense history text-book; however, it's even more true of, say, Plato, Faulkner, or Nietzsche.

7. Said students can usually get by without doing the reading. That means that they slide by with a superficial and confused understanding, and by basically being unmoved—much less improved—by the subject matter and purpose of the course.

8. One problem, of course, is that the "humanities," even these days, too often buy into the fact-value distinction. That means they're all about not the pursuit of truth but articulating value judgments that are basically relative. So, students in the humanities have a hard time understanding that their opinions are usually wrong or stupid without being educated. And professors too often facilitate their self-indulgence by speaking of the class

as a community of equal learners, and by adding that what matters is less understanding than engagement or activism.

9. This problem can also be called a democratic problem: As Alexis de Tocqueville explains, democrats are skeptical of claims for knowledge that aren't technical or scientific. If I defer to your personal judgment, then I'm letting you rule me. And so, the ideas of truth and virtue are transformed into the idea of the equality of all personal judgments. That way I get to rule myself, as you get to rule yourself.

10. As one of my students (Jacob Stubbs) astutely reminded me, students are too often taught that the various answers that have been given to the fundamental questions of the "humanities," such as "Why is there being rather than nothing at all?" or "Who or what is God," are little more than different values. But the truth is that those real questions can only be taken seriously by those who think that they might have real answers, and the way to those answers is rigorous investigation.

11. The humanities aren't really less difficult than the sciences. Understanding what Plato actually meant, for example, is tougher than experimental physics. It might also be indispensable for theoretical physics. Certainly understanding the true connection between the precise and imaginative use of words and the way things really are is both tougher and rarer than excellence in engineering or genetics.

12. Maybe we just live in a time when the truth about who we are is less valued than ever, or maybe we live in a time when we seem to be able so easily to do without it.

13. It is really true that the negative sides of these propositions apply far less at my Berry College than most places. And so my students are making these judgments less from their personal college experience than from their reading.

14. It's also true that Berry students are more likely to find a religious dimension to remedying what's wrong with higher education today than BIG THINK readers. But none of these propositions are specifically religious at all.

I Text! Therefore I Am!
(The Real Educational Issues Concerning Texting)

Sherry Turkle is at it again. When we expect more from technology, her story goes, we inevitably expect less from ourselves. In a high-tech world, we flee from the emptiness of ourselves into a world of virtual or emotionally impoverished connections. But such disembodied connections are no remedies for our loneliness (Turkle, "The Flight From Conversation," *New York Times*, April 21, 2012).

Texting, in particular, is a pitiful substitute for conversation, for an indispensable way for getting to know who you are. Consciousness, of course, means "knowing with," and being with others is only possible, the Platonic dialogue (for example) suggests, in the full sense when talking face-to-face with someone who has your full attention. A genuine conversation depends on all the interlocutors believing, for a while, that nothing is more important than what they have to say to one another.

Who can deny that texting, twittering, and such have impoverished the conversations we still have? Our exceedingly portable devices allow us to be talking and texting more or less simultaneously. And a rapidly developing skill, Turkle notices, is faking eye contact with the person physically with you while genuinely focusing attention on one or more texting partners.

It's surely self-deception to believe that such multitasking assists in cognitive development. Everything is said sloppily and superficially. Texting when driving, studies are showing in a big way, might be more dangerous than drinking when driving. Rapidly communicating with several people simultaneously surely contributes to our attention deficit disorder. The brain is surely over-stimulated, with quick calculations replacing reflection or even appropriate responses to social instincts. The overload of the "rapid response" portions of our brains isn't producing some "cognitive surplus" that technophiles celebrate.

So, a very obvious educational reform—one, I admit, I haven't had the guts to implement—is to make students check all electronic devices at the classroom door. The students allegedly or really taking notes on laptops are just about always also communicating to folks not in the class (at my nice college, I hear, a good number of girls are even chatting with mom) too. And laptops and smart (or even genius) phones produce plenty of gossipy side conversations in class. That might be in some ironic sense good for in-class bonding, but at the expense of any sustained focus on the content of—the conversation that is—the class.

You might say that this stuff wouldn't happen if professors were more entertaining or inspirational, if they had, for example, a more spectacular multimedia, PowerPoint and more, display going on in the front of the class. I readily admit that the pressure is on in our attention-deficit time for professors to be more engaging—although more in the way the young Steve Martin was on *Saturday Night live* than the way Socrates was.

But even the successfully demagogic professor produces, at best, ambiguous results. I sometimes hear about something deliberately per-verse or ridiculous I said in class from students not in the class just a few minutes after class is over. They heard it through the text-vine!

Let me change teams for a while by making a couple pro-techno points. I am sometimes touched by the use students make of Facebook. Things they would have said in their diaries or just left unsaid they post, imagining that their deep thoughts or emotional reactions will be immedi-ately shared and appreciated by others. Sure, that's not Socratic dialogue, but it's something. ... There's some poetry on those Facebook walls!

While it's impossible to have a real conversation through texting, it's very easy to do it, I think, through email. Socratic dialogues, after all, are written down for us. Email responses can be lengthy, considered, and leisurely, even if they usually aren't. An email conversation can last a lot longer than a face-to-face one.

Now to return to the beginning: The deepest of deep thinkers, Pascal, said that most of our misery comes from being unable to sit quietly alone in our rooms—to be, as Turkle says, alone with ourselves. Experiencing and enjoying solitude depends on having a real sense of personal identity, a truthful and confident inward life.

Who can deny that being online everywhere and all times—always being connected—makes us more miserable in exactly the way Pascal describes? The Beach Boys' celebration of the reverie of simply being "in my room" makes less and less sense to us.

Mitt and His Lit Major

Students at a small, liberal-arts college complained to Mitt Romney about having to borrow money to pursue a college major that doesn't lead to a job. He replied, sensibly, that some majors have a lot more job opportunities connected with them than others. He might have mentioned, it seems to me, stuff like accounting, nursing, and computer science (Sonmez, "Romney to College Students: Pursue Your Dreams, Even If You Have to Borrow to Do So," *Washington Post*, April 27, 2012).

Romney himself majored in English literature. His experience, he explained to students, is that with his major all you can do is go to graduate school. So, Mitt himself went on to get degrees in law and business. He managed to go on to make a good living for himself and his family.

Shouldn't Romney have talked up the obvious ways his major has been a great benefit to him in his life's work? He's the most able and most correct talker among Republican presidential candidates for a long time. He has grammar, syntax, and the correct and even subtle use of words down. We can wish he'd be more poetic, but that's not his style. The truth is that he's better off the cuff than even our eloquent professor-president.

Compare Mitt with Rick Perry the Aggie agriculture major. Don't major in agriculture, someone might say, if you're planning to run for president, although there are, I think, still plenty of jobs for agriculture majors. Or Hermann Cain, the math major, whose undeniable enthusiasm that often comes somewhere near eloquence is at the expense of correctness and ordinary clarity. Or even business major Rick Santorum, whose grammar gets confused when he gets excited. I could add comments here about the Presidents Bush and even President Reagan. (Actually, Reagan was better than people remember, but it turns out that he read a lot more good books for pleasure than people thought.)

So, should the lesson of Romney be that the perfect combination is an undergraduate major in liberal arts and a specialized graduate degree (or two)? Specialization too early is at the expense of eloquence and precision in language, among other qualities that every leader should have.

No specialization at all and you might end up like the young women displayed on the new HBO series *Girls*. I don't really enjoy the show, but it is done well. Those "girls" are whiny and inspire a combination of pity and contempt. Their literary studies and liberal-arts college experiences left them pretty clueless when it comes not only to earning a living, but also in their relationships, moral judgments, and their misguided and degrading sexual "adventures." If you want an indictment of what goes on at our allegedly sophisticated colleges, watch this show.

At my Berry College, students really are able—through the work program and many other ways—to pick up lots of skills and self-confidence outside of the classroom without getting college credit for every "experience" and "engagement." Our admissions people should show parents an episode of *Girls* and explain why our grads hardly ever turn out like *that*, even or especially if they choose a liberal-arts major.

They're more likely to follow a road not all that dissimilar from Mitt's, and there's nothing at all wrong with that.

B. H. Obama and T. S. Eliot

Vanity Fair has published some revealing letters from the young student Barack Obama to his girlfriend Alex McNear. Some conservatives have been mocking the heck out of them as evidence that our president is hard-wired to be a pretentious snob who's always saying a lot less than he thinks he is.

Postmodern conservatives, such as the erudite and profound Carl Scott, are fair-minded enough to actually be impressed. Obama's observations on T. S. Eliot are, in fact, pretentious and awkwardly phrased. But they were written to impress a girl! And the letters actually show our president knows some deep stuff about a hugely important (and now unjustly neglected by our literary critics) poet. More than that, it seems he thought pretty seriously about the relationship between poetic insight, the contemporary West, and his own life. Here's the key paragraph:

> I haven't read "The Waste Land" for a year, and I never did bother to check all the footnotes. But I will hazard these statements—Eliot contains the same ecstatic vision which runs from Münzer to Yeats. However, he retains a grounding in the social reality/order of his time. Facing what he perceives as a choice between ecstatic chaos and lifeless mechanistic order, he accedes to maintaining a separation of asexual purity and brutal sexual reality. And he wears a stoical face before this. Read his essay on Tradition and the Individual Talent, as well as Four Quartets, when he's less concerned with depicting moribund Europe, to catch a sense of what I speak. Remember how I said there's a certain kind of conservatism which I respect more than bourgeois liberalism—Eliot is of this type. Of course, the dichotomy he maintains is reactionary, but it's due to a deep fatalism, not ignorance. (Counter him with Yeats or Pound, who, arising from the same milieu, opted to support Hitler and Mussolini.) And this fatalism is born out of the relation between fertility and death, which I touched on in my last letter—life feeds on itself. A fatalism I share with the western tradition at times. You seem surprised at Eliot's irreconcilable ambivalence; don't you share this ambivalence yourself, Alex? [Scott, "Literary

Proclivities among Obama's Tangled Web," *First Things*, May 5, 2012.]

Here are some thoughts:

1. Sure, it's pretentious and probably somewhat misleading to admit to having not checked out all those famous footnotes. But Obama knows enough to know he doesn't know that much about what Eliot thinks for sure if he doesn't check them.

2. Not only has our president read "The Waste Land," which was a pretty standard introductory assignment when our literature programs were better than they are now, he's read an essay by Eliot that shows that literary excellence of any kind is necessarily situated in a tradition. I will hazard the guess that that's why our president understands why Eliot refused to choose between "ecstatic chaos" and "lifeless mechanistic order"—both of which, of course, dispense with the ennobling and realistic discipline of tradition. It's the tradition—and the poet in response to the tradition—that maintains the tension between the two extreme ways of dissolving the forms and formalities that constitute human life.

3. Eliot's poetic effort to maintain a profound tension or "irreconcilable ambivalence" Obama called "reactionary," because that kind of insight reveals so clearly the limits of any kind of modern political reform or technological advance. Eliot looked backward in some ways to pre-modern realism, and the hopes of the socialists were not hopes he could believe in. We postmodern conservatives might even agree that Eliot slighted what's good—or better—about modern life and thought in some ways.

4. But Obama knew enough to distinguish Eliot from his fellow poets by his not sharing for a moment the hopes of the Fascists either.

5. Eliot wrote, Obama reports, about "moribund Europe"—that is, Europe after "the death of God." Our president didn't seem to object to the thought that Europe is moribund. We wish he would reflect more on it now.

6. Obama shares, "at times," the fatalism of the Western tradition, the fatalism he finds in Eliot. Life and death feed off each other. We are born to die. Our fertility—every dimension of our eros—depends on our mortality. The poet is attracted by but refuses to succumb to the various efforts—imaginative or political—to escape who we are. In this respect, we could wish that our poetic president would be more critical of the transhumanist impulses of our techno-optimism, and maybe even more critical of the "birth dearth" that plagues the sophisticated West.

7. Fatalism, our president seemed to think at other times, is reactionary because it gets in the way of our hopeful or progressive political efforts to transform our condition. Our president is more socialist than Eliot, but his fatalism—what he learned about the Western tradition from poetry—chastens his political hopes at least to some extent. We would wish our poetic tradition would chasten those hopes more. The tension between fatalism and the belief in indefinite perfectibility is one that should characterize our best political reflections, and we postmodern conservatives are more with—although far from completely with—Eliot here.

8. Our president wrote he respects conservatives such as Eliot more than "bourgeois liberalism." He seems to mean that bourgeois liberals don't address our deepest longings, and they're blind to how flat-souled or one-dimensional bourgeois aspirations often are. This is not a political statement so much as an acknowledgment that poets and the study of the best poetry of our tradition are more indispensable than ever in bourgeois times.

9. Our president learned a lot that's *real* about himself and our world from the study of Eliot. Traditionalist conservatives who talk up the liberal arts should be proud (well, proud enough) to use him as an example of the *value* of a liberal education these days. They can add, of course, he might have studied harder and learned more.

B. H. and T. S.—Part 2

So, of all the sundry commentaries on young Obama as literary man, the one that's impressed me the most (except, of course, for my own) is the one by the liberal literary critic Adam Kirsch. Mr. Kirsch connects the musings of young Obama to the great themes of political philosophy:

> But the affinity with Eliot goes deeper than mere style. Mr. Obama speaks respectfully of Eliot's "reactionary" stance, because he sees that "it's due to a deep fatalism, not ignorance." That is, Eliot, like so many of the greatest modern writers, thinks of liberalism as an inherently shallow creed, because of its inability to reckon with the largest things — death and the meaning of life. Since Hobbes, liberalism has been defined as a form of government designed to preserve us from violent death. But death, Eliot reminds us, can't be avoided, and the trivial concerns of everyday life are just a distraction from that ultimate truth.
>
> That's the import of the mocking lines from the poem Mr. Obama cites, "Four Quartets": "O dark, dark, dark. They all go into the dark,/The vacant interstellar spaces, the vacant into the vacant,/The captains, merchant bankers, eminent men of letters...."
>
> It is rare for a politician to give the sense that he has genuinely encountered this kind of "fatalism," or despair. After all, politics in a liberal democracy is all about the distribution of worldly rewards; to believe with Eliot that such rewards are essentially futile is to nullify the whole purpose of politics. Mr. Obama's ability to recognize the poetic truth of Eliot's conservatism, while still embracing the practical truth of liberalism, is what makes his letter not just a curiosity but also a hint at the complexity of his mature politics.
>
> Yet the vicissitudes of his presidency prove that possessing an ironic, literary mind is not necessarily a help when it comes to day-to-day governing. The big revelation of the Obama presidency, for intellectuals, is that his authenticity and irony have not succeeded in making him a transformative figure—that the quality of the president can't be directly deduced from the quality of the man. [Kirsch, "Young Obama's Poetic Politics," *New York Times*, May 8, 2012.]

So, what's wrong with bourgeois or Hobbesian liberalism is that its foundation is fear of one's own death. It lacks both truth and depth because it's obsessed with avoiding what's unavoidable, with not facing up to both personal contingency and personal mortality. According to Eliot in "Four Quartets," we all seem to exist for a moment as kind of accidents in the vacant interstellar spaces that provide no support and no meaning for our particular existences. All human distinctions are meaningless in light of our cosmic insignificance. Captains, merchant bankers, eminent men of letters all equally and quickly go into the dark, and what they do is nothing in light of the eternity of meaningless matter and space. The pride that puffs up ephemeral human accomplishments is overwhelmed by the democracy of the dead.

If you can't face up to who you are, then it's impossible to give or find meaning in what you think and what you do. So, bourgeois lives are nothing more than a series of restless, meaningless diversions that end only in death.

Mr. Kirsch is wrong, however, to equate fatalism with despair. Obama actually called Eliot's insight Stoic. Fatalism means finding meaning in accepting and living well with what we really know about who each of us is. And fatalism itself is only one aspect of B. H. and T. S. or, for that matter, Stoics such as Marcus Aurelius or Atticus Finch or John McCain. Rational men and women are still called to do what they can to assume responsibility for human life being as just and as humane as it can be. Fatalism is no excuse for being amoral or withdrawing from political life.

Obama, in fact, distinguishes his fatalism from Eliot's: he refuses to lose himself in the "reactionary" mood that attributes too little significance to political action.

There are, we might say, three basic moods in Western thought: the fatalism of philosophic insight, the hope in salvation by a loving and gracious Creator by the Christians, and our hope (that perhaps originates in Hobbes) that we can achieve what the Christian God promised for ourselves through some combination of political and technological transformation. We can note that our president seems tone-deaf to that second form of hope, and there's no reason to believe he's evolved (as Eliot did) in its direction over the years.

We can also agree with Kirsch that our president has failed to become a transformative figure, to become in his example and accomplishments the hope we can believe in.

Science, Technology, and Modernity

Indefinite Longevity and Immortality—Part 1

These days, it seems like the reasonable promise of biotechnology has become *indefinite longevity*. Actually, that goal was first articulated by the French enlightenment thinker Condorcet. In order for our pursuit of happiness to be turned into real happiness and for our longings to be undistorted by the prospect of death, the duration of particular human lives have to become long enough and indefinite enough that literally we will not be able to count the days.

Condorcet was clear that goal would be achieved by medical science, although he was necessarily pretty vague about how. His somewhat reasonable faith was in the indefinite progress of science.

Condorcet knew, of course, that human beings longed for immortality. And he was just about as certain that there was no God to free us from our biological limitations. But he also was pretty certain that most of those biological limitations could eventually be overcome by us, by free beings with the ability to change nature with themselves in mind. Now, he didn't think they could be completely overcome. He never doubted that each of us would die eventually. But death, his scientific hope was, would need not come for any particular human being at any particular time. So, it would never seem necessary to any of us. The necessity of death, which for now is so important in determining who we are, would be turned into an accident.

We can be a lot less vague about what Condorcet had in mind. The transhumanists who talk about immortality, about human beings somehow becoming completely other than biological beings, don't make much sense. It's the body that animates the mind, and pure, disembodied consciousness—something like Aristotle's God—couldn't act, couldn't be aroused. Even if our bodies became something other than flesh and blood, even if they became wholly artificial or manmade, they would still be bodies, and so subject to accidental and eventual destruction.

So, the only way we could become immortal is to bring the whole cosmos under our personal control. Actually, the only way I could achieve immortality through my own efforts is to bring the whole cosmos under *my* personal control. As long as I don't control *you*, after all, you remain a threat to me. I could only become immortal if I'm free and rational enough to make myself into the God described in the Bible. And even the Biblical Creator didn't *make* himself who he is.

Living as we do at the dawning of the biotechnology of regenerative medicine, here's what really seems possible: maybe every part of the body—including, of course, the heart and the kidneys—could be regenerated or replaced. And perhaps the brain itself, although irreplaceable, could be kept from degenerating. Then an older person would become like a classic car. If well maintained (and with the ready availability of spare parts), he could go chugging along for who knows how long? Nobody could say that he would necessarily stop working at this or that age, especially if he was extremely prudent in attending to the risk factors—the accidental forces—that could stop his motor, extinguish his being. Regenerative medicine—aided by nanotechnology and all that (it goes without saying I don't understand the details)—provides the promise that we can overcome the necessity of bodily decay.

Will indefinite longevity be the secret to human happiness? Well, there's no denying that people would rather not die at any particular time, and that there's a lot of misery in being governed by the scarcity of time. Time, we can't help but notice, ruins or undermines at least most forms of human enjoyment. That's why we can say that human beings have always longed for immortality, to be freed from the miserable constraints of their self-conscious mortality. When thinking about immortality, we can't help but begin with the Greek gods—who were self-conscious but didn't die. They were, in many respects, like our vampires.

But the immortality of the Greek gods was never meant to make sense or be a realistic possibility. The poets invented them—like today's poets employ the Vampires—to show that immortality isn't only impossible but undesirable. And so if we thought about who we are, we'd actually choose the mortality with which each of us is stuck anyway. Our longing for immortality is best satisfied by accomplishments that stand the test of time—the immortal glory of the great political deeds or of the enduring beauty and wisdom of works of art or literature—although even our fame, we really know, doesn't last forever. And we can achieve a kind of immortality through our minds, through knowing the eternal truth about natural necessity, through philosophy. Everything great that we do—from having children to writing the *Republic*—depends on being mortal. The polymorphous human eros that animates us, in other words, depends upon death. Only mortals know what it means really to fall in love.

But the Greeks still didn't quite know what to do with the fact that, after all the realistic therapy of the poets and philosophers, we still really didn't want to die. The Greeks couldn't quite deny the wisdom of Woody Allen, who said he didn't want to achieve immortality through his work, he wanted to achieve it through not dying. A more vulgar way of expressing the same thought, of course, is, "I don't want to live on through my children; I want to live on by not dying."

Living the trivial, unerotic, and weightless life of a Greek God, someone might say (our transhumanists do say!), is better than being dead. Homer could come up with a character who would choose mortality out of love— like the occasional vampire does—but he still leaves us wondering both how many of us would have the wisdom to make that choice and whether, all factors considered, the choice was even reasonable. Avoiding death or embracing love! It seems like a choice way above the human pay grade. The vampires, we notice, aren't doing that well with it.

That's why the Greeks had to emphasize that that choice is not given to us. Philosophy is learning how to die, how to live as well as possible in light of the invincible truth of one's own mortality. But even Socrates would rather not die at any particular time, and his courageous confrontation with the Athenians at age seventy depended, in part, upon his knowledge that, no matter what he did, he didn't have much time left anyway. Philosophy may depend upon being mortal, but dead men don't philosophize.

Is the Transhumanist Pursuit of Immortality Coercive?

I debated the excellent libertarian author Ronald Bailey over this question at Wheaton College in Massachusetts. Let me share my talking points with you:

Here's what the debate was about: *The Future of Human Liberty.*

Here's Mr. Bailey's position: our pursuit of personal immortality through biotechnological eugenics—through the enhancement and eventually the transformation of our natural beings—is nothing but a new, unprecedented birth of freedom. So there's no need to worry about it or regulate it or limit in some way or another.

Everything about our lives will be more and more about free choice. Eventually we'll be able to choose whether to *live or die*—we won't be stuck with death, as we are now.

Mr. Bailey, of course, will choose *life*—meaning his life. But nothing will prevent me or anyone else from choosing *death*. Nothing will keep any of us from choosing death for himself or herself, however unreasonable Mr. Bailey might think such choices to be.

Here's my position: as we move toward indefinite longevity through biotechnology, we will be more free in some respects, but less free in others. It will be very difficult, maybe impossible, for anyone to choose against enhancement for themselves and their children. Because the world will be more pro-life in some ways, it will be less pro-choice in others.

Here's some background: biotechnological eugenics, for Mr. Bailey and many others today, is *personal*. It's not about improving citizens or the race or the species—the goals of the eugenics of Plato's *Republic* and the Nazis and the Progressives. It's about improving each particular person's chances to remain a person as longer as possible or just to be as personal as possible.

Nothing, in Mr. Bailey's mind, trumps the imperative to keep the people alive right now alive for as long as possible.

So Mr. Bailey is at war against nature. It's out to make him suffer and die for no good reason. To live according to nature is to submit to random indignities. Nature doesn't care about *me*. It treats me as species fodder. It's out to take me out—all particular persons out—for its own purpose. Because I'm *personal*, I don't want to be *natural*.

From a personal or unnatural view, nothing is more important than *me*. That's why we, in our freedom, are using technology and biotechnology to replace cruelly impersonal natural evolution with conscious and volitional evolution. We self-conscious beings are willing change into being that we can really believe in, changes that will keep particular persons around for a lot longer than nature intends.

So, it follows, the more we enhance who we are to make each of us more free from our natural or biological limitations, the more free we will be as persons.

But is it really true that free persons will be able to choose against enhancement?

Consider that we don't think that parents are free to choose against making their kids' lives as risk-free as possible. We don't let parents, for religious reasons, choose against indispensable medical treatment. We don't let two deaf parents choose deafness for their kid, that is, choose to make their kid's life more risky than it need be.

We won't let parents, soon enough, choose against genetic testing and genetic enhancement. They will be choosing against changes, in Mr. Bailey's words, any reasonable person would want. We can't let parents choose unreasonably when it comes to their children.

What if we reach a stage of scientific development where it's safe and easy to enhance kids—or give them genetic advantages that point toward much longer and less risky lives—by implanting upgraded embryos into wombs?

That process means, of course, the complete separation of sex from reproduction. To maximize health and safety, all sex would have to become safe sex. Unprotected sex would result, after all, in the birthing of unenhanced babies.

Right now, the pro-lifers say, we're all too ready to abort "defective" babies. But maybe the progress of science will allow for the correction of defects before the baby enters the womb, making the "therapeutic" reason for abortion obsolete.

What about Catholic or Mormon parents who want to be free to choose to have babies the old-fashioned way—by having unprotected sex and hoping and praying for the best?

We won't let them do it! Having all those comparatively stupid and disease-ridden Mormon and Catholic kids running around would be a danger to us all!

Sure, it's true enough that parents will usually feel compelled to enhance their kids just so they will be competitive in school. But the bigger point is that the other parents will demand that their kids not be exposed to the risky behavior and bodies of unenhanced kids.

Right now, there's no evidence at all that religiously observant people are less intelligent than those who don't believe. But what if religious belief became the cause of people being less intelligent and sicker or just more "according to nature"? Surely we will have reached a rather obvious limit to tolerance. Our religious tolerance is limited, everyone agrees, by the right to life.

Right now the progressives, the libertarians, and other trendy people are all pro-choice. Women should be free to choose whether or not to have babies.

Soon they will be pro-life, wanting laws supporting the eugenics that make their kids' lives as safe as possible. Who can deny that among our already paranoid parents today, the demand is there for health and safety legislation that limits our liberty? Don't we all choose health and safety over liberty? Consider the rapidly eroding right to smoke. Not to mention the right to ride a motorcycle without a helmet.

The pro-lifers will soon enough become the pro-choicers. They will clamor, probably unsuccessfully, for reproductive freedom, for the freedom to choose how they want to reproduce.

Our preference for *life* over *liberty* will also limit the autonomy of individual decision making in many ways.

Consider the physician. What if it becomes easy to enhance the cognitive abilities, memory, and so forth of the doctor? The libertarian view, of course, is that there's nothing wrong with the personal choice of enhancement. But will the physician be able to choose against his personal enhancement on behalf of personal autonomy, on being who he is as a person?

Would anyone go to a "natural" doctor who might kill you but has preserved his personal freedom and noble personality over an "enhanced" doctor who might be a mess personally and have a horrible bedside manner but has the souped-up skills that can actually save you?

There might not be a law making physicians enhance. But there might be, for the same reason that we now require physicians to have M.D.s. In either case, anyone who wants to practice medicine really won't be free to choose not to acquire the latest enhancements.

Someone might say that we require physicians to enhance themselves through their education, and so we should be able to expect them to make themselves better in every possible way. But you know there's a difference between educational expectations and the one that you change your nature, who you are. And no one can really believe that significant cognitive or even emotional enhancements won't change who you are in many ways, affecting, for example, your relationships with the people you most know and love.

Consider the most unproductive profession, the one full of pretentious and self-indulgent autonomy freaks—the college professor. Professors, or some of them, would resist enhancement on the ground that they have a right to the natural moods as indispensable clues to the truth about who we are. The novelist Walker Percy, for example, claimed a right to his anxiety. For many or most philosophers, the issue of which mood opens us to the truth about Being and the truth about ourselves is a fundamental one. For them, moods are a natural gift and not merely random collections of chemicals.

We used to tolerate professors' moodiness because we didn't think they could help it. But soon enough a dean might call a professor in and say: Your students' evaluations aren't so good—students say you're a downer. Not only that, you spend too much time brooding and not enough time publishing.

The dean says get yourself to the physician to get your mood enhanced. There's nothing wrong with that. Studies show moods are just collections of chemicals, and nowadays we're free to choose the chemical collection that makes us happiest and most productive.

The professor can't say no in the name of his autonomy. His freedom to choose his mood means he's free to choose the one that makes him most productive. And so he's free to choose for what the administrators require as a condition of his livelihood.

The requirements of life once again trump liberty understood as personal autonomy. That's bound to diminish the quality of philosophy and literature and music professors, although in the case of the computer science or accounting professor the result might be, as they say, win-win.

The demands of prolonging life will trump liberty in many ways. There will be massive social pressure and actual laws that limit our right to liberty in the name of our right to life. We won't know of a standard of autonomy, it appears, that trumps effectively the standards of security and productivity.

Is a Biotech *Brave New World* the Next Phase of Totalitarianism?

That's the conclusion of Flagg Taylor—one of the leading experts on totalitarian communism:

> I've spent and continue to spend a great deal of time thinking about totalitarianism. In what guise will it appear next? What if we don't need some dramatic revolutionary change in government, some new political ideology, but only an ever-gradual, barely noticeable change in our sense of ourselves? In other words, don't worry so much about Orwell's *1984* but about Huxley's *Brave New World*. The great dissidents knew that they were struggling against more than a deeply unjust political order—they struggled against (in the phrase of Chantal Delsol) the "systematic destruction of man's reality." As Václav Havel put it, "The natural world, in virtue of its very being, bears within it the presupposition of the absolute which grounds, delimits, animates, and directs it, without which it would be unthinkable, absurd, and superfluous, and which we can only quietly respect. Any attempt to spurn it, master it, or replace it with something else, appears . . . as an expression of hubris for which humans must pay a heavy price." Aristotle famously argued we are strange in-between beings—higher than beasts but lower than the gods. When we play God, do we not become even lower than the beasts? [Taylor, "The Nature of Nature," *Ricochet*, October 17, 2011.]

Totalitarianism, from Flagg's view, means that we're free from natural limitations and moral restraints; we're free to impose our personal wills upon reality as we please. He mentions the example of the woman who took advantage of the techno-ability to abort one of her twins. It's her preference as a consumer to have just one kid; therefore, she can alter freely the intention of nature to give her two.

From this view, Marxist communism was the effort to free ourselves definitively from natural limitations. At the end of History, scarcity, due to capitalist technology, will have disappeared, and we'll be free to do whatever we want whenever we want. We'll be free like gods to live unalienated and unobsessive lives. So, religion and the state will wither away, because we will be perfectly satisfied in this world without God and government. And of course we won't have to work unless we feel like it.

Because communism was based on an unrealistic view of who we are, Communist tyrants (such as Lenin, Stalin, Mao, etc.) attempted to will the end of History into being by extinguishing with all means necessary—including or especially terror—all manifestations of "bourgeois" or alienated human individuality. That futile effort to end real human freedom, as the dissident Havel said, was defeated by real human nature.

Does that mean totalitarianism has been forever defeated? Well, for one thing, natural scarcity wasn't really conquered by capitalism, at least in way that wouldn't require more individual productivity in an alienated division-of-labor system. People, it turns out, still have to work. And there's no "Historical" or merely political or ideological solution to that problem.

As Marx himself would have predicted, people, as long as they're alienated, would remain obsessed and even often religious.

But biotechnology promises to really change our *natures* to achieve the result Marx has in mind. Will biotechnology lead to new and improved means of social control in the name of human happiness or contentment, such as those we see described in Huxley's classic *Brave New World*? Will we surrender our freedom in the name of happiness? The new tyrants will be much more responsible and humane, thinking about what's best for us and not just their own lust for power.

We remember that the philosopher Nietzsche said that modern liberalism aimed to produce the "last man," a being without the risky and potentially self-destructive deep longings characteristic of human beings so far. And we have to ask whether our real goal isn't to flatten out who we are in the name of security and a shallow form of self-indulgence. So we willingly surrender our personal sovereignty to experts, bureaucrats, and various forms of immersion into virtual reality. Certainly, we've embraced mood enhancers that allow us to live more easily with who we are, that make us less miserable and more agreeable and productive.

I don't think that the *Brave New World* future is all that likely.

First of all, we can see that our individualism—having produced a world with too many old people and not enough young ones—has undermined productivity to the extent that our entitlement programs seem to be imploding. The "soft despotism" Tocqueville predicted—the omnicompetent nanny state—doesn't seem to be in our future now.

And if you think about the impulse to biotechnological eugenics at this point, it seems to be driven by people determined to take charge of their own futures, to not be replaced, to live for an indefinitely long time. In this respect, it's easy to see that particular persons are more discontented than ever with their present merely natural situation, and they're willing to work hard to escape from it. They do want to be gods, but they think in terms of personal survival more than controlling the lives of others. Their goal may be much less noble—but perhaps it's also much less dangerous—than the goal of the communist idealists of the past.

The easy criticism of Marxist communism was that people will remain self-conscious and mortal, and so aware of the fundamental human scarcity, scarcity of time. That Marxist error produced existentialism—people more morbid or death-obsessed than ever. And the most perverse and evil thinkers of the twentieth century might be thought of as Marxist existentialists.

The biotechnological promise, in its extreme or transhumanist forms, is to free us from the necessity of dying altogether. Only then will we really be free from nature, and beings that free, the thought is, wouldn't have the obsessions that produce tyrants, including Marxist tyrants.

But still, there's always tyranny—fueled by hatred of who we really are—in the thought that we can simply be whatever we happen to desire to be.

It's worth noting that the communist fantasy of Marx really seems to have been a libertarian fantasy. It's hard to know why he called it communism, given that it seems to be a world free from personal love and the other impulses that produce real communities.

Maybe It's Better to Be Alone
(Than to Be Lunch for Alien Predators)

So say some of our leading scientists. Of course, not all experts agree. Carl Sagan, the inspiration behind the films *ET* and *Contact,* thought that we should spend big bucks combing the cosmos for much more intelligent life somewhere else. He even thought that such life, being benign and otherwise more "evolved" than we are, could provide us with what we need to know to free ourselves from our self-destructive tendencies.

If Stephen Hawking, for one, is right, we should do everything we can to not make our presence known; the films *Independence Day* and *Men in Black* provide better insight into what will happen to us when we're found out. The aliens in *Independence Day* travel through the cosmos trashing one planet after another, with no regard at all for the life that might be found here or there. They're like modern imperialists and modern technologists; even Hawking, after all, says we should be thinking up some way of diversifying ourselves to other planets before it's too late. (Apparently, in Hawking's view, abandoning this planet is both good and bad for our species' survival.)

The more intelligent and techno-skilled members of our species have gotten, the more they've been about the business of making their planetary environment unfit for life, and the more they can imagine that they don't need earth to survive and flourish. Why shouldn't more techno-advanced life be like us, but much more so?

One failing among many of *Independence Day* is we don't get any sense of who the extraterrestrial mass-murderous predators really are. But in *Men in Black*, we learn that self-conscious mortals throughout the cosmos are pretty much as screwed up as we are, and intelligent life doesn't get any less screwed up by getting smarter and more scientifically advanced. That makes sense. People these days aren't less neurotic or disoriented or potentially violent than people have always been. The twentieth century gave us more murders than any other.

The fantasy of Sagan and *Contact* is that human beings have been moving from body to mind—evolving away from the basically primate (or even reptilian) causes of our territoriality, violence, and cruelty. So, the more scientifically advanced people are, the more they're all about peaceful coexistence and love and all that stuff John Lennon imagined. The transhumanists add that soon enough we'll all be smart enough to stop dying, and so all the misery of our mortality—such as jealousy and war—will wither away.

The opinion of the great author Walker Percy is that any self-conscious mortal would experience himself as alienated—as "lost in the cosmos"—without help he can't provide for himself or herself. It's silly to believe that we earthlings could be redeemed by aliens from some other planet or place in the cosmos. Any being smart enough to find us would be in some sense or another a "displaced person" (like us) in a way that makes himself a potential danger to himself and others.

Our Proud Human Future—Part 1

The conquest of space, from one view, is one stage among many in the conquest of nature, the human rebellion against nature's indifference or hostility to the importance of man or, better, particular men and women. The conquest of nature proceeds with the importance of me (that is, every particular me) in mind, and its success serves my being—my security and freedom. But the conquest of nature also depends on the science that denies the significance (or even real existence) of any particular being. That science depends on homogeneous, materialistic, impersonal premises that seem to have greater explanatory and practical power than the more anthropocentric views of nature they have discredited. Nothing that we can see with our own human eyes as moral and political beings, according to our scientists, turns out to be real. The eyes of the scientist—the being wholly detached from earthly concerns, the being abstractly and imaginatively orbiting the world of mortals—see us only as examples of natural or, more precisely, universal processes that account for all that really is.

Hannah Arendt wants us to wonder about the being with the capacities for abstraction and imagination. Our freedom from nature that comes with abstraction and imagination—including our capability to make our abstractions real—is at the root of both modern theoretical science and modern technology. Modern technology would not be possible without modern theoretical science, but the scientist as scientist is not concerned with either the great good or great harm modern technology can do for particular human beings. The scientist as scientist abstracts from the effects of his discoveries, and the technologist or autonomous individual abstracts from the question of the truth of those discoveries.

The scientist as scientist, Arendt contends, is not concerned about particular human beings or humanity at all and "does not even care about the survival of the human race on earth or, for that matter, about the survival of the planet itself." When scientists become concerned with the destructive capabilities unleashed by their discoveries and campaign for their peaceful uses, or when they lecture us on the ecological consequences of our techno-trashing of the planet, they are no longer thinking like scientists, but acting like citizens.

The modern scientist's desire to see the reality behind the deception of anthropocentric experience, Arendt suggests, is actually one that has always been shared by all scientists. The theoretical progress of science has necessarily been made at the expense of illusions about human stature. But those illusions, arguably, were already thought to be dispelled in principle at the beginning of science. Aristophanes, in *The Clouds*, mocks the scientist Socrates that he portrays suspended in a basket above the world, who thinks of himself as being detached from the concerns of merely ephemeral beings, even those regarding his own body. As an atheistic materialist, he should consider the core of his being. Even Plato's Socrates explained that philosophy (which in those days was not different from science) is about learning how to die—that is, how to achieve a sort of abstracted indifference to all personal considerations, to see the particular individual as unreal. The physicist's demonstration of the reality of the physical world is much more rational than the humanistic poet's concern for the fate of any particular man. Modern science, from this view, is simply a series of breakthroughs in accord with the intention of science all along to become a genuinely universal account of all that exists, one that does not privilege any anthropocentric consideration.

A universal science, Arendt explains, is different from a merely natural science, because nature itself is finally incomprehensible in terms of the common-sense human perception of lawful regularities. As Aristophanes himself predicted, surely the philosophers or scientists would eventually figure out that even the idea of the beautiful natural order that animated their inquiry is an illusion. Scientists err when they think of themselves as escaping from the deluded world of the earthly "cave" that guarantees personal significance to what mere mortals do into a cosmos that is the home of the human mind. It turns out that even that abstract perception of the mind being at home depends on the mind's imposition of structure upon a reality deeply incomprehensible to any human perspective.

Ultimately, the question of whether the success of modern science enhances the stature of man or, more precisely, of particular men is of no concern to the scientist. Carl Sagan explained that modern science was one "Great Demotion" after another of all our claims to excellence or distinctiveness in nature or the cosmos. This cold and atheistic obliteration of all human pretensions, Harvey Mansfield complains, was a cause of the "manliness run amok" of the twentieth century—horrifyingly cruel and futile ideological attempts to replace scientific truth with something else. But the scientist as scientist cannot help but be baffled by all that sound and fury, by so many people who care about their importance or dignity or some made-up God. It is, as Arendt says, the scientist's "pride and …

glory" to be indifferent to "his own stature in the universe or about his position on the evolutionary ladder." It is his pride and glory to show that pride and glory signify nothing.

Genuine human pride, of course, does not come simply from an extension of one's material powers. It is always a form of self-transcendence, an understanding of oneself as more than a merely biological being. The pride taken in the success of modern science is, from one view, really pride in the display of man's freedom from natural determination, in his ability to assume conscious and volitional control over his environment. From another view, though, modern science is rooted in the scientist's proud transcendence of all personal concerns in favor of anonymous truth. Modern progress feeds on the interdependence of these two incompatible views of pride—that of the self-obsessed individual and that of the self-denying scientist. Both forms of pride, of course, depend on abstraction and imagination, and so both are finally incomplete.

Our Proud Human Future—Part 2:
The Scientist's Proud Transcendence

Of course, a real criticism of "the scientist" is that he himself is an abstraction. The distinction between the scientist and "the layman" (and so the sciences and the humanities) does not correspond to the whole lives of real human beings. The scientist, Arendt notices, "spends more than half of his life in the same world of sense perception, of common sense, and of everyday language as his fellow citizens." It is only when acting as a scientist that he leaves behind part of himself in his quest for the truth, imaginatively detaching himself from various dimensions of his earthly home to enter into a universality which has no place for him as he ordinarily experiences himself. It is a strange and wonderful testimony to our powers of abstraction and imagination that men have purged science of its anthropological elements.

Arendt concludes with the dehumanizing possibility that, completely detached from the anthropological or earthly perspective, human life—even science—might appear to be just another impersonal natural process. Perhaps scientists will come to comprehend and control "laymen" in ways completely incomprehensible to them; then the key common sense distinctions that separate us from rats will disappear in practice as well as in theory. It is this conquest "from space"—from the perspective of the scientist orbiting earthly life through his powers of imagination and abstraction—that threatens to transform our existence far more than men merely traveling in space.

Space travel, itself theoretical, scientists rightly consider the accomplishment of mere "plumbers" exploiting certain merely technical features of theoretical truth. Knowing the truth about "space," our scientists have already concluded, does not depend on people actually going there. Modern science's displacement of particular human beings from the world of proud personal significance would be complete whether we stay on this planet or settle others.

Arendt actually provides plenty of evidence that our dehumanization by the science discovered by perfectly abstracted imaginative scientists is quite unlikely. Because the scientist as scientist characteristically does not reflect sufficiently on who and what make science possible, a fully abstract science cannot sustain itself. Only mortal, temporal beings in spirited and erotic pursuit of various forms of self-transcendence have the desire to fund science, or for that matter to become scientists; the disappearance of such beings would bring science to an end. Through abstraction and imagination, the scientist diverts himself from "the who," the real existence of the whole human being who remains incomprehensible to his science. But the scientist himself remains a "who." He can never, in truth, be reduced to just a mind; he necessarily remains, for example, a citizen, too.

The scientists' proud and abstract indifference to the stature of man and particular men and women is, in part, a diversion from what they really know. Like all human inquiry, theirs is distorted by pride. Arendt reports that Greek philosophers like Aristotle thought it absurd that anyone could regard man as the highest being in the cosmos. Those philosophers reached that conclusion by proudly identifying their own highest activity with a kind of divine transcendence of human insignificance. At their best, they did not really deny that the wondering and wandering philosopher and scientist—the being captured in the character Socrates—is more wonderful than the stars securely situated in invariable orbits. Plato's Socrates did not understand himself, finally, as an orbiting philosopher-king but as a seeker located in the "cave" with his fellow citizens—a far cry from the self-denying, self-transcending scientist.

The Romans, Arendt adds, were the first to be obsessed with the stature question, but she does not explain why. It seems to me that only with the influence of the Biblical view on the Roman world that man was—or particular men and women were—raised above the rest of natural existence, even as they were also equally located under a personal God. And modern science, from a moral and political view, was driven by the Christian insight about personal stature or significance, by the insight that the beings alienated—and not just abstracted—from the rest of nature are both the most wonderful and incomprehensible of beings.

Human beings, in their freedom, use the results of scientific inquiry to overcome their alienation from the rest of nature, to secure their importance or stature. Our efforts have the perverse effect of displacing ourselves further from the personal significance we enjoy in our particular moral and political homes on earth. As increasingly rootless or displaced persons, we are in many respects more free and secure. Still, we seem to experience ourselves in many ways as more contingent, accidental, and deeply insignificant than ever before. We have absurdly tried to make our stature completely dependent on our conquest of nature, and we have neglected the evidence that we are elevated in many ways above the rest of creation by God and nature. Our scientists have encouraged us in that neglect.

The simple truth is that we cannot do anything to enhance or diminish the singular stature we have been given all that much. Human beings will remain as strange and wonderful—and as uniquely great and miserable—as ever. It is part of our stature and our undeniable greatness that we lack the power to make ourselves more or less than we really are. And our ineradicable alienation from the world our scientists can otherwise perfectly explain will continue to be a clue to an unabstracted or genuinely realistic account of the lives of whole human beings. Changing our location to some other planet will have an insignificant effect on our stature in the cosmos. Conquering all of space (as Arendt explains) is just out of the question, so we cannot help but remain (as Walker Percy says) to some extent "lost in the cosmos." Being the only beings who truly wander is a precondition for being the only ones who truly wonder; just knowing that can make us at home enough with our homelessness on whatever planet we might find ourselves.

Scientists so abstracted that they cannot see the real world of human beings become irrelevant to that world. Their discoveries will be deployed, but not by them. Our world will remain in the decisive respect anthropocentric—or, better, theocentric—insofar as what we really know about the being who knows and loves points in the direction of a personal, loving God.

Does NASA Need a Philosopher?

One of the most disappointing moments in an otherwise fairly encouraging Republican New Hampshire debate was that none of the seven candidates would continue federal funding for human space flight. Newt was about "a real space program that works"; but, for him, that now means privatization as the key to innovation.

My own view is that space exploration is a project that our government should believe in. So, I'm taking the liberty of sharing with you a defense of space exploration and even, in a limited sense, space conquest as both necessary and a choice worthy of American efforts that I wrote a couple of years ago.

According to Tom Wolfe, NASA's best journalistic poet, our space program needs a philosophic justification to get the "godlike" adventure that gave us all that heroic right stuff going again. Here are a few random thoughts in that direction. I'm not saying that I'm volunteering to be a pioneer to Mars or that I'm not aware that there's a powerful case in the other direction. But it's always a mistake not to give Tom Wolfe a hearing.

1. JFK understood that the space race with the Soviets was a key part of a military contest that we were stuck with taking with dead seriousness. We still need a space program for military reasons, although that probably doesn't involve going to Mars. We have no choice but to remain techno-dominant, and our likely eventual war with the Chinese may well be fought in space. People can retreat to their porches or not as they please, but technology will continue to develop whether we like it or not. I'm saying this first because Wolfe doesn't say it and because President Obama (contrary to the sagacious advice of Bill Gates) doesn't even see clearly enough that modernizing our nuclear weapons is the best way to save lives and liberty. I could say something similar about the need to keep ahead in nanotechnology, no matter how scary or potentially "dehumanizing" it may be. Describing the prospect of nanotechnology combined with space travel is above my pay grade.

2. Actually, Wolfe says NASA did have a philosopher, Werner von Braun, whose word didn't catch on, he speculates, because he was a German with a Nazi background. But Americans are pretty open to listening to Germans (like Leo Strauss) and even Germans with Nazi backgrounds (like Martin Heidegger). I can't help but add that von Braun's word just didn't get out.

3. Wolfe heard that word in a dinner speech and can't point us to any text. Here's my version of it: only human beings are open to the truth about all things. Only human beings live meaningful lives. With their disappearance, the truth about Being would have no one to know it, and the universe would become meaningless matter and nothing more. So far, we're stuck in a very vulnerable position on this planet. It might be pulverized by an asteroid at any time; we might accidentally blow it up or trash it beyond repair. The sun will stop shining someday, no matter what we do. We have a duty—in the name of meaning and Being—to spread ourselves out around the cosmos, giving philosophy, as Strauss would say, the longest possible future, not to mention virtue, dignity, poetry, and (some would impiously say) God.

4. That duty seems deeper, from an anthropocentric view, than merely our duty to "the environment." No matter how well we treat our planet, eventually it will turn on us. We're getting increasingly paranoid about "climate change," forgetting that we have no "natural right" to a stable climate, one that will support lives such our ours. Surely, our duty to preserve "man" is more profound than our duty to do what we can to preserve earthly nature. (The two duties are obviously not incompatible.)

5. It seems pretty likely that we can employ our technological freedom to make other planets inhabitable. That will increase our experiences of "displacement" and produce various neuroses connected with earth deprivation and earth nostalgia. But it won't change fundamentally who we are. If we find other meaningful life, that won't prove there's no God, and we'll remain stuck with virtue and "born to trouble" out there, as we are here.

6. Von Braun's philosophizing makes a lot more sense than Carl Sagan's silly thought that planet hopping be justified by making conscious and sacred our natural inclination to species preservation. To the extent animals become conscious, they become less driven by what's best for the species. But the way the German describes the duty does seem noble and distinctively human.

7. Sagan was also animated by the silly thought that we search the cosmos for much more intelligent and so benign extraterrestrial intelligences that can cure us of what ails us. If there are super-intelligent ETs, we should not make ourselves known to them. We have no evidence that there's any connection between being really, really smart and techno-advanced and being peaceful. The ETs in *ET* and *Contact* are baloney. *Men In Black*—the first one—seems closer to the truth. Really smart

beings—like Heidegger—are likely to be really perverse, screwed up, and a danger to themselves and others. Von Braun's philosophizing is based on what is to me the more reasonable thought that there are no other really brainy beings out there, that we are in crucial respects on our own in the cosmos.

Spacey Philosophy

1. So my thoughts on NASA provoked a variety of most thoughtful responses. The ones by Brendan Foht were the most detailed and philosophic, but they were all worthwhile.

2. Their relevance is heightened by this being the BIG THINK day where we question the wisdom of economic and technological progress from the point of view of *stability*. Being detached from our home planet would be mighty destabilizing. Another German philosopher, Hannah Arendt, actually feared that possibility as one culmination of the disorienting, inhuman logic of modern science.

3. On BIG THINK I was attacked, once more, for being a conservative. But in other places I was more reasonably attacked for being a liberal, or at least libertarian. A fiscal conservative could reasonably say we don't have money for this techno-luxury these days, and a social conservative could add that playing around in space just distracts us from doing what's required to lead decent and virtuous lives right here.

4. The post about NASA needing a philosopher ended with a question mark. It was, as they say, a thought experiment. America's most philosophic novelist of the twentieth century, Walker Percy, said our job is to put back together what's true about Anglo-American empiricism (science generally) with what's true about European existentialism (which is really various forms of the dumbing down of the evil and pretty unreadable genius Martin Heidegger).

5. So, even in departments of philosophy you see that division. Analytical philosophy is very rigorous and attuned to scientific inquiry, but it's boring because it says so little about who we really are. What is usually called "continental philosophy" is pretty interesting (to the extent it can divorce itself from bad translations of Heideggerian terminology) because it deals with real people in real situations (Sartre, Camus), but it's usually between pretty and really undisciplined and usually has an unreasonable contempt for what scientists (such as our friend Carl Sagan) really know. (I didn't say Carl Sagan was silly about everything; he wasn't only an effective popularizing physicist—he was one heck of a theoretical physicist.)

6. So here's, exactly, where Sagan was silly: he thought we should make conscious our natural inclination to indefinitely perpetuate our species, and make that project our sacred cause. He also thought that the

ETs would be benignly wise "pure minds"—check out *Contact* or *ET* for the most boring aliens imaginable. Those advanced minds, he thought, could tell us what we really needed to know to save ourselves from destruction, from our seemingly fatal combination of very high technology and residually reptilian brains.

7. Given that we don't really have a duty to the species, we might follow the Germans and say we have a duty to preserve what distinguishes human beings—openness to Being, the truth. We have the duty to preserve the only source of meaning in the universe. There are realistic objections to this conclusion. Brendan Foht had a great one—what has Being ever done for *me*?

8. To which I would add the obvious, what has the species ever done for *me*? Sagan and Heidegger, each in his own way, is too impersonal to be realistic about who each of us is.

9. Percy asked why it makes sense to be all excited about searching the cosmos for "aliens" when the strangest and most wonderfully alienated beings imaginable—us—live right here on earth. That's not to say there aren't "aliens" elsewhere in the cosmos. But, following Percy and Foht, I am saying we already know pretty much what they'll be like. Sagan's problem is that he didn't really appreciate how strange and wonderful *we* are—and even *he* was. (And Heidegger didn't see that it it's our *natural* capacity for wondering that leads to our wandering …)

10. I said before that we tend to exaggerate the ontological and theological significance of successfully cloning a human being. Just because we, in a way, make the clones doesn't mean they won't have souls, display unique and irreplaceable individuality or the inwardness of personal identity. Successful cloning won't be any decisive evidence one way or another for the possibility that we're beings made in the image and likeness of a personal God.

11. The same goes for discovering highly intelligent and in some way or another embodied life elsewhere in the cosmos.

Looking For Love with All the Wrong Devices (Because People I Only Like)

Our famous novelist Jonathan Franzen gave quite the challenging commencement address at Kenyon. Here's what he said about technology and *eros*:

> Let me toss out the idea that, as our markets discover and respond to what consumers most want, our technology has become extremely adept at creating products that correspond to our fantasy ideal of an erotic relationship, in which the beloved object asks for nothing and gives everything, instantly, and makes us feel all powerful, and doesn't throw terrible scenes when it's replaced by an even sexier object and is consigned to a drawer.
>
> To speak more generally, the ultimate goal of technology, the *telos* of *techne*, is to replace a natural world that's indifferent to our wishes—a world of hurricanes and hardships and breakable hearts, a world of resistance—with a world so responsive to our wishes as to be, effectively, a mere extension of the self.
>
> Let me suggest, finally, that the world of techno-consumerism is therefore troubled by real love, and that it has no choice but to trouble love in turn. [Franzen, "Liking Is For Cowards. Go For What Hurts," *New York Times*, May 28, 2011.]

Franzen doesn't mean that our devices—such as our BlackBerries—are really sexual. I admit I have days when I spend a good deal of time fondling mine, but not in a creepy way. There's no such thing as a sexy machine, and contrary to Mr. Kurzweil, it's clear that if and when we become conscious robots, we'll cease being sexy and, of course, loving. We may still like other robots, though.

Franzen means that our fantasy is to be able to take all the risk out of our relationships. We want to receive without having to give, and we want enough control that indifference to our wishes and "rejection" aren't possibilities. We want to replace natural relationships with technological ones; with ones that we made with our "self"-ish or personal needs in mind. (We already have robots who seem to be better versions of dogs, the animal we also invented millenia ago to be of uncritical service to us. The dog, of course, remains natural to a degree, and so capable, unlike the BlackBerry, of biting the hand that feeds him.)

So, from the beginning, the modern, technological project has been at war with the unpredictability of love and the elusiveness or incomprehensibility of anyone we can't control. As Franzen goes on to explain, we'd rather like and be liked than love and be loved. There are reliable techniques to get people to like you, and you like them back, but with a bit of contempt. But to be satisfied with liking is "cowardly." It's about, as they say, fear of the unknown, diverting oneself from the irreducible mystery of one self in love with another. It's true, as the song says, I don't have to like you to love you. And there's nothing you can (reliably) do that will make me love you.

Franzen concludes that we're all really angry we're going to die, and love is the compensation we have for death. The transhumanists—or techno-enthusiasts on steroids—want to bring death to an end, and then we won't need to love to curb our anger. But our increasingly technologized world won't really end death, but it makes love, in some ways, tougher than ever.

A Few Thoughts from Sherry Turkle's *Alone Together: Why We Expect More from Technology and Less from Each Other*

The theme of Turkle's indispensable book is in its title. It's an old theme, originating, maybe, with the philosopher Rousseau. Technological progress is at the expense of personal virtue and the relational lives of persons.

I'm going to share just a few observations from one of Turkle's notes (p. 308, note 11):

1. "As preteens, the young women of the first Google generation (born roughly from 1987 to 1993) wore clothing widely referred to as 'baby harlot'; they listened to songs about explicit sex well before puberty. Their boomer parents had few ideas about where to draw lines, having spent their own adolescences declaring the lines irrelevant."

2. "One might say it is the job of teenagers to complain about constraints and the job of parents to insist on them, even if the rules are not obeyed. Rules, even unheeded, suggest that twelve to fifteen are not good ages to be emotionally and sexually enmeshed."

3. "Today's teenagers cannot easily articulate any rules about sexual conduct except for those that will keep them 'safe.' Safety refers to not getting venereal diseases or AIDS. Safety refers to not getting pregnant. And on these matters teenagers are eloquent, unembarrassed, and startlingly well informed."

4. "But teens are overwhelmed with how unsafe they feel in relationships. A robot to talk to is appealing—even if currently unavailable—as are situations that provide feelings of closeness without emotional demands."

5. "Rampant fantasies of vampire lovers (closeness with constraints on sexuality) bear a family resemblance to ideas about robot lovers (sex without intimacy, perfect)."

6. "And closeness without the possibility of physical intimacy and eroticized encounters that can be switched off in an instant—these are the affordances of online encounters."

7. "Online romance expresses the aesthetic of the robotic moment. From a certain perspective, they are a way of preparing for it."

So we can say that transhumanists want to become robots not only to be freed from the necessity of decay and death characteristic of biological bodies. They want to be free from the shared responsibility and real intimacy characteristic of free and rational beings with biological bodies. Relationships are unsafe. Real love (and the corresponding real hate) are too scary and otherwise more trouble than they're worth. We seem free to choose—and so we increasingly do choose—virtual lives, lives without the perception of real rules and constraints. An online relationship is almost as virtual or disembodied as a relationship with a robot.

Beer, Other Beverages,
and the Future of Self-Government

Let me share with you the conclusion of an alarming study that came to my attention a couple of years ago.

Americans are now drinking more bottled water than beer. The people who reported on the study comment that this has got to be bad for our future as relational and political beings.

We drink beer to loosen up, to clamp down on our inhibitions. Then, we anxious autonomy freaks can open up to others, be conversational, tell the truth with uncalculated abandon. Bars, of course, are among the most conversational places in America; and beer, we all know, is the mean between the extremes of hard liquor (that will get you too drunk to talk and cause you to lose any control over your moods and so might make you more solitary and melancholic than ever) and not drinking at all (which is a sure sign of a lack of conviviality and openness to the joys of life).

Beer, of course, is somewhat unsafe. I'm not going to lecture you on the dangers of drunk or even tipsy driving. Because having a real beer is sort of like drinking a loaf of bread, it doesn't take much to make you fatter. I don't know of any diet plan that includes beer. Not only that, beer can cause you to loosen up too much, and so your conviviality might too easily slide into more than mere talk. It can make you into a sucker in general, easy prey for all the evildoers that surround us all these days. That's why beer is best consumed at the neighborhood bar, where friends look out for friends and everyone walks or staggers home.

I myself am getting too old and fat to pretend that I'm completely unafraid of beer. I've tried—with uneven success—to switch to the safer and allegedly more tasteful wine. Wine, in my opinion, does facilitate the social virtues about as well as beer. It was an excellent replacement for the martini (which tastes ridiculous and gets you drunk fast) among sophisticates such as us BIG THINKERS. So, I endorse wine as long as it's fairly cheap. The movie's passionate argument against Merlot, to me, is an argument for it—it's impossible to screw Merlot up, and that can't be said of even Cabernet.

I rarely drink water unless I'm really thirsty. After all, what's the point? Where's the pleasure, the fun? If I do drink water, I make sure it's from a tap. Bottled water is the biggest scam going; it's not really less dangerous or better for you. I have to admit I do like carbonated water a little, especially the very cheap Kroger brand (and I guess Walmart has some equivalent). Drinking water is a shamefully privatized, narcissistic act.

What about coffee? Well, I really like it and drink a lot of it. Some say I don't believe in progress, but who can deny that there's been remarkable progress in the coffee readily available to Americans over the last generation? Starbucks coffee is swill. But there are many better kinds of designer, grind-your-own bean coffee everywhere now. Coffee shops that serve all kinds of special roasts are even in the sticks of our country.

The new coffee we all enjoy (and lots of us to excess even in this safety-conscious time) is much stronger than the traditional *Maxwell House*. And so, we're more wired than ever. Someone might say that the resulting paranoid edginess is keeping us from being relaxed enough to reproduce.

But I tend to think that multiple large cups of powerfully caffeinated beverages assist us in our efforts to find genuinely relational ties in our lonely, ghostly time.

In my profession, coffee is indispensable. Studies show it makes you smarter in the short term (that term being about as long as a typical class), and it induces you to talk fast and straight. It releases you from some inhibitions and triggers others, making you charmingly quirky and vulnerable.

Coffee is certainly the beverage for philosophers. Wine might lead some to speak the truth, but often in a stupid, blowhard way. Coffee, take it from me, is the more *erotic* beverage.

Fat, Smoking, and Stupid Is No Way
to Go Through Life

I'm distorting, of course, the legendary admonition of the evil Dean Wormer to the fat loser Delta pledge Flounder in the classic film *Animal House*.

I had to add "smoking" and delete "drunk" from the original quote, because they weren't particularly judgmental about smoking in 1962. That is, alcohol abuse and not smoking was associated with being a loser back in those less enlightened days. Smoking, in fact, doesn't get in the way much of being a good student or a productive citizen. Alcohol abuse was the main culprit for the self-destructive (if witty and somehow enlightened) behavior of the Delta guys. (The Sixties vibe of the film was most clear in the postscripts that assured us that the Deltas all turned out to be, despite being expelled for very good reasons, huge successes, while the Omegas who stayed in school all met deservedly bad ends.)

(More digression: the best thing about the film is the motto of Faber College: "Knowledge is good." Nobody could for a moment defend that Platonic faith on that campus, least of all the one professor we get to know a little—the aging hippie and failed novelist played by Donald Sutherland.)

Back to the story: cigarettes, used as directed, will very probably shave years off your lifespan. And the biggest loser these days is someone who makes the huge error of short-sighted indifference to "risk factors." That may be why, as I also learned on BIG THINK, studies show smokers can't get dates these days. (I'm not at all sure that's true: a not negligible percentage of Berry College students smoke, and the lookers among them still seem to be doing okay.) Smoking is certainly less sexy than ever.

Animal House came to mind when I read the excellent BIG THINKER David Berreby's post on the trinity of evildoing for our sophisticates today—obesity, smoking, and not saving for retirement (Berreby, "Obese? Smoker? No Retirement Savings? Perhaps It's Because of the Language You Speak," *Big Think*, February 5, 2012).

The study Dave cites (by a Chinese guy touting, in effect, the superiority of his language) connecting differences in syntax among various languages as a key to variations in prudence about the future is completely implausible to me.

Here's one reason: Americans pretty much speak English. But there are huge variations in behavior among Americans on the obesity, smoking, and savings fronts. As I said before, the most recent studies (by Charles Murray, David Brooks, and others) connect those differences to class or, better, tribe. Americans, Brooks says, are divided into an upper and a lower tribe.

The upper tribe is more prudent than ever: Its members are thin, fit, don't smoke, and save their money. It used to be weight didn't correlate with class much at all. Lots of rich guys used to be fat and smoke; they were in every respect, as we learn from *Mad Men* and many movies, not particularly health conscious. It even used to be that men were much more attracted to women with considerable body fat as a sign of prosperity and even health. Now body fat is more unerotic than ever because it calls death to mind in neon letters.

Meanwhile, I've said before, the lower tribe is still plagued with smoking and a genuine obesity epidemic. Its members have steadily gotten worse (until maybe very recently) when it comes to saving. Some people would say that consumerist materialism or the welfare state is to blame. Others would talk about the instability of families and the growing number of single parents. Others still would say with considerable evidence that families have to work more hours than ever to make ends meet. Our high-tech, globalized economy has caused wage stagnation, with a contributing factor being women flooding the workforce. Wage increases have lagged behind productivity increases and the cost of living. It's easy to add, of course, a lot about the declining quality of the education available to the ordinary guy's kids.

There is also the tendency to connect these vices with the lower tribe's desperate attachment to guns, God, and sundry forms of oppressive and superstitious fundamentalism.

What's interesting to me is why BIG THINK writers and readers (reflecting, as they do, the upper-tribe consensus) are so judgmental about the obesity, smoking, and lack of savings of others. Those judgments seem contrary to the libertarian drift in the way they talk about morality generally.

Maybe they care that their fellow Americans are making erroneous choices when it comes to their health, happiness, and security. Maybe they care about these behavioral threats to personal productivity and so our nation's future prosperity.

Or maybe they're afraid that those they'll end up having to pay for the consequences of the "bad choices" of those screw-ups.

If the members of the lower tribe don't start getting more prudent when it comes to their future security or retirement, for example, they'll become so impoverished in their old age that we'll be stuck with taking them on as dependents. With the general movement from defined benefits to defined contributions, the ordinary working stiff is no longer guaranteed a pension but only the opportunity to save his own money for his old, unproductive years. He better save a lot, and he'd better manage his funds wisely.

If he (or she, of course) continues to smoke and stuff his (or her) face with refined carbs, of course, we can have the solace of hoping that his (or her) money lasting as long as he (or she) does won't be such a big problem after all.

The Change We Can Actually See

The progress of American individualism in the past generation has not been toward apathetic contentment (Tocquevillian individualism) but toward the intensification of personal self-obsession (Lockean individualism). People are more detached from others than ever, or less animated by personal love or less moved by thinking of themselves as part of a whole greater than themselves. That means that, in the Lockean sense, we are thinking more personally or individually; we believe that the "bottom line" is keeping the free person alive as long as possible. The result can only be, we now see, the increasing anxiety of individual responsibility. Americans have not been living any Progressive or Marxist dream of having freed themselves from scarcity for unalienated self-fulfillment. And they know, now more than ever, that such a dream can never become real in some postproductive age.

In this respect, the vision of our libertarians (Lockeans on steroids) turns out to have been, to a point, most realistic. The Marxian idea that the modern techno-conquest of nature could allow people to live unobsessive, and so unalienated, lives was naïve—a naïveté present, for example, in the 1960s version of our Progressivism. Naïve, too, was the idea that government planning could remove worry and anxious planning from individual lives. People are, it turns out, stuck with working. And the demands of productivity actually accelerate as technology progresses. They are also in some ways more future-obsessed than ever.

Free individuals tend to believe that their own deaths are the extinction of being itself; but, as Lockeans, we are less whiny-existentialist and fatalistic about that than we are powerfully resolved to do what we can to stay around as long as possible. (We can exempt our religious minority of observant believers from this view of who we are, just as we can notice that they are actually the ones who are mitigating our birth dearth with their many babies. It is always possible that there could be a religious solution to the crisis of our time.)

Our libertarians were wrong, however, to think that we could flourish in abundance by understanding ourselves with ever-more-perfect consistency as free and productive individuals progressively untethered by biological direction. It turns out that it is not free individuals but men and women in touch with who they are by nature who have enough babies to secure our productive future and so to pay for our minimalist entitlement programs.

It also turns out that the hyper-Lockean attempt to detach individual autonomy from birth and death and love is the wrecking ball of the welfare state. The least that can be said is that the free individual has triumphed over the feckless dependent.

Our demographic "crisis" has destroyed the Progressive dream of a schoolmarmish social democracy humanely enveloping us all. The good news is that Tocqueville was wrong to worry that we would slouch into subhuman contentment. The road to serfdom, we see now, will never get to serfdom. The bad news is that, to the extent that we understand ourselves as free individuals (and nothing more), we pursue happiness, as Locke himself explains—but hardly ever find it.

The next stage in American progress, we can hope, is that we will discover, or rediscover, the truth that the free or personal being is necessarily a relational being. That would, however, take us a step beyond Locke in thinking about who we really are.

Health Care, Pensions, and Our Demographic "Issue"

According to BIG THINK's Mr. Daylight Atheism, birth control will save the world. He writes as if it were 1962 and all that Malthusian stuff about the population explosion was still plausible. But the truth is that the "advanced" world from the United States to Europe to Japan is actually plagued by a "birth dearth." The birth rate has dropped below the rate of replacement, and that fact seems to have made welfare or social insurance states unsustainable over the long term.

The demographic issue is not a crisis—although it's a big problem—in our country because of the reproductive behavior of observant religious believers, which, for now, is causing our birth rate to be hovering just above the rate of replacement. In most of Europe, Japan, and so forth, that rate is well below replacement, no doubt for many reasons. But one is the dearth of observant religious believers.

Here's a taste of what James Capretta is going to say at Berry College on Thursday:

> The social welfare programs that were erected in the postwar era were premised on assumptions of robust fertility rates, perpetually growing workforces, and never-ending economic growth.
>
> Indeed, Paul Samuelson, one of the intellectual fathers of pay-as-you-go pension systems, had this to say about them in 1967:
>
> "The beauty of social insurance is that it is actuarially unsound. Everyone who reaches retirement age is given benefit privileges that far exceed anything he has paid in—exceed his payments by more than ten times (or five times counting employer payments)!
>
> "How is it possible? It stems from the fact that the national product is growing at a compound interest rate and can be expected to do so for as far ahead as the eye cannot see. Always there are more youths than old folks in a growing population. More important, with real income going up at 3 percent per year, the taxable base on which benefits rest is always much greater than the taxes paid historically by the generation now retired.
>
> ". . . A growing nation is the greatest Ponzi game ever contrived."

Unfortunately, almost from the moment Samuelson uttered that statement, the population of the industrialized West has been rapidly aging, birthrates have been anemic, workforces are stagnant or declining, and global economic competition has suppressed the wage growth of the West's middle class.

The United States isn't exempt from these problems. The Baby-Boom generation is on the verge of retirement, which will swell the ranks of enrollees in entitlement programs. The U.S. workforce is still growing, but not nearly as rapidly as the population age 65 and older. And the middle class has gone through a long period of stagnant wage growth.

Well, here's one more taste:

> But there is substantial evidence that a particular relationship between public pension schemes and fertility does indeed exist. Foreign as it may sound to the modern ear, a motivation for having children in earlier times was economic security in old age. As parents became frail and less productive, it was expected that one or more of their adult children would take care of them. Married couples thus "invested" in numerous children, in part to ensure the next generation would have the economic capacity to provide for them in their final years. With state-run Social Security schemes, the government has largely absorbed this family responsibility. Married couples have a much diminished economic incentive to have children because now they are counting on—and paying for—government-based old-age support.

Capretta is certainly right that our entitlement programs are in trouble because we have more and more old people and fewer and fewer young ones. The ratio between productive and unproductive Americans is shifting in the direction of the latter, even as we put more of a premium on being productive than ever.

That's why traditional pension plans—based on defined benefits—have been and are being replaced with defined contribution schemes, such as 401(k)s. The good news is that there's more choice for the individual. The bad is that risk is being transferred from the government or the private employer to the individual. Anyone can see that Social Security and Medicare will eventually have to be reformed along those same lines.

I disagree with Capretta—at least in the American case—by not putting so much weight on welfare-state dependency for the declining size of families. He exaggerates the extent to which people have stopped relying on their own children and started relying on the government to provide for their old-age support. People can't actually live on Social Security alone, after all. And studies show that the Americans differ from the Europeans in still regarding themselves as primarily responsible for their aged parents.

I actually think the primary cause of our "demographic issue" is our creeping and sometimes creepy individualism. Sophisticated people have taken much more responsibility for their individual futures by focusing much more intentionally on personal health and safety. They're all about prudently avoiding risk factors. So the good news is they're living longer than ever. We used to think only the good die young, now we think only the stupid and self-indulgent do so.

By thinking of themselves more insistently as individuals, people are thinking of themselves less and less as biological beings to be replaced by children. Their reproductive behavior is less and less that of the social animals Darwin described. They can't relax enough or be spontaneous enough to have unprotected sex. Why generate replacements when I'm working so hard to stay around for an indefinitely long time?

So the welfare state depended on the "Baby Boom" demographics of the late 1950s and early 1960s, when so many men dropped dead of heart disease in their fifties—having not drawn a dime of Social Security and later Medicare and after having had three or more children to pay for those programs in the future. Those demographic facts made Social Security a Ponzi scheme we could believe in.

The welfare state depended, in other words, on the human behavior displayed for us as insane on TV's *Mad Men*.

Here's a joke I probably tell students too often: I want you to embrace my two-point program for saving Social Security and Medicare. First, start smoking and really stay with it. Second, start having babies right now (although preferably after class). It goes without saying I'm not really pro-smoking, although I do love those babies.

The primary experience of the typical American today is the erosion of the various safety nets on which he or she has come to rely. The last thing, perhaps, we have to worry about is increased dependency on big government. The good news is that the so-called road to serfdom never gets to serfdom. The bad news might be that each of us might be more on his or her own than ever.

Is My Redundant Kidney
Part of My Net Worth in Dollars?

As we can see on BIG THINK and elsewhere, libertarians are especially attracted to the organ market issue. In this case, the pro-choice and pro-commodification position is also clearly the pro-life one. Pro-lifers can't locate the transplantation transaction with abortion in the "culture of death."

Contrary to what some of the more radical libertarians might risk, we still draw a line when it comes to the buying and selling of fetuses, because even our Supreme Court concedes that fetuses share some qualities with human babies.

Commerce in kidneys does not seem to be commerce in human beings. A kidney's moral status, the pro-lifer notices, is incomparably less than an embryo's, and consider how little our law does to protect embryos. I am the same person with just one kidney in an absolutely complete way I wouldn't quite be with just one eye or just one leg. I can go about my business without it being distorted in any way by my number of kidneys. A guy with one kidney has the same reproductive fitness and the same likelihood of picking up girls in bars as a guy with two, whereas many young ladies find one leg or one eye a turn-off for reasons an evolutionary psychologist could give.

But, as Ray Robertson says, we naturally recoil from the idea that human bodies are natural resources to be mined. A human kidney—or any part of a human body (including a woman's eggs, but that's a topic for another day)—is surely deeply different from a tree or an apple or even a pig kidney.

We are rightly revolted by what might well be the resulting redistribution: Healthy kidneys in the healthy bodies of the young would gradually become, via transplantation, failing kidneys in the sick bodies of the old. Surely there's at least something creepily un-Darwinian in taking organs from fit reproductive machines to allow those who are years beyond their gene-spreading to linger for no species-based reason.

Our sophisticated libertarian response might be: As long as the kidney market is properly regulated with health, safety, and genuinely informed choice or consent in mind, we have to let people decide their self-conception for themselves. Rich old guys need kidneys, and poor young guys have them to spare. And we're been okay so far with having the government step in to help out with the poor who are kidney-deprived. It would be cheaper for the government to give top dollar for kidneys than to fund years and years of dialysis at six figures per year for each patient.

The adequacy of this libertarian response has to be judged in light of the excessively low opinion we have of our embodiment. People these days seem to hate their bodies more than people ever have. Contrary to what you might think at first, we live in one of the least erotic times ever. The allegedly highly repressed Puritanical or Victorian male was very easily aroused: The sight of a bare ankle got him going. Today, our young men see perfectly sculpted almost bare women everywhere, both on TV and in real life, and they yawn. They just can't relax enough to see all that's good about the bodies they've been given.

Most sophisticated people these days identify themselves and their pursuit of happiness less than ever with the bodies they've been given by nature. One disturbing feature of a live kidney donation is that it turns a healthy person—the donor—into a sick patient, at least temporarily, and surely the physician should never intentionally do harm to anyone's health. But the cosmetic surgeon also makes healthy people sick, and, unlike the transplant surgeon, with no intention of improving someone else's health.

Plastic surgery allows people to choose, to some extent, the body they have imagined over the body they have been given. The small-breasted woman can become amply endowed; a man can, with some mutilation, become a woman. Whatever we think about the morality or even the sanity of these procedures, they are perfectly legal and becoming more common.

"Enhancement" or "transformational" surgery that makes us better than or something other than well involves both commerce and body parts. It is rightly not covered by medical insurance, and the doctors who do it make some of the biggest money in the surgery business. At the same time, people often submit to such surgery for profit: They connect their new appearance—looking younger and better—with personal success. Although it is the individual's choice whether or not to submit to the knife to look prettier, there is sometimes a subtle coercion at work. If people can look better, employers may come to expect it, and those who refuse the available therapy will be at a competitive disadvantage.

There was a lot to be said for the old-fashioned or true interpretation of the Hippocratic Oath: a doctor should never turn someone into a patient for reasons having nothing to do with his or her own health. The exception of "gifting" a kidney out of love is easily justified—but surely not the motivation of profit or personal productivity. Allowing people to be patients when their own health isn't on the line is a form of exploitation—a way of forcing them into deals they can't easily refuse.

Surely the freedom to sell a kidney contains within it its own forms of coercion. One expert says we should allow the poor to sell kidneys to improve their condition, because our unjust society isn't doing so adequately in other ways. But won't turning a kidney, in effect, to part of one's net worth make government even less likely to step in on behalf of the unfortunate with extra kidneys (that could be for sale). I can imagine college financial aid officers requiring students and parents to list healthy kidneys among their personal resources.

I could go on and might later, but in this case as in many others, the libertarians are naive to believe that commodification is the key to free us from coercion.

This is a tough issue.

Update: In a comment, reader RainbowExplorer says this post did or should have made her vomit. What she says is thoughtful and eloquent, and we should pray that things turn out as well as possible in her rare and most difficult situation. Actually, though, I'm not sure where we disagree. I used the word "redundant" with a bit of irony. And my point was to examine the case on both sides of regulated kidney markets. One conclusion of mine I thought was clear is that we probably shouldn't be turning people into patients—or have them take on even minor risk factors—for reasons have nothing to do with their own health. I also thought I was clear that one problem I have with organ markets is that they could actually could come very close to coercing people to take chances with their health with productivity and profit in mind. So let me quote with nothing but admiration Rainbow's conclusion, based as it is on personal experience:

> So, when you speak of your second kidney as being "redundant," I hear a profound level of ignorance coming out of you. There are reasons human bodies were designed with two kidneys. Kidneys are *major* organs, not redundant pieces of flesh, like an appendix or something. All it takes is *one* illness or injury to kill a person living with a single kidney. Most of us living with serious kidney disease know how fragile our bodies are. It seems clear to me that you do not. Remember, no matter how much money you might receive for your "redundant" kidney, you can't take *any* of it with you, when you die.

Is My Redundant Kidney a Natural Resource?

Dr. Benjamin Hippen, a nephrologist and a philosopher, has had lots of firsthand experience with people stuck on dialysis. That's why he's for regulated organ markets—for developing a fairly safe way of buying kidneys for the something like 100,000 Americans on dialysis who need them.

When Congress passed the entitlement legislation covering the cost of dialysis, the argument was that this medical care would get people back to work. But that's hardly ever true. Dialysis is kind of a full-time job for those who must have it to stay alive. One day is spent having dialysis, the next getting over it.

Next to the brain, the kidney is my most complicated organ. It works wonderfully well in cleansing my blood of waste. Dialysis doesn't work nearly as well. So, even in the best case, it's a kind of very slow poisoning. Although the occasional person lives for a long time on dialysis, it's usually a slow killer over a fairly small number of years. People usually get sicker and sicker.

There is surely a very admirable kind of virtue in living well on dialysis, on not giving up, on making the most of the life you have. But we can't expect our poets to celebrate that virtue. The people actually on dialysis we can't expect to be poets themselves; they are surely among the most marginalized of Americans.

I've talked to people cruel and judgmental enough to blame the people on dialysis for their tough situation. The most common cause of kidney failure is type-2 diabetes, the kind you typically get through getting fat by eating way too many carbs.

But for one thing, we have to remember that the Americans with the worst diets are often stuck in positions without the time to reflect on what they're eating or the money to eat much better. Scientific eating and exercising tends to be the privilege of fairly rich folks with fairly easy jobs (and often no or hardly any kids). We also have to remember that African-Americans suffer disproportionally from kidney failure, even when we control for diet and class and such.

We should certainly push preventative medicine and all that, but it's not clear that the big effort would reduce the number of people with failed kidneys all that much. There's still type-1 diabetes, which is found among kids and leads much more certainly to eventual kidney failure. And kidney failure plagues the elderly even without diabetes or who aren't overweight. Living longer is going to put more Americans in need of new kidneys.

So far, we've been relying on kidneys from the newly dead that checked out with their kidneys in good shape. A young person who died by head trauma is one especially good source of such a kidney, and so a dumb joke is that one way to increase our cadaver kidney supply is to repeal those prohibitionist laws requiring motorcyclists to wear helmets.

The number of "harvested" cadaver kidneys doesn't come anywhere near meeting the need of people on dialysis. And there is really no way of pushing that number up all that much higher.

Not only that, cadaver kidneys just don't last, even the best cases, nearly as long as a kidney transplanted from a live person. It appears the body treats the cadaver kidney as a diseased kidney, and it starts to die slowly almost immediately.

The time will come when there are really effective artificial kidneys. And maybe they will figure out of way of tweaking pig kidneys so they can be implanted in people without being rejected.

But for now, what people who need new kidneys really need is live kidneys transplanted from other people.

It's true that each of us is free to give our second or redundant kidney as a gift. But those gifts, not surprisingly, are almost all to relatives or very close friends. Having only one kidney is a very minor risk factor, and the removal operation is close to as safe as an operation can be. Still, it's unreasonable to expect people to become patients and be mutilated—even in a pretty insignificant way—for a stranger.

Some libertarians also worry about "the tyranny of the gift." If I give you a kidney, to some extent I "own" you emotionally for the rest of your life. It's reasonable to say that you can't thank me enough.

With that thought in mind, we can say that what a person on dialysis really wants is a kidney purchased from someone else at a fair price. Once I've paid you my money, I owe you nothing.

Biotechnology and American Principle

The first book we're reading for my seminar on bioethics is *Biotechnology: Our Future as Human Beings and Citizens*, edited by Sean D. Sutton. This is undoubtedly the most balanced collection of essays by the leading public intellectuals in our debate over the implications of the coming biotechnological age. I hope to get around to talking about each of these instructive and genuinely pithy contributions here. But let me begin with some general observations about the case for welcoming biotechnological change—change we can and, in fact, already do believe in.

The first thing anyone would notice about this conflict is that it can't be captured by the Founders (=Locke=good) vs. Progressives (=Hegel/History=bad) dichotomy. Those least fearful and most welcoming of biotechnological progress present themselves as consistent Lockeans or libertarians. And those who oppose at least some features of that progress are defending, in one way or another, a non-Lockean view of nature. The latter remind us of the Progressives insofar as they favor more government regulation. Insofar as the Progressives were Darwinians, we see another similarity: Darwinian conservative Larry Arnhart is one of the defenders of the goodness of our social natures in service to the species against this self-obsessed liberationism.

Now some of the opponents to the unlimited progress of biotechnology do worry that changing human nature will ruin our natural rights republic. Beings with certain natural characteristics have rights, and right now we can say all human beings are alike enough to equally have rights. All that could change, and the result would be tyranny of the sort you see, for example, in the *Brave New World*. We could engineer natural masters and natural slaves into existence, and Confederate Alexander Stephens's notorious *Cornerstone* speech would suddenly be right. In a way he wouldn't have expected, the progress of science, as Stephens claimed, has become on his and not our Framers' side. His assertion that slavery is just by nature would have become true. The blacks enslaved by the South weren't actually natural slaves, and they weren't actually happy to be deprived of their freedom. But why couldn't we consciously create natural slaves who are content to be who they are as most of the people are in the *Brave New World*? All men are created equal doesn't necessarily apply to men we make ourselves. We could engineer a reconciliation of the greatness made possible by aristocratic leisure and genuine justice or according each man the dignity of who he is in the eyes of his Creator that Alexis de Tocqueville thought impossible.

Today's libertarians respond that biotechnology is not so much about changing nature as increasing free beings' control over it. Locke himself was all about not submitting to the tyranny of Nature's lottery, which cruelly deals out futures blighted with ill health, stunted mental abilities, and early death. Nature is no respecter of persons, and that's why Locke encouraged us to change the almost worthless stuff we've been given by nature to make it infinitely more supportive of the life, liberty, and happiness or at least comfort of each of us. The intrinsic value of human life is a given for all sides in this debate. Bailey is especially certain about the value of his own life, and he's especially anxious that our scientists do everything possible to keep Bailey from dying or ceasing to be as a person or individual. And he's all for the rest of us staying around so long as we don't get in his way. So, for Bailey, the battle is really between those who want to use the gifts of human reason and human compassion to ameliorate illness and death and those who counsel fatalistic acceptance of the manifold cruelties randomly meted out by nature. He surely thinks of himself as the new Jefferson defending the light of (Lockean, modern) science against monkish ignorance and superstition.

The quacks who used to identify science with History—the Progressives, Marxists, and so forth—were all too ready to kill the persons around today in the name of the coming of a perfected man at some indefinite point in the future. The new libertarians are way too self-obsessed to commit that error. Their devotion to the individual and to the Lockean principle of consent is undeniable. They really believe that hardly anyone would choose to die if he or she could get out of it. (They're all for those suckers who think life is meaningless etc., choosing death if they want.) They refuse to be history fodder, of course. But they also refuse to be nature fodder, and they believe that the Creator made us free to make the latter great refusal as effective as possible. Locke's past-tense God, remember, seems to have given us freedom and nothing else to secure our personal beings, and so he left us alone to do what we can to—play god—in a hostile environment.

Bailey even says that his hyper-Lockean position is the genuinely ecological one: Why do we want to stay married to Nature anyway? She certainly has been an inconstant wife, literally afflicting us with many surprises like birth defects, diseases, earthquakes, hurricanes, famines, and so forth. Actually, an amiable separation might be good for Nature and humanity. The less we depend on Nature for our subsistence, the less harm we do to her.

It goes without saying I don't agree with that (although it's certainly true that many ecological problems do turn out to have technological solutions). But I can't help but admire one version of thinking through a fundamental American principle and one piece of evidence that it's tough to keep Locke in the Locke box.

I also admire, in a way, Bailey's resolution not to get way existential in view of the contingent and momentary presence of Bailey in the world (or anywhere else). Like a good American, when presented with a problem, he's determined to find a solution. Bailey's not going anywhere if he can help it. And who am I to deny him the hope in freedom that he can? The genuinely outstanding popularizing scientist Lee Silver adds to the Lockean case for optimism concerning unfettered biotechnological development by reminding of us of a time not so long ago: Then the entire biosphere was pushed beyond its human-carrying capacity. We can just imagine what Dr. Pat Deneen and other Front Hutters of the time were predicting about impending collapse as just punishment for our unnatural acquisitiveness and greed. The truth is, as Silver says, that any other species would have collapsed under the weight of its own voracious appetites. But not us!

Thanks to evolutionary nature, human genes had endowed human beings with the capacity to initiate a revolutionary lifestyle change that blew apart the traditional equation of adaption and survival. That is, we might say (even if Silver doesn't quite), the theory of evolution as described by Darwin was no longer true for them (us). Instead of fitting into a natural world as best they could like every creature before the human species consciously took control away from Mother Nature and into its own hands through a process we now refer to as the Agricultural revolution. Conscious, volitional, and unnatural evolution began not with biotechnology but with agriculture (as Locke himself explains). But Locke might make more sense than Silver in suggesting that no impersonal theory of evolution can really explain why one species alone turned on nature and has increasingly brought the planet under its conscious and personal control.

We discovered the truth about genes, and so we developed the ability to create novel organisms displaying domesticated characteristics built to satisfy human needs and the newly emerging desires. We changed what nature gave us to meet the needs of free beings with bodies, and both biological nature and our desires change over time. In changing nature, we changed ourselves in an increasingly free or unnatural direction. We invented out of wild and inhospitable natural material, among other things, corn, the cow, the pig, the chicken, the sheep, and the dog. In the animals we domesticated through genetic transformation, wild human-threatening, and human-fearfulness instincts are eliminated and replaced by tameness, an acceptance or desire to be near humans, and often, other specific human-serving personalities.

We did violence to nature by turning selected wild and free animals into our slaves, into beings willing to be led to the slaughter for our benefit. In the case of dogs, we also created craven suck-ups bred to alleviate our loneliness and bolster our self-esteem. (The cat, to his or her natural credit, continues to put up some admirable resistance.)

We agrarian, southern Porchers can't imagine life without cows, pigs, corn, chicken, sheep, and dogs. But life with them is hardly life according to nature. It's life in an environment we used our knowledge and freedom to domesticate or make less alien or unfriendly with each of our lives, liberty, and even happiness in mind. From this view, biotechnology is nothing more or less than a more conscious, effective, and quick way of continuing the revolution we're conducting on our behalf against nature. It's not that biotechnology doesn't need to be managed without our true needs and desires in mind, but it's far from an alien force out to extinguish who we are. It is, instead, a revelation of who we are as free persons.

Being Personal

We are the species that believes in change. We are the beings that can take nature personally and do something about it. We have personal objections to the limited and precarious character of our biological existence: nature is cruelly indifferent to my personal existence; nature does not care about me as a person; nature is out to replace me. We are the animals who care about me, who think in terms of personal identity, who can orient ourselves around the insight that each member of the species is unique and irreplaceable.

Each of us is an animal who refuses to be wholly reduced to merely a part of a species or a part of some impersonal natural process. When we try to dispense with participation, we are engaged in a mission impossible that might well make us miserable more than anything else. Our personal identity depends upon being relational beings, and even consciousness is knowing with ("con" means together, "sci" means knowing). Of course, nature does provide indispensable guidance for knowing who each of us is. But still, it is quite wonderful what we can do for ourselves.

Impersonal natural evolution continues gradually to be displaced by conscious and volitional evolution—evolution caused by members of our species with ourselves in mind. All of nature has been altered by our personal willfulness, and it is almost impossible to find anything that is purely nature or merely impersonal on our planet any more. We have engineered whole species, dogs and pigs and cows and chickens, into existence for our personal convenience and even with our personal vanity in mind. Although the human race has not been changed by nature in any fundamental way since it showed up, it has changed the rest of nature with itself in mind. Now we are on the edge of a biotechnological revolution that promises to allow us to fundamentally change our own natures.

Scientists tell us that we are pretty much like dolphins—cute and smart, dependent, rational, social mammals. And we are like dolphins in some ways, of course. But now, the very being of the dolphins depends on us, rather than the other way around, for we think they are cute enough and smart enough and entertaining enough to protect, while the tuna are ugly enough and dumb enough (not to mention tasty and nutritious enough!) to die. But we could easily switch things around and take the dolphin out—perhaps as a threat to our species self-esteem—and gain a strange Rousseauian or Buddhist appreciation for the noble simplicity of the tuna.

The dolphins do not have what it takes to be out to get us, because they do not have what it takes to be in technological rebellion against their natural existence. Our being will never be dependent on them. One reason is that they cannot think personally enough to raise the question of being. Another is that they are not equipped to act freely enough to consciously and willfully change their own nature, or ours. And not only is there no dolphin technology, but there are no dolphins physicists, no dolphin priests or preachers, no dolphin princes or presidents, no dolphin poets or philosophers, and even dolphin parents are not like our parents.

The evolution of nature produces ontological differences—that is, different kinds of beings. Being changed when plant emerged from rock, and biology emerged from physics, bringing the distinctions between life and nonlife, and life and death. How life emerged from inanimate nature remains a mystery to us. Being changed when the animal emerged from the plant—this changed all the capabilities and behavior that turned the distinction from life and death into birth and death. And being changed again when the social, rational, free, or technological animal who can raise the question of being, began to take things personally, love personally, be aware of, reflect on, and rebel against personal contingency—and mortality emerged.

The questions that surround the mystery of being, including who we are, what we are, and who or what God is, could not be raised without us. The "what" questions could not be raised by anyone but a "who," a being with a name who can name. (Certain other animals have names and even know them, but we give them their names to personalize them in our own image.) That "who" cannot be reduced to a "what," the human person to some impersonal, wholly necessitarian natural process. The "who" is the being open to the "what," and the mystery of the "who" is much more wonderful than the famous question, "why is there being rather than nothing at all?"

Physics cannot explain the physicist. Perhaps physics can explain the correspondence between the physicist's mind and the invincible laws of nature. But the physicist is not simply a mind; he is a whole human being. The physicist cannot explain the uniqueness of the scientific effort of human beings to deny the uniqueness of our species—and especially particular members of our species—in the cosmos. We do not look to the physicist to explain the experience of the particular human being existing for a moment between two abysses. We can look to penetrating psychologists from Aristophanes to Pascal to Nietzsche to Walker Percy to remind us that the physicist's attempt to lose himself in an impersonal account of nature is really, in part, an always-partly-failed attempt to divert himself from what he really knows about himself, the "who," the particular being with a name who can name.

Physicists from Aristotle onward have said that the most wonderful thing in the cosmos is the stars, because of the majestic regularity of their impersonal, inanimate behavior. The Bible says that nothing we can see is more wonderful than the behavior that characterizes the personal destiny of the particular human being. But maybe we can wonder most of all about the behavior of the being who can so easily know what moves the stars but seems to remain an elusive, even impenetrable, mystery to himself. Aristotle, following Socrates, says we are most deeply moved by wonder, and the Bible says we are most deeply wanderers or pilgrims in this world. Surely, the truth is that because we wonder we wander, or because we can wander we wonder. It is because of our personal detachment that we are open to the truth and we always fall far short of integrating ourselves into the nature our physicists and biologists so perfectly describe. That does not mean being personal means that we are nothing but absurdly purposeless leftovers or miserable aliens stuck inside our puny particular selves. Sure, we have miseries not given to the other species that flow from our contingency as wanderers, but we are also given joys—such as wonder and deeply personal love—and obligations—such as those that flow from being open to the truth and taking responsibility for the very future of life on our planet—not given to the other species.

American Cartesianism
and the Emerging Right to Same-Sex Marriage

So, I'm sorry for yet another relatively pointy-headed post. I'm still thinking about the twin pillars of our modern, scientific self-understanding:
Descartes and Darwin. For today, I'm thinking about how the right to
same-sex marriage might emerge from a Constitution understood in a consistently Lockean/Cartesian way. I'm not taking a stand on any issue for
today.

I am not saying that this understanding of our Constitution is complete
or accurate. I am saying that there's a certain individualistic or personal
logic that can explain recent Court decisions.

Alexis de Tocqueville, in the best book on America and the best book
on modern liberal (or individualistic, Lockean/Cartesian) democracy,
observes that the Americans are Cartesians who've never read a word of
Descartes. The Cartesian method—the radical doubt that produces the conclusion that the only certainty is the self-conscious "I"—is also the democratic method. The democrat achieves intellectual liberty by methodically
or habitually doubting the word—the authority—of other persons. If I trust
what you say, then I'm ruled by you, and I surrender my self-sovereignty.

Democratic Cartesianism is full of words like "deconstruct" (good)
and "privilege" (bad). The democratic theorist deconstructs any theory that
privileges one person's word over another. So, the democratic theorist—
say, Whitman or Emerson—preaches nonconformity, or personal resistance to being absorbed into a personal whole greater than oneself. To be a
democratic "I" is to be liberated from the authority of priests, poets,
philosophers, preachers, politicians, (theoretical) physicists, parents, and
the personal, judgmental God. It's also to be liberated from personal claims
about what is according to nature. As Whitman explained, American personal freedom is the unlimited, indefinite movement away from nature.

This Cartesianism, for some Americans, is clearest in the
Constitution. Our Constitution treats humans as free or wholly detached or
self-sufficient persons. The "I" is not subsumed into some class or category—as a part of religion or race or class or even gender or even country.
The Constitution, of course, can't help but recognize the distinction
between citizen and non-citizen, but even that distinction is treated as artificially constructed or not some deep statement about who anyone is.

The Constitution of 1787 is maybe most striking in its silence on God, in its decision not to employ theology politically. But not only are persons freed from "civil theology"—from the degrading and destructively seductive illusion of being part of a political whole, they are in a way free from biological nature. The Constitution does not recognize the natural division of members of our species into men and women. Americans are understood to be free to consent to be governed by God and even nature, and the idea of consent, of course, dissolves the authority claimed on behalf of God and nature by the word of the philosophers and theologians of the past.

The founding American limit to this democratic Cartesianism or Lockean individualism was federalism. The states were free to treat people as men and women, black and white, and even Christians and Jews. The Bill of Rights, after all, was constructed to be limits only on the power of the national government. Laws concerning marriage and the family— which necessarily understand persons to be intrinsically social or relational beings with duties to others—were reserved to the states.

From a purely Cartesian perspective, the states were allowed to be unjust by treating persons as other than free individuals. The result was legalized racism, sexism, and so forth. The result also strongly discouraged divorce and marital infidelity and supported parental and especially paternal responsibility. From a Darwinian view, the result supported the pair-bonding, reproducing, and young-raising that are indispensable for the flourishing of the species. The states even thought of themselves as supporting religion in a nonsectarian way to support a common social morality that went beyond the mere protection of rights.

Our Court has understood the Fourteenth Amendment to be the completion of our Cartesian Constitution, to have overcome a defect that was, in truth, the product of an unprincipled founding compromise. The Bill of Rights, it decided, is implicitly incorporated in the Fourteenth Amendment. So, it can now be applied to strike down non-individualistic state laws concerning religion, gender, sexual orientation (also, of course, not mentioned in the Constitution), race, even citizenship, and so forth.

The Court actually has largely abandoned that idea of "incorporation," replacing it with an expansive interpretation of the single word "liberty" in the Fourteenth Amendment. (One reason among many for this replacement, of course, is to overcome the embarrassment that "the right to privacy" doesn't actually appear in the Bill of Rights.)

The Court, in *Planned Parenthood v. Casey*, explained that the state can't unduly interfere with a woman's right to choose an abortion because women have the right not be treated as biological women under the law. They have the right to be free persons fully engaged in political and economic life, and they can't be understood to be reproductive machines for the state. Women, just like men, have the right to define for themselves the mysterious freedom that constitutes the "I" that is each of their existences.

In *Lawrence v. Texas*, the Court added that free persons have the right to define for themselves the content of their intimate relationships. The law can't compel that those connections be limited or shaped by the biological distinction between the sexes. The consensual, relational connection between "I" and "I" is to be unconditioned under the law by what are only said to be natural or traditional or political or religious imperatives.

The word "liberty" in the Constitution, the Court went on, doesn't refer to any fixed understanding of who we are by nature. Instead, it's a weapon to be used by each generation of Americans to liberate themselves from limits once regarded as necessary and proper but are now revealed to be merely arbitrary. The "I" becomes less blinded or deluded over time. That's why the Court will probably conclude that same-sex marriage didn't used to be, but is now, part of personal, constitutional liberty. It became a right as we freed marriage from any necessary dependence on social or relational duties.

But surely, the last stage in this evolution will be the deconstruction of marriage itself. By affirming the right to same-sex marriage, won't our law still privilege marital over non-marital autonomous relationships? Won't it still degrade the autonomous persons who choose to express themselves intimately outside of a social institution that doesn't really express the truth about who each of us is?

Is Social Science an Oxymoron?

Believe it or not, I'm continuing my theme of Cartesian America. As I explained, the Cartesian/Lockean American understands science basically to be technology. Its point is to make free persons more secure, comfortable, and "autonomous" in their natural environment. That means, of course, that science is all about understanding, predicting, controlling, and transforming bodies or "natural resources." Science is about making our country and our species more powerful or productive.

Science, so understood, is all about medical, engineering, commercial, communications, and military applications. It is most of all about inventions. Because we consent to government to get our rights (particularly life and liberty) secured better than they are by nature, we naturally expect government to devote lots of its resources to facilitating technological progress. That can explain why every major scientific and engineering project in recent decades has been supported by the National Science Foundation.

It's true that some of that money goes to scientific theory with no obvious practical applications—to highly abstract and even speculative math and physics, for example. Our friendly French critic Tocqueville helps us understand why the Foundation has been correcting a democratic prejudice for our own good. Democrats have a skeptical prejudice against pure theory. One reason is that they—being too busy to have appreciated the truthful joy of theoretical insight for themselves—don't "get" the necessary connections between theoretical breakthroughs and technological progress. Theory is more practical than we think it is, just as practice—technology—is more theoretical than we think it is. So, Tocqueville concludes it's more important than ever to talk up the leisurely and high-minded enjoyments of theoretical inquiry of all kinds in democratic times.

Partly because of the great authority quantitative (or demonstrably productive) science enjoys in our time, the social sciences (political science, sociology, economics, and so forth) have tried to establish credibility by configuring themselves along the methodological lines developed by the natural sciences. Truth is identified with what can be precisely measured. All else is "values" or ideology.

Many social scientists have been successful in getting the National Scientific Foundation to fund their work as science.

Members of Congress think the NSF has been suckered. Social

science—especially political science—is ideology masquerading as science. The studies are "cooked" to produce results that conform to the controversial opinions of the investigators. Nobody would say that a biologist studying fruit flies or a physicist studying particles or an engineer building bridges has been distorted by such bias. Members of Congress may be weak on science, but they know politics or partisanship when they see it. They know it isn't science. Most social science is liberal propaganda. We note that there's the occasional social scientist, such as Jonathan Haidt, who agrees.

Well, there's one nerdy physicist who agrees. In his opinion, the progress of science on which we all so depend is based on a measurable, peer-driven rigor that's just not found in the social sciences. So, the physicist agrees with the Republican Congressman that social science isn't science (Tom Hartsfield, "NSF Should Stop Funding Social Science," *Real Clear Science*, May 16, 2012).

Everyone knows that "real scientists" are very unimpressed with the level of mathematical sophistication of social science. From the point of view of the physicist, the sociologist is way too easy on herself as a scientist. My highly nerdy and very liberal University of Chicago math professor brother and I agree on one thing: the status of the mathematics of most social science.

Following Aristotle, my own view is that political science rightly understood is less precise but far more difficult than at least most natural science. Medicine, he says, deals with bodies and has the uncontroversial goal of health. Political science deals with the soul, the reality and true content of which is much more controversial. (By soul, in this case, Aristotle means no more than what animates human thought and action.) The soul, we naturally think, is higher than the body, and anyone with eyes to see knows that the soul can't be reduced to the body, that human action is much more fundamentally different from that of bees and ants than, say, E. O. Wilson thinks.

The political scientist is particularly concerned with moral virtue or ethics. Moral or ethical distinctions really exist, but they are particularly hard to see. One error is to think of them, Aristotle explains, as mere "rhetoric" or persuasive baloney spewed out by the clever as an instrument of domination. That error emerges as the result of another one—thinking of the only standard of truth as mathematical precision. The world of praise and blame, virtue and vice exists somewhere between the extremes of mathematics and rhetoric. Seeing that world requires not only theoretical insight but the judgment and chastened expectations that come through practical experience.

The political scientist such as myself notices that natural or "cognitive" scientists—such was E. O. Wilson or Dawkins or Dennett—know a lot less than they think they do when they write about what people think and do. They're no match for Aristotle, for example, when it comes to politics and ethics, although they most likely have far surpassed him in physics. If science is nothing more than knowledge of the way things really are, then we shouldn't look to physicists to know who we are and what we're supposed to do. They're no experts when it comes to political science. That might be one reason why conservatives balk at deferring to the authority that scientists so often claim for themselves.

But all this is a diversion from my conclusion: Whatever the scientific status of social science, it is not a reliable source of the scientific knowledge that produces the technological progress on which we Cartesian Americans depend. In this time of burgeoning deficit and all that, I see no reason for the NSF not to be commanded to cut at least most social science off. I might be accused of being a traitor to my discipline. Or it may be my perverse self-interest that's driving my analysis: I'm not the kind of political scientist who could ever hope to get a dime from the NSF.

History/Localism

The End of the End of History

Modern thinkers aren't quite atheists because they can't account for the mysterious emergence of human persons from an impersonal nature. But if there is a God, he's not living or giving or loving; he made us free and then took a permanent vacation. So some modern thinkers may really be Deists. But the more radical ones—such as Rousseau—believe that human freedom is a kind of cosmic accident, and we accidents make our existences more accidental or contingent over time.

Human beings act freely to negate nature. By doing so, they become more self-conscious, or conscious of being free. They become aware of their contingency and their mortality as particular beings. They become more aware that their existence is temporary, and so their lives become more and more defined by time.

The more people move away from nature, the more they live in their self-created or invented world. The proper name for that self-created world is *History*—the world defined by past and future or time, the world that only could have been created by beings that become more and more aware that their existence is merely historical or temporary.

So the key modern distinction is between impersonal nature and personal history. And that distinction, it seems, is quite judgmental. Nature is bad; history is good. History is our success in satisfying the desires we've been given as free beings that have no natural satisfaction. History is the same as technology in the broadest sense; our use of what we can know and do to make our lives more comfortable, free, and secure. The other animals aren't free; they don't make history; they're not in technological rebellion against their worthless natural existence. Even the super-smart dolphins seem okay with their natural gifts; their lives are not defined by time, and they aren't obsessed with fending off non-being.

As people become more historical, they become smarter. The only thing they can know for sure is what they've made, and so the more they've made—the more history they've created—the more they know. So, modern philosophers think they're sure they know more than classical philosophers. Classical philosophy was uncertain speculation about nature or the eternity beyond our grasp. Modern philosophy is certain knowledge about History or the record of human self-invention, about the effectual truth, or the real truth about our successful overcoming of nature. So, modern philosophers, like Marx, speak of rural idiocy, and Rousseau says that to be perfectly natural is to be perfectly stupid or unconscious. History, from the modern view, is the record of enlightenment.

But the modern philosophers were also stuck, from the beginning, with the thought that historical development makes us smarter but not necessarily happier. John Locke explained that what distinguishes free persons is not happiness or contentment but the pursuit of happiness. The fundamental human experience is uneasiness, which spurs us to historical or technological action. Every time we satisfy a desire, we create one that's more difficult to satisfy. And so the result of our work is misery that produces harder work.

Really historical people invent air conditioning, which makes them more sensitive than ever to the heat and miserable, in a really historical way, when it breaks. They have to work or sweat harder than ever to secure their historical right never to sweat. And then to fend off the historically created heart disease that comes from sitting around too much in climate-controlled comfort, they have to go to the gym to sweat most scientifically or historically or artificially. Living with natural sweat was certainly easier.

According to Marx and Rousseau, history also makes people miserable by depriving them of the illusions that there's more to human existence than money or power or productivity. It rips off the veils that hid the vanity of virtue, of charm and chivalry, and it makes work itself—in the name of efficiency—more monotonous and repetitive. For Marx, most lives get reduced to meaningless subsistence and nothing more. For more empirical thinkers, such as Tocqueville or even the early or psychological Marx of "On the Jewish Question," lives get more miserably restless in the midst of prosperity. Most people, as the Christians say, can't live with secure personal love and God. People are more isolated and self-obsessed, and they work harder than ever to divert themselves from their emptiness. As political life gets perfected in the direction of the equality of free citizens, private life comes to resemble—in a nonviolent or businesslike way—the Hobbesian war of all against all for money and status.

The truth is that people become more free and prosperous, but at the cost of happiness. At least, they're not as happy as people seemingly should be living in the most fortunate environment ever. There's also a cost in human excellence, insofar as people have to believe that they're more than historical or productive beings to produce accomplishments that stand the test of time. They also have to believe that they really are naturally or supernaturally social and loving beings to produce accomplishments meant to move others deeply to experiences and thoughts they can share in common.

So, at a certain point, the modern philosophers were stuck with the fact of all the evidence being history—or the record of enlightening human freedom—has made people more powerful and free, but in some ways more miserable and less virtuous. History, the philosophers thought, is all there is, but historical results are the disoriented and confused record of restless and alienated beings. So, knowing history can hardly be satisfying to the human mind. History seems to have no *Logos*—a fact that would have hardly surprised classical or Christian thinkers.

At a certain point, the philosophers decided to declare victory or talk about *The End of History*. Hegel claimed to show the *Logos* in History in order to show that history was a whole; that history had ended in a perfectly logical way. More compelling, though, was Marx's thought that the end of History is coming, is just around the corner, can be achieved with just a little more work.

For Marx, the unprecedented misery people had accidentally created for themselves through their hugely successful historical effort was good news. Natural scarcity had been conquered, but the great mass of people weren't sharing in that abundance. Their misery would turn their stabilizing fear into recklessly destructive hatred. Having nothing left to lose, they would turn to inevitably successful revolution. The many without property would overthrow the few with it, and the revolution would be against the very idea of property, in the sense of the means required to exploit the labor of others.

The end of History overcomes the miserable alienation of modern life—of capitalism—not by going back to some earlier stage in History or the division of labor. Once people are enlightened, they stay enlightened. They can't and don't want to return to the drudgery or the illusions of a more natural past. The repression that scarcity made necessary, but not good, was defeated by capitalism, as were the illusions that chained us to love and virtue. The only standard remaining was productivity, and at the end of History the machines we've invented work so well on their own we don't have to be concerned much with that.

So it's hard to know why Marx calls communism, communism. The people who live there are more or less completely free from being obsessed by or even particularly concerned with communal or personal obligation. They're really on their own to do what they please. They have perfect freedom from natural determination for self-determination, without any alienating external guidance at all about how to determine a self. The true slogan of Marx's communism is that of the American Sixties, "Do your own thing," because nothing or nobody can tell you what your thing is. Or, as self-help experts say, "Be your own person."

At the end of History, every person will be free from nature to be whoever he or she pleases. And seeing History as a whole will be the really empirical evidence that we're free. At the end of History, philosophy will be replaced by wisdom. We'll know all there is for us to know—what we've made to secure our freedom. And then we'll also know that nature means nothing to us. At the end of History, we become perfect atheists by knowing that History is all there was, and so there was no divine or natural dimension to genuinely human existence.

Historical thinking in this strong sense has been discredited by a fatal contradiction; the people in the present are miserable and worthless. The people in the future will be happy and completely free. Philosophers today still are confused about what they know; the philosophers of the future will actually be wise men and women. The people and philosophers of today gain significance, it seems, in what they do for a future they will never see. So, historical thinkers, such as the various Marxist-Leninists, thought nothing of sacrificing them for the future.

The twentieth century saw hundreds of millions of people slaughtered in the name of History. Historical thinking, which began to secure the existence of unique and irreplaceable beings in this world, culminated in turning the great mass of people into "history fodder." And it turned out, of course, to be far more personally destructive or dehumanizing to think of people as merely part of History than it was to think of them as merely part of nature or merely part of their political communities. History ended up reducing the particular person around today to nothing, at least in thought. And so the idea of History caused particular persons to be treated like nothing.

It's undeniable progress to say that nobody dies for History any more. And there was nothing stupider to die for than History. It was much stupider to die for the end of History than Rome. Rome, after all, was a real place that could inspire real loyalty. Nobody really thinks the end of History in the strong Marxian sense is coming any more, and nobody thinks that the sacrifice required to try to make us all unalienated and wise is worth it anymore. We can, in this sense, only speak of History with a capital H in the past sense, and we reject it in the name of the unique and irreplaceable human person.

The Christian Contribution to History
(with a Capital H)

The Christians rejected the Greek view of what a human being is—the natural being who makes history. For the Christians, the human being is not merely a part of nature or his political community, but a whole free being with a unique and irreplaceable personal destiny. Even the *Logos* that governs the world is personal. *Logos* must be animated by the eros or love that's only present in persons and is, in fact, most deeply personal. Persons are both the strangest and the most wonderful beings in the cosmos; the stars and even the flowers and the dolphins are boring by comparison. The being that wonders can't help but wander or see himself as an exception to what might otherwise be an impersonal cosmic order.

For the Greeks, each of us and God is a "what"—a being that can be described according to the impersonal principles of natural necessity. Aristotle's God isn't a person, but a sort of giant magnet. For the Christians, each of us and God Himself is a "who"—a being free from merely natural or political determination. Each person is a social or relational being—but one who maintains his personal identity even or especially in his relationship with a personal God. For the Christian, the person, in truth, is always to some extent an alien or pilgrim in his or her political community. Even the personal love between man and woman—between husband and wife—points beyond itself to a more secure and transparent "relational" foundation of personal identity.

For the Christians, the point of human life is not to understand what is eternal or to learn how to die or to free oneself from concern for personal being. It's reasonable to despair at the prospect of not being, and there's no higher concern than personal love. The philosopher who claims to transcend personal concerns and to live entirely beyond hope and fear and love is finally sustained through proud self-deception, by an illusory self-sufficiency that really depends on willful self-forgetfulness.

For the Christian, the destiny of each of us is personal, not historical. And history doesn't, because of our sinfulness, point to any kind of perfection in this world. The Christians, in their way, agree with the classical philosophers that the glory that was Rome is nothing in light of eternity—although by eternity they mean the life beyond death that the personal God makes possible for each particular person. For the Greeks, only a philosopher wins a compensation for his mortality better than that gained by the noblest Roman hero. For the Christians, every person is more than a Roman, and everyone who looks to Rome for security and happiness is looking in the wrong place.

But the Christians disagree with the Greeks by claiming that there are fundamentally unprecedented historical events: The creation of the world by God, the special creation of human persons—both the creation of the first person and the creation of each person, and God becoming man—the word becoming flesh and so becoming a historical being–and dying for each of us.

To be a person is to be rational and loving and creative, and so human work and creativity is dignified for the Christians as it never was for the Greek and Roman philosophers. That's not to say that the creativity of sinful human persons could ever free them from dependence on the Creator to whom they owe their very being. The unique and irreplaceable character of every human creature doesn't need to be secured by human work.

The Christian criticisms of the classical philosophy on behalf of the free, rational, loving, social, and creative person—the being who's not merely part of some larger whole—paved the way for modern thought and for the emergence of History with a capital H. Certainly, the modern thinkers thought that the Christians understood who we are in certain key ways better than, say, Plato and Aristotle. They take the side of creativity over eternity in describing who—as opposed to what—we are. They think that each person is justified in regarding himself or herself as unique and irreplaceable and in employing his creativity or inventiveness to fend off non-being or death as long as possible. Each person or individual exists for himself or as not merely a part; the modern thinkers agree with the Christians that individuals are necessarily alienated or emotionally detached from the claims of any political community and even the family. They disagree, of course, on the real existence of the personal, relational God, and so they don't agree that personal identity is relational all the way down.

My View of Classical History

Are human beings fundamentally *natural* or *historical* beings? This seems to be the question of Leo Strauss's *Natural Right and History*. Common sense suggests that this is a false dichotomy. Of course, we're both! We have natures—we're given capabilities and limits we didn't make for ourselves. Birds do it, bees do it, and we do it. We're impelled by nature to have sex and babies, and we're stuck with dying, as are all the animals. Biologists can explain a lot—if not everything—about what we do.

We, unlike the other animals, also have and make history. We can't help but know about—and live in reference to—past and future. We can't help but think in terms of time—which is the stuff of history. We can think up projects to accomplish the unprecedented, and we can't help—or maybe almost can't help—but remember and be very judgmental about the dead, not only about Hitler and Churchill but about your selfless mother and your alcoholic, abusive, racist great uncle who abandoned his kids and blew the family fortune.

Everyone knows, it would seem, that we're like the other animals in having natures and different from the other animals in having history. We're hardwired by nature—unlike the chimps and dolphins—to make history, especially political history. There are no dolphin politics, no dolphin presidents or prime ministers or princes; no dolphin poets, priests, or philosophers to find meaning in history.

Because we can think historically—or think in time—each of us knows his or her own existence is temporary. Each of us knows he or she was born to die. And so, each of us—experiencing life or one's particular being as good—can't help but be moved by an intense aversion to the prospect of not being. That's partly a reasonable fear of change away from what's good to what's unknown. And it's partly an anxiety about how contingent or utterly unsupported any particular being's life is. Being a natural in the sense of being a biological being isn't enough for the being with time in him. There's no biological support for personal significance.

History is, in part, a limited overcoming of the limits of biological being. Human beings can produce all sorts of accomplishments that stand the test of time. They can live on in the memories of others, as they can live on, in a way, through their children. They can win a sort of immortal glory with genuinely extraordinary deeds, especially those that inspire gratitude in those who are living after them. Much about who you are—beginning

with your name—can be much more durable than anyone's merely biological existence. History is both caused by our self-conscious mortality and
is to some extent a compensation for it. There are no dolphin cemeteries,
no dolphin equivalent of the Lincoln Memorial, no dolphin tributes to
saints and heroes, and no dolphin "historical districts."

But, of course, history—or even the fame won through the noblest
deeds—is an inadequate compensation. Fame, as the song says, is all about
wanting to live forever; however, it comes up short in two ways. Fame
eventually fades, even if it takes centuries or millennia to do so. And
Lincoln, of course, has never really been to the Lincoln Memorial.
Immortal glory is—of course—not a real indefinite perpetuation of your
being.

So, people have always hoped for or longed for real immortality—the
perpetuation of my real being or identity after death. From the earliest
times, they have neglected their own real self-preservation in favor of serving gods that could guarantee their personal significance or preserve their
being against natural indifference. They've always known the difference
between historical memories and real immortality.

The Greek philosophers—such as Plato and Aristotle—acknowledged
the reality of the human desire not to not be, and so the existence of longings for immortality. They even thought that most men and women had to
believe in immortality in some sense to live well with death. But they also
thought that the hope for personal immortality was supported by no real or
natural evidence at all. As far as we can tell, one's real personal identity—
one's real experiences of conscious existence—disappears with death,
although, Socrates added reasonably, that's not something we know with
absolute certainty. Whether death is better than life is known only by someone who's experienced both, and dead men just aren't talking. But we do
know life is good—both just being alive and what we can know and who
we can love. Nothing we can see about death—or lifeless nonbeing—is
good for the dead guy, at least.

The therapy offered by the Greek philosophers was that our desire for
immortality—or to avoid personal nonbeing—is really the desire to know
what's eternal, what is always, what is natural in the precise sense. They
offered us the drama of the person with the name Socrates in search of the
impersonal or anonymous, eternal truth about the "whole"—of which each
of us is a part. The being on that quest can have the experience of not living "in time" and being a lot less concerned about his temporary existence.

The only beings open to the eternal are beings that aren't really eternal, and so they know that death is a price that must be paid for the satisfaction of what is really our deepest longing. That doesn't mean death is good—it's not good that any particular person's enjoyment of eternity is finally only temporary. But it does mean death need not be that big a deal. This therapy, finally, isn't really some airtight argument, but an appeal to the experience of Socrates and other philosophers. Most men, they say, may be miserable without God and even live rather desperate lives, but not us.

The natural world may not be experienced as the secure home of most human beings, but it is the home of the mind. And so those who live most rationally or most according to the longing of the mind can be most at home in the cosmos. That's why we're mostly deeply not historical but natural beings. History—being a temporal or ephemeral record of contingent events—is not an altogether serious concern. History or historical action doesn't really win freedom for any of us from natural necessity, and it can't change eternity or what really is.

Darwinian Conservatism?

There's a lot of talk on BIG THINK about evolutionary explanations of this or that human behavior. They're all pretty fascinating, although far from completely convincing.

Darwinian explanations, for what it's worth, usually strike me as pretty conservative. In fact, the best Darwinian political scientist, Larry Arnhart, has written a book and writes a blog called "Darwinian Conservatism." Larry distinguishes Darwinian conservatism from "metaphysical conservatism." His conservatism flows from a Darwinian understanding of the human being as a wholly natural animal, one whose behavior can be completely explained through an understanding of natural evolution.

Metaphysical conservatives tend to emphasize what distinguishes the human being in his or her freedom, self-consciousness, personal love, technological power, awareness of his personal contingency and mortality, and longing for God.

But all conservatives tend to agree that a considerable amount of our happiness comes from doing our social duties to our families, friends, community, and country. Understanding oneself as a liberated individual— someone who finds freedom and dignity in being autonomous or freed from relational and biological imperatives—leads one to pursue happiness but never find it. Darwin's understanding of who we are by nature— although incomplete—frees us from transhumanist and other techno-liberationist fantasies about the possibility or desirability of transforming ourselves into something other than natural beings.

The Darwinian conservative tends to say stuff like members of our species are political animals, but so too are the chimps, bees, and ants. And we're cute, smart, social mammals, but so are the dolphins.

The metaphysical conservative argues: If the other animals are so smart and political, where are the dolphin presidents and princes? And where are the dolphin poets, philosophers, physicists, preachers, priests, poets, and even plumbers?

The metaphysical conservative doubts there could be a completely satisfying evolutionary explanation of the behavior of Socrates or Jesus or Solzhenitsyn or Mother Teresa or Mozart or Shakespeare or Nietzsche or Pascal or Churchill or Lincoln, or even, for that matter, Hitler or Stalin.

The smarter Darwinians (like Arnhart) aren't all for atheism, of course. They can see that religion is an indispensable social bonding mechanism for animals such as ourselves. Religion generates pro-social behavior, and that can't be bad.

For Darwinians, religion only goes wrong when it becomes all otherworldly or too personal, but they really can't explain why it takes those wrong turns. A Christian would say that religion is really all about personal significance and personal love. It's about the being who can't be reduced to merely a part of nature or anything else. That's not to say we're not natural beings (see Thomas Aquinas), or that evolution didn't happen (see Walker Percy).

But it might be true that once evolution produces an animal smart enough to discover the theory of evolution, that animal would inevitably exhibit behavior that would show the theory to no longer be wholly true.

Darwinian Larry Responds ...

The leading Darwinian conservative has done me the honor of responding to my previous thoughts, including the excellent comment by Brendan Foht. According to Larry, the criticism of him for rejecting the idea of eternity of the human species is misguided.

The basis of the objection comes from the philosopher Leo Strauss. There are two bottom-line possibilities: the world is eternal or the world is in some sense personally created. If the world is eternal, then it is governed by an endless process of impersonal necessity, and that process is comprehensible to the human mind. This understanding is that of the "Nature's God" of our Declaration of Independence, who is the same God of the physicists (of, say, Einstein). Eternity so understood—as in, for example, matter is neither created nor destroyed—is what makes the world the home of the human mind.

The objection to this understanding of nature or the cosmos is that there's no place for individual personal identity, and no place for our real experience that particular beings are born and die. Individuality or personal significance becomes illusory. As Socrates said, philosophy becomes learning how to die or getting over illusions about one's own significance in a basically impersonal, indifferent, and unchangeable world. So, from the view of this criticism, the world may be the home of the human mind, but whole human persons become alienated, inexplicable leftovers in the "systematic" account of the eternity of nature.

The idea of the eternity of nature has generated two extreme possibilities in terms of our self-understanding. The first is existentialism; we, in our inexplicable freedom, are absurd, but stuck with living with who we know we are. The other is pantheism; we should surrender our illusory, misery-filled personalities by being reabsorbed into a whole where everything is indistinguishable and everything is somehow divine.

Against the eternity of nature, believers in Biblical religion have said the world was created by God, and the fundamental fact is willful and loving personal creativity. I—a particular person—am not eternal. I didn't exist forever, and, as a natural being, I won't exist forever. My transcendence of the laws of biological nature is guaranteed by the Creator who made me in his image. When Christians speak of eternal life, they often are quite imprecise. God himself might be considered eternal insofar as he alone was not created.

Distinctively modern thought tends to replace divine creativity with human creativity and to call what free beings create in the world History. We free beings are in rebellion against natural indifference to each of our personal beings. We're about changing nature with *me*—with the desire to have more personal significance and a much longer and more secure existence than stingy nature offers each of us—in mind. Over time, we become more Historical (including Technological) and less natural beings.

Eventually, Marx thought, we'll conquer natural scarcity and live in abundance with very little work, and our libertarians come close to agreeing with him. Very soon, Ray Kurzweil and other transhumanists think, we will no longer be natural or perishable, finite beings. We will have created our way out of the bad deal nature gives each of us. We will have proven that not only are we the only species full of discontent with who each of us is by nature, but we—with no help from the Creator/God—are the only species that can replace impersonal natural evolution with conscious and volitional evolution, an anti-natural change that each of us who wants to never die can believe in.

Brendan calls Darwinians Historicists for not believing in the eternity of nature. But a consistent Darwinian wouldn't believe in History either. Nature itself changes. Human beings, members of our species—came into existence at a certain stage of evolution; and our species, like every other species—won't always be around. The human mind is no evidence of our transcendence of nature. It is, finally, a tool for species perpetuation that will eventually fail us.

Our species is toast, despite our best efforts to perpetuate itself forever against nature's intention. And every particular member of our species is toast; nature doesn't want any of us staying around too long. Nature, in fact, is not about each of us. Conscious and volitional evolution with *me* in mind will be vanquished by the natural evolutionary process that is, in its way, sovereign over us all.

So, Darwinian conservatism returns us to the Socratic thought that we should get over obsessing over our personal existence. It is a way of learning how to die through persuading us that we don't really long for eternity or indefinite personal being. But why is it that only philosopher-members of our species have believed that longing for eternity is actually part of our natures, and the price for the surrender of that longing is losing our most sublime faculties?

Despite all the Darwinian pop-scientific propaganda, people these days are more personal or death-haunted than ever, less able to think of themselves as being fulfilled by being a part of some whole greater or bigger than themselves. People these days increasingly think, Solzhenitsyn observed, that *my* demise is the extinction of being itself. The Darwinian lullaby doesn't work. The transhumanists are just extreme examples of a widespread thought that being natural couldn't be good. But Darwinian evolution is no place to look for hope that we can create our way out of nature's intention for each of us.

Localism

1. A couple of readers suggested that I drop the pointy-headed Strauss stuff and comment on the trendy localism posts of the Porchers, the First Thingers, and all that. My real experience is that most of them were kind of boring—no offense.

2. It goes without saying that I'm against "localism" or "traditionalism" or any other "that's-the-ticket-ism" as a solution to the pathologies specific to modern life. Jody Bottum and some others are right to remind us that local life has its own pathologies. That's a good shot against the selective nostalgia of all romanticism. It also means a stronger local life might balance out us cosmopolitans (like Deneen, who jets all over the place evangelizing localism). A lot of localist "theory" is an admirable self-help program, and certainly many are improved by it. But self-constructing roots—or trying to horn in on the roots grown by others—is going to work less than perfectly. And it often deserves to be poked fun at in the style of the classic *Green Acres.* This is not exactly real criticism either—all forms of human life have their laughable and screwed-up parts.

3. Because of nationalizing influences (which give us stuff like justice and prosperity), local life is a lot less racist and anti-Semitic than it used to be. So localism and localists aren't even unwittingly encouraging those "redneck" (hardly the same as localist) pathologies now. We do have to remember that a lot of nationalization was in response to racism, and even that it might have been better had the South been more reconstructed than it actually was. It wasn't Lincoln who destroyed the sense of place in the South, but the South's refusal to give up what it should have given up. Too many localists (although not so much those in blogland) remain nativists, forgetting the greatness of America—which is about the romance of citizenship or a home for all the homeless—described by Chesterton.

4. The distinctively local features of life in Floyd County, GA are God, family, and country. This is a land of evangelical patriots, and they always tearfully stand up when they hear Lee Greenwood. I would like to see the localist theorists say more good about those actually living the homegrown life. Their faith and their churches lack aesthetic sense, they shop at Walmart, they talk a lot about hunting, God, cars, football, and golf, they are very charitable and neighborly, and they have huge-screen TVs. They like both country and rock. They vote Republican for pretty legitimate God-and-country reasons. I can't say it's bad that their lives have been

improved by anti-racist and (yes) anti-sexist justice and even by having enough prosperity to travel around some in jet planes and on interstates. They don't have to choose, often, between making money and staying near the extended family. Hardly anyone farms for a living.

5. We do have people living the more totally organic life around here: aging hippies, home-schoolers of a certain kind, a few professors, and others too. But they're "secessionists." They have their own little communities and often their own little churches. They don't run the place, and the major charitable and community undertakings aren't theirs.

6. The most localist thing Rome, GA has done in recent years is to get its own minor league baseball team and a cute little stadium. Everyone goes there, and people drive up from Atlanta for the excellent cheap seats and fine concessions.

7. I am really, really for *subsidiarity*. That is, government policy ought to promote voluntary caregiving based on love. We should take pride that, even now, most Americans still believe the sick, the disabled, and frail elderly are the responsibility of the family. In the European social democracies, most people regard them as the government's problem. Thinking about that fact alone should have been reason enough both not to have voted for Obama and worked instead, with Yuval Levin and others, to get McCain to read, take seriously, and really defend his health care alternative.

Is Walmart Change We Should Believe In?

1. I was glad to learn from BIG THINKER Daniel Honan that Walmart has become a catalyst for change on the Green or environmental front. That's good news, because what that corporation's brains decide to do makes a big difference.

2. But someone might say that the most important issue could be "social ecology." When Walmart comes to town, do human beings live better as social beings?

3. Walmart is surely, on balance, good for consumers. The stores have a huge variety of stuff at mostly low prices—including, of course, cheap prescription drugs. Walmart might be understood as a blessing for a large American family, especially if both parents have to work. Almost every imaginable need can be efficiently satisfied with one stop.

4. Still, when Walmart comes to town (meaning a relatively small town), "Main Street" closes down. Locally owned stores—such as hardware and grocery stores—go out of business. People just don't make the choice for quality service and the personal touch over affordable convenience often enough. Main Street is sometimes eventually revitalized, but hardly ever as a retail district. It becomes a fake-historic place full of restaurants, coffee shops, etc., and so not a real center of the social and economic life of the community.

5. Walmart makes small-town America stupider. The brains of the store are at some undisclosed location, and specific orders are issued to the locals, who are pretty much stuck with doing what they're told. American brainpower is centralizing in the cities. A Marxist might even say that the sticks are being proletarianized. Marx says that the development of capitalism saves people from rural idiocy (by forcing them into the cities), but he forgot to add it would make the remaining rural people more idiotic.

6. Walmart is a central part of the drab homogenization of country into depressing strip malls. Major urban areas and fancy bourgeois bohemian towns are semi-excluded, but ordinary America is getting increasingly boring and predictable from the perspective of the consumer. From that view, even consumers in general are getting stupider or more easily satisfied.

7. Localities usually just don't have the power to keep Walmart out to defend a particular way of life. So someone might say that Walmart is a main vehicle holding ordinary Americans hostage to the impersonal imperatives of globalization.

Change and Walmart—Part 2

My previous thoughts on Walmart being change that's, on balance, bad for us as social beings was one of my most popular and, apparently, least controversial. That's because many so-called liberals and many traditionalist or "Agrarian" conservatives (followers of Wendell Berry and such) unite in being anti-capitalist and anti-libertarian and anti-globalization. The post got a point across that I've been trying to make over the months; being a conservative is not being a libertarian, including not being automatically for whatever the free market brings.

The routinely excellent conservative blogger, John Fea, did me the favor of reorganizing the ideas in my post to make them even more clear, and then concluded that my conservative case against Walmart is "compelling."

But I only meant it to be semi-compelling—a kind of "lawyer's argument" that should generate a case in the other direction. I had to search hard to find a critic of my case (usually that's no problem at all!). I found a good one in the comments section of the blog mentioned above.

Here's a taste what the man says:

> I am in complete agreement with Lawler on point #3; all too often Walmart's critics ignore the beneficial consequences for consumers. I would intensify his point by noting that Walmart's benefits are actively progressive in the sense that lower income consumers spend a much larger percentage of their income on basic, weekly purchases than wealthier consumers. By offering lower prices and forcing competitors to do the same, Walmart is a boon to poorer consumers.
>
> As much as I agree with point 3, Lawler's 4th point smacks of bourgeois smugness. He simply assumes the superiority of "quality service and personal touches over affordable convenience." That's easy to say as a comfortably middle class academic. Customer service and intimacy may be goods, but they are luxuries as well. I am bothered when politicians and NIMBY activists unite to prevent the working classes from having access to "affordable convenience." [Fea, "Does Walmart Make Small-Town America Stupider?," The Way of Improvement Leads Home (blog), June 2, 2011.]

To highlight the main points, Walmart benefits people who are relatively poor and can't afford luxuries. It's progressive in forcing prices down, helping people stuck with using most of their incomes on basic needs. Lawler doesn't shop at Walmart (it's true, I hardly ever go there) because he's a smug, bourgeois, comfortable, middle-class academic who can afford not to shop there, who can afford to amuse himself by paying more to be flattered by the personal servants found at more aesthetically pleasing places.

It would be possible, of course, to take this line of attack even further. Lawler, as a bourgeois academic with tenure, has an easy job with flexible hours. Plus, he's not caring for a large number of kids. This means that he can take his sweet time shopping here and there, going for totally organic this or that at little shops or stands at inflated prices. The case against Walmart is bourgeois bohemian elitism.

Last night, my wife and I ate dinner with a very affluent and sophisticated (but also down-to-earth) couple at (of course) a chain Japanese restaurant (Rusan's—pretty darn good) that's come to our Southern, Walmart town. The wife remarked that she hated Walmart. The husband said he loved it, and that he's proud that Rome (GA) is a Walmart town.

Real men (if I may be so sexist) are proud to shop at Walmart (and Home Depot). It's the sensible thing to do. Most everything you need to fix up the house, maintain your own car, and all that can be found there. Real men who do real chores (the chores the Agrarians romanticize) don't care about the aesthetics of some store. They pour their imaginations and creativity into the families, their homes, (sometimes) their jobs, (sometimes) their cars, their churches, and their hobbies (like hunting and fishing and flying one's own plane).

So, one reason I rarely go to Walmart is that I'm not so "manly" when it comes to chores and so forth. If I want something done right, I have to hire someone to do it (and being a middle-class academic I can usually afford to do that).

What I said about Walmart in the previous post remains true to a point. But real conservatives don't go so far as to say that the average American has been reduced to a proletarian cog-in-a-machine. Nor do we take Heidegger or T. S. Eliot so seriously as to really believe that America has been a techno-wasteland that continues to grow. (Nonetheless, we learn from Heidegger and especially Eliot, knowing that their instructive exaggerations need to be taken seriously, just not as the whole truth.)

Scattered, Smothered, and Covered at the Waffle House

The *New York Times* has a predictably pointless or just randomly conde-scending article on America's leading diner. The long and diverse thread is a lot more interesting than the article.

Sure Waffle Houses are robbed more than most restaurants. It's actu-ally amazing that they aren't robbed more. They're cash-only concerns in sketchy parts of town or right on the Interstate. They're easy marks.

It used to be (and may still be, for all I know) that the Waffle House was one of the top examples used at Harvard Business School of an extraordinarily successful entrepreneurial achievement.

Maybe no other chain combines a huge number of locations with real intimacy at each and every one. Going to a Waffle House is like going to bar. For one thing, late at night at least some of the customers will be drunk. And many of them will obviously be struggling to get by in life or just down and out. But all things considered, everyone is well behaved, and there's a kind of an easygoing friendliness with people you've never met before.

Well, you may actually know the people if it's your local Waffle House. But the experience is not so different if you've just pulled off the Interstate in the middle of nowhere in some pretty depopulated part of some south-ern state.

I know northerners who put the Waffle House in the general category of features of the scary, redneck South. They call it the "Awful House," and they stop there only if they must on the way to Atlanta or Florida or what-ever. They're not properly grateful for the all-day, everyday reliable service and general tastiness of the food so conveniently located next to the exit.

It's true that if you ate at the Waffle House all the time you'd die young. But the effect on your arteries is clinically insignificant if you drop by once in a while.

The Waffle Houses rather conscientiously fulfill a neglected social need. They're clean, well-lit, warm, and inviting places that are always open. The one piece of useful information the *New York Times* shares with us is that they knock themselves out never to close, even in blizzards, hur-ricanes, and other disasters. They have their own generators, the employ-ees always show up, they stock up on food on the basis of forecasts, and so forth.

There are lots of unfortunate Americans who really need such a place. They need a cheap, hot meal when the power is out, and they often have been rendered homeless by personal disasters not shared by most of us.

The typical Waffle House crowd is mostly lower middle-class people, people who work with their hands, the class of Americans that was hit hardest by the economic downturn. But, late at night especially, the Waffle House is a classless society. It is fashionable for young people of all classes to go there (at least in Rome, GA). College students study for exams there, and they can stay as long as they want, all night, if need be.

One great thing about the Waffle House is that you can sit at the counter and watch your food being prepared. Nothing is hidden. If someone spits in your food, you can see it happen. (So it doesn't happen.) Can you say that about your fancy French restaurant with the snotty service persons who you really know have nothing but contempt for you?

I've observed many times the high level of professionalism of the staff at Waffle House. You don't usually have young people working their way through school. The people behind the counter are generally older, and their "career" is what they're doing right now. They really know what they're doing, and they fill lots of orders quickly and cheerfully. Let me emphasize cheerfully. The staff is mostly responsible for what nice places Waffle Houses always seem to be.

The waffles are really delicious. The best thing to eat at the Waffle House are the scattered, smothered, and covered hash browns—that is, covered with cheese, ham, onions, tomatoes, chili, and other stuff too. All the food groups are represented.

If you want a low-carb option, order either the ham and cheese or steak and cheese omelet, with, of course, no grits or toast and a side of bacon. If you want a vegetable, ask for a side of tomato slices (okay—technically not a vegetable).

The coffee at Waffle House is much better than the swill at Starbucks. It's also cheaper, and your cup is bottomless.

Reagan Was Right about Human Nature and History

Reagan, through his powerfully eloquent applications of moral criteria to politics, restored American confidence that we stand for a purpose higher than empty materialism, fueling the progressive thought that human nature, moral right, and history all support the future of our way of life. "It is the Soviet Union," the president confidently asserted in a remarkable 1982 speech to the British Parliament, "that runs against the tide of history by denying freedom and dignity to its citizens." "The decay of the Soviet experiment," the president argued, is both political and economic, and the "constant shrinkage of economic growth combined with the growth of military production" will prove to be unsustainable. The Soviet suppression of "man's instinctive desire for freedom" can't help but always be inherently unstable.

Reagan, against Solzhenitsyn's excessive pessimism, saw "[t]he hard evidence of totalitarian rule" as the source of "an uprising of the intellect and will." In the most genuinely advanced currents of Western thought, "there is one unifying thread." All of "mankind" was being united by the "refusal to subordinate the rights of the individual to the superstate," and by "the realization that collectivism stifles all the best human impulses." The president presented our country's aggressive resistance to the evil empire of the Soviet Union as part of the sacrifice and struggle for freedom that historians had chronicled from "the Exodus of Egypt" to "the Warsaw Uprising in World War II." And, while remaining prudent and peace-loving in the choice of means, Reagan unflinchingly proclaimed mankind's "ultimate objectives" when it comes to all forms of totalitarian oppression.

We can say, with confidence, that Reagan's dignified moral aggressiveness on behalf of what is best about who we are turned out to be more realistic and more prophetic than the conservative defenders of mere containment, and those who feared that we lack the courage and determination to prevail against ideological totalitarianism. Reagan was right, or right enough, about human nature.

David Brooks on Communitarian Conservatives

David Brooks has a generous and eloquent column on the decision of "crunchy conservative" Rod Dreher to move back to his hometown of St. Francisville, LA. Dreher is embracing the "limitations" of small town life in order to be "enmeshed" in the rituals, traditions, and virtue of genuine community. It's in the small towns that people know what to do when confronted with the inevitabilities of vulnerability, suffering, and death. So it's in such places that the virtue of charity is routinely practiced.

Charity, in principle, should be equally for friends and strangers, but it flows more strongly and reliably in the direction of those we know and love in our daily lives. Dreher's decision is based on gratitude for the personal support he and his family received in his sister's struggle against cancer. It's also based on wanting his kids to be raised knowing who they are and what they're supposed to do as loving, relational, dutiful beings.

Brooks finishes up by reminding us that there are two basic kinds of American conservatism:

> Dreher is a writer for *The American Conservative* and is part of a communitarian conservative tradition that goes back to thinkers like Russell Kirk and Robert Nisbet. Forty years ago, Kirk led one of the two great poles of conservatism. It existed in creative tension with the other great pole, Milton Friedman's free-market philosophy.
>
> In recent decades, the communitarian conservatism has become less popular while the market conservatism dominates. But that doesn't make Kirk's insights into small towns, traditions and community any less true, as Rod Dreher so powerfully rediscovered. [Brooks, "Going Home Again," *New York Times*, December 29, 2011.]

First big point: conservatism in America isn't one thing but a kind of "creative tension" of conflicting principles—devotion to a particular place or community and the cosmopolitanism of economic freedom. Adherents to the two principles work together against big, centralizing government that undermines local self-government. But they diverge in their view of, say, Walmart, which undermines communal economic self-reliance when it comes to town.

Generally, the centralization caused by high technology, economies of scale, and such have removed real economic decision-making from towns in the sticks and relocated brain-work or "mental labor" to distant locations. As Marx says, capitalism saves us from rural idiocy, but he should have added at the price of making the rural areas more idiotic still.

The communitarian conservatives are all about exposing the damage globalization, multinationals, the displaced, virtual world of social techno-networking, and so forth do to the distinctiveness of particular places and the "enmeshed" lives of particular people. The economic conservatives celebrate the prosperity and freedom that come when the market displaces local prejudice and laziness with liberated productivity.

Dreher calls himself a "crunchy" conservative because he believes that true conservatives share "ecological" concerns of the Birkenstock wearing, small-is-beautiful, Granola crunching children of the Sixties. The conservatives are more concerned with the "ecology" that sustains life on an appropriately human scale. That means, of course, conservation of our natural environment. But it also means sustaining indispensable social institutions—traditions, manners, morals, churches, schools, families, neighborhoods, and the locally controlled economy.

It also means sustaining the discipline—or "tough love"—of the daily habits or "moral virtue" that are equally indispensable for true human flourishing. Nothing is less ecological, for Dreher, than the Sixties principle of moral liberation: "Do your own thing."

That leads to Brooks's second big point: communitarian conservatism continues to lose ground to economic conservatism. We often call consistent economic conservatism libertarianism—that is, the application of the principles of individual freedom, contract and consent—to all areas of life.

America, anyone can see, is now characterized by creeping and sometimes creepy libertarianism. The conservatives are probably winning when it comes to persuading people to distrust big government and put their faith instead in entrepreneurial productivity.

The libertarians are certainly winning when it comes to personal morality: people are increasingly persuaded that they should liberate themselves from communal prejudice for autonomous moral choice, and that moral tradition is really a name for prejudice and repression.

The enmeshing community of the small town still attracts us, but not at the price of accepting the loving discipline and binding responsibilities of the community's distinctive way of life. Our libertarians often move to small towns, bringing their demands for sophisticated amenities and with no intention of surrendering their personal freedom. In that respect, they're ecological hazards.

There's a lot more to say, and I don't want to leave you with the impression that I simply agree with the communitarian conservatives.